DAILY LIVES OF

Civilians in Wartime Africa

Recent Titles in the
Greenwood Press "Daily Life Through History" Series

The Byzantine Empire
Marcus Rautman

Nature and the Environment in the Twentieth-Century American Life
Brian Black

Nature and the Environment in Nineteenth-Century American Life
Brian Black

Native Americans in the Twentieth Century
Donald Fixico

Native Americans from Post-Columbian through Nineteenth-Century America
Alice Nash and Christoph Strobel

Cooking in Europe, 1250–1650
Ken Albala

The Black Death
Joseph P. Byrne

Cooking in America, 1590–1840
Trudy Eden

Cooking in America, 1840–1945
Alice L. McLean

Cooking in Ancient Civilizations
Cathy K. Kaufman

Nature and the Environment in Pre-Columbian American Life
Stacy Kowtko

Science and Technology in Medieval European Life
Jeffrey R. Wigelsworth

DAILY LIVES OF

Civilians in Wartime Africa

From Slavery Days to Rwandan Genocide

EDITED BY JOHN LABAND

The Greenwood Press "Daily Life Through History" Series
Daily Lives of Civilians during Wartime
David S. Heidler and Jeanne T. Heidler, Series Editors

GREENWOOD PRESS
Westport, Connecticut • London

Library of Congress Cataloging-in-Publication Data

Daily lives of civilians in wartime Africa: from slavery days to Rwandan genocide/edited by John Laband.

p. cm.—(The Greenwood Press Daily life through history series: daily lives of civilians during wartime, ISSN 1080–4749)

Includes bibliographical references and index.

ISBN 0–313–33540–0 (alk. paper)

1. Africa—History, Military. 2. Africa—Social conditions. 3. War and society—Africa. 4. Combatants and noncombatants (International law) 5. Civilian war casualties—Africa. 6. Civil-military relations—Africa. 7. Civil war—Africa. 8. Ethnic conflict—Africa. I. Laband, John, 1947-

DT21.5.D35 2007

960.3—dc22 2006026178

British Library Cataloguing in Publication Data is available.

Library of Congress Catalog Card Number: 2006026178
ISBN: 0–313–33540–0
ISSN: 1080–4749

First published in 2007

Greenwood Press, 88 Post Road West, Westport, CT 06881
An imprint of Greenwood Publishing Group, Inc.
www.greenwood.com

Printed in the United States of America

The paper used in this book complies with the Permanent Paper Standard issued by the National Information Standards Organization (Z39.48–1984).

10 9 8 7 6 5 4 3 2 1

Contents

Series Foreword

Few scenes are as poignant as that of civilian refugees torn from their homes and put to plodding flight along dusty roads, carrying their possessions in crude bundles and makeshift carts. We have all seen the images. Before photography, paintings and crude drawings told the story, but despite the media, the same sense of the awful emerges from these striking portrayals: the pace of the flight is agonizingly slow; the numbers are sobering and usually arrayed in single file along the edges of byways that stretch to the horizon. The men appear hunched and beaten, the women haggard, the children strangely old, and usually the wide-eyed look of fear has been replaced by one of bone-grinding weariness. They likely stagger through country redolent with the odor of smoke and death as heavy guns mutter in the distance. It always seems to be raining on these people, or snowing, and it is either brutally cold or oppressively hot. In the past, clattering hooves would send them skittering away from the path of cavalry; more recently whirring engines of motorized convoys push them from the road. Aside from becoming casualties, civilians who become refugees experience the most devastating impact of war, for they truly become orphans of the storm, lacking the barest necessities of food and clothing except for what they can carry and eventually what they can steal.

The volumes in this series seek to illuminate that extreme example of the civilian experience in wartime and more, for those on distant home fronts also can make remarkable sacrifices, whether through their labors to support the war effort or by enduring the absence of loved ones far from home and in great peril. And war can impinge on indigenous populations in eccentric ways. Stories of a medieval world in which a farmer fearful about his crops could prevail on armies to fight elsewhere are possibly exaggerated, the product of nostalgia for a chivalric code that most likely did not hold much sway during a coarse and vicious time. In any period and at any place, the fundamental reality of war is that organized violence is no less brutal for its being structured by strategy and tactics. The advent of total war might have been signaled by the famous *levee en masse* of the French Revolution, but that development was more a culmination of a trend than an innovation away from more pacific times. In short, all wars have assailed and will assail civilians in one way or another to a greater or lesser degree. The Thirty Years' War displaced populations just as the American Revolution saw settlements preyed upon, houses razed, and farms pillaged. Modern codes of conduct adopted by both international consent and embraced by the armies of the civilized world have heightened awareness about the sanctity of civilians and have improved vigilance about violations of that sanctity, but in the end such codes will never guarantee immunity from the rage of battle or the rigors of war.

In this series, accomplished scholars have recruited prescient colleagues to write essays that reveal both the universal civilian experience in wartime and aspects of it made unique by time and place. Readers will discover in these pages the other side of warfare, one that is never placid, even if far removed from the scenes of fighting. As these talented authors show, the shifting expectations of governments markedly transformed the civilian wartime experience from virtual non-involvement in early modern times to the twentieth century's expectation of sacrifice, exertion, and contribution. Finally, as the western powers have come full circle by asking virtually no sacrifice from civilians at all, they have stumbled upon the peculiar result that diminishing deprivation during a war can increase civilian dissent against it.

Moreover, the geographical and chronological span of these books is broad and encompassing to reveal the unique perspectives of how war affects people whether they are separated by hemispheres or centuries, people who are distinct by way of different cultures yet similar because of their common humanity. As readers will see, days on a home front far from battle usually become a surreal routine of the ordinary existing in tandem with the extraordinary, a situation in which hours of waiting and expectation become blurred against the backdrop of normal tasks and everyday events. That situation is a constant, whether for a village in Asia or Africa or Europe or the Americas.

Consequently, these books confirm that the human condition always produces the similar as well the singular, a paradox that war tends to amplify. Every war is much like another, but no war is really the same as any other. All places are much alike, but no place is wholly separable from its matchless identity. The civilian experience in war mirrors these verities. We are certain that readers will find in these books a vivid illumination of those truths.

David S. Heidler and Jeanne T. Heidler, Series Editors

Introduction: African Civilians in Wartime

John Laband

THE TIMELESSNESS OF TOTAL WAR

Civilians have always suffered in war, but many argue that what is different in present-day conflicts is that they, rather than soldiers, have become the primary target. Certainly, since the Second World War the overwhelming majority of those killed in conflicts have been civilians rather than soldiers, and in Africa in the late twentieth century they make up more than 90 percent of the casualties. Unspeakable violence and destruction has been brought into civilian life through the waging of what is commonly called "total war." Such warfare, which is usually said to date from the final stages in 1864–1865 of the American Civil War, and which blurs—if not entirely eliminates—the demarcation line between combatants and civilians, requires the mobilization and participation of entire societies and not just the armed forces that represent them. This, in turn, exposes civilians as well as soldiers to comprehensive military retaliation by their enemies.[1] Taken to extremes, such retribution culminates in the mass extermination of peoples. Indeed, systematic genocide is regarded as a measure of modernity, an expression of the ability of the bureaucratic, industrial state (such as Nazi Germany) to intervene comprehensively in the lives of its subjects and to apply the new technologies of mass destruction against its internal and external enemies. Yet the Rwandan genocide of 1994, perhaps the very worst occurrence of its kind of the late twentieth century, took place not in the First, but in the Third World, in a failing postcolonial African state, largely by means of crude weapons such as clubs and machetes instead of modern armaments.

Not that this should be surprising. During times of war, conquest, and civil strife, helpless civilian noncombatants in most cultures from the earliest of times have suffered a brutal fate from massacre, the destruction of their means of livelihood, captive forced labor, slavery, and general maltreatment.[2] And today, while the great industrial military powers ponder the tactical implications of a "revolution in military affairs" based on futuristic weaponry and control systems supposed to minimize collateral damage, vicious low-intensity "subconventional" conflicts proliferate around the globe. These are in essence waged (despite the use of modern small arms and landmines) exactly like the so-called primitive wars of the distant past.[3]

Lawrence Keeley, in his seminal book, *War before Civilization,* which effectively rebuts the long-held anthropological notion that warfare was introduced to primitive societies through contact with civilization, points out that "primitive warfare is simply total war conducted with very limited means."[4] For millennia warriors have been conducting raids and campaigns that might have been on a smaller scale than modern ones, but that were certainly just as ruthless and "total" because their objective (as it still is today) has been to destroy their enemy's economic and social ability to resist. Then, as now, a few hours of warfare could see the plunder of resources such as food stores and livestock that would have taken years to accumulate, and the burning of dwellings and crops. The devastated area would be rendered temporarily uninhabitable and the inhabitants put on an instant famine footing. As a consequence, the targeted social unit might (as was the case in the Zulu wars of expansion in the early nineteenth century [see Chapter 2]) be displaced, dispersed, exterminated, incorporated, or (as regularly occurred as a result of raids and wars in West and Central Africa) enslaved (see Chapter 1).

Indeed, there is an ugly sameness when the fate of civilians in wartime is contemplated, for in every age all are exposed to variations on the dismal themes of death, rape, pillage, enslavement, flight and exile. In Keeley's view, primitive and prehistoric warfare (like low-intensity and guerrilla conflict today) was actually more deadly than that waged between "civilized" states on account of the cumulative effects of low-casualty but more frequent raids and battles, the systematic plunder of valuable commodities, the destruction of the means of production and shelter, the atrocious treatment of enemy women and children, and the massacre of entire communities.[5] Archaeological evidence shows quite clearly that even prehistoric, Stone Age communities were subject to massacre. Site 117 in northern Sudan on the banks of the Nile contains the bones of 59 individuals (male and female adults as well as children) dating from 12,000 to 10,000 B.C.E. Evidence from projectiles lodged deep within certain skeletons and from the damage inflicted to bones clearly indicates that these people had been buried after suffering a violent death, as had the 18 adults and 16 children piled in a common grave in Talheim in southwestern Germany about 7,000 years ago.[6]

In many precolonial societies, like that of the Zulu (see Chapter 2), no adult males were taken alive in battle lest they live to avenge their defeat. Boys were spared, however, as were women of marriageable age and young girls, because they were of material benefit and could be incorporated more easily than male adults into the society of the victors, or sold more readily into slavery (see Chapter 1). Women were generally held to be the legitimate spoils of victory. Indeed, those studying gender in war would argue that the gendering of social life along a male-female divide builds discrimination into accepted patterns of behavior. During war these may resurface in an aggressive fashion and be sanctioned, even though women have primarily been defined as a group in need of protection. Consequently, women in war are likely to be systematically raped and terrorized to rub home the totality of male conquest.[7] Thus, even if women did not suffer death like the adult men of their community, they still experienced the crushing loss of their homes and families, capture, rape, and exile. But for their captors they were an invaluable asset. Not only did women's agricultural labor usually provide the staple food upon which society relied, but the augmented presence of fertile women in a polygynous society (such as was common in Africa) was vital for population growth. Indeed, one of the central themes of the history of Africa is that of the peopling of an environmentally hostile continent. This involved the pressing forward of frontiers of settlement and the formation of nodes of population in favored regions that could sustain dense agglomerations of people.[8] However, this process of internal colonization created fault lines among foragers, pastoral nomads, and village farmers, which, in regions like Darfur in the western Sudan, are still basic to the prevailing violence (see Chapter 8).

AFRICAN CIVILIANS AND WARFARE IN AFRICA

States, such as those that developed in many parts of Africa between the mid-thirteenth century and European conquest in the nineteenth,[9] had a stronger material interest than less sophisticated pre-state social formations in preserving the lives of defeated enemies (even of adult males) because of their potential as tribute-paying subjects, serfs, or slaves. Population, which was increased through relentless raiding and conquest and the incorporation and redistribution of the defeated in various forms of dependency, including slavery, encouraged further aggression and provided a larger manpower pool to absorb losses (see Chapter 1). Economically the African state, such as the Zulu kingdom, was best served by the submission of its enemies and not by their destruction or dispersal in flight. Of course, slaughters of noncombatants may occur when the aggressors are consumed by ethnic or religious hatred, or by vengeance, or when a calculated attempt is being made to terrorize and cow a conquered populace.[10] Such self-defeating acts have occurred all too often in the horrific conflicts of late twentieth-century Africa (see Chapters 6–9).

European conquest of Africa during the course of the nineteenth century eventually suppressed internal warfare. However, during the process of conquest and subsequent pacification, African civilians, such as the Zulu, suffered repeatedly under brutal military methods (see Chapter 2); and in the case of the Anglo-Boer War the internment of Boer women and children and their African farm workers in concentration camps verged in its disastrous effects on genocide (see Chapter 3). In other theaters, such as German South West Africa, suppression of revolt did indeed become genocidal.[11] And although colonial rule imposed its rule of law and put an end to endemic conflict, for ordinary Africans this came with loss of land; subordinate political, social, and economic status; and (in many cases) forced labor. Colonial rule also meant that Africa was drawn into two World Wars (see Chapters 4 and 5) and renewed fighting on its soil. Civilians again suffered the effects, but these were not all deleterious. The Second World War in particular shook the foundations of European rule in Africa and paved the way for independence in the 1960s. Although this came about in most cases through a peaceful transfer of power, in several white-ruled territories independence was won only through protracted liberation struggles, which, as in the case of Angola (see Chapter 6) merged into decades of civil war exacerbated by Cold War rivalries.[12] The consequences for civilians of these seemingly never-ending, generally low-intensity struggles proved disastrous, exposing them to every evil from massacre (regularly employed as an intimidatory and coercive tactic) to forced dispersal from their communities.

Yet it is the wars of the late twentieth century that have had the most fatal consequences for unarmed civilians, destroying villages, towns, and infrastructures; stalling investment and development; displacing millions internally or into refugee camps; exposing them to famine, rape, mutilation, bondage, massacre, ethnic cleansing, and systematic genocide at the hands of regular, paramilitary, and irregular forces. In independent states right across Africa armed bands have continued to operate long after original ideological or related motives had lost their meaning. Endemic warfare serves as a system of profit and power in the conditions of post–Cold War insurgency where (now that international backing has dried up) a conflict group has to find its own financial resources to survive through illegal trading, looting, tribute, and seizure of assets. For armed bands and the conflict entrepreneurs who command them in countries such as Angola, Liberia, Sierra Leone, Sudan, the Democratic Republic of the Congo, and Uganda (see Chapters 6–9), actually winning the war becomes secondary to profiting from the general chaos that it is in their selfish interests to maintain.

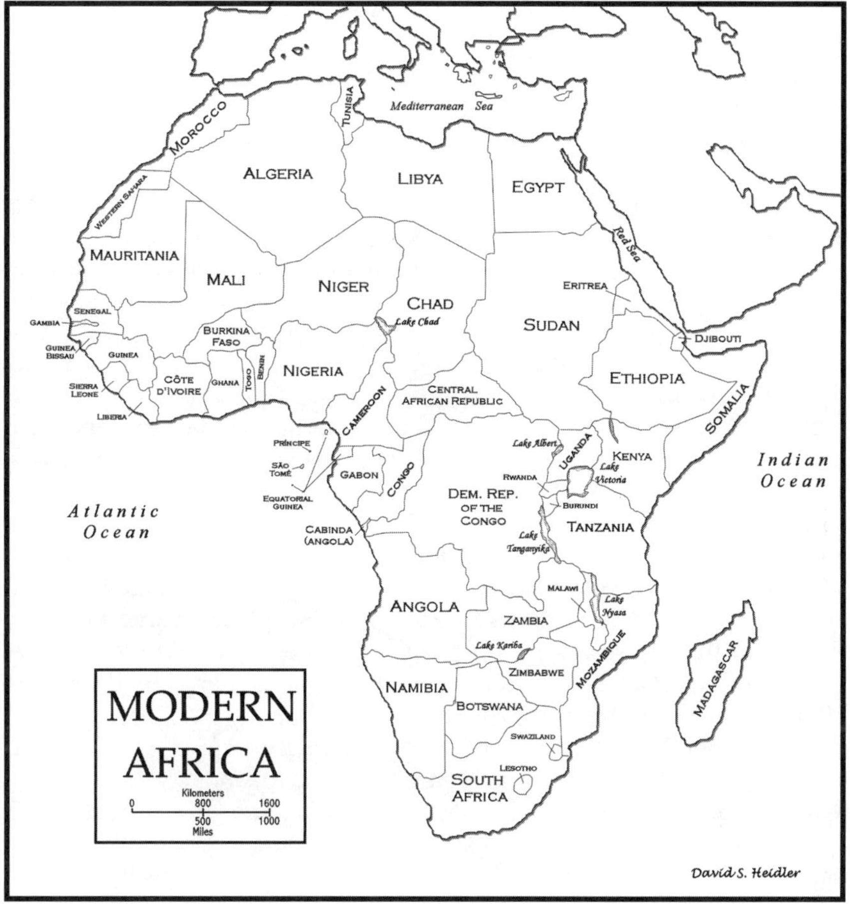

Modern Africa

The criminal goals of these entrenched warlords have led inevitably to a change in strategy toward civilians. Because there is no point in winning over the hearts and minds of the people as is standard procedure in classic insurgency operations that aim at capturing the state, these groups concentrate instead on terrorizing the population into compliance in the areas they control, and in pillaging resources for all they are worth. Such methods are unremittingly brutal: mass killings, rape, and torture. In the process there is a hellish blurring of war, organized crime, profit-seeking, and violence for its own sake. Unfortunately, the armed forces of the state can be as terrible to the state's own subjects as the rebels and insurgents if, as in Rwanda and Sudan (see Chapters 8 and 9), the state decides to adopt policies that single out minorities for ethnic cleansing or genocide and mobilizes the majority of the population to act as its willing executioners.

The true horror of such massacres is that local people are persuaded to kill their own neighbors and even close families, to cut down people known personally to them while spectators stand by in complicity.[13]

THE AMBIGUITIES OF BEING A CIVILIAN IN WARTIME

If it is conceded that "total war" is a phenomenon not confined to the modern age, and if it is accepted that in all ages and in all places civilians have experienced the sharp edge of war, even then to define what being a civilian actually means in the context of wartime is not as straightforward as it may seem. Thus, if most British public opinion at the time considered Bomber Command's fire-bombing of Dresden on February 13, 1945 entirely legitimate because of the city's designation as an industrial and communications center—even though "collateral damage" included the deaths of between 25,000 and 40,000 German civilians[14]—then why the public disquiet in Britain in the first years of the twentieth century over the concentration camps of the Anglo-Boer War in which 26,000 Boer women and children perished?[15] If all Dresdeners (in or out of uniform) were acceptable targets because they were aiding the German war effort through their work in factories and along the line of communications and supply to the Eastern Front, then were not Boer women on their farms prolonging the war by actively supplying and sheltering the Boer guerrilla groups still in the field?

When in the 1960s and early 1970s the Portuguese herded Angolan peasants working on the white-owned farms of the highlands into prison-style villages at night (see Chapter 6), was not the justification that this prevented them providing supplies and intelligence to nationalist guerrilla fighting the colonial regime for their independence?[16] Considered logically, were not German, Boer and Angolan civilians all enmeshed in their respective war efforts, and therefore undeserving of tender treatment from the military? A Zulu army on campaign depended for its supplies on cooperative civilians along its line of march. So to strike at Zulu fields and herds as the British did in 1879 was considered militarily necessary, and civilian livelihoods could not be spared in the process (see Chapter 2). And there is an additional factor: whether the civilian targets were Germans, Boers, Angolans, or Zulu, it was recognized by their enemies that "de-housing" them, sweeping them into camps, confining them in fortified villages, or burning their huts had a shattering effect on morale for everyone involved in the war effort and weakened the soldiers' will to continue fighting. Home front and battle front are thus intimately connected, and the distinction between civilian and soldier begins to dissolve.

In this regard, slavery in Africa causes particular difficulties (see Chapter 1). The institution of slavery was widespread in Africa. It long predated the notorious Atlantic slave trade and survived its abolition well into the colonial era; it flourishes to this day in Mauritania and Sudan, where 50 years of civil war have led to a resurgence of the slave trade despite the special provision prohibiting slavery in the Universal Declaration of Human Rights adopted by the United Nations General Assembly on December 10, 1948.[17] The difficulty is that African slavery is a slippery category. Slaves might be captured in war, kidnapped, bought, born into slavery, inherited, sentenced for a crime, received in settlement for a debt, or even self-enslaved in need. Non-Islamic states incorporated slaves and employed them not only as agricultural laborers, but as administrators and soldiers. Likewise, in Islamic states slaves could be tributary cultivators settled in slave villages, urban laborers and craftsmen, and concubines and domestic servants, as well as becoming soldiers and rising to high civil and military office.[18] The line between civilian victims and perpetrators dissolves and slaves themselves become slavers.

During the period of colonial rule in Africa, colonial administrations made wide use of armed African levies and permanent formations of soldiers, like the British King's African Rifles, French Senegalese *tirailleurs,* or the German *Schütztruppen,* in order to augment the small numbers of white troops available. Whether or not it is appropriate to consider these African soldiers as mercenaries, they certainly must be regarded as combatants in the two World Wars into which Africa was sucked (see Chapters 4 and 5). But how should the 827,5000 carriers Britain and her allies employed during the First World War to keep their armed forces supplied in the field be regarded? Most were impressed or conscripted and thousands died of disease and exposure.[19] They carried no arms, but can they be regarded as civilians?

In the civil wars that have bedeviled postindependence Africa, rebel forces tend not to wear uniforms so as to blend into the civil population. For government troops trying to hunt them down it can become an impossible dilemma to identify who among the populace poses a threat. It becomes even more problematical when rebel groups employ child soldiers who can slip unsuspected past guard posts and patrols. The active presence of children has become a fact of modern combat, and Africa (especially West Africa and the Great Lakes region) is at the epicenter of this phenomenon. Child soldiers, 60 percent of whom are 14 or under and sometimes as young as 11, are present in almost every one of Africa's postindependence wars. In Angola alone 36 percent of all Angolan children went into combat, and the notorious Lord's Resistance Army in Uganda is made up almost entirely of child soldiers. Children are targeted for abduction or recruitment because they are a quick, cheap, easy way of building up a force, and the relative simplicity of modern weaponry means that they can be rapidly trained in their use. Civilians bear the brunt of the rape and other atrocities committed by child soldiers because they are targeted as softer targets for inexperienced fighters. Because the predatory and cruel child soldier groups are so feared, the rebels use them to terrorize local communities into acquiescence or to punish those who have not cooperated.

Usually, a few refugees from targeted villages are deliberately allowed to escape to spread fear among the wider populace. Yet in child soldiering, as in slavery, the perpetrators are also the victims. Child soldiering is nothing less than a new form of slavery in which abducted children are turned (as in slave societies in the past) into predators on their own civilian communities.[20] Once again, the categories of civilian and combatant dissolve into each other.

ETHNIC CLEANSING, GENOCIDE AND MASS CRIME

Ethnic cleansing and genocide, understandably regarded as the supreme crimes against civilian populations, offer difficulties of their own. Ethnic cleansing in principle involves the purification of a territory, the removal of a so-called alien nationality, or ethnic or religious group and all traces of them, whether physical, cultural, or linguistic. Ethnic cleansing is inevitably violent because people resist their forced deportation, and it often (but not always) bleeds into genocide. Genocide has been defined as "a one-sided mass killing" when the victims are unarmed civilians and when the killings (as well as the systematic mass rape of women in traditional societies) form part of a deliberate attempt to destroy the target group. In this sense the practical difference between ethnic cleansing and genocide is no more than a matter of intent.[21] Yet, as with the double-think over strategic bombing and the acceptable death of civilians because of their participation in the wider war effort, so it is with ethnic cleansing and genocide. Article XIII of the Potsdam Protocol of 1945 provided for the "orderly and humane transfer of German populations" from all territories of the former Reich to Allied-occupied Germany. It is estimated that while nearly 12 million Germans survived the expulsion, over 2 million died in a process that was all too often neither orderly nor humane.[22] Yet this blatant case of ethnic cleansing has determinedly never been recognized as such by those who ordered and effected it. Identically, in Africa today the indisputable genocide in Rwanda and the continuing ethnic cleansing in Sudan are not officially defined as such by the world community because of the dictates of *realpolitik* (politics based on realities rather than on ideals) and selfish economic interests (see Chapters 8 and 9).

Of course, too much can be made of tight definitions and the need for consistency, and too much attention can be paid to arguments in the United Nations over whether certain terrible acts properly fit the definitions contained in the Genocide Convention of 1948 (Resolution 260 (III) A of the General Assembly), definitions that were themselves the product of Stalin's concern that his own purges and ethnic cleansings be overlooked. Rather, when considering the fate of civilians in war, it is perhaps most useful to adopt Jacques Semelin's broad concept of "mass crime." He defines "mass crime" as the destruction of a large segment of the civilian population (often accompanied by atrocities) in the context of war. He includes in his definition acts such as forced deportation, mass rape, massacre, and mass murder, and insists that the passivity of the rest of the world when faced by a mass crime is a vital key to its implementation.[23] Civilians, in every one of the cases included in this book on African civilians in wartime, must be described as the victims of mass crimes as defined by Semelin.

THE LAWS OF WAR

For some moralists all war is immoral and to distinguish between moral and immoral acts of war is to blur the main issue. Others accept war as an inescapable human activity and try to humanize it by proposing rules to govern it. Such rules derive their immediate force from law, but they draw their ultimate sanction from moral precept. Lawyers make the distinction between *Ius ad Bellum,* the rules regulating the justified resort to war, and *Ius in Bello,* the rules regulating conduct in war. The category of *Ius in Bello,* which has exercised European theologians, philosophers, and lawyers since the Middle Ages, prescribes what a belligerent may or may not do even though the state of war legitimizes many acts that are illegal in peacetime. It applies primarily to individual behavior, and *Ius in Bello* was always intended to regulate and humanize war by banning excesses. The rule that has evolved is that destruction should be proportionate, in other words that the force used and the damage inflicted should be no greater than what is necessary to achieve the war's just purpose.[24]

During the course of the late nineteenth and the first half of the twentieth centuries, lawyers, confronted by the increasing destructiveness of warfare as a result of the improving technology of armaments and the growth in the scale of warfare, evolved ever more precise definitions of the laws of war in the sequences of the Geneva and Hague conventions and in United Nations resolutions.[25] The 1907 Hague Convention (IV) Respecting the Laws and Customs of War on Land, Annex to the Convention, was grounded on the principle that the infliction of unnecessary suffering is contrary to law, and it condemned the killing of prisoners, and attacks on undefended towns and on civilians.[26] Article 6 (c) of the 1945 Charter for the International Military Tribunal at Nuremberg defined crimes against humanity as "murder, extermination, enslavement, deportation and other inhuman acts committed against any civilian population before or during the war, or persecution on political, racial or religious grounds …" In Article 6 (b) the Tribunal laid down that "murder, ill-treatment or deportation to slave labour or for any other purpose of civilian population of or in occupied territory … plunder of public or private property, wanton destruction of cities, towns or villages, or devastation not justified by military necessity" constituted war crimes.[27] In other words, these "Nuremberg Principles" defined clearly what constitute crimes against humanity and war crimes and laid down that as offences against customary international law they are thus subject to universal jurisdiction. In December 1946 the General Assembly of the United Nations unanimously adopted the Nuremberg Principles. Subsequently, the 1949 Geneva Convention (IV) Relative to the Protection of Civilian Persons in Time of War laid down in great detail how civilians should be safeguarded;[28] the 1977 Protocols I and II additional to the 1949 Geneva Conventions relating to the protection of victims of both international and noninternational armed conflicts further defined the prosecution and punishment of war criminals.[29]

THE PROBLEMATIC ENFORCEMENT OF THE LAWS OF WAR

A major problem with all these apparently clear statements regarding the proper treatment of civilians in time of war is that in the post-1945 period so many conflicts—and those in Africa in particular—have been civil wars.[30] The Geneva Conventions and Protocols do specify minimal rules to be applied in civil wars, but the extent to which the laws of war actually apply to civil wars has long been open to debate. Because the distinction between soldier and civilian, basic to the modern laws of war, is not nearly so clear in practice as in theory and is especially indistinct in the case of civil wars, governments have routinely been reluctant to treat rebels or insurgents as legitimate belligerents. Concerned at the repeated and major violations of the rules of war as recognized by many members of the world body, the United Nations has made attempts to improve implementation. The UN Security Council's decision to establish Ad Hoc International Criminal Tribunals on the model of Nuremberg and Tokyo for Yugoslavia in the Hague in 1993, and for Rwanda in Arusha, Tanzania, in 1994 is significant in affirming the principle that individuals can be personally held responsible for war crimes, even if committed with the authority of the state. The conviction in September 1998 of Jean-Paul Akayesu, the Hutu mayor of Taba, on counts of genocide, torture, rape, murder, crimes against humanity, and breaches of the 1949 Geneva conventions is crucial in that the judgment established that rape and sexual violence can be considered genocidal. Of course, there are huge difficulties in applying the law supranationally, although in 1998 the Rome Statute established a permanent, free-standing International Criminal Court with its own, independent prosecutor to hear cases of war crimes wherever and whenever they may have been committed. Articles 5 to 8 of the Rome Statute (4) contain extensive provisions applicable to civil wars as well as a summary relating to the crime of genocide, crimes against humanity, and war crimes. The court came into being in 2002, but it was opposed by the United States, China, India, and a number of other states, which makes its effectiveness problematical. Unfortunately, law that is not rigorously enforced inevitably withers, and although war criminals can be left in no doubt as to where they stand in relation to the law, in most cases they can flout it with impunity.

An alternative means of diminishing the deleterious effects on civilians of the plethora of small wars and insurgencies still taking place in Africa and most other regions of the globe is to place limits on the actions of belligerents. One such initiative was the 1997 Ottawa Convention Prohibiting the Use, Stockpiling, Production, and Transfer of Anti-Personnel Mines, a practice that has proved so lethal to civilians even after hostilities have ceased, and that has so disrupted efforts to rehabilitate war-torn economies and infrastructures. Similarly, in May 2000 the UN General Assembly, concerned for the plight and future rehabilitation of child soldiers, adopted a new "optional protocol" to the 1989 Convention on the Rights of the Child that raised the minimum age of recruitment for soldiers from 15 to 18. And in August 2005 the UN Security Council passed a resolution to set up a comprehensive mechanism to monitor and report on the illegal use of children in armed conflict.[31] Yet laudable as all these initiatives are, the continuing ethnic cleansing in Darfur (see Chapter 8) is but one example of the persistence of the dreadful plight of civilians caught up in Africa's vicious little wars, and the unwillingness or inability of the world community to intervene with any effectiveness.

Yet even when intervention is attempted, the consequences are often not what might be hoped for. The generally unsuccessful peacekeeping record of the United Nations in Africa has demonstrated again and again the limited capacity of external forces to shape the outcome of local conflicts.[32] Indeed, in the case of the Rwandan genocide, the inadequate UN contingent was rendered helpless while partisan French armed involvement proved positively baleful in its consequences (see Chapter 9). Nor have interventions by African states proved any more effective; witness the interminable and sometimes counterproductive presence of the forces of the Economic Community of West Africa (ECOWAS) in war-torn Liberia and Sierra Leone (see Chapter 7). The African Union has detailed plans for more productive interventions to contain African conflicts (see Chapter 9), but these still have to prove their worth. The African Union's (AU) record thus far in Darfur has not been encouraging (see Chapter 8).

DEALING WITH THE AFTERMATH OF WAR

The plight of civilians does not end when the fighting stops. Refugees have to be resettled, destroyed dwellings and infrastructures rebuilt, shops and businesses restocked and reopened, jobs created, abandoned fields won back from the encroaching bush. Lethal landmines buried along paths and roads and in fields must be located and removed. And, most difficult of all, considering that almost all the recent wars in Africa have been civil wars, shattered communities must be recreated and helped to function again through a process of reconciliation. The process of mourning may never end, and may indeed not prove recuperative.

Yet whether as victims or survivors, people suffering injustice, injury, or trauma as a result of war should be prepared to demand public recognition of their harrowing experiences and must seek a space to present their testimony. This is a very difficult process. War memory is the personal possession of those who have experienced war, even if solely as civilians. In the end it may never be articulated in any wider arena, either because it is too private or painful to share, because it is suppressed through a community sense of shame, or because of fear of the political repercussions of bringing war memories into public debate.[33] The establishment of truth and reconciliation commissions, sometimes accompanied by a criminal tribunal for prosecuting war crimes, is one path to be followed, especially in UN-sponsored peace accords (see Chapters 7 and 9). However, African communities do not always find these Western-style initiatives culturally fulfilling or effective and, as in Rwanda, have turned to traditional community courts as a means of healing the wounds of the past and readmitting transgressors into the community.[34]

The situation of former child soldiers is a particularly poignant one, and their case may be taken to stand for all those other Africans whose lives have been ruined by war, and who are trying to build them afresh in a civil community. Because child soldiering is a form of child abuse, the psychological and moral development of child soldiers has been severely disrupted. On top of this, many suffer from forms of Post-Traumatic Stress Disorder (PTSD), sexually transmitted diseases including HIV/AIDS, and drug dependency. Their future prospects are thus severely compromised, not only because of the lasting mental and physical effects of their vile experiences as child soldiers, but because they lack the literacy and numeracy skills and the vocational training necessary to make a living as civilians. Yet little can be done for them because most essential health facilities and schools have been destroyed in the fighting. In any case, existing demobilization programs are inadequate to the task, and it is exceedingly difficult to reabsorb former child soldiers into society. Besides the problems already mentioned, many are orphans with no home or family to return to, while others face retribution and ostracism by the community they all too often have played an active and atrocious part in harming.[35] Civilian victims of war in Africa have much to forgive, not least the actions of their children.

THE ARRANGEMENT OF THE BOOK

The nine essays in this book have been selected and arranged so as to provide a representative range of civilian experiences during wartime in Africa. They extend in time from the late eighteenth century to the present and represent every region of Africa (as they are usually defined) except North Africa. The geographical situation of this particular region between the Mediterranean Sea and the Sahara Desert, combined with its overarching Arab-Islamic culture, distinguishes it from the rest of sub-Saharan Africa and unites it with the Arab-speaking world of the Middle East.[36]

In temporal terms, the book begins with Paul E. Lovejoy's study of the ubiquitous experience of African slavery, which for such an extended period has so profoundly affected the development of the continent and the lives of its people. The second chapter, by John Laband, examines the rise of the Zulu kingdom in the early nineteenth century and its subsequent conquest by Britain, thus charting the fate of civilians during the formation of an African kingdom and their experiences during colonial conquest. The Anglo-Boer War is situated at a crucial crossroads between colonial and modern warfare, and the concentration camps the British set up for Boer and African civilians pioneered a new form of modern savagery. In the third chapter Bill Nasson examines this war's complex effects on various categories of noncombatants in South Africa. Because it was under colonial rule, Africa was dragged into the two World Wars. Tim Stapleton shows in the fourth chapter that while the African civilian response to the war of 1914–1918 was often contradictory and ranged from collaboration to revolt, the effect of the conflict was only to confirm colonial rule.

In the following chapter, David Killingray explains how and why the impact of the Second World War on African civilians was rather different from that of the First in that it undid colonial rule and paved the way for the future independence of Africa under modernized African leadership. The Portuguese held on to their African empire long after the other colonial empires had relinquished theirs in the 1960s. Angola, the subject of Chapter 6, passed seamlessly out of an independence struggle against Portuguese rule into civil war that soon involved Cold War rivalries and interventions. Inge Brinkman describes the dismal sufferings and displacement of Angolan civilians during four decades of interminable fighting. Liberia and Sierra Leone declined from relative stability and prosperity into horrific civil war, and in Chapter 7 Lansana Gberie traces the deadly consequences for civilians and the efforts to stabilize society once peace was tentatively restored. The Sudan has suffered decades of ethnic and religious strife between the government and the people of the southern and western periphery, and in Chapter 8 Jane Kani Edward and Amir Idris analyze what this has meant, and still means, for the myriad civilian victims. Chapter 9 concludes the book with the most horrific single episode of recent African history: the Rwandan genocide. Alhaji Bah explains its genesis and canvasses the subsequent search for reconciliation. The chapter ends with his discussion of African mechanisms that should—and even might—be put in place to ensure effective peacekeeping in Africa, and so save civilians in future from the swarm of war's horrors.

NOTES

1. Christon I. Archer, John R. Ferris, Holger H. Herwig, and Timothy H. E. Travers, *World History of Warfare* (Lincoln: University of Nebraska Press, 2002), 410, 414, 416, 426–27, 510–12.

2. See Kurt Jonassohn with Karin Solveig Björnson, *Genocide and Gross Human Rights Violations in Comparative Perspective* (New Brunswick, NJ and London: Transaction Publishers, 1998), chaps. 17–20.

3. See Williamson Murray and MacGregor Knox, "The Future behind Us," in *The Dynamics of Military Revolution 1300–2050,* ed. MacGregor Knox and Williamson Murray (Cambridge: Cambridge University Press, 2001), 188–94; Martin Van Crefeld, *The Transformation of War* (New York: The Free Press, 1991), 206–8; Martin Van Crefeld, "Technology and War II: Postmodern War?" *The Oxford History of Modern War,* ed. Charles Townshend (Oxford: Oxford University Press, 2000), 350–59; Jeremy Black, *Rethinking Military History* (London and New York: Routledge, 2004), 234–35.

4. Lawrence H. Keeley, *War before Civilization* (Oxford: Oxford University Press, 1996), 175.

5. Ibid., 88–93, 174–75; see figure 6.2.

6. Jean Guilaine and Jean Zammit, trans. Melanie Hersey, *The Origins of War: Violence in Prehistory* (Oxford and Malden, MA: Blackwell Publishing, 2005), 36–39, 67–72, 86–91.

7. See Joshua S. Goldstein, *War and Gender: How Gender Shapes the War System and Vice Versa* (Cambridge: Cambridge University Press, 2001), 332–36, 349, 356–57, 362–71.

8. John Iliffe, *Africans: The History of a Continent* (Cambridge: Cambridge University Press, 2000), 1–5.

9. See Roland Oliver and Anthony Atmore, *Medieval Africa 1250–1800* (Cambridge: Cambridge University Press, 2001).

10. Keeley, *War before Civilization,* 83–88, 108–12, 129.

11. See Bruce Vandervort, *Wars of Imperial Conquest in Africa, 1830–1914* (London, UCL Press, 1998).

12. See Anthony Clayton, *Frontiersmen: Warfare in Africa since 1950* (London: UCL Press, 1999).

13. For useful collections of essays on contemporary conflict in Africa, see Christopher Clapham, ed., *African Guerrillas* (Oxford, Kampala, Bloomington, and Indianapolis: James Currey, Fountain Publishers and Indiana University Press, 1998); and Taisier M. Ali and Robert O. Matthews, eds., *Civil Wars in Africa: Roots and Resolution* (Montreal, Kingston, London, and Ithaca, NY: McGill-Queen's University Press, 1999).

14. See Frederick Taylor, *Dresden, Tuesday 13 February 1945* (London: Bloomsbury Publishing, 2005), esp. 450–76, 503–9.

15. For the controversy in Britain over the concentration camps, see Paula M. Krebs, *Gender, Race, and the Writing of Empire: Public Discourse and the Boer War* (Cambridge: Cambridge University Press, 1999), 32–79.

16. David Birmingham, "Angola," in *A History of Postcolonial Lusophone Africa,* ed. Patrick Chabal, with David Birmingham, Joshua Forrest, Mary Newitt, Gerhard Seibert, and Elisa Silva Andrade (Bloomington and Indianapolis: Indiana University Press, 2002), 141.

17. Martin Klein estimates that in the first decade of the twentieth century over 30 percent of the population of French West Africa (or up to 3.5 million people) was slaves. The descendants of slaves still face social sanctions. See Martin A. Klein, *Slavery and Colonial Rule in French West Africa* (Cambridge: Cambridge University Press, 1998), 240–46; 252–56: Appendix 1. For the contemporary accommodation of slavery in Africa, see Ronald Segal, *Islam's Black Slaves: A History of Africa's Other Black Diaspora* (London: Atlantic Books, 2002), chap. 12.

18. See John Iliffe, *Honour in African History* (Cambridge: Cambridge University Press, 2005), chap. 8.

19. Hew Strachan, *The First World War in Africa* (Oxford: Oxford University Press, 2004), 6–9, 143, 157.

20. P. W. Singer, *Children at War* (New York: Pantheon Books, 2005), 7, 19–20, 24, 29, 41–44, 47–49, 95, 101–4, 111–12, 139, 155, 157.

21. See Norman M. Naimark, *Fires of Hatred: Ethnic Cleansing in Twentieth-Century Europe* (Cambridge, MA and London: Harvard University Press, 2002), 2–5; and Edward Kissi, "Genocide in Cambodia and Ethiopia," in *The Specter of Genocide: Mass Murder in Historical Perspective,* ed. Robert Gellately and Ben Kiernan (Cambridge: Cambridge University Press, 2003), 311.

22. For the figures see Alfred M. De Zayas, *Nemesis at Potsdam: The Anglo-Americans and the Expulsion of the Germans: Background, Execution, Consequences* (London, Henley, and Boston: Routledge and Kegan Paul, 1977), xxv.

23. Jacques Semelin, "Analysis of a Mass Crime: Ethnic Cleansing in the Former Yugoslavia, 1991–1999," in *The Specter of Genocide,* 354–57, 362.

24. See Yehuda Melzer, *Concepts of Just War* (Leyden: A. W. Sijthoff, 1975), chap. 2; Ian Clark, *Waging War: A Philosophical Introduction* (Oxford: Clarendon Press, 1988), chap. 2.

25. See Geoffrey Best, *War and Law since 1945* (Oxford: Clarendon Press, 1996).

26. The text of the Convention can be found in W. Michael Reisman and Chris T. Antoniou, eds., *The Laws of War: A Comprehensive Collection of Primary Documents on International Laws Governing Armed Conflict* (New York: Vintage Books, 1994), 47–48.

27. See ibid., 319.

28. See ibid., 233–83.

29. See ibid., 385–86.

30. The following account of initiatives taken to define and implement the laws of war in the late twentieth century is based on Richard Holmes, ed., *The Oxford Companion to Military History* (Oxford: Oxford University Press, 2001), 494–95, 976–78.

31. *Globe and Mail* (Toronto), 2 August 2005.

32. See Norrie Macqueen, *United Nations Peacekeeping in Africa since 1960* (London: Longman, 2002), 257–64.

33. Jay Winter and Emmanuel Sivan, "Setting the Framework," in *War and Remembrance in the Twentieth Century,* ed. Jay Winter and Emmanuel Sivan (Cambridge: Cambridge University Press, 2000), 32; T. G. Ashplant, Graham Dawson, and Michael Roper, "The Politics of War Memory and Commemoration: Contexts, Structures and Dynamics," in *The Politics of Memory: Commemorating War,* ed. Timothy G. Ashplant, Graham Dawson, and Michael Roper (New Brunswick and London: Transaction Publishers, 2004), 1, 18–20.

34. See S'ifiso Ngesi and Charles Villa-Vicencio, "Rwanda: Balancing the Weight of History," in *Through Fire with Water: The Roots of Division and the Potential for Reconciliation in Africa,* ed. Erik Doxtader and Charles Villa-Vicencio (Claremont, South Africa: Institute for Justice and Reconciliation, 2003), 19–25.

35. Singer, *Children at War,* 112–13, 185–86, 194, 210, 204, 207.

36. For the logic behind such African regional divisions, see F. Jeffress Ramsay and Wayne Edge, *Global Studies: Africa,* 10th ed. (Guilford, CT: McGraw-Hill/ Dushkin Company, 2004), 20, 54, 111, 112, 118, 162.

ONE

Civilian Casualties in the Context of the Trans-Atlantic Slave Trade

Paul E. Lovejoy

INTRODUCTION

What does *civilian* mean in the context of the slave trade? The story of Lucy Fagbeade and her daughter, Ogunyomi, as recorded in her journal for May 6, 1867 by Anna Hinderer, a German missionary among the Yoruba people in what is now southern Nigeria, sheds some light on this issue. The story of both mother and child, reproduced here as an appendix, was written in German for children, with the intention of raising support for the Christian mission among the Yoruba. The established religion was associated with the worship of various *orisa (orisha)* [deities], traditionally 404 in number, the more important including *sango (shango)* of the Oyo; *ifá*, associated with divination, *ogun, obatala, osun,* and others.[1] By 1867, after nearly 50 years of war, Yorubaland was in the midst of religious upheaval that was closely associated with issues of enslavement as well as belief. The catalyst in this upheaval was the Muslim holy war (jihad) emanating from the north, which undermined the main Yoruba kingdom, Oyo, eventually engulfing much of northern Yoruba country, as well as Nupe and the Hausa state, into the Sokoto Caliphate, which had been founded in jihad in 1804–1808 (see map).

An uprising in 1817 at Ilorin, the military center of Oyo, is particularly important in the accounts that are discussed here. Enslaved Muslims, who constituted a significant portion of the Oyo army, and particularly its cavalry forces, revolted in 1817 in sympathy with the jihad further north. Efforts to contain the uprising were not very successful, resulting

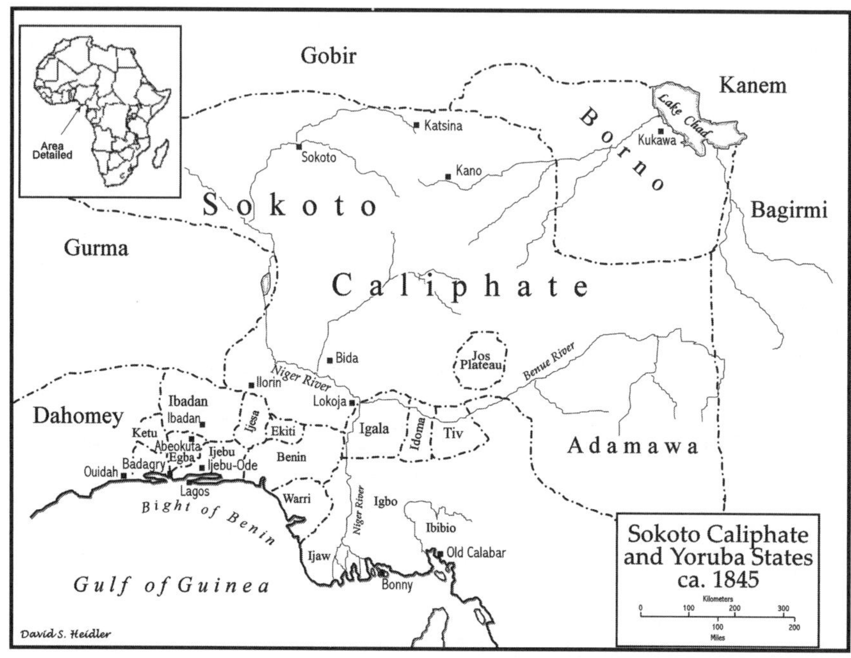

Sokoto Caliphate and Yoruba States ca. 1845

in the enslavement of many people and retaliatory raids by Muslims on Oyo towns and villages. By 1823, Ilorin was constituted as an emirate within the Sokoto Caliphate, and Oyo entered a period of collapse, resulting in its destruction through a series of wars lasting into the 1830s and with reverberations beyond, as Fagbeade's story reveals. After the demise of Oyo, new towns, walled for defense, were founded; these were filled with refugees, and hence their plight was similar to that of many other refugees in modern times, with the exception that enslavement was an ever-present danger in nineteenth-century Yorubaland. The events in which Lucy Fagbeade and her daughter became entangled were a result of these upheavals. As John Peel has argued, the confrontation and accommodation among Muslims, Christians, and adherents of *orisa* were instrumental in the definition of Yoruba ethnicity after the collapse of Oyo.[2] Hence the fact that Fagbeade's story comes to us through a Christian lens is neither irrelevant nor unusual.[3] Moreover, the case reveals the importance of biography in the reconstruction of the history of the Atlantic slave trade and the corresponding social history of the regions from which slaves came,[4] although such accounts have to be treated with caution because stories are always filtered. As Natalie Zemon Davis reminds us, there is much room for misinterpretation and confusing (mis)-representation.[5]

CIVILIANS IN THE CONTEXT OF ENSLAVEMENT

It might be argued that all victims of enslavement were a casualty of a system of slavery that had to find mechanisms of procurement. This has been characterized as a mode of production, in which the Marxist paradigm explains the interconnections among enslavement, slave trading, and slave use in Africa, and the distinctions between the African experience and the trans-Atlantic, and indeed trans-Saharan, experiences. My initial idea of transformations in slavery focused on the recognition of a separation in functions between the Americas and Africa.[6] In the Americas, slave trading and slave use were determined by market demands emanating from an Atlantic, indeed world economy, but where the process of enslavement, which involved insecurities and risks, was divorced from the areas of slave use. The generation of new slaves, a process of enslavement, did ensue, but it was through birth into slavery of a "creole" generation, born in the Americas or, as more recently appreciated, born under slavery in Africa as well as in those areas connected with the Americas. This paradigm is incomplete unless it allows for the enslavement of the Amerindian population as part of the slavery nexus. Nonetheless, the disjunction involved in the use of slaves in Jamaica, for example, and the use of slaves in the African kingdoms of Oyo or Asante, has to take into consideration the relationship between the enslavement phenomenon and the status of people in different contexts. In West Africa, free people were reduced to slavery, and hence can be considered, in part at least, as civilians subjected to the fluctuations of the political arena, whereas in Jamaica slaves were brought in from outside through the trans-Atlantic market. Issues of ethnicity and identity are important in this regard and have been the subject of extensive research.[7]

As a proxy, all enslaved women and all enslaved children in the trans-Atlantic slave trade can be considered to have been civilian casualties. As Joseph C. Miller has noted for Angola, "[t]he wars of the slaving frontier zone—in fact, wars generally—supplied the additional females [that were wanted], since warriors captured mainly women and children, killing the elderly and leaving them for the consumption of starving marauders and driving the male survivors into flight into the hills and woods."[8] There is nothing that I have found in any of the biographical accounts that have been identified that suggest that women were directly involved in war, although often they supported military campaigns and defense in subsidiary ways, such as with food preparation and transport of food supplies. For purposes of argument, I am allowing that most men were captured in war and therefore perhaps in some legal contexts were eligible to be sold into slavery as prisoners of war. And to some extent this was true, since there was allowance made for ransoming, which usually affected males from families who could raise the requisite funds, sometimes twice the sale price as a slave. In discussing casualties, it is perhaps best to exclude soldiers, and perhaps even potential soldiers, in the calculation, although this begs a question, since some soldiers were in fact slaves and hence their involvement in military campaigns was not necessarily voluntary.

There is considerable evidence that many males harbored belligerent intentions and therefore might well be excluded in estimating the impact of enslavement on the civilian population. For example, Ali Eisami, who was born in the later 1780s in Gazir, the metropolitan province of the empire of Borno, found himself in the capital of Oyo at the time of the Muslim uprising at Ilorin in 1817 and, because he was a Muslim, was suspected of thinking rebellious thoughts.[9] His father was a Muslim cleric and scholar, a *mallam,* and he in turn had received a good education in the Islamic tradition of Borno. He was about 20 years old when, in 1808, the jihad spread to his part of Borno. He was present when the Fulbe destroyed Birni Gazargamu, the capital of Borno, and later his hometown was sacked and he was enslaved. He was taken to Kano and Katsina before being sold south to Oyo in about 1813, where he lived for four years. In 1817, when the general of the Ilorin army, Afonja, offered freedom to slaves who enlisted in his forces, he was, in fact, recruiting the army that later sacked Osogun, the hometown of Samuel Crowther, later West Africa's first black Anglican bishop. Ali's Yoruba master, however, sold him to the coast to prevent his escape. As Ali recounted:

> After I had been there four years, a war arose: Now, all the slaves who went to the war, became free; so when the slaves heard these good news they all ran there, and the Yoruba saw it. The friend of the man who had bought me said to him, "if you do not sell this slave of yours, he will run away, and go to the war, so that your cowries will be lost, for this fellow has sound eyes." Then the man took hold of me, and bound me, and his three sons took me to the town of Ajashe [Porto Novo].[10]

At Porto Novo, he was sold to a slave ship, but a British patrol captured the ship at sea, and the fortunate slaves on board were landed at Sierra Leone. His Oyo master's suspicions were not unfounded. Many Muslim slaves joined the jihad, thereby gaining their freedom. For the next 30 years Ali lived in Freetown, where he was known as William Harding. S. W. Koelle, the German linguist and Church Missionary Society (CMS) missionary, employed him in his linguistic studies during most of 1848 and again for a period of two years during 1849–1852. The results of this work were the construction of a Kanuri grammar and dictionary, and the compilation of Kanuri readings with English translation.

Ali, a civilian casualty of the jihad in Borno, was a potential belligerent in Oyo. Nonetheless, for my purposes here, males are assumed to have been potentially rebellious and politically conscious and hence can be dismissed in assessing the impact of enslavement on civilians. Many males were captured in war or as a result of slave raiding that was politically motivated, if not also motivated by profits to be derived from ransoming and gains from the theft of livestock, grain, and other material goods. The profiles of enslaved Muslims from the central Sudan taken to Brazil provide excellent examples of this conscious policy of enslavement as a political weapon.[11] Moreover, newly captured males may have already have been slaves, since many armies were comprised of slave soldiers. Moreover, raiding was often directed into rural areas against unprotected plantations and villages where slaves lived, with the result that many people who were already enslaved were re-enslaved and simply changed masters. These same men could easily be impressed into the armies of their new masters and become active belligerents in war themselves.

ENSLAVEMENT OF WOMEN AND CHILDREN

Women and children were another matter, however. In most cases, they can be considered to have been civilian casualties. In some cases women and children were captured in the supporting camps of the military and hence could be classified as noncombatant belligerents. Even with this qualification it can be assumed that most women and children who entered the trans-Atlantic slave trade were civilians, and their enslavement was a punishment directed at the unprotected and those vulnerable to enslavement.

Women and children fitted into the Muslim slave trade more readily than men, and hence the disparity in the gender and age composition of the enslaved population on the coast of West Africa. Women and children tended to come from near the coast, but that does not mean that women and children from the interior were not also enslaved. Quite the contrary, there was a large trade in women and children in the interior where the markets, which were dominated by Muslim merchants, connected with the trans-Saharan trade.[12] Indeed, relatively speaking, women—at least young women and children, particularly girls—were worth more than men, even young men. The prices for slaves in the interior of West Africa (as presented in Table 1.1) indicate that there was a steady demand and a ready supply of slaves that were governed by market conditions, and therefore available for purchase. The price data also show that women were worth more than men, and girls were almost always worth more than young males. Examples of the price differential among categories of slaves based on age and gender, valued both in cowries and silver dollars that were current in much of West Africa, show not only that slave prices were low by comparison with the Americas, but that they ranged considerably between 1805 and 1850. For example, in 1841 at Eggan on the Niger River in Nupe, at a time of civil war and depressed prices, they were as low as $12 (or 40,000 cowries); however, in Sokoto in 1826, when there was high demand for young women as concubines among the increasingly large

Table 1.1
Slave Prices by Age and Gender, Central and Western Sudan

Date	Place	Woman	Man	Boy	Girl	Older Slave
1805	Sinsani[1]	K 80–100	K 40			
		$ 40–50	$ 20			
1826	Sokoto[2]	K 40–50	K 20	K 10	under K 30	
		$ 20–25	$ 10	$ 5	$ 15	
1832	Idah[3]	K 60–110	K 30–50	K 10–30		
		$ 18–36	$ 10–16.7	$ 3–9		
1835	Katsina[4]	K 50–60	K 30	K 45	K 35–45	K 10–15
		$ 25–30	$ 15	$ 22.5	$ 17.5–22.5	$ 5–7.5
1841	Rabba[5]	K 60–120	K 30–50	K 10–30		
		$ 18–36	$ 9–15	$ 3–9		
1841	Eggan[6]	K 40	K 20	K 20		
		$ 12	$ 6	$ 6		
1850	Kano[7]	K 40–100	K 30	K 20	K 20–30	K 10
		$ 20–50	$ 15	$ 10	$ 10–15	$ 5

Key: K = 1000 Cowries; $ = Silver Dollars

[1]Mungo Park, *Journal of a Mission into the Interior of Africa in the Year 1805* (London: John Murray, 1815), 162.

[2]According to Hugh Clapperton, at Sokoto in 1826 "a young male slave, from thirteen to twenty years of age, will bring from 10,000 to 20,000 cowries [$5–10]; a female slave, if very handsome, from 40,000 to 50,000 [$20–25]; the common price is about 30,000 [$15] for a virgin about fourteen or fifteen." See Clapperton, *Journal of a Second Expedition into the Interior of Africa* (London: John Murray, 1829), 59.

[3]According to William Allen and T.R.H. Thomson, *A Narrative of the Expedition Sent by Her Majesty's Government to the River Niger in 1841*, vol. 1 (London: Frank Cass, 1968 [1848]), 401, a young female cost 60,000–120,000 cowries, a young man 30,000–50,000 cowries, a boy 10,000–30,000 cowries, and a common slave 10,000–30,000 cowries.

[4]Daumas reported that a man with a beard cost 10,000–15,000 cowries, an older woman 10,000–15,000 cowries, an adolescent boy 30,000 cowries, a small boy 45,000 cowries, a small girl 35,000–45,000 cowries, and a young woman (price varying with beauty) 50,000–60,000 cowries. See M.J.E. Daumas and Ausone de Chancel, *Le grand désert: Itinéraire d'une caravane du Sahara au pays des Nègres-Royaume de Haoussa* (Paris: Lévy frères, 1856), 241–42.

[5]Allen and Thomson, *Narrative of the Expedition*, 401.

[6]James Frederick Schön and Samuel Crowther, *Journals of the Rev. James Frederick Schön and Mr. Samuel Crowther* (London: Frank Cass, 1970 [1854]), 176.

administrative, merchant, and intellectual class in the capital of the Sokoto Caliphate, they reached as high as $40 to $50. Prices at Kano, the largest city in the Caliphate, which had a very prosperous merchant and industrial class, ranged from $20 to $50 (or from 40,000 to 100,000 cowries) for a slave woman. Children could be bought for as low as $5 to $10 in Sokoto in 1826 but could cost as much as $20 to $30 in many other places in the first half of the nineteenth century, regardless of gender. Older slaves were consistently valued at $5 to $10 dollars, certainly depending upon their skills and usefulness.

An analysis of the age and gender profile of the trans-Atlantic trade allows some basis for estimating the impact of the population displacement on Africa and thereby addresses such issues as collateral damage. This analysis is possible because of the voyage database constructed by Eltis, Behrendt, Richardson, and Klein, which allows estimates of the number of females and children taken across the Atlantic as slaves.[13] As can be seen in Table 1.2, the proportion of females decreased over time. In the second half of the seventeenth century, the proportion of females, initially at 45 percent in 1651–1675, fell to 41.3 percent in the last quarter of the century. The decline in the proportion of females continued, dropping to roughly one-third in the first half of the eighteenth century—which in fact was the proportion that is often cited as the ideal among slave traders at the time and is reflected in the scholarly literature. Thereafter, the proportion of females again increased, rising to 38.5 percent in 1751–1775 and 45.1 percent in 1776–1800, before declining radically to 31 percent in the first half of the nineteenth century and to about 24.5 percent in the last years of the trade. The shift in preference was toward males, and increasingly boys. In terms of assessing civilian casualties, this profile suggests that civilians were increasingly the victims of enslavement. The shift in gender and age in the trans-Atlantic trade reflects nothing more than the destinations of this civilian population. It can be assumed that if boys were increasingly sent to the Americas, then girls were retained in relatively equal numbers within Africa. The resulting social subordination and displacement, which were perhaps of differing value and impact, nonetheless are factors in assessing casualties.

---

[7]At Kano in 1850, according to James Richardson, a man with a beard cost 10,000–15,000 cowries, a youth with a beard beginning, 30,000 cowries and under, a boy without a beard 30,000–35,000, a small boy 20,000 cowries or less, an older woman 10,000 cowries or less, a woman "with breasts hanging down" as much as 80,000 cowries, a woman with "plump" breasts as high as 100,000 cowries, girls with "little breasts" 40,000 cowries, smaller girls 30,000 cowries or less, and a female child less than 20,000 cowries. See Richardson, *Narrative of a Mission to Central Africa Performed in the Years 1850-51*, vol. 2 (London: Chapman and Hall, 1853), 102–3.

Table 1.2
Proportion of Females among Enslaved Africans Crossing the Atlantic (Percent)

Region	1651–1675	1676–1700	1701–1725	1726–1750	1751–1775	1776–1800	1801–1825	1826–1850	1851–1867
Senegambia	–	27.0	31.0	21.3	37.8	31.6	46.8	32.6	–
Sierra Leone	–	23.2	31.9	–	41.4	34.8	32.0	28.1	–
Windward Coast	–	–	–	39.7	38.4	33.0	26.3	25.7	–
Gold Coast	42.7	46.8	32.9	32.2	37.9	34.2	28.1	28.7	–
Bight of Benin	41.3	41.0	36.0	40.8	46.2	34.3	24.3	34.9	27.7
Bight of Biafra	50.3	41.1	48.3	24.6	39.9	42.6	35.0	34.3	–
West Central	–	40.1	26.2	32.8	32.5	35.2	29.1	26.8	24.7
South East Africa	–	–	–	47.3	–	28.5	30.5	19.4	13.2
Origin Unknown	38.5	40.6	34.5	33.6	43.4	30.1	31.3	24.8	27.3
Average	45.0	41.3	33.9	33.8	38.5	45.1	31.2	31.7	24.5

Source: David Eltis, Stephen Behrendt, David Richardson, and Herbert Klein, *The Atlantic Slave Trade: A Database on CD-Rom* (Cambridge: Cambridge University Press, 1999).

The proportion of children rose from approximately 10 to 11 percent of the numbers of slaves transported across the Atlantic in the second half of the seventeenth century, reaching 28.8 percent in 1751–1775, before leveling off at 22.2 percent for the remainder of the eighteenth century (Table 1.3). The increased proportion of children in the mid-eighteenth century probably related to growing demand for slaves in the Americas and the inability of African suppliers to provide the numbers required without resorting to the sale of more children. The proportion of children increased dramatically in the nineteenth century, especially after the British abolition of the slave trade in 1807 and the attempt to impose abolition through the seizure of slave ships. The proportion of children rose to 42.6 percent in the first quarter of the nineteenth century, remaining at 40.7 percent in the second quarter, before declining slightly to 35.9 percent in the last years of the trans-Atlantic trade. The increase in the number of children was particularly striking in west-central Africa and in southeastern Africa, where the proportion of

Table 1.3
Proportion of Children among Enslaved Africans Crossing the Atlantic (Percent)

Region	1651–75	1675–1700	1701–25	1726–50	1751–75	1776–1800	1801–25	1826–50	1851–67
Senegambia	–	5.4	9.1	12.0	30.2	16.7	25.7	19.7	–
Sierra Leone	–	7.3	6.5	–	34.3	25.5	41.1	41.9	–
Windward Coast	–	–	–	35.3	42.7	24.9	34.5	29.3	–
Gold Coast	6.4	8.8	17.5	15.1	21.4	19.4	38.0	46.2	–
Bight of Benin	6.5	12.3	19.6	26.1	19.3	14.4	22.5	36.1	18.8
Bight of Biafra	12.8	9.7	23.9	18.4	34.3	19.7	29.7	39.3	–
West Central	–	19.8	24.5	32.1	30.4	18.3	41.0	52.9	41.6
South East Africa	–	–	–	–	–	29.6	47.0	62.4	–
Origin Not known	9.1	18.1	22.9	23.7	27.1	34.5	46.0	29.6	–
Average	10.5	11.3	19.3	22.6	28.8	22.2	42.6	40.7	35.9

Source: David Eltis, Stephen Behrendt, David Richardson, and Herbert Klein, *The Atlantic Slave Trade: A Database on CD-Rom* (Cambridge: Cambridge University Press, 1999).

children, many of them boys as well, reached 52.0 percent and 62.4 percent respectively.[14] Between 1600 and 1800 over one million children, who were mostly aged between 6 or 7 and about 13 or 14, crossed the Atlantic. It has been estimated that the scale of this forced migration was such that probably as many as four million newly enslaved children would have remained behind in Africa, assuming a demographic profile for the enslaved population that matches a normal population.[15]

These estimates of the proportion of children, and also females, in different branches of the trans-Atlantic trade in different time periods are presented in Table 1.4, based on material summarized by David Geggus from a variety of sources.[16] His data show that the number of males per females was almost equal in the Dutch trade between Angola and Brazil in 1636–

Table 1.4
Gender and Age Composition of Enslaved Africans in Selected Branches of the Atlantic Slave Trade

Carrier	Destination	Date	Males per 100 Females	Children (%)	Number of Slaves
Dutch	Angola-Brazil	1636–43	105	33	2,064
Dutch	Guinea-Brazil	1636–45	138	13	3,086
British	Barbados	1663–67	108	9	2,269
British	British West Indies	1673–1725	158	14	73,990
Dutch	West India Company	1675–1740	228	13	36,121
British	Spanish America	1715–38	197	34	17,080
French	French colonies	1714–56	186	27	59,705
British	South Carolina	1735–40	–	14*	11,562
Dutch	Free trade	1730–90	144	22	25,051
French	French colonies	1764–78	171	27	101,533
British	Jamaica	1764–88	165	19*	74,546
Danish	Danish Caribbean	1777–89	175	23	15,203
British	Grenada	1784–88	154	32	13,561
French	French colonies	1784–92	196	19	13,197
Spanish and Cuban	Cuba	1811–67	229	39	51,577
Portuguese and Brazil	Brazil	1811–67	188	42	27,365

* Children defined as those under 4′ 4″ in height.

Source: Derived from David Geggus, "Sex Ratio, Age and Ethnicity in the Atlantic Slave Trade: Data from French Shipping and Plantation Records," *Journal of African History* 30, 1 (1989): 24.

1643, and that the trade to Barbados in 1663–1667 was comprised of almost equal numbers of males and females. However, the proportion of children was very different, being only 9 percent of Barbados imports but one-third of Dutch shipments. How children were identified may account for some of this discrepancy. The proportion of females to males varied greatly, dropping from virtual parity in the seventeenth-century trade to as low as 30 percent of the enslaved population moved in the Dutch trade of 1675–1740, and in the trade to Cuba in 1811–1867. The ideal of loading cargoes of one-third females was attained in the Dutch trade of 1730–1790, the British trade to the West Indies in 1673–1725, and the British trade to Grenada in 1784-1788. Otherwise rather less than one-third of cargoes were females, virtually all of whom can be considered to have been nonbelligerent casualties.

In considering the damage to civilians resulting from war and raiding, it is necessary to recognize that many enslaved individuals remained in Africa. Hence estimates of the number exported across the Atlantic, Sahara Desert, and Indian Ocean, while important in themselves, are also significant because they are some indication (as Patrick Manning has attempted to simulate) of the scale of slavery within Africa.[17] Typically, in 1834 a merchant called Soho purchased "six young women, three of whom had children at the breast," at the Niger-Benue confluence and was intent on taking them further inland to buy ivory, not to the coast for shipment to the Americas.[18] The differentials in slave prices in the interior of West Africa, in which females generally cost a quarter or a third more than males, reflected an internal West African market for slaves, which to some extent was autonomous.[19] Muslim merchants played a key role in this internal slave trade in West Africa, as much as mulatto merchants did in Portuguese Angola; whereas in west central Africa where merchants funneled slaves to the coast, Muslim merchants were as likely as not to transfer slaves for retention within Africa.

The slave trade tended to be concentrated at major commercial entrepots in the interior of West Africa, as well as at particular ports on the African coast. The towns and cities that dotted the savanna and sahel [the semi-arid fringe of the southern Sahara] of West Africa all had thriving slave markets, not only for purposes of export but also for local use. In the nineteenth century, these urban centers included such places as Kano, Kukawa, Jenne, and Timbuktu, and by mid-century there were probably 500 or more towns with populations of several thousand inhabitants, some with as many as 50,000 people.[20] At the coast, there were similar concentrations, with most slaves sent to the Americas leaving from a relatively small number of large ports and coastal towns including Ouidah, Bonny, Old Calabar, Luanda, Benguela, Elmina, Cape Coast Castle, Anomabu, and Koromantin.[21] The interlocking slave markets of the coast and the interior were characterized by the widespread use of slaves internally and by an external trade that was multidirectional: across the Sahara, Red Sea, and Indian Ocean, as well as the Atlantic. It might be asked how it is possible to talk of "civilians" in a continent in which slavery was pervasive.

Although regional variations in the impact on the civilian population were significant, it is even more significant that the impact of the violence associated with slavery was pervasive.

THE SLAVE TRADE OF THE BIGHT OF BENIN

The region that is the primary focus of this chapter, the interior of the Bight of Benin, was tied to the slave trade through a series of ports located on the lagoons just behind the beach, which characterized the stretch of the Guinea coast from the edge of the Niger delta in the east to the Volta River in the west. None of the towns on the "Slave Coast" from Lagos in the east to Badagry, Porto Novo, Ouidah, Grand and Petit Popo, and Agoué in the west actually had harbors, and slaves had to be embarked through heavy surf in large dugout canoes. Representative of the merchants of these ports were Brazilians, often of mixed African and Portuguese descent, and returning former slaves who were from the interior of the Bight of Benin.

The most important merchant family who dominated the slave trade was that of Francisco Felix de Souza (c. 1779–1849) and his sons, especially Isidoro Felix (c. 1802–1858).[22] Francisco Felix de Souza came from either Bahia or Rio de Janeiro in Brazil. He first went to the Bight of Benin in about 1793, staying initially for three years and establishing a factory at Badagry, which was called Ajido.[23] According to one report, he was 23 when he first arrived, suggesting a birth date of 1770.[24] He returned to Brazil for several years, where he was allegedly involved in political intrigue and may have been forced to flee. In any event he moved back to the Bight of Benin in about 1800 and remained there, except for several trips to Brazil, until his death in 1849.[25] Although his headquarters were at Ouidah, he also settled at Petit Popo to the west of Ouidah, where he established another factory, which he also called Ajido. He married Jijibou, daughter of Comlagan, chief of Popo, who, according to family tradition, bore his first son, Isidoro Felix, in 1802.[26] By 1825 he allegedly had been resident at Whydah and Popo "upwards of twenty five years—and [had] partly adopted the fashions and customs of the natives—He having upwards of fifty wives and nearly as many children."[27]

By 1803 Isidoro Felix was the scribe and book-keeper at the Portuguese fort in Ouidah.[28] Soon after, the governor, Jacinto José de Souza, who was apparently his brother, died in 1804. Thereupon, de Souza became acting governor, at least until 1806.[29] Subsequently, he abandoned the fort and concentrated on the flourishing slave trade to Brazil and Cuba. The British naval patrol seized one of his ships in 1816,[30] which is one of the earliest examples of a merchant resident in West Africa owning ships involved in the slave trade. In 1818 he supported Gezo in the coup d'état that ousted Gezo's brother Adandozan as king of Dahomey. Thereafter de Souza had an official position in the Dahomean government; he was known by his nickname as the *chacha* of Ouidah and "almost entirely" dominated the slave trade of the Bight of

Benin in the following years.[31] In 1824 (according to Hugh Clapperton, who met him in 1825) he ran afoul of Spanish authorities, who accused him "of not fulfilling his contracts" and "plundered his vessels of upwards of twelve hundred slaves besides other property." Still, as Clapperton revealed, de Souza had "several vessels running between Whydah and Bahia these five or six years, which have been generally fortunate in escaping His [British] Majesty's cruizers on the Coast, and must have realised him immense profits."[32] By the 1840s, because of his advanced age, his son Isidoro was running the business and, because of the British blockade, was shipping slaves from Popo. De Souza died on May 8, 1849 and Isidoro in 1858.

While the de Souza family dominated the trade of Ouidah and Popo, their activities as slave traders were representative of other ports in the Bight of Benin, notably Porto Novo and Lagos. The Bight of Benin was unusual in that relatively fewer children came from this region than other parts of Africa, most notably the Bight of Biafra, Angola, and Mozambique. Before 1700, about 12 percent of Bight of Benin exports were children. The proportion rose to 26 percent in the second quarter of the eighteenth century, which was higher than the average for all regions of Africa (Table 1.3). Thereafter the proportion of children in shipments from the Bight of Benin was consistently lower than other parts of the coast, constituting about 19.3 percent in 1751–1775, 14.4 percent in 1776-1800, but rising to 22.5 percent in 1801–1825 and peaking at 36.1 percent in 1826–1850. Although it appears that proportionately fewer children entered the export trade to the Americas from the Bight of Benin, there is no reason to believe that fewer children were actually enslaved. In this region in particular children and women tended to remain in slavery within West Africa, and this was more likely the case further from the coast. Comparatively, a higher proportion of adults were sent to the Americas from the Bight of Benin than from most other regions along the African coast.

ENSLAVEMENT AND THE SEPARATION OF KIN

The dangers of being exposed to slavery in Africa not only related to the possibility of sale across the Atlantic, but were also connected to the local market for labor and the reliance on various forms of dependency that overlapped with slavery. Moreover, local demand included the purchase of slaves for human sacrifice, and in some places ritual cannibalism was practiced, in which the execution of enemies was an alternative to their sale into slavery. Similarly, in many places twins were killed rather than being sold into slavery. Finally, in some places individuals threatened with slavery could attach themselves to religious shrines for protection from a worse fate, since sale into slavery risked execution, not just oppressive working conditions or sale across the Atlantic. One orphaned child whose relatives sold him into slavery (and who subsequently passed through the hands of various masters) was destined for sacrifice, escaped, attempted suicide, was recaptured, and finally was sold to a Brazilian slave merchant, which (as he put it) "was the end of my bondage under men of my own colour." By this time, he had lost contact with anyone whose language he knew.[33] In some cases, slavery was related to the prevalence of polygyny, in which having multiple wives was perhaps not unrelated to the disposability of children in cases of debt, contracted marriage, or simply because of insubordination.

Any analysis of casualties, of course, has to allow for those killed during the enslavement process, particularly the impact on the elderly and infants. Moreover, the corresponding impact of disease and famine, sometimes politically induced because of the disruption of raiding and warfare, were after-effects of enslavement and related acts of violence and domination. Joseph Wright, for example, was by origin Egba Alake, one of the three major subdivisions of the Egba Yoruba.[34] He provides an account of his capture after his town, which had been under siege, was taken in the early 1820s during the Owu war:

> The enemies satisfied themselves with little children, little girls, young men, and young women; and so they did not care about the aged and old people. They killed them without mercy. Father knew not the son, and the son knew not the father. Pity had departed from the face of mothers. Abundant heaps of dead bodies were in the streets, and there were none to bury them. Suckling babies were crying at the point of death, and there were none to pick them up. Mothers looked upon them with contempt—a lamentable day![35]

Other documented accounts include the case, as analyzed by José C. Curto, of Nbena and her daughter, who were illegally enslaved in 1817-1820,[36] and the case of Catherine Mulgrave-Zimmermann, kidnapped in 1834 by Brazilian slavers on the coast near Cape Town.[37] Usually, enslaved girls from the interior were retained locally, but in neither of these cases were the girls from there. Rather, they came from the coastal zone where, based on local custom of "original freedom" or British law, individuals were supposed to be protected. Separation from kin was common, as the case of Thomas King demonstrates. As a boy, he was enslaved in about 1825 in a war that destroyed his village, one of the old Egba towns. He was educated at the school of the CMS and graduated from Fourah Bay Institute in 1849. He was sent to Badagry in 1850 and was subsequently reunited with his mother in Abeokuta, where he worked as a catechist, becoming a deacon in 1854, and being ordained in 1857.[38] The accounts have survived because of the British campaign against the slave trade, which resulted in the occupation of Lagos in 1851 and the establishment of a formal protectorate in 1861. Various Christian missions, especially the CMS, were active in repatriating former slaves who had been liberated and had lived in Sierra Leone.

A particularly poignant account of the separation of kin was provided to the Parliamentary Enquiry into the Slave Trade in 1789. James Arnold, who had been on a ship to the Bight of Biafra, recounted that he had witnessed the pathos of siblings who had been separated through slavery, only to be reunited for the Middle Passage.[39]

The first Person who was purchased … was a young Girl of about Fifteen Years of Age, whom we called Eve; for it is usual on board the Slave Ships to give the Appellation of Adam and Eve to the first Man and Woman that are brought on board. This Girl, who was extremely clever and intelligent, told … the following Tale: "That a Goat had been found in her Father's Garden, which, she said, had been purposely put there: That one of the Traders and great Men of the Place came in the Morning, and finding the Goat there, charged her Father with having stolen it, and said, moreover, that nothing less would satisfy him for the Offence than One of his Daughters as a Slave. In consequence of this, he was obliged to produce them, or abide by the Consequences himself. They were Three in Number, and the great Man, liking her the best whom we called Eve, took her and sold her to those Traders, who afterwards brought her to the Vessel." She came from a Place called Bunje, which is on the opposite Continent of the Cameroons. About Three Months afterwards, a young Girl of about Eight Years old was brought on board. On being placed on the Quarter-deck, she either saw, or attracted the Notice of the other young Girl just mentioned. They soon embraced each other, and went below. Their Features were much alike, and it appeared, upon Inquiry, that they were Sisters.

Although Arnold did not enquire into how the younger girl was enslaved, it is clear that these girls were victims who had been forced into slavery.

Another notable example is Bishop Samuel Ayaji Crowther (c. 1807-1891), who came from one of the Ibarapa towns, north of Egba country and west of Ibadan, which had been subject to Oyo.[40] He was enslaved in 1821 in the course of the jihad in the interior of the Bight of Benin that destroyed the Oyo kingdom, including his hometown, Osogun. In 1822 he was sold in Lagos to a Portuguese slave ship but was freed that same evening by two Royal Navy vessels and taken to Freetown in Sierra Leone, where he was cared for by missionaries of the CMS. He was ethnically Yoruba but, as he was liberated in Sierra Leone, he did not reach Brazil or Cuba as so many other Yoruba did. His history personified the interaction among Islam, Christianity, and *orisa* worship. His allegiance to the *orisa, obatala,* was part of his upbringing at Osogun.[41] He was taken through enslavement, at the hands of Muslim jihadists, although his conversion to Christianity led him to a position as the first African bishop in the Anglican Church. Unlike most slaves, he was fortunate in being reunited with his mother and sister and indeed has left an account of their enslavement.[42]

ENSLAVEMENT AND RANSOMING

Ransoming was an important mechanism for reducing the number of civilian casualties from enslavement. In many places, and especially in areas of Muslim influence, captives were often provided with the opportunity to regain their freedom through the practice of ransoming.

Relatives were notified of their captivity or were able to learn about it and thereby arrange for payment of the redemption fee. This system of ransoming was tied closely to the instruments of slave raiding, war, jihad, and politically sanctioned actions intended to enslave. Ransoming also failed, as it did in the cases of many Muslim men, such as Mahommah Gardo Baquaqua (c. 1820, and still alive, in England, in 1857).[43] Baquaqua was enslaved twice. The first time was in northern Asante, but fortunately he was redeemed by his brother. In his second enslavement in 1845, he was not so fortunate. He found himself moved rapidly to the coast and sold to a Portuguese ship through the notorious hands of Francisco Felix de Souza and his son. Baquaqua was a Muslim and Hausa who arrived in Brazil 10 years after the Malês uprising in Bahia, which Muslims, especially Hausa and Yoruba, had staged. A slave in Brazil for two years, he was able to jump ship in New York City (where his master took him with an assignment of coffee in June 1847), and he gained his freedom with the aid of the New York Vigilance Society. The account of his Brazilian experiences, his life in urban settings, and his residence in Haiti are unique. He was a Muslim who became a Baptist. He did not marry but was involved with the daughter of a white abolitionist in upstate New York, before he fled to Canada. Again the case establishes the significance of narrative; we have a detailed biography, and we know what he looked like—there is a lot of information on his life.[44]

Many people were not ransomed, for various reasons. In 1841 a boy who had been seized by "Felatah" raiders near the confluence of the Niger and Benue was sold into slavery because the ransom offered by his parents "was not sufficient."[45] James Macaulay, a liberated slave who returned to his home in 1841, located his sister and discovered that she had had two of her children seized by "Fulatahs" and taken to Sokoto. She was trying to arrange their ransom.[46] Kidnapping was a form of lawlessness, although there were many attempts to restrict the incidence of arbitrary seizure. In some cases, the capture of people was a form of *panyarring,* which in West Africa denoted collective action to obtain redress through arbitrary seizure of anyone associated with a complaint. Although the results for the victim could be the same, in cases of outright kidnapping no justification was provided. In both cases, the institution of human pawning was an attempt to develop an alternate system of defining credit relationships. However, those held in pawn were not usually volunteers and were really little better than kidnap victims.

Osifekunde was from Epe in Ijebu Ode, although he was born in Makun in about 1795. His father, Adde Sounlou, an Ijebu warrior, had fled to Makun after killing another Ijebu soldier in a fight. As a boy, Osifekunde also spent time in the Kingdom of Benin, once again as a result of his father fleeing to seek asylum. He was about 20 when Ijaw pirates seized him in the lagoons that connected Lagos with the Niger delta, apparently in the 1810s. He was taken to Brazil, where he spent almost 20 years and was known as Joaquim. In the mid 1830s his master took him to Paris, where

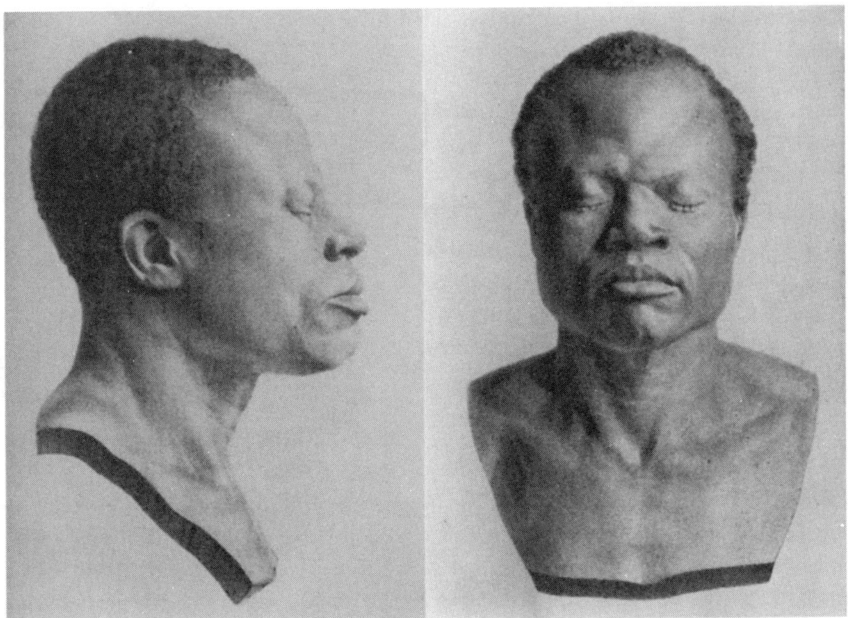

Osifikunde (c. 1805–after 1841) B Marie Armand Pascal d'Avezac-Macaya, "A Notice sur le pays et le peuple des Yébous, en Afrique," in the *Mémories de la Société Ethnologique*, 2:2 (1845).

he worked as a servant. He came to the attention of Marie Armand Pascal d'Avezac-Macaya, vice-president of the Société Ethnologique of Paris and member of numerous geographical societies with interests in Africa and the Orient. D'Avezac was a proponent of the new science of ethnography and, in that capacity, interrogated Osifekunde, asking questions of his homeland and its language. D'Avezac arranged for Osifekunde to travel to Sierra Leone, but Osifekunde preferred servitude under his former master in Brazil, where he could be with his son, and disappeared from Le Havre leaving behind only a life-size bust commissioned in about 1838. D'Avezac published his account in 1845.[47]

It is clear, therefore, that many, if not most, enslaved individuals should be considered civilian casualties with justifiable claims for "collateral damage." It should also be recognized that the social order of enslavement was closely associated with local instruments of power and domination. For example, on Monday, March 7, 1870, at Lokoja at the confluence of the Niger and Benue rivers, "two of the school children that [word illegible] one was ransomed but the other was sold with some of our class members to Bidda but the rest ran away with their parents [word illegible] to Bassa, A great hope for them to redeem back as soon as Massabas men [i.e., the Nupe army from Bida] can be away out of this place."[48] The trauma of separation was widely recorded. At the Parliamentary Committee hearings on the slave trade in 1789, Arnold responded to the question, "Were the Slaves commonly dejected when first brought on board?" by giving the following testimony:

I had an opportunity of going down the coast from Bonny, as far as the Island of Bimbe, and upon the passage we purchased nine slaves, most of which were very much dejected—one in particular, a girl, when she found that she was sold, clung fast about the neck of her disposer, and eagerly embraced him—he did all that laid in his power to make her easy under her situation; but notwithstanding his exertions, accompanied with ours, it was impossible, though a child of about ten or twelve years of age, to give her any comfort, and she continued for three or four days in that situation; indeed, all the rest of the cargo, and which we received from the Garland, appeared to me more or less afflicted when they found that we had left their country.[49]

Pawnship was widespread, as numerous studies have demonstrated, and the prevalence of this institution also involved the subjugation of individuals who were not necessarily, and usually not all, involved in the decisions of their own subordination. As in the case of slaves, the fate of pawns become a preoccupation of Christian missionaries who believed that it was their responsibility to protect pawns. Are these individuals who were being protected from potential abuse to be considered civilians?[50] In 1863, Elizabeth Alady, who had fled to the CMS mission, reported that she and her three- year-old son, who had been born into slavery, were to be sold together to pay off a debt of her master.[51] But this also raises the question: are the children of slaves who inherit slavery as a status and a mechanism of control in fact civilians?

ENSLAVEMENT AND CIVILIAN CASUALTIES—AN ASSESSMENT

The overwhelming evidence from western Africa and the areas bordering the Atlantic, as well as those extending along the Indian Ocean at least as far as Mozambique, suggests that the hazards of childhood and gender were pervasive. A large proportion of children and women found themselves in conditions of slavery, and the overwhelming portion of these appear to have been victims of war and political oppression. Hence they can be considered to have been civilian casualties. This designation is not intended to trivialize the experiences of slavery, but to suggest that a comparison with modern forms of collateral damage to civilian populations should be perceived in historical perspective. Structurally, slavery involved the redistribution of population through coercive means, which included a gross level of inefficiency in the form of death and destruction. When asked how old children were when brought to be sold, whether they were in age from 8 to 12 or 13, and whether they were brought with or without their parents or near relations (for whose crimes they might be supposed to have been condemned, and in whose punishment to be involved), John Ashley Hall answered that he had "frequently seen Slaves brought on board from eight to thirteen years of age; they always came without any relations; I never knew but one instance to the contrary, which was a woman with a child, about six weeks old, sucking at the breast."[52] According to Hall,

> I remember an instance of a woman being purchased, with her child about six weeks old; the child was very cross from indisposition, and had made much noise at night; the boatswain wished much to have permission to throw it overboard, he even solicited the captain for that permission, and gave as a reason, that the child would not live, and if it did it would fetch nothing in the West Indies; which request the captain received with horror and detestation.[53]

Similarly, at Gbebe, on the Niger River, James Thomas reported on November 19, 1858 that "today I am very sorry to say that our mind is always perplexed in this place on account of the unsettled state of the town." He continued:

> some time ago one Igbira man sold a woman which belong to a Nupe man they found her in another village So the owner of the woman redeemed her for the sum of 120,000 cowries[;] they took the matter before the King and the King asked the woman[;] she pointed the man out who sold her to another village so the man confessed[,] then the King told him pay the amount 120,000 cowries, from that time the Nupe party agreed altogether to leave this place. Though the man promised faithfully to pay the cowries he never fulfilled his promise[;] on account of this the Nupes party made ready to go out of this place even our landlord, Daganna told Mr. Newland in the same evening that he was ready to sent his people to Bassa Town after which they will try to cut bush over the river to built their houses today matter was very strong. The Nupe people wish to leave this place, their wives and their children tied boundles to remove at once.[54]

Thomas reported that on December 4,

> the King sent a person to call us after eight o clock … last time we pass one Nupe man was going up the river by chance he met a man brought for sold this poor man bought him without money to pay it the same time and bring the slave. He promised to pay as soon he sell [sic] the slave. When he reached home another day then the slave died and there is no money to pay to the owner the man himself was oblige to put himself under another man to work hardly for to pay the money.[55]

Finally, there is the case of Joaquim d'Almeida, known as "Zoki Azata" ("Zoki" being an abbreviated form of Joaquim), who lived at Agoué near Grand Popo and was associated with the lagoon slave trade of the Bight of Benin. Originally from Mahi country, north of Dahomey, Joaquim d'Almeida was the exception among liberated slaves in that he became a large-scale slave trader himself.[56] In fact, he became the most important trader in the area in the early nineteenth century and was described by a contemporary observer as having monopolized the trade of Agoué, which was close to Little Popo where the de Souza family were located. D'Almeida's career is well documented. As a boy he had been captured by the Fon and shipped to Bahia. There the captain of a slave ship by the name of Manoel Joaquim d'Almeida bought him and taught him the trade. He was baptized, adopted the name of his owner, and eventually was freed. As early as 1835 he was making slave-trading voyages to the West African coast and finally settled in Agoué, probably in 1845. He later established himself at Ouidah, founding the quarter Zokikomé. He built a church, inviting missionaries from Brazil and Sao Thomé, and was granted the post of "director" of customs on the beach between Agoué and Little Popo (equivalent to the office of *yevogan* at Ouidah) by the king of Glidji. This meant that he was in charge of the collection of taxes from European traders, which gave him considerable power. He was friendly with the Lawsons, the most important merchants at Little Popo. He died in May 1857 after (according to local tradition) being poisoned by Pedro Kodjo, another Afro-Brazilian, following a quarrel over money.[57]

These vignettes enhance the richness of the story of Lucy Fagbeade, Ogunyomi's mother, as recorded in her journal by Mrs. Hinderer and reproduced here as an appendix. The tragedy of kin seeking the locations of relatives and then arranging their ransom raises the issue of reparations for the collateral damage affecting society as a whole that resulted from slavery. The prevalence of slavery cannot be isolated from historical context. The level of insecurity was related to factors such as the expansion of states, Muslim advocacy of jihad, and forms of social organization involving secret societies that behaved like Mafioso. The demand for slaves in the Americas certainly reinforced the enslavement of people, providing an alternate market to local use and exploitation. The sordid history of slavery encompasses all the stories and tragedies of the enslaved, whether they were retained within Africa or exported to the Americas, North Africa, or elsewhere. Many of their stories have been preserved because when they converted to Christianity people recounted their sad tales. In attempting to understand the impact of slavery and the slave trade on African societies and cultures, this process of "confession" in the course of conversion has left us with biographical accounts of the enslaved population—men, women, and children—that flesh out the concept of slavery in its personal dimensions.

APPENDIX: OGUNYOMI FINDS HER MOTHER, LUCY FAGBEADE

By Anna Hinderer[58]

In 1854, a war broke out between Ibadan and Efon.[59] Until that time Ogunyomi was a happy child at home, living in peace with her father, mother, and two brothers, in the town of Efon. When the war began, all the able-bodied men were compelled to join the army, and amongst them was Ogunyomi's father. He was never heard of again, and most probably had fallen in battle. His town was destroyed, the men and youths were killed; and the women and children, after wandering about in despair and misery, were taken prisoners, and sold for slaves. A few, stronger than the rest, contrived to escape into the bush, and amongst them were Ogunyomi and her mother. Fear drove them farther and farther. Their only food was roots and leaves. When they had threaded their way for two or three days, through the dark and pathless thicket, they began to hope that they were safe from their enemies. But they were afraid to speak above a whisper, lest they should be heard and overtaken. Exhausted with hunger and fatigue, they at last lay down to rest, under the shelter of a great tree. At once two men sprang upon them, one seized the mother, and the other the child. Their tears and entreaties were useless, they were torn from each other, and hurried off in different directions. The little girl, who was only seven years old, was taken to Ibadan, and put up for sale in the market. A Christian man, who himself had once been a slave, touched by her sorrowful face, took her in his arms, and tried to comfort her.[60] Hearing that she was soon to be taken down to the coast and stowed away in a slave ship, he longed to purchase her and set her free; but it was beyond his power. He therefore went to the mission-house, told her sad story to Mr. and Mrs. Hinderer, and entreated them to redeem her.[61] They gladly gave him money for her ransom, and in a few minutes the kind-hearted man brought the little girl to her new home. The poor child had never before seen a white face, and she screamed with terror when she found herself in the presence of the missionaries. The other children in the compound gathered round her, and told her how happy they were, and that all who lived in the mission-house were safe from slavery. She soon learned, herself, to love her "white mother," and was constantly found at her side. When strangers came to the house, she clung closely to her, fearing lest they should carry her away. But her great delight was to sit on the floor near to Mrs. Hinderer, and puzzle over the alphabet, or the still greater mysteries of needle and thread. Singing was a pleasure to her, and she quickly learned simple prayers and easy texts. She was a child of a happy disposition, and often her hearty laugh rang through the compound. But a change came over her. Her laugh was heard no more, and her countenance was sad and troubled. Mrs. Hinderer asked, "What is the matter, Ogunyomi? Is any one unkind to you?" "Oh, no," she said quickly. "Then what makes you sad?" She burst into tears, and sobbed out, "Iya mi, iya mi!"—"My mother, my mother!" Mrs. Hinderer tried to comfort her, and promised to have a diligent search made for her mother. But, in a large town of more than a hundred thousand people, this was no easy task, especially as slaves usually received a new name; besides which, it was not known whether the poor woman was in Ibadan, or had been carried away to some other place. Meanwhile she said to Ogunyomi, "You have learned to pray to God, He loves to receive the prayers of little children. Pray to Him, if it be His will, to restore your mother to you." From that time forward, to all her prayers she added the simple petition, "O God, give me back my mother." Ogunyomi gradually became happier, but there was still an expression of sorrow upon her face, stamped there by her longing for her lost mother. When she had lived about six months in the mission-house, she went one morning, as usual, with the other little girls, to draw water from the neighbouring brook. The children were laughing and playing together, when a woman passed by, and, being attracted by the unusual sight of their white clothes, she stood still for a moment, and watched them as they played. One voice appeared to be familiar to her. She raised the basket from her head, placed it on the ground, and listened attentively. Yes, it was her child's voice! Trembling in every limb, she cried out "Ogunyomi!" Ogunyomi turned round, stared for a long time at the woman, and then, with the cry "My mother, my mother!" threw herself into her arms. The other children ran to the house, exclaiming, "Ogunyomi has found her mother!" It was difficult to believe the joyful news. The poor woman was at first afraid of the white people; but when she heard from Ogunyomi how kind and good they were, and that they had rescued her from slavery, she was at a loss for words wherewith to express her joy and gratitude. She threw herself on the ground and sobbed aloud. When her mind was somewhat more composed, she listened with interest to the story of her child, and then explained that she herself had been sold for a slave in Ibadan, but that happily she had been bought by a kind master. She was obliged to hurry away, but she was comforted by the thought of Ogunyomi's happiness, and rejoiced in the prospect of being able to see her, whenever she might have permission from her master. Ogunyomi's heart that night overflowed with gratitude to God, who had so graciously heard and answered her prayers. For many weeks all went on well. The mother often came to see her child. Then her visits ceased, without any explanation. Mr. and Mrs. Hinderer were troubled for the child, and, after much enquiry, they discovered that the mother was seriously ill, and that all hope of her recovery was gone. For Ogunyomi's sake they paid the poor woman's ransom, and removed her to the mission-house. For ten months she was nursed and cared for by these new friends, and then, to the joy of all, especially of her own child, she recovered. When her health was sufficiently re-established, she was employed as cook for the children, and found much happiness in the altered circumstances of her life… On June 20th [1867] … In the midst of all this noise and confusion, these dark and evil doings, our dear Lucy Fagbeade, Ogunyomi's mother, fell asleep in Jesus. She was a very sincere woman, who extremely disliked much talking and noise about things in religion. On the third day before her death, some of the Christians gathered round her, and asked what she saw. Poor Lucy was vexed, and spoke roughly, "I see nothing," and again, "I shall see when I have done with earth, and not till then." Afterwards, when alone with me, she said, "Oh, Iya, I have no faith in what people say they can see, all my hope is in the blood of Jesus to wash me clean; I can only go behind Jesus, and beg Him to beg God for me," and she covered her face with her hands, as if she would hide herself then and there.... Eleven years ago we redeemed her from slavery, when she was apparently sick unto death, that her child might nurse her, and soothe her dying hours; and God has spared her eleven years, and redeemed her soul by the precious blood of Christ, and has now taken her to dwell with Him forever.

TIMELINE

1804–1808	Jihad of the Sokoto Caliphate
1807	British abolition of the trans-Atlantic slave trade
1817	Muslim uprising at Ilorin
1818	Coup d'etat in Dahomey brings Gezo to power
1821–1822	Owu war
1834	Emancipation of slaves in British colonies
c. 1834–1836	Collapse of Oyo and evacuation of capital district
1845	Establishment of CMS Mission at Abeokuta
1849	Establishment of CMS Mission at Ibadan
1851	British occupation of Lagos
1854	War between Ibadan and Efon
1861	Formal establishment of British Protectorate at Lagos

GLOSSARY

Names and Places

Abeokuta. Founded by Egba refugees and location of first Christian mission (CMS).

Agoué. Minor port on the Bight of Benin, located to the west of Ouidah.

Bight of Benin. West African coast between the Niger River delta in the east and the Volta River in the west.

Central Sudan. The region of northern Nigeria and neighboring countries, derived from Arabic, *sudan,* land of the blacks.

Church Missionary Society (CMS). British missionary society associated with the Anglican Church.

Efon. Yoruba town destroyed in 1854 in war with Ibadan.

Egba. Subgroup of the Yoruba, who founded Abeokuta as a city of refuge after the Owu war (1821–1822).

Fulbe, Fulani. Ethnic group associated with the jihad movement; also language and occupational specialization associated with livestock herding.

Hausa. Dominant ethnic group in the Central Sudan.

Ibadan. Major Yoruba city founded by refugees from Oyo after its collapse in the 1830s.

Igbira. Ethnic group and kingdom on the Niger River below the confluence with the Benue River, in central Nigeria.

Ilorin. Center of the Oyo military, and site of Muslim uprising in 1817, leading to the incorporation of Ilorin as an emirate in the Sokoto Caliphate.

Kano. Largest city and most populous emirate within the Sokoto Caliphate, in the central Hausa country.

Lagos. Yoruba town on the Bight of Benin, also known as Eko in Yoruba and Hausa.

Mahi. Region and ethnic group north of the Kingdom of Dahomey.

Nupe. Region and ethnic group near the confluence of the Niger and Benue Rivers, incorporated into the Sokoto Caliphate through jihad.

Ouidah (Whydah). Major port on the Bight of Benin, located near modern Cotonou in Republique du Benin.

Oyo. The major Yoruba state in the interior of the Bight of Benin in the eighteenth and early nineteenth centuries, subjected to civil war after 1817, and destroyed by mid 1830s.

Porto Novo. On the lagoon between Lagos and Lake Nokoué.

Sokoto. Capital of the Sokoto Caliphate, in Hausaland.

Sokoto Caliphate. Founded in the jihad of 1804–1808, and named after the capital city of Sokoto, located on the Rima and Sokoto Rivers in Hausaland.

Yoruba. Language and ethnic term for people of southwestern Nigeria and neighboring Republique du Benin, and by extension descendants of people from this area in Brazil, Cuba, Trinidad, and elsewhere.

Terms

creole. First and subsequent generations of Africans and Europeans born in the Americas.

cowries. Small shells from the Indian Ocean used as currency in large parts of West Africa.

jihad. Muslim holy war, specifically the jihad of the Sokoto Caliphate, 1804–1808.

pawnship. The use of humans as collateral for debts, usually relatives of the debtor.

orisa. Deities in Yoruba religion, including *ogun, abatola, shango, ifá,* and others.

NOTES

This chapter was originally presented at the conference on "Collateral Damage," University of Toronto, May 2004. I would like to thank Olatunji Ojo for his assistance.

1. Anna Hinderer, *Seventeen Years in the Yoruba Country: Memorials of Anna Hinderer, Wife of the Rev. David Hinderer, C.M.S. Missionary in Western Africa*, ed. C. A. Hone and D. Hone, with an Introduction by Richard B. Hone (London: M. A. Piccadilly, The Religious Tract Society, 1872), 143–47, 292–93.

2. J. D.Y. Peel, *Religious Encounter and the Making of the Yoruba* (Bloomington: Indiana University Press, 2000). For the collapse of Oyo, see R.C.C. Law, "The Chronology of the Yoruba Wars of the Early Nineteenth Century: A Reconsideration," *Journal of the Historical Society of Nigeria* 5, no. 2 (1970): 211–22; R.C.C. Law, "The Owu War in Yoruba History," *Journal of the Historical Society of Nigeria* 7, no. 1 (1973): 141–47; R.C.C. Law, "Making Sense of a Traditional Narrative: Political Disintegration in the Kingdom of Oyo," *Cahiers d'études africaines* 22 (1973); and R.C.C. Law, *The Oyo Empire, c. 1600–c.1836: A West African Imperialism in the Era of the Atlantic Slave Trade* (Oxford: Clarendon, 1977).

3. A biographical database of enslaved Africans, from which material in this essay is drawn, is under construction. See Paul E. Lovejoy, "Biography as Source Material: Towards a Biographical Archive of Enslaved Africans," in *Source Material for Studying the Slave Trade and the African Diaspora,* ed. Robin Law (Stirling: Centre of Commonwealth Studies, University of Stirling, 1997) and www.yorku.ca/nhp. Also see Francine Shields, "Palm Oil and Power: Women in an Era of Economic and Social Transition in 19th Century Yorubaland (South-western Nigeria)" (Ph.D. thesis, University of Stirling, 1997), 296–30, Appendix, "Domestic Slaves of Yoruba Origin;" Femi James Kolapo, "Military Turbulence, Population Displacement and Commerce on a Southern Frontier of the Sokoto Caliphate: Nupe c.1810–1857" (Ph.D. thesis, York University, 1999), 297–317, Appendix 4, "All Incidents of Slavery and the Slave Trade for the Areas of Study 1820–67," and Appendix 5, "Profile of Slaves Exported from the Lower Middle Niger Area, c. 1800–1850"; and Paul E. Lovejoy, "The Central Sudan and the Atlantic Slave Trade," in *Paths to the Past: African Historical Essays in Honor of Jan Vansina,* ed. Robert W. Harms, Joseph C. Miller, David C. Newbury, and Michelle D. Wagner (Atlanta, GA: African Studies Association Press, 1994), 345–70.

4. For examples of unusually rich accounts of children and women, see Robin Law and Paul E. Lovejoy, eds., *The Biography of Mahommah Gardo Baquaqua: His Passage from Slavery to Freedom in Africa and America* (Princeton, NJ: Markus Wiener Publisher, 2001); José C. Curto, "The Story of Nbena, 1817–20: Unlawful Enslavement and the Concept of 'Original Freedom' in Angola," in *Trans-Atlantic Dimensions of Ethnicity in the African Diaspora,* eds. Paul E. Lovejoy and David V. Trotman (London: Continuum, 2003), 43–64; Marcia Wright, "Women in Peril: A Commentary on the Life Stories of Captives in Nineteenth Century East Central Africa," *African Social Research* 20 (1975): 800–819; Wright, *Strategies of Slaves and Women: Life-Stories from East/Central Africa* (New York: L. Barber Press, 1993); and E. A. Alpers, "The Story of Swema: Female Vulnerability in Nineteenth-Century East Africa," in *Women and Slavery in Africa,* eds. Claire C. Robertson and Martin

A. Klein (Madison: University of Wisconsin Press, 1983), 185–219. Also see Paul E. Lovejoy, "The Children of Slavery—the Trans-Atlantic Phase" (Colloque avignonnais sur l'Esclavage et la Main-d'œuvre forcée: L'Enfant dans l'esclavage, Avignon, May 19–21, 2004).

5. Natalie Zemon Davis, "Non-European Stories, European Listeners," *Zeitsprünge Forschungen zur Frühen Neuzeit* 7, nos. 2/3 (2003): 200–219.

6. See Paul E. Lovejoy, *Transformations in Slavery: A History of Slavery in Africa*, 2nd ed. (Cambridge: Cambridge University Press, 1983, 2000).

7. For a consideration of this approach see Gwendolyn Midlo Hall, *African Ethnicities in the Americas: Restoring the Links* (Chapel Hill: North Carolina University Press, 2005) and various collections of essays, including Paul E. Lovejoy, *Identity in the Shadow of Slavery* (London: Continuum, 1999); Paul E. Lovejoy and David V. Trotman, eds., *Trans-Atlantic Dimensions of Ethnicity in the African Diaspora* (London: Continuum, 2003); José C. Curto and Paul E. Lovejoy, eds., *Enslaving Connections: Changing Cultures of Africa and Brazil during the Era of Slavery* (Amherst, NY: Humanity Books, 2004); Paul E. Lovejoy, ed., *Slavery on the Frontiers of Islam* (Princeton, NJ: Markus Wiener Publisher, 2004), also at http://www.yorku.ca/nhp/jccurto/enslaving; and José C. Curto and Renée Soulodre-La France, eds., *Africa and the Americas: Interconnections through the Slave Trade* (New Brunswick, NJ: Africa World Press, 2005).

8. Joseph C. Miller, *Way of Death: Merchant Capitalism and the Angola Slave Trade 1730–1830* (Madison: University of Wisconsin Press, 1988), 163.

9. The narrative was dictated by Ali Eisami to Sigismund Wilhelm Koelle in Sierra Leone in about 1850; see S. W. Koelle, *African Native Literature* (Graz: Akademische Druck-und Verlagsanstalt, 1968 [1854]). For the original text in Kanuri, see pp. 115–21, and for the English translation, see pp. 248–56. Also see H.F.C. Smith, D. M. Last, and Gambo Gubio, eds., "Ali Eisami Gazirmabe of Bornu," in *Africa Remembered: Narratives by West Africans from the Era of the Slave Trade*, ed. Philip D. Curtin (Madison: University of Wisconsin Press, 1967), 248–56.

10. Smith and Gubio, "Ali Eisami Gazirmabe of Bornu," 212–13.

11. Francis de Castelnau, *Renseignements sur l'Afrique centrale et sur une nation d'hommes à queue qui s'y trouverait, d'après le rapport des nègres du Soudan, esclaves à Bahia* (Paris: P. Bertrand, 1851). For an analysis, see Paul E. Lovejoy, "Jihad e Escravidao: As Origens dos Escravos Muculmanos de Bahia," *Topoi* (Rio de Janeiro) 1 (2000): 11–44.

12. As discussed in Paul E. Lovejoy, "The Sahara-Atlantic Divide, or How Women Fitted into the Slave Trade," in *Women and Slavery*, eds. Gwyn Campbell and Suzanne Miers (Athens: Ohio University Press, forthcoming).

13. David Eltis, Stephen Behrendt, David Richardson, and Herbert Klein, *The Atlantic Slave Trade: A Database on CD-Rom* (Cambridge: Cambridge University Press, 1999).

14. In an earlier study, David Eltis and Stanley L. Engerman estimated that the proportion of children rose from approximately 12.2 percent in the late seventeenth century to 22.7 percent by the early nineteenth century. Thereafter the proportion of children rose dramatically, rising to 40 percent in the 1820s and reaching almost 50 percent from Angola and Mozambique. See Eltis and Engerman, "Fluctuations in Sex and Age Ratios in the Transatlantic Slave Trade, 1663–1864," *Economic History Review* 46 (1993): 308–23.

15. Lovejoy, *Transformations in Slavery,* 65–66, 143; and Patrick Manning, *Slavery and African Life: Occidental, Oriental, and African Slave Trades* (Cambridge: Cambridge University Press, 1990), 99.

16. David Geggus, "Sex Ratio, Age and Ethnicity in the Atlantic Slave Trade: Data from French Shipping and Plantation Records," *Journal of African History* 30, 1 (1989): 24.

17. Manning, *Slavery and African Life.*

18. MacGreggor Laird and R.A.K. Oldfield, *Narratives of an Expedition into the Interior of Africa by the River Niger in the Steam Vessels Quorra and Alburkah in 1832, 1833, and 1834,* vol. 2 (London: Frank Cass, 1971 [1837]), 312.

19. Paul E. Lovejoy and David Richardson, "Competing Markets for Male and Female Slaves: Slave Prices in the Interior of West Africa, 1780–1850," *International Journal of African Historical Studies* 28 (1995): 261–93.

20. See Paul E. Lovejoy, "The Urban Background of Enslaved Muslims in the Americas," *Slavery and Abolition* 26, no. 3 (2005): 349–76.

21. See David Eltis, Paul E. Lovejoy, and David Richardson, "Slave-Trading Ports: Toward an Atlantic-Wide Perspective," in *Ports of the Slave Trade (Bights of Benin and Biafra),* ed. Robin Law and Silke Strickrodt (Stirling: Centre of Commonwealth Studies, University of Stirling, 1999), 12–34.

22. Robin Law, "Francisco Felix de Souza in West Africa, 1820–1849," in *Enslaving Connections,* eds. Curto and Lovejoy, 187–212; Robin Law, *Ouidah: The Social History of a West African Slaving "Port"* (Oxford: James Currey, 2004); and Alberto da Costa e Silva, *Francisco Félix de Souza: Mercador de escravos* (Rio de Janeiro: Ed. da UERJ/Nova Fronteira, 2004).

23. According to what de Souza told Archibald Ridgway, "Journal of a Visit to Dahomey," *New Monthly Magazine* 81 (1847): 195, as cited in Law, "Francisco Felix de Souza," in *Enslaving Connections,* eds. Curto and Lovejoy, 187–211.

24. According to Law ("De Souza in West Africa"), the de Souza family tradition dates his birth to Oct. 4, 1754, which would make him 38 in 1792. Observers in the 1840s give differing estimates of his age but agree in making him substantially younger than the traditional account suggests.

25. In November 1825, Clapperton understood that he had been "resident at Whydah and Popoe upwards of twenty-five years;" and two French visitors in 1843 believed that he had been living locally for either 42 or 43 years. See Jamie Bruce Lockhart and Paul E. Lovejoy, *Hugh Clapperton into the Interior of Africa: Records of the Second Expedition 1825–1827* (Leiden: Brill, 2005), 90; André Brue, "Voyage fait en 1843, dans le royaume de Dahomey," *Revue coloniale* 7 (1845): 56; Prince de Joinville, *Vieux souvenirs (1818–1848)* (Paris, 1894), quoted in Pierre Verger, *Flux et reflux de la traite des nègres entre le golf du Bénin de Todos os Santos, du dix-septième au dix-neuvième siècle* (Paris: Mouton, 1968), 463. The date 1800 is also commonly given in family tradition; see Law, "De Souza in West Africa."

26. Law, "De Souza in West Africa," citing Norberto Francisco de Souza, "Contribution a l'histoire de la famille de Souza," *Études Dahoméennes* 15 (1955): 18.

27. Lockhart and Lovejoy, *Clapperton into the Interior of Africa,* 90.

28. In a document no longer extant, but seen in the fort at Ouidah in 1865, according to Carlos Eugenio Corrêa da Silva, *Uma Viagem ao estabelecimento portuguez de S. Joao Baptista de Ajudá na Costa da Mina em 1865* (Lisbon, 1866), 77, as cited in Law, "De Souza in West Africa."

29. Verger, *Flux et reflux,* 460.

30. Ibid., 638.

31. Subsequently, *chacha* became a title that was used by his sons who inherited his position; see Law, *Ouidah,* 167.

32. Lockhart and Lovejoy, *Clapperton into the Interior of Africa,* 90.

33. "A Liberated African's Account of his Slavery, and Subsequent Course," *Church Missionary Gleaner* 6 (1846): 16–18.

34. The others being Gbagura and Oke-Ona; see Philip D. Curtin, "Joseph Wright of the Egba," in *Africa Remembered,* ed. Curtin, 317.

35. For Wright's account, see Curtin, ed., *Africa Remembered,* 317–34.

36. Curto, "Story of Nbena, 1817–20," 43–64.

37. Various accounts state that Catherine came from Luanda, but her description of her home clearly refers to Cape Town, not Luanda. See "Account of Converted Negress In Jamaica," *Church Missionary Gleaner* 4 (1844): 131–32; P. Steiner, "Frau Missionar C. Zimmermann," 1891, Basel Mission Archives, Basel, Switzerland; Johannes Zaimmermann, on Catherine Mulgrave, Usu, 18. XI. 1852, Basel Mission Archives; Peter Haenger, "Sklaverei und Sklavenemanzipation an der Goldküste 1860–1900: Ein Beitrag zum Verständnis von sozialen Abhängigkeitsbeziehungen in Westafrika" (Ph.D. thesis, University of Basel, 1996); *Periodical Accounts Relating to the Missions of the Church of the United Brethren, Established among the Heathen* (London, 1834–44); and John Henry Buchner, *The Moravians in Jamaica: History of the Mission of the United Brethren's Church to the Negroes in the Island of Jamaica, from the year 1754 to 1854* (London: Longman, Brown, 1854).

38. Jean Herskovits Kopytoff, *A Preface to Modern Nigeria: The "Sierra Leonians" in Yoruba, 1830–1890* (Madison: University of Wisconsin Press, 1965), 291. King died on October 23, 1862.

39. Sheila Lambert, ed., *House of Commons Sessional Papers of the Eighteenth Century* (Wilmington, DE: Scholarly Resources, 1975); Vol. 69, Report of the Lords of Trade on the Slave Trade 1789, Part 1, 50, evidence of James Arnold, surgeon in His Majesty's Navy for five years, and later voyaged to Africa on three occasions on Bristol ships as surgeon and surgeon's mate. His first slaving voyage was to Bonny, on board the *Alexander,* Captain Mactaggart, in quality of surgeon's mate, under Mr. Alexander Falconbridge, surgeon of the vessel. The second voyage was on board the *Little Pearl,* Captain Joseph Williams. On his third voyage, on the *Ruby,* commanded by Captain Williams, he went to the Island of Bimbe, "a small Island situated opposite to that Part of the Continent of Africa distinguished by the Name of the High Lands of the Cameroons."

40. P.C.C. Lloyd, "Osifekunde of Ijebu," in *Africa Remembered,* ed Curtin 249n.

41. For a photograph of the tree that marks the site of the shrine to *obatala* in the ruins of Osogun, see Curtin, ed., *Africa Remembered,* photograph opposite p. 309.

42. J. F. Ade Ajayi, "Samuel Ajayi Crowther of Oyo," in ibid., 289–316. According to the account in "Bishop Crowther: His Life and Work," *Church Missionary Gleaner* 5 (1878): 10–11, Crowther was 11 at the time of his enslavement. Also see "A Liberated African's Account of his Slavery, and Subsequent Course," *Church Missionary Gleaner* 6 (1846):16–18; "Meeting of the Rev. Samuel Crowther with his Mother," *Church Missionary Gleaner* 7 (1847): 63–65; and James Frederick Schön and Samuel Crowther, *Journals of the Rev. James Frederick Schön and Mr. Samuel Crowther*

(London: Frank Cass, 1970 [1854]). Later scholars have held that Crowther was 15 at the time of his enslavement; see Kopytoff, *Preface to Modern Nigeria,* 285; and Ajayi, "Crowther of Oyo," 289.

43. Law and Lovejoy, eds., *Biography of Baquaqua.* Also see various accounts of enslaved Muslims in Philip D. Curtin and Allan D. Austin, eds., *Africa Remembered; African Muslims in Antebellum America: A Sourcebook* (New York: Garland Publishing, 1984).

44. Law and Lovejoy, eds., *Biography of Baquaqua.* Also see Paul E. Lovejoy, "Identidade e a Miragem da Etnicidade: A Jornada de Mahommah Gardo Baquaqua para as Américas," *Afro-Ásia* 27 (2002): 9–39.

45. Willaim Allen and T.R.H. Thomson, *A Narrative of the Expedition Sent by Her Majesty's Government to the River Niger in 1841,* vol. 1 (London: Frank Cass, 1968 [1848]), 92.

46. Schön and Crowther, *Journals of Schön and Samuel Crowther,* 204.

47. Marie d'Avezac, "Notice sur le pays et le peuple des Yébous, en Afrique," in *Mémoires de la Société thenologique* 2, no. 2 (1845): 1-10; 13-27, 30–46, 53-105, and reproduced in Lloyd, "Osifekunde of Ijebu," in *Africa Remembered,* ed. Curtin, 217–88. A picture of the bust was published in D'Avezac, "Notice sur les Yébous."

48. James Thomas, Letters and Journals, 1858–79, "The Journal of James Thomas Native Teacher Lokoja From 1869–1870," entry for March 7, 1870, Church Missionary Society (CMS) Niger Mission CA3/O38.

49. Lambert, ed., *House of Commons Sessional Papers of the Eighteenth Century,* Vol. 82. Slave Trade 1791 and 1792, 32–34; testimony of Ecroyde Claxton, surgeon, who traveled to Bonny in 1788 on the *Young Hero,* a brig under Capt Molineux. The ship carried 250 slaves, of whom 132 died of "flux."

50. Paul E. Lovejoy and Toyin Falola, eds., *Pawnship, Slavery, and Colonialism in Africa* (Trenton ,NJ: Africa World Press, 2003).

51. Thomas, Letters & Journals, 1858–79, April 16, 1864, CMS Niger Mission CA3/O38.

52. Lambert, ed., *House of Commons Sessional Papers for the Eighteenth Century,* Vol. 72, Minutes &c., 1790 (Monday, 1st March 1790), 515, testimony of Captain John Ashley Hall, who had been to West Africa in 1772–1776.

53. Ibid., 513, 558.

54. Thomas, Letters and Journals, 1858–79, November 19, 1858, CMS Niger Mission CA3/O38.

55. Thomas, Letters and Journals, 1858–79, December 4, 1858, CMS Niger Mission CA3/O38.

56. Another example of a former slave who became a major slave trader was Pierre Tamata, of Hausa origin, who as a boy was taken to France and educated, returning to Porto Novo in the late 1780s, where he was the agent for French shipping to the Caribbean; see Verger, *Flux et reflux.*

57. Silke Strickrodt, "Afro-Brazilians on the Western Slave Coast" (Stirling, Scotland: University of Stirling, unpublished, 2000).

58. Hinderer, *Seventeen Years in the Yoruba Country,* 143–47, 292–93.

59. Efon was the largest town on the Ekiti-Ijesa border. During the nineteenth century, Efon also referred to the district now called Ekiti. For a discussion of the war of 1854, see Samuel Johnson, *The History of the Yorubas from the Earliest Times to the Beginning of the British Protectorate* (Lagos: CSS Books, 1976 [1921]), 317–21;

Isaac B. Akinyele, *Iwe Itan Ibadan* (Ibadan: Board Publications, 1980 [1911]), 54–63; Bolanle Awe, "The Rise of Ibadan as Yoruba Power 1851–1893" (D.Phil. thesis, Oxford, 1964); and Stephen A. Akintoye, *Revolution and Power Politics in Yorubaland, 1840–1893: Ibadan Expansion and the Rise of Ekitiparapo* (London: Longman, 1971), 41–45.

60. The identity of this man is unclear, although he was an early convert in Ibadan.

61. The German David Hinderer joined the CMS Yoruba Mission in 1848, making his first visit to Ibadan in 1851. He returned to England after three months. With Anna, his new wife, he went to Abeokuta in 1853, but after three months the couple moved to Ibadan, where for 17 years they lived at the Kudeti Church Mission house. On the Hinderers, see Anna's journals in *Seventeen Years in the Yoruba Country,* and the account of David Hinderer in CA2/049 (a) and (b), CMS.

SELECT BIBLIOGRAPHY

Alpers, E. A. "The Story of Swema: Female Vulnerability in Nineteenth-Century East Africa." In *Women and Slavery in Africa.* Edited by Claire C. Robertson and Martin A. Klein. Madison: University of Wisconsin Press, 1983.
This study follows one woman's experience of slavery in East Africa in the nineteenth century, and her ultimate redemption by missionaries.

Austin, Allan D. *African Muslims in Antebellum America: A Sourcebook.* New York: Garland Publishing, 1984.
A collection of primary source materials on enslaved Muslims who were taken to the Americas. Accounts include the biographies of individuals taken to North America and the Caribbean.

Curtin, Philip D., ed. *Africa Remembered: Narratives of West Africans from the Era of the Slave Trade.* Madison: University of Wisconsin Press, 1967.
A collection of annotated memoirs and autobiographies that consists of accounts from the eighteenth and nineteenth centuries by enslaved individuals, all males, as well as a travel account of a free Muslim from Turkistan who was in West Africa.

Curto, José C. "The Story of Nbena, 1817–20: Unlawful Enslavement and the Concept of 'Original Freedom' in Angola." In *Trans-Atlantic Dimensions of Ethnicity in the African Diaspora.* Edited by Paul E. Lovejoy and David V. Trotman. London: Continuum, 2003: 43–64.
Account of the trials and tribulations of a woman in Angola who was arbitrarily seized in the nineteenth century. One of the most detailed narratives available on enslavement and the successful attempts to regain freedom in Africa.

———, and Paul E. Lovejoy, eds. *Enslaving Connections: Changing Cultures of Africa and Brazil during the Era of Slavery.* Amherst, NY: Humanity Books, 2004.
This collection of essays examines the important cultural connections between western Africa and Brazil. Provides information on Brazil, which received approximately 10 times as many enslaved Africans as mainland North America.

———, and Renée Soulodre-La France, eds. *Africa and the Americas: Interconnections through the Slave Trade.* New Brunswick, NJ: Africa World Press, 2005.

This collection of essays explores various interconnections across the Atlantic that continued despite the trauma and tragedy of slavery.

Eltis, David, Stephen Behrendt, David Richardson, and Herbert Klein Herbert. *The Atlantic Slave Trade: A Database on CD-Rom.* Cambridge: Cambridge University Press, 1999.

Database that is the starting point for any study of the demography of the "slave trade" across the Atlantic, it allows an examination of the regional origins of the enslaved population in Africa and their distribution in the Americas.

———, and Stanley Engerman. "Fluctuations in Sex and Age Ratios in the Transatlantic Slave Trade, 1663–1864." *Economic History Review* 46 (1993): 308–23.

Demonstrates that the demographic composition of the enslaved population on board European slave ships changed over time.

———, Paul E. Lovejoy, and David Richardson. "Slave-Trading Ports: Toward an Atlantic-Wide Perspective." In *Ports of the Slave Trade (Bights of Benin and Biafra).* Edited by Robin Law and Silke Strickrodt. Stirling: Centre of Commonwealth Studies, University of Stirling, 1999, 12–34.

Based on a study of the coastal origins of enslaved Africans, this paper shows that most enslaved Africans left from relatively few ports on the African coast, demonstrating a degree of concentration of trade that has only recently been appreciated.

Geggus, David. "Sex Ratio, Age and Ethnicity in the Atlantic Slave Trade: Data from French Shipping and Plantation Records." *Journal of African History* 30, no. 1 (1989): 23–44.

Draws on documents on the French slave trade and plantation inventories in the French-controlled areas of the Caribbean, thereby examining the extent of concentration of certain African ethnic groups and the gender composition of the population in French colonies.

Hall, Gwendolyn Midlo. *African Ethnicities in the Americas: Restoring the Links.* Chapel Hill: North Carolina University Press, 2005.

Overview that examines the extent to which specific ethnic groups were dominant among the enslaved population in the Americas.

Kopytoff, Jean Herskovits. *A Preface to Modern Nigeria. The "Sierra Leonians" in Yoruba, 1830–1890.* Madison: University of Wisconsin Press, 1965.

Explores the return of freed slaves to their homeland from Sierra Leone, where they had been liberated by the British anti-slave trade campaign after 1807.

Lambert, Sheila, ed. *House of Commons Sessional Papers of the Eighteenth Century.* Wilmington, DE: Scholarly Resources, 1975. Vol. 69: Report of the Lords of Trade on the Slave Trade 1789.

These papers are the transcripts of the Parliamentary enquiry into the slave trade in 1789 in Britain.

Law, Robin, and Paul E. Lovejoy, eds. *The Biography of Mahommah Gardo Baquaqua: His Passage from Slavery to Freedom in Africa and America.* Princeton, NJ: Markus Wiener Publisher, 2001.

One of the most detailed autobiographies available of an individual born in Africa who was enslaved and taken to the Americas, in this case to Brazil and then New York City.

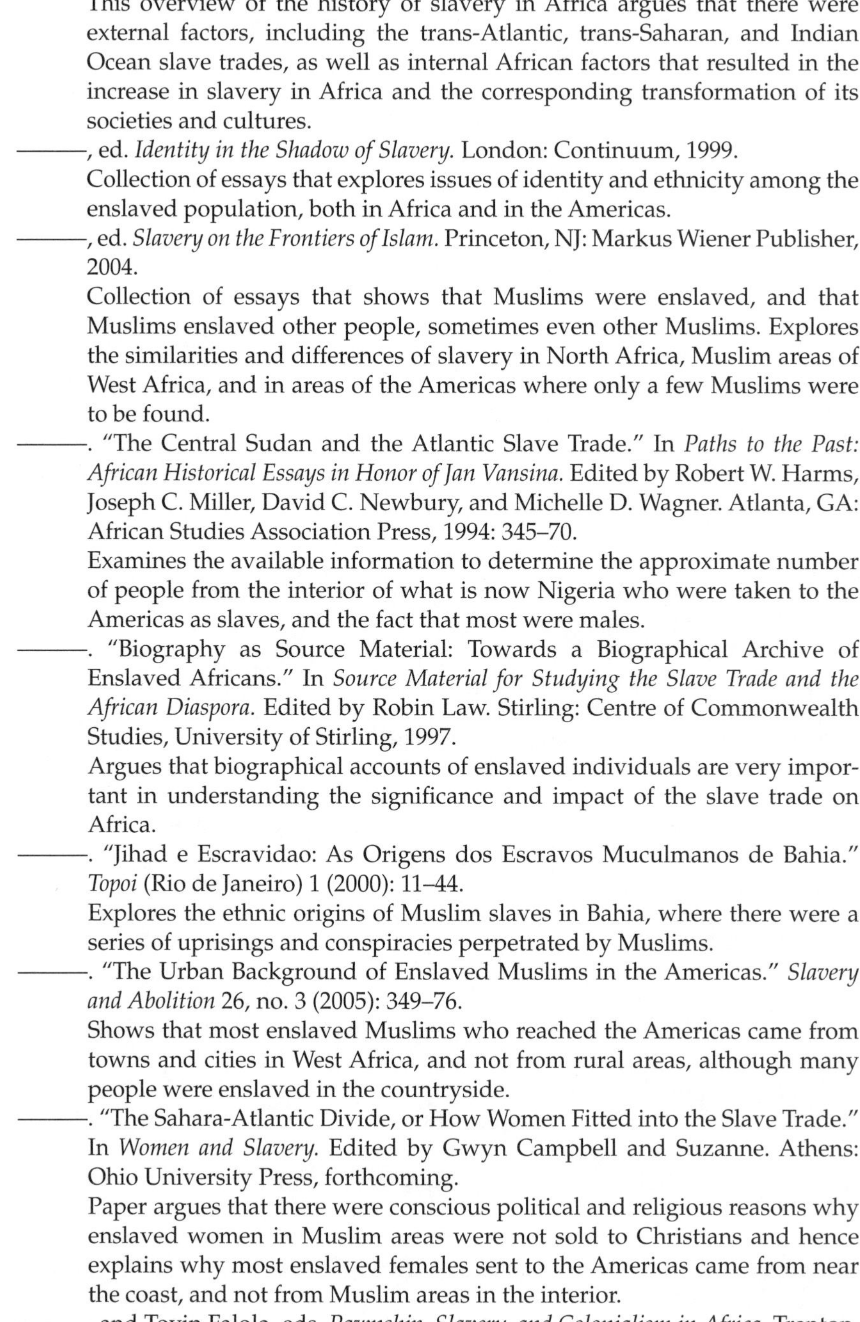

Lovejoy, Paul. E. *Transformations in Slavery: A History of Slavery in Africa.* 2nd ed. Cambridge: Cambridge University Press, 1983.2000.

This overview of the history of slavery in Africa argues that there were external factors, including the trans-Atlantic, trans-Saharan, and Indian Ocean slave trades, as well as internal African factors that resulted in the increase in slavery in Africa and the corresponding transformation of its societies and cultures.

———, ed. *Identity in the Shadow of Slavery.* London: Continuum, 1999.

Collection of essays that explores issues of identity and ethnicity among the enslaved population, both in Africa and in the Americas.

———, ed. *Slavery on the Frontiers of Islam.* Princeton, NJ: Markus Wiener Publisher, 2004.

Collection of essays that shows that Muslims were enslaved, and that Muslims enslaved other people, sometimes even other Muslims. Explores the similarities and differences of slavery in North Africa, Muslim areas of West Africa, and in areas of the Americas where only a few Muslims were to be found.

———. "The Central Sudan and the Atlantic Slave Trade." In *Paths to the Past: African Historical Essays in Honor of Jan Vansina.* Edited by Robert W. Harms, Joseph C. Miller, David C. Newbury, and Michelle D. Wagner. Atlanta, GA: African Studies Association Press, 1994: 345–70.

Examines the available information to determine the approximate number of people from the interior of what is now Nigeria who were taken to the Americas as slaves, and the fact that most were males.

———. "Biography as Source Material: Towards a Biographical Archive of Enslaved Africans." In *Source Material for Studying the Slave Trade and the African Diaspora.* Edited by Robin Law. Stirling: Centre of Commonwealth Studies, University of Stirling, 1997.

Argues that biographical accounts of enslaved individuals are very important in understanding the significance and impact of the slave trade on Africa.

———. "Jihad e Escravidao: As Origens dos Escravos Muculmanos de Bahia." *Topoi* (Rio de Janeiro) 1 (2000): 11–44.

Explores the ethnic origins of Muslim slaves in Bahia, where there were a series of uprisings and conspiracies perpetrated by Muslims.

———. "The Urban Background of Enslaved Muslims in the Americas." *Slavery and Abolition* 26, no. 3 (2005): 349–76.

Shows that most enslaved Muslims who reached the Americas came from towns and cities in West Africa, and not from rural areas, although many people were enslaved in the countryside.

———. "The Sahara-Atlantic Divide, or How Women Fitted into the Slave Trade." In *Women and Slavery.* Edited by Gwyn Campbell and Suzanne. Athens: Ohio University Press, forthcoming.

Paper argues that there were conscious political and religious reasons why enslaved women in Muslim areas were not sold to Christians and hence explains why most enslaved females sent to the Americas came from near the coast, and not from Muslim areas in the interior.

———. and Toyin Falola, eds. *Pawnship, Slavery, and Colonialism in Africa.* Trenton, NJ: Africa World Press, 2003).

This collection of essays explores the institution of human pawning, in which individuals were held as collateral for debts. In some cases, default could result in enslavement, and often the treatment of slaves and pawns in Africa was similar, unless relatives could intervene to protect pawns who were their kin.

——— and David Richardson. "Competing Markets for Male and Female Slaves: Slave Prices in the Interior of West Africa, 1780–1850." *International Journal of African Historical Studies* 28 (1995): 261–93.

Demonstrates that enslaved women were in greater demand within Africa than they were in the trans-Atlantic trade, suggesting that most females who were enslaved remained in Africa.

——— and David V. Trotman, eds. *Trans-Atlantic Dimensions of Ethnicity in the African Diaspora.* London: Continuum, 2003.

Collection of essays that explores the trans-Atlantic dimensions of ethnicity, demonstrating the links and ruptures of cultural expression and survival under slavery.

Manning, Patrick. *Slavery and African Life: Occidental, Oriental, and African Slave Trades.* Cambridge: Cambridge University Press, 1990.

Overview that examines the demographic impact of the external slave trade across the Atlantic, Sahara, and Indian Ocean on the population of Africa. Develops a model of demography that allows some estimate of the loss of life associated with enslavement.

Miller, Joseph C. *Way of Death: Merchant Capitalism and the Angola Slave Trade 1730–1830.* Madison: University of Wisconsin Press, 1988.

Monumental exploration of the links between Portugal, Angola, and Brazil, which demonstrates how the economics and politics of slavery impinged on African societies in West Central Africa.

Wright, Marcia. *Strategies of Slaves and Women. Life-Stories from East/Central Africa Women and Slavery.* New York: L. Barber Press, 1993).

One of the few collections that focuses specifically on the life stories of enslaved women, concentrating on East and Central Africa.

two

Zulu Civilians During the Rise and the Fall of the Zulu Kingdom, c. 1817–1879

John Laband

A WARRIOR PEOPLE?

"We Zulus come from a warrior nation who know what valour and bravery are all about," proclaimed Prince Mangosuthu Buthelezi at a commemoration held in January 1992 at Isandlwana mountain, the site of the famous battle on January 21, 1879 when the Zulu army routed one of the British columns invading their kingdom. Yet Buthelezi, the leader of the Zulu nationalist Inkatha Freedom Party, was more than simply conjuring up a distant heroic age of Zulu military honor. His stirring invocation of the Zulu warrior in the pride of his physical strength, adorned in his spectacular military costume of exotic skins and feathers, was meant to appeal to the alienated contemporary Zulu migrant worker searching for dignity and a worthy heritage within the dehumanizing context of the dying days of South African apartheid. Identification with the idealized warrior image connected the modern worker directly to that definitive model of Zulu manhood, Shaka kaSenzangakhona, the creator and first king of the Zulu state in the 1820s, military genius and ferocious conqueror. This warrior identity, Buthelezi was claiming, was nothing less than a Zulu ethnic characteristic, fundamental to the national ethos.[1] Indeed, as Ngidi kaMcikaziswa affirmed when questioned in 1904 by James Stuart, a white magistrate taking down Zulu oral history, "We are always talking of war and battles, even at this day."[2] Nearly ninety years later Buthelezi knew he could still effectively appeal to this established cultural predilection.

Yet if many Zulu continue to regard themselves as a quintessentially warrior people, this is equally the perception of them in the West where they have captured and held the imagination as the epitome of the courageous African "tribal warrior." Perhaps the reason why the Zulu maintain pride of place in the warrior pantheon to which their stunning victory over the British at Isandlwana elevated them is, as Bruce Vandervort has suggested in his work on wars of imperial conquest in Africa,[3] the reiteration of the stereotype in cult films like Joseph E. Levine's swashbuckling *Zulu* (1964), in the epic television series, *Shaka Zulu* (1986)[4] and in popular histories such as Donald Morris's much reprinted *The Washing of the Spears: The Rise and Fall of the Zulu Nation* (1966).

Nevertheless, no matter how romantic the Zulu warrior might appear to the postindustrial imagination (which stereotypically pictures him rhythmically beating his fearsome stabbing spear against his great ox-hide shield as he stamps the earth in his fierce war dance) the reality is that he needed to demonstrate his prowess and confirm his masculinity through the death of other men, the capture of their property, and the abduction of their women. Violence encompassed the Zulu kingdom. It was born of conquest in the 1820s at the expense of its African neighbors, nearly succumbed in 1838 to the armed migration of white settlers from the Cape Colony (the Great Trek), and was wracked by vicious civil wars in 1840 and 1856. Within the span of a single lifetime it rose and fell, going down in final military defeat to the British in 1879 when its own territory was overrun and its people suffered all the pains of invasion and conquest it had once visited upon others. Zulu fighting men perished in all these conflicts, but noncombatants died too—and sometimes in greater numbers—of violence, starvation, exposure, and deprivation.

PRECOLONIAL ZULU SOCIETY

To gauge the effects of war on Zulu civilians, it is necessary to understand how their society functioned. Although the daily life of the Zulu people naturally changed somewhat over time and exhibited many local variations, it remained constant in its fundamental aspects throughout the existence of the Zulu kingdom.

The Homestead *(Umuzi)* Economy

The Zulu were essentially pastoralists.[5] Wealth (in a society that had little other means of storing it) was counted in terms of cattle. The Zulu kept no slaves, so women's labor and fertility had a high value expressed in the cattle transferred to the father of a bride at the time of her marriage in exchange for the loss of her domestic labor (*ilobolo*). Cattle were of ritual significance, for it was only through their sacrifice that the spirits of the ancestors (*amadlozi;* singular—*idlozi*) could be propitiated. They were of basic material importance too, as providers of milk (which, sour and clotted, constituted part of the staple diet), of meat for festive occasions, and of hides for garments and shields. So great was the value of cattle, that war in Zulu society as often as not had as its primary purpose the enrichment of the victor with the captured herds of the enemy.

The Zulu also tilled the soil in small, scattered fields. Indian maize appears to have become fully established by the eighteenth century, and by the early nineteenth had supplanted sorghum (increasingly restricted to brewing beer) and millet as the favored food crop. When turned into various forms of porridge, accompanied by other boiled vegetables, it constituted the staple item of diet. Confirming the relatively inferior status of agriculture in a strongly patrilineal, cattle-herding society, it was normally the woman's task to cultivate and reap the crops (although men of low rank might help their wives with sowing, hoeing, and weeding). Routine domestic duties were also the woman's responsibility. To men exclusively fell the more prestigious

Zulu woman returning from work in the fields carrying a hoe over her shoulder. G. F. Angas, *The Kafirs Illustrated* (London: J. Hogarth, 1849).

activities of caring for livestock, building and repairing the homestead, discussing politics, and going out to hunt or fight.

Tens of thousands of scattered homesteads (*imizi;* singular: *umuzi*), looking like so many tiny villages, dotted the rolling countryside, supported by their own grazing and agricultural land. Each was the home of a married man (*umnumzane;* plural: *abanumzane*) and his two or three wives and their children, though a man of wealth and status might have as many as a dozen wives. Every *umuzi* was circular, and built on dry, sloping ground with the main entrance at the bottom of the incline. The huts (*izindlu;* singular: *indlu*)—which should really be regarded as separate rooms in a single home—were arranged hierarchically in a crescent with that of the chief wife at the top and dropping progressively in status to those of retainers or dependants nearest the entrance. They surrounded the central *isibaya* (plural: *izibaya*) or cattle-fold, where deep pits, in which grain was stored during the winter, were dug and their funnel-shaped mouths carefully disguised. The storage huts for beer, vegetables, and grain were usually built between the dwelling huts and the outer protective palisade, constructed on similar lines to the fence forming the *isibaya.*

All Zulu huts were alike in both construction and furnishings, but those of the great were distinguished (as in any society) by their luxury in the choice of materials and in their workmanship. Those in nineteenth-century Zululand were circular and domed, much in the shape of a

Typical mid-nineteenth-century Zulu *umuzi* (homestead) near Umlazi, Natal. G. F. Angas, *The Kafirs Illustrated* (London: J. Hogarth, 1849).

beehive, and constructed from thousands of curved intersecting saplings and sticks, rather like compact wicker work, tied together with grass where they crossed. The average hut was three meters in diameter, but those occupied by chiefs were double the size with several poles (rather than a single central one) supporting the structure. A neat thatch of long, tough grass covered the huts. The floor was made of a mixture of the earth from ant-heaps compressed with cow dung, and polished to a blackish dark-green, glossy smoothness.

Every *umuzi* was essentially self-sufficient, supported by its own labor and resources. The household fed itself off its own cattle and agricultural produce. There was still sufficient wood in Zululand, except in the western highlands, to provide fuel and the materials for building huts. Basic items of clothing were made from hides of slaughtered cattle (more decorative furs came from hunted wild animals), while cooking and eating utensils were manufactured from grass, wood, and clay. Iron for weapons and agricultural tools (such as hoes) was mined, smelted, and forged within the country. But the working of iron was increasingly a matter for specialist smiths, and most households had to obtain their metal implements through trade, as was the case with luxury items, such as beads. During the course of the nineteenth century increasing activity by traders from neighboring colonial Natal meant that manufactured blankets began to displace skins as clothing, and mass-produced hoes and luxury items like beads and alcohol were introduced.

The Clan and Chiefdom

On the death of an *umnumzane,* his household would break up, or segment, and each of his sons would establish his own *umuzi.* All the men and women who believed that they, through this process of segmentation, had descended from a common ancestor strictly through the male line, formed a social unit that anthropologists call a clan. Marriage within the clan was prohibited, and wives had to be taken from other clans. The clan was not an egalitarian social unit, and a wealthy, dominant lineage would usually emerge, forming the chiefly house. Clans were not political units as such. Rather, the major political unit was the chiefdom. A number of clans—or some elements of these clans—constituted a chiefdom, where political power was vested in the dominant lineage of the strongest clan. Thus, while membership of a clan was an immutable matter of ancestry, being part of a chiefdom involved a political choice—or necessity. Chiefs attracted followings especially if they offered a haven in times of war and upheaval. Incorporation into a chiefdom meant taking on the identity, language, and customs of the dominant lineage. It was always remained possible (if hazardous) to tender allegiance (*ukukhonza*) to another chief if circumstances required it. Chiefdoms thus rose, fell, and regrouped in response to times of drought and hardship, internal dissension, and war with rivals.

The Military *(Ibutho)* System

In a society where the possession of cattle was synonymous with power and wealth, oral traditions tell of constant raiding from earliest times in what would later be the Zulu kingdom to acquire herds by force from neighbors. The warriors who raided each other would have had their fighting skills honed by participation in organized hunting parties. European sailors in the late seventeenth century saw them using long throwing spears and finishing off their prey with short stabbing spears. By the mid-eighteenth century at the latest these hunting parties were developing into large-scale military formations, or "regiments"—known to the Zulu as *amabutho* (singular: *ibutho*)—which were based on age-grade units that had developed out of circumcision schools marking the transition from youth to manhood. It is impossible to say which particular grouping invented the *amabutho,* but it is certain that they were increasingly used as the chiefs' instruments of coercion. To keep them fed and rewarded necessitated raids against neighboring chiefdoms, and this added to the growing cycle of violence. Nevertheless, because the acquisition of cattle rather than the death of opponents still remained the main purpose of warfare, the number of casualties and scale of destruction in these brief localized campaigns must have remained limited.

Amabutho (warriors) of the uNokhenke *ibutho* (age-grade regiment) photographed c. 1879. They are arrayed for the hunt or war. Courtesy of the Cecil Renaud Library, University of KwaZulu-Natal.

ZULU WARS OF CONQUEST

The Rise of the Zulu Kingdom

In the sixteenth century the largest of the chiefdoms in the lands between Delagoa Bay and the Thukela River was probably that of the Mbo, which for reasons unknown fragmented in the early eighteenth century. Norman Etherington speculates that several splinters, notably the Ndwandwe, later attempted to rebuild their lost power, while rival chiefdoms, of which the Mthethwa were the most powerful, attempted to impose their hegemony.

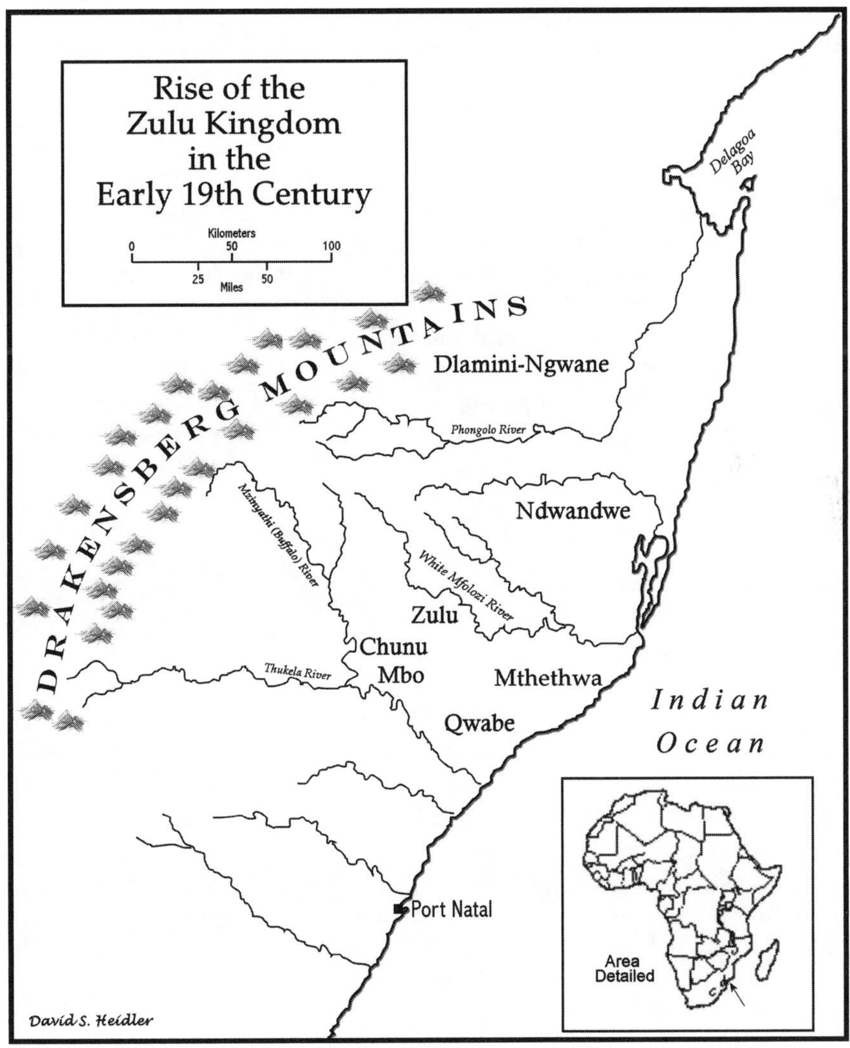

Rise of the Zulu Kingdom in the Early Nineteenth Century

By the end of the eighteenth century they, and other more aggressive chiefdoms such as the Qwabe, Dlamini, Chunu, and Hlubi, were deploying their well organized *amabutho* as they struggled with each other for control of cattle and grazing land and vied to incorporate adherents at the expense of their rivals.[6] The future Zulu kingdom was fully part of this unstable world of fierce raids and cattle rustling. Despite later legend it did not emerge unheralded as a terrible war machine to fall upon its astonished neighbors, the peaceful inhabitants of some bucolic, pre-Shakan Eden. Rather, in its rise it overcame its equally ambitious and ferocious rivals in the lands between the Drakensberg Mountains and the sea.

In 1816 Shaka seized the throne of the little Zulu chieftainship from his half-brother with the aid of his overlord, Dingiswayo, ruler of the Mthethwa. The following year the Ndwandwe overthrew the Mthethwa, and all that then stood between them and dominance of the entire region was the determined defiance of the little Zulu chiefdom. Shaka increased his army, improved its capability, and went on—through the exercise of skilful diplomacy and military might—to extend and consolidate his position over the entire region between the White Mfolozi and Thukela rivers. Smaller chiefdoms who submitted were incorporated into his burgeoning kingdom and provided additional manpower for the Zulu *amabutho.*

Shaka fully developed the *amabutho* system so that for him and his successors it became the central instrument of royal power for holding together the political structure of the Zulu kingdom. All the men as well as the women of the Zulu kingdom were grouped into *amabutho* under the king's ritual authority. Through this institution the monarch exercised social, economic, and political control over his subjects, for without his consent the male *amabutho* could not marry designated female *amabutho* and establish their own *imizi* as fully fledged *abanumzane.* This meant that until given royal permission to marry, they technically remained youths under the supervision of their elders, and their labor was diverted away from their own *imizi* and chiefs to the service of the king. Their military potential was also taken away from the chiefs and placed exclusively in the hands of the king, for the male *amabutho* operated as his instruments of tribute collection, internal control (which included being deployed against recalcitrant regional chiefs), as well as his army against external enemies. They were concentrated in the great military homesteads, or *amakhanda* (singular—*ikhanda*), which could range in size from about a hundred to well over a thousand huts, and which formed the nodes of royal authority in various strategic places around the kingdom. It is essential to remember, though, that the *amabutho* were a militia, and not a standing army, directly serving their king in their *amakhanda* for only a few months a year. For the rest of the time they reassumed their places in the *imizi*-based economy of the nation.[7]

As Zulu might grew, large neighboring chiefdoms were faced with the options of resistance, flight, or acceptance of Zulu overlordship. In 1819 the Ndwandwe were pushed north over the Phongolo River and Shaka established control over their former territory. Shaka broke up and absorbed chiefdoms to the south and west of the original Zulu territory as well, and these new subjects reformulated their traditions to fabricate a new collective identity based on the myth of a common Zulu ancestry. The *amantungwa,* as these assimilated people of the Zulu heartland came to be known, benefited fully as members of the Zulu kingdom. In contrast, the people of the southern chiefdoms between the Thukela and Mzimkhulu rivers conquered slightly later, and those subjects or tributaries generally living along the peripheries of the kingdom, were more heavily exploited and oppressed. Their Zulu overlords gave them the derogatory designation of *amalala,* or menials, with the attached stigma of social inferiority, and they differed in dialect and custom from the dominant *amantungwa.*[8]

Shaka's interminable military campaigns and his high-handed domestic rule led to his assassination in 1828 by his half-brothers and leading nobles. But he was already a legend. Magema Fuze, who in 1922 penned the first history in Zulu of his people, wrote of Shaka: "And there was wild confusion amongst the people, who began to lift their ears and say, 'What sort of king has now arisen?' And he conquered everywhere." He also quoted with awe from Shaka's praise-poem, chanted to invoke the spirit of the great king at public festivals, and in which, as Shaka's image crystallized during the nineteenth century, praise-singers surrounded his name with violent metaphors and allusions:

> The blade that vanquishes other blades with its sharpness. He who roars like thunder as he sits ... Shaka, a fearful name I dare not utter. The long-armed robber who robs with violence, Who destroys always in a furious rage, With his ever-ready shield on his knees.[9]

The *Mfecane* Debate

White historians early associated Shaka and the rise of the Zulu kingdom with appalling devastation and bloodshed that decimated the population and turned thousands into terrified refugees or desperate cannibals. It was the first white traders in Zululand in the 1820s, wishing to establish Cape commercial interests in southeast Africa, who first popularized the idea that the regions south of the Thukela were devastated and depopulated. From the late 1830s the missionaries, who were very influential in molding opinion in Britain, reinforced this image. Like the merchants, they were anxious to open up the interior to the Western civilizing mission and justified their intervention in terms of rescuing Africans from what they characterized as their barbaric culture and history of pointless war and destruction. This denigratory picture of savage Zulu society equally suited the purposes of the British settlers who started arriving in the British Colony of Natal, established south of the Thukela in the late 1840s. It helped assuage any sense of guilt they might have felt as colonizers if they could present themselves as bringing peace to a land devastated and depopulated by war. Colonial officials in charge of Africans in Natal, as well as settler historians, continued through their writings to reinforce the stereotype of Shaka's violent conquests and wars of extermination, uncritically recycling previous texts and adding sensationalist glosses of their own. And because reliable, empirical evidence of Shaka's reign was largely lacking or only obtainable through Zulu oral sources, it was easy to reinforce the established Zulu cultural stereotypes against which white superiority could be advantageously measured.[10] In 1900 the influential imperial historian, George McCall Theal, extended the conventional settler portrayal of Shaka to a wider audience. "In all history, ancient or modern," he insisted, "there is no name with which more ruthless bloodshed is associated than with that of Tshaka." He further claimed (on no possible basis of evidence) that "two million lives were lost" in his depredations.[11] So persuasive was this assertion of raw African savagery that as recently as 1990 the eminent American anthropologists Frank Chalk and Kurt Jonassohn stated:

> Shaka's success was based on terror. He was the first African state leader to wage a war of complete annihilation in Southern Africa ... To maintain the security of his empire, Shaka surrounded it with traffic deserts—devastated areas in which anyone found trespassing was automatically killed. Shaka's exterminatory campaigns—known as the *Mfecane,* or the great crushing—triggered a mass exodus of African peoples fleeing his reign of terror.[12]

The concept of the "*mfecane,*" which became firmly established in the 1970s as the orthodox means of explaining the tumultuous period of state-building in the early nineteenth century in southeastern Africa, was John Omer-Cooper's formulation.[13] He argued that the sudden rise and expansion of the Zulu kingdom, based on a new state structure and military innovation, set off waves of unprecedented dislocation across the subcontinent. Omer-Cooper's notion of the seismic Zulu explosion was abrasively challenged by Julian Cobbing, who in turn sent shock waves through the academic community. Though Cobbing's critique has subsequently come under considerable critical review and several aspects of it have been modified,[14] what is relevant to this discussion is the hardening consensus that the Zulu kingdom was hardly as novel and unprecedented a state as Omer-Cooper believed, and that the level of violence traditionally associated with the *mfecane* was not on the scale supposed. Certainly, there are no accurate or trustworthy counts of the casualties of the wars in which the Zulu under Shaka played so prominent, but hardly singular, a part. Nor is there any basis of evidence to compare casualties with previous periods of warfare in the region. It is therefore impossible to do more than speculate what the actual impact on civilians might have been during the rise of the Zulu kingdom. That is not to suggest that it was negligible, or that the dislocation, suffering, and death should in any way be underrated. As Shaka's praise-poem puts it:

The newly planted crops they left still short,
The seed they left among the maize-stalks,
The old women were left in the abandoned sites,
The old men were left along the tracks,
The roots of the trees looked up at the sky.[15]

The Extent of Civilian Suffering

The evidence of the "crushing" was there for the first white adventurers to see, although it should be kept in mind that certain areas, particularly the coastal lands south of the Thukela, had suffered worse devastation than others. The young Charles Maclean (known in settler legends of South Africa as "John Ross"), journeying in 1825 through this very region, called it a "comparatively depopulated country," and commented that there was "no evidence wanting in our travels by the wayside to show what the fate of the many had been. The heaps of human skulls and bones blanching the plains were sad monuments of the fearful conflicts."[16]

Yet the degree of devastation must be kept in perspective. John Wright, in his exhaustive study of the Thukela-Mzimkhulu region in the late eighteenth and early nineteenth centuries, suggests what it meant to be a civilian during that time of upheaval. Without minimizing the degree of violence, he reminds us that nothing in the evidence shows that huge numbers of people were being massacred.[17] He argues that the violence that accompanied the turbulence was primarily the result of fights over cattle, which were an absolutely essential resource for leaders who were trying to maintain or increase the size and cohesion of their followings. When communities resisted the seizure of their cattle, combat was doubtless widespread and fierce but would have involved relatively few numbers of men at any one time and would have been quite short and sharp. Casualties were probably not generally very large, even though it was usually generally the Zulu custom to give no quarter in battle. In Shaka's time this practice was probably mitigated by his desire to draft brave survivors into his army. However, although we must beware of overestimating the technological and physical capacity of the Zulu to kill untold numbers, Lawrence Keeley reminds us that the cumulative losses suffered by a small community in a series of clashes could mount surprisingly quickly to an unacceptable level.[18]

Certainly, expanding chiefdoms did their best to destroy the leadership and political organization of subjected groups, and chiefs and their close adherents were often put to death by the conqueror, but not invariably. There is evidence that Shaka could be considerate to the conquered, that he might treat subordinates in a conciliatory manner, and that he allowed some of the chiefs on the peripheries of his kingdom to live and rule as his tributaries. It must always be remembered that both Shaka and the leaders of those larger groups set into motion to escape Zulu aggression were intent on breaking up the polities they encountered so as to incorporate

The return of a Zulu war party c. 1850; driving off captured cattle laden with booty from an *umuzi* (homestead) that has put to the torch. Courtesy of the late S. B. Bourquin.

as many as possible of their components into their own followings. It made no political sense to annihilate people rather than to compel them to submit. It is thus Wright's contention that the period was consequently characterized not so much by the destruction of peoples as by two alternative and linked processes: the displacement and migration of populations and the associated fragmentation of political units, followed by their reaggregation into new, enlarged entities, of which the Zulu state was one of the greatest.

All the same, there were indubitably occasions when civilians suffered directly and heavily in the fighting. This occurred primarily when a ruler and all his adherents came under attack while they were migrating. Then the noncombatants had no option but to stand by and watch, hoping desperately that their menfolk would successfully defend them. It seems that in 1826 at the battle of the izinDolowane hills, where Shaka finally defeated the Ndwandwe who were trying to return *en masse* to their former territory, that when the Ndwandwe warriors broke and fled the Zulu surrounded and butchered their women and children as well as rounding up their cattle. The same would happen in the future during the reigns of Shaka's half-brothers. On January 29, 1840, Mpande defeated King Dingane at the battle of the Maqongqo hills in order to seize the crown and killed the women and children of Dingane's household who did not make good their escape when his army crumbled. The greatest known slaughter of civilians in the kingdom's history (this time substantiated by many eyewitness accounts) occurred on December 2, 1856 at Ndondakusuka. Cetshwayo, King Mpande's son, pinned Mbuyazi (his hated half-brother and rival for the royal succession) and his entire following against the flooded, crocodile-infested Thukela River, which they had been hoping to cross to sanctuary in British Natal. Once Mbuyazi's warriors were routed, Cetshwayo's men remorselessly slaughtered the hysterical and defenseless mob of women, children, and old people or drove them into the raging river to drown. Bodies washed up all along the coast, and for decades afterward bones littered the river banks. Colonial officials estimated that several thousand must have been massacred.[19]

Of course, numbers of people, particularly in areas where social and economic disruption was severe, would have perished from starvation and privation. When the Zulu attacked a community, many might take refuge in the surrounding bush, in caves, or on mountain tops to reemerge once the Zulu had passed on. The raiding Zulu might carry captives off to the heartland of the Zulu kingdom where they would be incorporated into the households of Zulu notables in various menial capacities, the women and girls as concubines and domestic servants, the men and boys as cattle herders. As people shifted into regions dominated by the larger and more stable chiefdoms to find security, the areas they left became relatively denuded. Yet even in these denuded areas small groups clung to the more broken or forested parts, living by hunting and gathering to avoid attracting attention, or by banditry and raiding neighboring communities. Some of the most desperate inevitably took to cannibalism to survive, though the frequency of this practice has undoubtedly been much sensationalized in the settler literature and has been kept alive in Zulu oral tradition as a metaphor for dire social breakdown.[20]

Although dating from the period of civil war in 1883–1884, which was the consequence of the breakup in 1879 of the defeated Zulu kingdom, Nomguqo Dlamini's reminiscences of the months she spent taking refuge in a mountain cave from marauding armed bands gives a vivid impression of what it would have been like in similar circumstances in Shaka's time:

> On the day on which we moved into the cave a white goat was sacrificed. The ancestral spirits were implored [to preserve them from their enemies].... By the friction of two sticks ... fire was made and all parts of the cave were lit up, enabling us to select nice dwelling-places within that large cave.... [W]e found deep inside a large pool of water ... fed by a spring.... The smoke from the fires was dissipated through fissures in the rocks; they were such that no sunlight ever penetrated....
>
> One day [enemy forces] took up position at the cave, but did not find us, because we had withdrawn deep into the cave. Our enemies were afraid to enter. They sat

on top of the rocks and called to us: "Come out and show us where the cattle are; if you do as you are told, we will not harm you." But we kept very quiet and stayed inside the cave, till they moved off again.... Our men, who were concealed near the mouth of the cave, would have immediately stabbed any entrant to death ...

They also failed to get hold of the cattle, which were kept inside the cave.... The cattle suffered no hardship; there was sufficient grazing and water.... We, however, nearly perished from hunger; because we stayed there nearly a year and were unable to till any fields or do any planting. We were reduced to searching for and digging up the tubers of a grass-like plant.... We cooked them, but ate them without salt, because we had none. We also picked ... berries. These berries we cooked and then ground them on stones, as we do with boiled mealie [maize] grains. We also searched the forest for edible tubers ... which are only eaten in time of famine; wild figs; and ... tuberous veld [grassland] plants, which we dug up. All these could be reached from our cave. I shudder to think of the famine! The Lord preserved us; but our suffering was great. [21]

Besides suffering the depredations of marauding bands, civilian communities, if they lived along the line of march of a Zulu army, were always vulnerable to pillage since, for lack of sophisticated logistical support, warriors on campaign had to live off the countryside. It is true that boys accompanied the army as carriers and to drive the accompanying cattle, that girls with supplies kept up with the army for a few days until their stocks were exhausted, and that the men carried iron rations in a skin sack. But these sources of food soon gave out. The hungry *amabutho* tried to spare their own civilian population as far as possible, slaughtering the cattle they brought with them, and camping if they could at *amakhanda* where stores of food had been amassed. When an army entered enemy territory, however, it began to forage ruthlessly as it advanced. The grain-pits in the abandoned *imizi* were raided, vegetable gardens stripped, and livestock driven off. Huts were demolished for firewood. Yet when forced to operate on their own soil, as in 1879, the hungry *amabutho* could not afford to be squeamish about pillaging their own people, and Zulu civilians took the same precautions against them as against an enemy, removing their grain, which was so vital as seed for the next season's planting, driving off their cattle, and taking refuge themselves out of the army's path.[22]

THE BRITISH INVASION OF 1879

A Zulu Genocide?

The direct effects of the British invasion of 1879 on Zulu civilians have not been much addressed in any of the plethora of books on the Anglo-Zulu War. The reason lies to some extent in the sheer difficulty of the task. It is nearly impossible to compute with any real degree of accuracy the losses the Zulu armies sustained in battle, let alone the number of ordinary people's huts the British burned and the grain-stores they looted, or the size of the herds and flocks they drove away. But some attempt can and must be made, particularly in the light of Michael Lieven's recent claim that the war stopped "just short of the demands of genocide."[23] It is certainly true that there were colonial campaigns of genocide in Africa, most notoriously the suppression in 1904–1907 of the Herero and Nama uprising in German South West Africa, and that until recently there has been a deep failure to acknowledge the extent of destruction intentionally inflicted by colonialism on indigenous peoples.[24] However, Lieven's thesis is based more on a subjective and impressionistic response to a variety of contemporary sources than on empirical data, which, problematic and incomplete as they undoubtedly are, are nevertheless available in considerably more profusion and detail than anything comparable for the period of the wars of Shaka, Dingane, and Mpande.[25]

Conducting a Colonial "Small War"

To appreciate the nature of the Anglo-Zulu War, and in particular its impact on noncombatants, it is necessary to place it in the context of contemporary colonial campaigns and the manner in which they were normally conducted. In devising their Zululand strategy, Lieutenant-General Lord Chelmsford and his staff were following certain military principles later formalized in Colonel C. E. Callwell's *Small Wars.* Callwell's work was adopted in 1896 by the British Army as an official handbook on the required techniques to be used by organized regular armies against "tribal" irregulars generally inferior in armaments, organization, and discipline, although exhibiting varied and unpredictable military styles. The experience of small wars, Callwell insisted, proved beyond doubt that those that were the most decisive were marked by pitched battles. What had at all costs to be avoided was the degeneration of a campaign into protracted, irregular warfare, which would favor the enemy fighting on their own ground. Fortunately for the British in 1879, Zulu military tradition did not favor a protracted, guerrilla-style defensive strategy, and the Zulu were willing to risk all in a pitched battle.[26]

At the time of the Anglo-Zulu War the Zulu population of probably somewhere around 300,000 people was living in something like 85,000 huts, or in 21,250 *imizi.* We can say that 45 percent of the Zulu population was male, or a maximum of 135,000. The nominal strength of the Zulu army was about 40,000, although the actual effectives, who were in an age-band between the early twenties and late forties, numbered no more than 29,000. If we also include the rather less than 5,000 irregulars who participated in the war but were not formally part of the *amabutho* system, this brings the percentage of the male population who went to war in 1879 up to only 25 percent of the total. Zulu battle fatalities in major engagements where *amabutho* (and some irregulars) were involved amounted to 6,160 men or more. Casualties in actions where irregulars alone were engaged came to about 400. In other words, 21 percent of the

Zulu who were deployed in battle were killed in action, and these losses were concentrated among men who were in their prime of life, when they would have been of their greatest value to Zulu society. (See Table 2.1.) Unlike the *amabutho,* the great majority of the Zulu population, including boys and older men, took no part in actively resisting the British invasion, although they were also its victims.

Although Chelmsford intended to conclude the Zululand campaign swiftly with a decisive battle, he soon came to realize that on account of the broken terrain and rain-sodden ground a rapid advance of the invading columns was impossible. Instead, he decided very early in the campaign to send out flying columns to occupy and devastate those parts of Zululand under King Cetshwayo's control, and only to resume the general advance once conditions improved sufficiently. When he did recommence the advance in May after a three months' halt to regroup after the Zulu victory at Isandlwana, Chelmsford's intended strategy was to drive "all of the Zulu population into the North-East portion of Zululand" precisely because he believed it was "unhealthy and not well cultivated."[27] This was in accordance with the strategy he had formulated as early as November 1878, by which he calculated that by pushing the increasingly hungry, shelterless, and desperate Zulu into this inhospitable countryside he might provoke them into deposing their king and surrendering.

Encouraging Zulu Submissions

Indeed, an essential element of Chelmsford's overall strategy was his belief, regularly confirmed by intelligence, that the Zulu kingdom was riven by existing tensions between the king and his ambitious royal relations and great chiefs. Chelmsford hoped to exploit these divisions to the British advantage by encouraging disaffected chiefs and their adherents to defect. Even before the beginning of the campaign, therefore, he instructed his commanders and border officials to pursue negotiations with Zulu notables and laid down guidelines for the accommodation of Zulu refugees and defectors in Natal. As he wrote to Colonel Evelyn Wood, the commander of No. 4 Column:

> When you advance every effort should be made to induce those Zulu tribes, who are averse to war, to come under our protection—They should be sent to the rear as soon as they come in, and a special civil officer told off to locate them and feed them—[28]

Once the tide of war turned irreversibly against the Zulu, the previous trickle of defections and submissions became a flood. This was particularly the case along the coastal plain where the wholesale surrender of the civilian population—even before the final battle of Ulundi had been fought on July 4—was not simply a consequence of the disheartening record of absolute lack of Zulu military success in this theater (crushing defeats at Nyezane and Gingindlovu and the failed blockade of Eshowe). It was

Table 2.1
Zulu Military Casualities

Actions where the *amabutho* were engaged		
Date	**Battle**	**Casualties**
22 January	Battle of Isandlwana	1 000+
22 January	Battle of Nyezane	400+
22-23 January	Battle of Rorke's Drift	600+
28 March	Battle of Hlobane	50?
29 March	Battle of Khambula	1 400+
2 April	Battle of Gingindlovu	1 200
3 July	Recce at White Mfolozi	10?
4 July	Battle of Ulundi	1 500
	Total:	***6 160+***
Actions where irregulars were engaged		
Date	**Action**	**Casualties**
12 January	Action at Sokhexe	67+
12 January	Action at lower Bivane	7
15 January	Action at upper Batshe	10?
20 January	Action at Zungwini	12
22 January	Skirmish on Phindo heights	30?
24 January	Action at Zungwini Nek	50?
1 February	Action at ebaQulusini	6
10 February	Action at Ntombe	15
15 February	Action at Ntombe caves	34
15 February	Action at Talaku Mountain	7
21 February	Action at Makateeskop	9
12 March	Action at Ntombe crossing	30+
5 April	Skirmish at Ntombe	2
18 May	Action at Jagpad	2
4 June	Action at Elandsberg	18
5 June	Skirmish at Zungeni	25+
15 June	Skirmish at Thabankulu	12
23,23,26, 30 June	Raids Ngoye/Mhlathuze	5
25 June	Raid at Middle Drift	10
4 September	Prisoners killed in Ntombe caves	7
8 September	Action at Ntombe caves	30+
	Total:	**388+**
	Total (*amabutho* and irregulars)	**6 548+**

Sources: John Laband, "Kingdom in Crisis: The Response of the Zulu Polity to the British Invasion of 1879" (Ph.D. diss., University of Natal, 1990), 186, 210, 227, 240–43, 244, 252, 255, 258, 315–18, 336, 354, 379, 442; John Laband and Paul Thompson, *The Illustrated Guide to the Anglo-Zulu War* (Pietermaritzburg: University of KwaZulu-Natal Press, 2004), 83, 87, 99, 109, 129, 159, 165, 177, 181.

also the result of the methods employed by the methodically advancing British 1st Division. Repeated and ruthless mounted patrols were sent out to burn *imizi* and *amakhanda* and to drive off livestock with the specific and successful intention of demoralizing the civilian population. As one newspaper correspondent ruthlessly put it:

> By deprivations of all kinds the Zulu ... must "feel" the miseries of war, and nothing will bring home to them the horrors of war better than being deprived of the shelter of huts in these cold nights. Fire, sword and rifle must never rest, day or night, to make every Zulu man, woman or child at last cry for peace.[29]

The submission of the disheartened Zulu civilians was made much easier by Chelmsford offering their leaders a carrot to go with the stick he was wielding. His message of June 11 to the Zulu chiefs promised those wishing to submit easy terms. Between January 10 and July 4 an estimated 3,359 Zulu surrendered and were taken under British protection. General Sir Garnet Wolseley, once he had superseded Chelmsford in early July, consolidated and hastened the process of submissions. He assured the Zulu chiefs on July 26 that all those who surrendered with their arms and royal cattle[30] would be permitted to retain their own cattle, land, and chiefly status in the new Zululand, where both the monarchy and the military system were to be abolished. Wolseley thus placed the chiefs in a position where they could preserve or even augment their positions by coming to terms with the British, while the livelihood of ordinary people was not disrupted. In the wake of the battle of Ulundi, fought on July 4, the Zulu everywhere openly acknowledged to the British that their defeat was complete and that the war was over. The predominant Zulu attitude was that they had seen enough of fighting, and that they wished for peace and the opportunity to go home to resume the normal course of their lives.

J. W. Colenso, the Anglican Bishop of Natal, early antagonized settler opinion by preaching in March 1879 that in Zululand too the people were suffering "the terrible scourge of war" and required mercy. By September he was arguing that, since the country was occupied by the British, the people would be threatened by starvation unless they were allowed to return to their homes in safety to plant their crops, for the last harvest had been destroyed by British patrols.[31] Yet Colenso's view was alarmist and ill-informed. Fighting and devastation in 1879 had been concentrated to limited areas, and even when in late July and August pacification columns moved out into fresh parts of the country, they failed to penetrate vast areas of northeastern and south-central Zululand. (See map.) By August most of the country directly affected by the war had already been pacified, with the people returned to their fields. In late July a newspaper correspondent wrote of the coastal plain, which the 1st Division had subjected to heavy mounted raids in May to July:

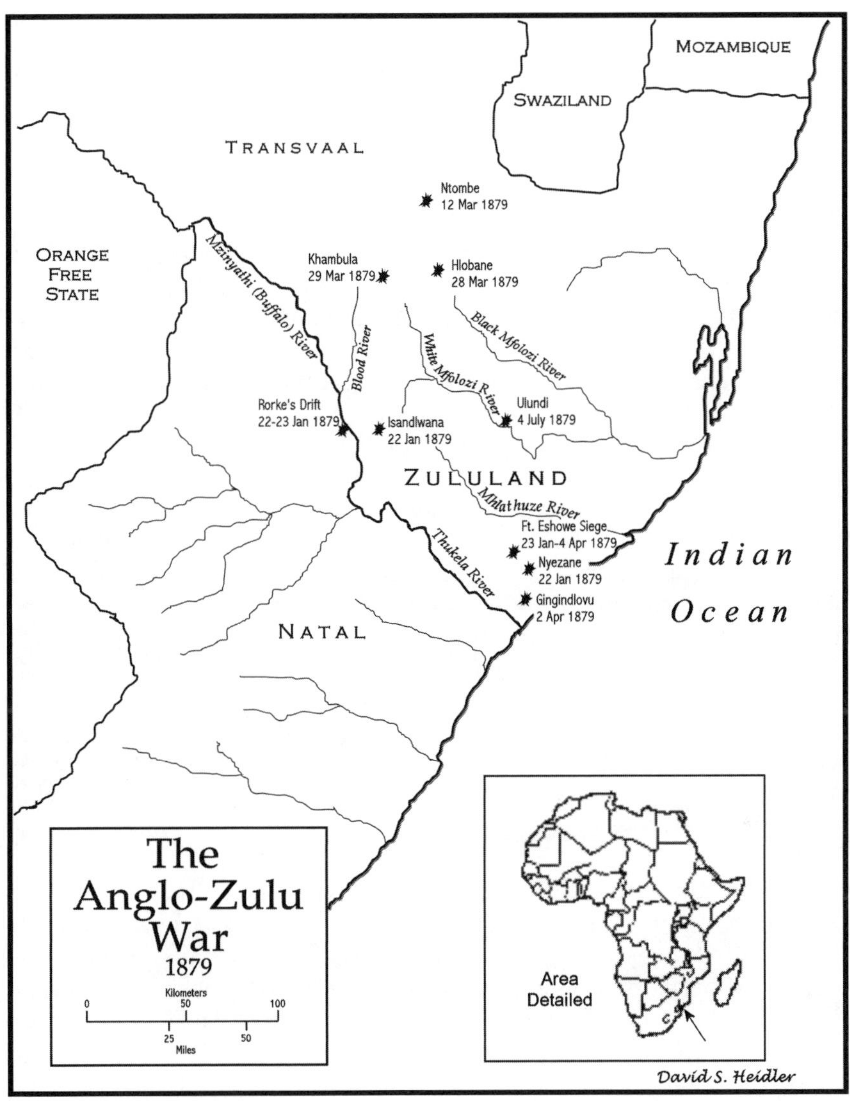

The Anglo-Zulu War 1879

Riding through the country one is struck by the marked contrast between the appearance of the country at the present time and a few weeks ago. Not long since the neighbouring fertile lands were the scene of battle, desolation, and other evils attending war.... Now everything presents a peaceful aspect, and those who until very recently were anxious to meet the invading forces of the white man in battle, are now industriously engaged rebuilding their old kraals [*imizi*], which have been fired and otherwise destroyed by the invading army.... Visits are repeatedly paid to camp by these Zulus ... as if the war had never disturbed them ... [yet] there is scarcely a family which has not lost one of its members, while numbers of them have lost some of their cattle, which is the Zulus' treasure; and many have even felt the pangs of hunger, which has probably hastened their surrender,—which none regret.... [32]

Waging War against Civilians

Chelmsford, as his military secretary, Lieutenant-Colonel J. N. Crealock wrote of him in late June 1879, did "not wish to prolong the war or in any way inflict any unnecessary hardship on the Zulus; but war can't be made with kid gloves."[33] In going to war, the British officially had no quarrel with the Zulu nation, only with its king. Accordingly, Chelmsford initially forbade any excesses against the Zulu population. The penalty for any African auxiliary "wilfully killing a woman or child or a wounded man" was hanging; while burning huts "except under the special orders of the officer commanding the column" meant a flogging for all British troops, black or white.[34] However, after the Isandlwana debacle on January 22, the distinction between the Zulu king and his "savage" subjects ceased to be observed. As the war correspondent Charles Norris-Newman wrote in the heat of Isandlwana's aftermath:

The fallacy of fighting with an uncivilised race with the same feelings of humanity that dictate our wars with civilised races was thoroughly proved; and it thus was shown that in Zululand neither men, kraals, cattle, nor crops should be spared on any pretence whatever, except on the complete submission and disarmament of the whole nation.[35]

No restrictions were henceforth placed on military operations other than the "laws of civilized warfare"—meaning what was permitted practice in Europe. The *amakhanda,* which were the regional centers of the king's authority, the rallying-points for the *amabutho,* and the depots of Zulu supplies, were obviously prime military targets, just as an enemy convoy, magazine, or fort would have been in a European theater of war. There were 24 *amakhanda* positively identified as existing at the time of the Anglo-Zulu War, and of these the British burned 23. What this comprehensive destruction of *amakhanda* meant in terms of huts actually burned is not easy to say precisely because the size of *amakhanda* varied enormously. If we take an average of about 500 huts to an *ikhanda,* that means over 12,000 huts were destroyed.

The British (unfortunately for the Zulu), besides eliminating primarily military targets like the *amakhanda,* also believed in waging war against the civilian population in an effort to diminish both their ability to sustain their fighting men in the field and their own morale. The systematic burning of ordinary *imizi* or the demolition of huts for use as fuel, and the destruction of standing crops and grain stores, as well as the capture of cattle, goats, and sheep were deemed to be militarily justified since such measures were bound to be efficacious in ending resistance among a people whose very livelihood was threatened. (See Table 2.2.) Mounted troops were essential for this raiding activity, so one reason why Chelmsford dispersed his invading columns so widely was to maximize the impact of the limited number of horsemen at his disposal. Chelmsford was well aware that if a decisive engagement eluded him, such methods (although slower), by wearing down the Zulu resolve to continue resistance, would fatally weaken the king's ability to prosecute the war. Tactically too, systematic pillaging in the area of operations denied the opposing Zulu forces bases, shelter, and supplies and created an extensive zone free of Zulu forces around the vulnerable British columns, which were dangerously extended while on the march.

The British operating in Zululand were nevertheless sensitive to charges in England that unnecessary destruction was being visited upon the Zulu. Even newspaper correspondents who witnessed the destruction of homes and crops and the loss of cattle could not help recommending a "little sympathy" for the enemy, even if "in campaigns of this kind one is apt to look lightly on the sufferings of the enemy who, happening to be of a darker hue, is often supposed to be utterly devoid of the gentler feelings possessed by the superior white man."[36] Aware of this viewpoint, the cavalrymen Major Ashe and Captain Wyatt-Edgell disingenuously declared in their partisan history of the campaign:

> Coming now to the farming and domestic kraals, it may without fear of contradiction be asserted, after minute and careful enquiries, that no single instance can be adduced in which her Majesty's troops ever attacked or molested such unless first attacked and fired upon.[37]

However, their tendentious statement has been contradicted in numerous reports and reminiscences by eyewitnesses who participated in the methodical burning of *imizi* along the British line of march, or in raids across the Natal border. In a typical account, a correspondent with the force raiding on May 20 across the Thukela River near Kranskop reported:

> No enemy was to be seen.... In the valley there were two kraals, a large and small one. The native contingent fired them by Major Twentyman's orders. The kafirs [Zulu] had evidently left only a few hours before. A large quantity of grain—mealies [maize] and kafir corn [sorghum]—was destroyed. It had been freshly gathered and stacked inside the kraals. Two other kraals nearer the river were also fired. There was a great deal of grain burned altogether. The natives pointed out some cattle in an open space underneath a very high hill some distance away. They were very anxious to capture them, but Major Twentyman did not consider it prudent to advance further into the country. After committing such unlimited havoc and devastation as was possible, we retired to the drift [ford].[38]

Table 2.2
Destruction of *Imizi* and *Amakhanda* and Loss of Livestock

Date	Place	*imizi*	*amakhanda*	cattle	sheep	goats
10:1	White Mfolozi			800+*		
11:1	White Mfolozi			4000	2000	
12:1	lower Bivane			538		
12:1	Sokhexe	1		413	235	332
13:1	White Mfolozi			400		
21:1	kwaGingindlovu		1			
22:1	Zungwini			250	400	
22:1	Nyezane/Eshowe	5?				
26:1	Phongolo/Ntombe			365		200
01:2	ebaQulusini		1	270		
10:2	Hlobane			490		
15:2	Ntombe caves	5		375	8	254
15:2	Talaku			197	44	70
21:2	Makateeskop			25	20	100
01:3	Ntumeni	3	1			
28:3	Hlobane			300		
01:4	Ngoye	7				
02:4	Middle Drift	2				
03:4	Middle Drift	1				
03:4	Ntumeni	1				
09:4	Batshe Valley	12				
24:4	Port Durnford			30****		
13:5	Buffalo/Batshe	25 ?				
20:5	Middle Drift	19		150		
21:5	Batshe	5?				
28:5	Lower Thukela	2				
03:6	Phoko	1				
0.2125	Zungwini	4				
07:6	Zungwini	4?				
08:6	Phoko	3?				
10:6	Phoko			300		
15:6	Thabankulu	24		300	100	
19:6	Babanango	10?				
19:6	patrol Ft Marshall			74		

Table 2.2 (Continued)

Date	Place	*imizi*	*amakhanda*	cattle	sheep	goats
26:6	patrol Ft Marshall	8				
26:6	emaKhosini		9			
23-30:6	Mhlathuze/Ngoye	50+		378	27	29
04:7	emaNgweni	12	1	600		
04:7	coastal surrender			1327*		
04:7	Mahlabathini		9			
06:7	oNdini		1			
07:7	KwaMagwaza			300		
09:7	patrol Ft Newdigate	6				
31:7	St Paul(s			20*		
13:8	Middle Border			28*		
14:8	Mahlabathini			617*		
25:8	Fort Cambridge			300**		
15:9	Middle Border			6*		
15:9	Middle Border			279***		133***
16:9	Middle Border			250***		100***
17:9	Middle Border			47***	11***	
19:9	Middle Border			150**		
19:9	Middle Border			300***		
20:9	Middle Border			20*		
20:9	Middle Border			50***		
20:9	Middle Border			92**		
Sept	Buffalo Border			471*	495**	8
05:9	Ntombe caves	1				
Total		**211**	**23**	**14 512**	**3 311**	**1 226**

Key: * = royal cattle surrendered; ** = livestock confiscated as fines; *** = raided livestock recovered; **** = cattle bombarded from the sea. If there is no symbol the livestock were captured in a British raid.

Sources: John Laband, "Kingdom in Crisis: The Zulu Response to the British Invasion of 1879" (Ph.D. diss., University of Natal, 1990), 218, 227, 239, 240, 241, 252, 262, 290, 324, 337, 354, 355, 378, 379, 381, 457, 461; John Laband, "Mbilini, Manyonyoba, and the Phongolo River Frontier" in John Laband and Paul Thompson, eds., *Kingdom and Colony at War: Sixteen Studies on the Anglo-Zulu War of 1879* (Pietermaritzburg and Cape Town: University of Natal Press and N & S Press, 1990), 195, 196, 197; John Laband and Paul Thompson, *War Comes to Umvoti: the Natal–Zululand Border 1878–79* (Durban: University of Natal, Research Monograph No. 5, 1980), 49, 60, 61, 82;—with Sheila Henderson, *The Buffalo Border 1879: The Anglo-Zulu War in Northern Natal* (Durban: University of Natal, Research Monograph No. 6, 1983), 64, 69, 73, 80.

Nevertheless, the graphic nature of such accounts should not be allowed to divert us from the incontrovertible fact that the British only destroyed a small percentage of the number of *imizi* in Zululand as a whole, for most were out of the reach of the mounted patrols. British records make specific mention of only 211 *imizi* burned. If we accept the figure arrived at earlier that there were probably some 21,250 *imizi* in Zululand as a whole, this means that only 1 percent were torched. An identical percentage is reached in terms of huts, for accepting that there were four huts to an *umuzi,* this means that only 844 out of the 85,000 huts in Zululand (excluding those in *amakhanda*) fell victim to the British. Even if we double, or even triple, the British figure of 211 *imizi* burned, this still comes to only a tiny percentage of the whole.

As with the number of huts burned, it is tempting, based on graphic contemporary accounts, to arrive at an impressionistic conclusion regarding the number of livestock taken that far exceeds the actual reality. A reasonable calculation would suggest that in Zululand in 1879 there were at least 300,000 cattle, 200,000 goats, and 40,000 African sheep. British tallies (which seem relatively complete) of livestock captured, surrendered, confiscated, or recovered from the Zulu who had raided them from the colonial population, give Zulu losses as 14,512 cattle, 1,226 goats, and 3,311 sheep. If we accept the figures arrived at above of the number of livestock in Zululand in 1879, this translates into

A patrol of mounted men from the Eshowe Relief Column burning Prince Dabulamanzi kaMpande's eZuluwini *umuzi* (homestead) on April 4, 1879. *Graphic,* June 7, 1879.

a Zulu loss of only 5 percent of cattle, 6 percent of goats and 8 percent of sheep. As with the number of huts destroyed, even if we were to double or even triple the figure, the loss was far from catastrophic and would have been made up over a few years through the natural increase of flocks and herds.

Ashe and Wyatt-Edgell complained that "accusations of shooting down women and children were not infrequently brought against the troops."[39] Yet, in truth, there were the scantest recorded occasions on which atrocities were perpetrated against the Zulu civilian population. Doubtless, one of the reasons for this was the general reluctance of the Zulu to wage guerrilla-style warfare. As a result, the British were not stung (as is typical in such situations) into wild reprisals against civilians who might be harboring guerrillas. There was only one atrocity of any note when, in the very last action of the war, on September 8 in northwestern Zululand, men of the 2nd Battalion of the 4th (King's Own Rifles) Regiment blew up some caves in Mbilini's mountain, killing about 30 die-hard defenders and the civilians sheltering with them. Yet even here it could be debated whether this action breached the laws of war by the calculated and purposeless killing of civilians for, strictly, they had not surrendered and the warriors with them were still fighting back.

Limited Civilian Suffering?

Apart from the very infrequent incidents such as the one described, civilians in the Anglo-Zulu War suffered little direct harm. Some might have been the indirect casualties of the fighting, such as the women watching the battle of Ulundi from the hilltops who were probably struck by shrapnel-bursts from the six British 9-pounder guns brought up to disperse groups of defeated Zulu warriors regrouping nearby. In most cases, civilians were able to flee in good time before the British attacked. For example, in western Zululand where Colonel Wood's No. 4 Column was very active, sending out effective mounted patrols, the abaQulusi abandoned the open country for their mountain fastnesses, and then, on King Cetshwayo's orders, fell back further east with their cattle out of Wood's range. The Mdlalosi people to Wood's rear, by contrast, returned home from the mountain tops where they had taken refuge once the war swept on past them. During the advance of the 2nd Division, the British caught sight of women and children swarming out of their *imizi* toward the security of the nearest mountain with what possessions they could carry on their heads. The problem, though, is that in their precipitate flight people not only abandoned their huts to destruction, but left their grain stores to be looted, their livestock to be driven away, and belongings such as mats, guns, and gourds, which they might have hidden away nearby, to be carried off.

However, and this is the vital point, for the few who did not manage to flee and were rounded up by British patrols, the worst was the loss of their possessions, for there was little or no danger of being killed by their captors. A newspaper correspondent with the 1st Division described a typical incident during a mounted raid on July 4, during which over 600 cattle were captured:

> As usual, some Zulu women and children were brought in. It was strange to see a Kaffir woman in tears. Most likely, she had had her home burnt, and all that she cared for was scattered.[40]

In seeking a decisive battle with the Zulu army, and in destroying Zulu crops and *imizi* and running off livestock in order to induce civilians to submit, the British were following the normal practices of "small wars" of conquest in Africa. The war was not as devastating as it could have been, particularly since it never entered the guerrilla phase, and large areas of Zululand never saw so much as a British patrol. Hostile activity and damage to civilian property were largely confined to the coastal plain as far north as the Mhlathuze River, the countryside around Khambula and Luneburg in the extreme northwest, and the route taken through west-central Zululand by the 2nd Division from the Ncome (Blood) River to oNdini. Though many civilians in the theater of operations were forced temporarily to abandon their homes for mountain fastnesses and forests, they were nevertheless able to return in time to plant for the new season. Indeed, the Zulu were in a position everywhere to make good the relatively limited losses to *imizi,* grain stores, and livestock within a season or two of peace being restored. The immediate impact of the war on the fabric of Zulu society was consequently limited. Doubtless, the biggest impression on society was made by the considerable number of Zulu battle casualties, which inevitably were concentrated in a narrow age-band of men in their prime. Yet even these losses were not so extraordinary that the economy was crippled for lack of manpower, even in the short term.

Rather, the most telling blow administered to the fabric of Zulu society was represented by the spectacular destruction of the *amakhanda,* those centers of royal authority. Since in his settlement of Zululand on September 1 the victorious Sir Garnet Wolseley abolished both the Zulu monarchy and the *amabutho* system that sustained it, the *amakhanda* were not rebuilt. Instead, political power devolved once more to the great chiefs and British appointees, and the young men of Zululand, rather than serving the king in their *amabutho* as they had since the days of Shaka, fell once more under their chiefs' localized authority. Forged first in war, Shaka's kingdom was undone by war in the reign of his nephew, Cetshwayo. Yet, resilient to the repeated horrors of war, in the late nineteenth century the *imizi* of the Zulu people, and their herds, continued to cover the hillsides and the broad plains of Zululand as they had done 80 years before when the kingdom was first formed. In the end, it was not war that would transform the Zulu way of life. Rather, it would be the forces of an industrializing subcontinent, the irresistible pull of the mines and cities, migrant labor, proletarianization and urbanization, the allure of a globalized, increasingly Americanized, culture that, in the course of the twentieth century, would irrevocably change the world of ordinary Zulu men and women.

TIMELINE

1816	Shaka kaSenzangakhona seizes the Zulu chieftainship
1817	The Ndwandwe overthrow the Mthethwa
1819	The Zulu defeat the Ndwandwe
1824	First white settlement in southeast Africa at Port Natal
1824	Assassination attempt on Shaka by Qwabe dissidents
1826	September: Zulu finally crush the Ndwandwe at the izinDolowane hills
1828	September 24: Assassination of King Shaka; half-brother Dingane seizes the Zulu throne
1837	October: Boer invasion of Zululand
1838	December 16: Boers defeat the Zulu at the battle of Blood River
1838–1844	Boer Republic of Natalia
1840	January 29: Mpande overthrows his half-brother Dingane at the battle of the Maqongqo hills
1843	October 5: British recognize the Zulu kingdom north of the Thukela River
1844	May 31: British annexation of Natal south of the Thukela
1856	December 2: Cetshwayo defeats his rivals for the royal succession at the battle of Ndondakusuka
1873	August 25: Cetshwayo crowned king in succession to his father Mpande
1879	January 11: British invasion of Zululand January 22: Zulu victory over the British at Isandlwana July 4: final British victory over the Zulu at Ulundi September 1: British dictate peace terms and break up the Zulu kingdom

GLOSSARY

Names

Bulwer, Sir Henry Ernest Gascoyne (1836–1914). Lieutenant-Governor of Natal, 1875–1880.

Buthelezi, Prince Mangosuthu Gatsha (b. 1928). President of the Inkatha Freedom Party since 1994 and South African Minister of Home Affairs, 1994–2004.

Cambridge, Field Marshal Prince, George William Frederick Charles, Duke of (1819–1904). Commander-in-Chief of the British Army, 1856–1895.

Cetshwayo kaMpande (c.1832–1884). Succeeded his father, Mpande, as fourth King of the Zulu in 1872.

Chelmsford, Lieutenant-General Sir Frederic Augustus Thesiger, 2nd Baron (1827–1905). Commander-in-Chief of the Forces in South Africa, 1878–1879.

Colenso, John William (1814–1883). First Anglican Bishop of Natal, 1853.

Dingane kaSenzangakhona (c.1788–1840). Assassinated his half-brother, Shaka, in 1828 and succeeded him as the second King of the Zulu.

Goodwill Zwelithini Mbongizozwa kaBhekuzulu (b. 1948). Succeeded King Cyprian in 1968 as eighth King of the Zulu.

Mpande kaSenzangakhona (c.1798–1872). Overthrew his half-brother, Dingane, in 1840 and succeeded as third King of the Zulu.

Shaka kaSenzangakhona (c.1787–1828). First King of the Zulu.

Shepstone, Sir Theophilus (1817–1893). Secretary for Native Affairs, Natal, 1856–1876; Administrator of the Transvaal, 1877–1879.

Wolseley, General Sir Garnet Joseph (1833–1913). High Commissioner in South Eastern Africa, Governor of Natal and the Transvaal, and Commander-in-Chief of the Forces in South Africa, 1879–1880.

Wood, Colonel Henry Evelyn (1838–1919). Commander of No. 4 Column and then the Flying Column in Zululand, 1879.

Terms

In accordance with modern practice, Zulu words are entered under the stem and not under the prefix.

isiBaya (pl. iziBaya). Enclosure for livestock (kraal).

iButho (pl. amaButho). Age-grade regiment of men or women; member of age-group; warrior.

iDlozi (pl. amaDlozi). Ancestral spirit.

inDlu (pl. izinDlu). Hut.

Drift. Shallow fordable point in a river.

Kafir Corn. Sorghum.

iKhanda (pl. amaKhanda). Royal military homestead where age-grade regiments were stationed.

ukuKhonza. To pay allegiance to king or chief.

Kraal. Enclosure for livestock or settler term for *umuzi.*

iLobolo. (sing. only) Cattle or goods handed over by man's family to formalize marriage transaction.

Mealie. Maize.

umNumzane (pl. abaNumzane). Married headman of a homestead.

ukuSisa. To pasture livestock in care of a subordinate.

umuZi (pl. imizi). Homestead of huts under a headman.

NOTES

1. See Thembisa Waetjen and Gerhard Maré, "'Men amongst Men': Masculinity and Zulu Nationalism in the 1980s," in *Changing Men in Southern Africa,* ed. Robert Morrell (Pietermaritzburg, London, and New York: University of Natal Press and Zed Books, 2001), 199–201, 205. See also John Iliffe, *Honour in African History* (Cambridge: Cambridge University Press, 2005), 6, 140–41, 202–4, 223–24, 312–13. Prince Buthelezi is descended through his mother from Mpande, Shaka's half-brother.

2. C. de B. Webb and J. B. Wright, eds., *The James Stuart Archive of Recorded Oral Evidence Relating to the History of the Zulu and Neighbouring Peoples* (Pietermaritzburg and Durban: University of Natal Press and Killie Campbell Africana Library, 2001), 5: 57: testimony of Ngidi ka Mcikaziswa, 6 November 1904.

3. Bruce Vandervort, *Wars of Imperial Conquest in Africa, 1830–1914* (London: UCL Press, 1998), 102.

4. For a full discussion of *Shaka Zulu* and how this historical television drama was manipulated in the turbulent political atmosphere of the dying days of apartheid, see Carolyn Hamilton, *Terrific Majesty: The Powers of Shaka Zulu and the Limits of Historical Invention* (Cape Town and Johannesburg: David Philip, 1998), 171–87.

5. For the precolonial Zulu way of life, see John Laband, *The Rise and Fall of the Zulu Nation* (London: Arms and Armour, 1997), 4–10.

6. Norman Etherington, *The Great Treks: The Transformation of Southern Africa, 1815–1854* (London: Longman, 2001), xxi, 23, 33–35.

7. For a detailed description of the Zulu military system, see John Laband and Paul Thompson, *The Illustrated Guide to the Anglo-Zulu War* (Pietermaritzburg: University of Natal Press, 2004), 9–19.

8. John Wright, "The Dynamics of Power and Conflict in the Thukela-Mzimkhulu Region in the Late 18th and Early 19th Centuries: A Critical Reconstruction" (unpublished Ph.D. thesis, University of the Witwatersrand, 1989), 310–13, 318–19; Dan Wylie, *Savage Delight: White Myths of Shaka* (Pietermaritzburg: University of Natal Press, 2000), 39–66, 239–45.

9. Magema M. Fuze, *The Black People and Whence They Came: A Zulu View,* trans. H. C. Lugg, ed. A. T. Cope (Pietermaritzburg and Durban: University of Natal Press and Killie Campbell Africana Library, 1979), 50, 53.

10. Wright, "Dynamics of Power," 66–73, 79–80.

11. D. G. McC. Theal, *Progress of South Africa* (London: Linscott, 1900), 169.

12. Frank Chalk and Kurt Jonassohn, *The History and Sociology of Genocide: Analyses and Case Studies* (New Haven and London: Yale University Press, 1990), 233.

13. See J. D. Omer-Cooper, *The Zulu Aftermath: A Nineteenth-Century Revolution in Bantu Africa* (London: Longman, 1966), 3–8, 180–82.

14. See the range of essays in Carolyn Hamilton, ed., *The Mfecane Aftermath: Reconstructive Debates in Southern African History* (Johannesburg and

Pietermaritzburg: Witwatersrand University Press and University of Natal Press, 1995).

15. T. Cope, ed., and D. Malcolm, trans., *Izibongo: Zulu Praise Poems Collected by James Stuart* (Oxford: Oxford University Press, 1968), 92.

16. Charles Rawden Maclean, *The Natal Papers of "John Ross,"* ed. Stephen Gray (Durban and Pietermartizburg: Killie Campbell Africana Library and University of Natal Press, 1992), 99.

17. For the following discussion on civilian victims see Wright, "Dynamics of Power," 231, 240, 270–73.

18. Lawrence H. Keeley, *War before Civlization* (New York and Oxford: Oxford University Press, 1996), 88–94.

19. For details of these battles see Laband, *Zulu Nation*, 40–41, 116–17, 144–46.

20. Wright, "Dynamics of Power." 274–75.

21. *Paulina Dlamini: Servant of Two Kings*, comp. H. Filter, ed. and trans., S. Bourquin (Durban and Pietermaritzburg: Killie Campbell Africana Library and University of Natal Press, 1986), 77–79.

22. Laband, *Zulu Nation*, 38.

23. Michael Lieven, "'Butchering the Brutes All Over the Place': Total War and Massacre in Zululand, 1879," *History* 84, 276 (October 1999): 616.

24. Isabel V. Hull, "Military Culture and the Production of 'Final Solutions' in the Colonies: The Example of Wilhelminian Germany," in *The Specter of Genocide: Mass Murder in Historical Perspective*, eds. Robert Gellately and Ben Kiernan (Cambridge: Cambridge University Press, 2003), 144–60; and Elazar Barkan, "Genocides of Indigenous Peoples: Rhetoric of Human Rights," ibid., 117, 136–38.

25. The following analysis of the impact of the Anglo-Zulu War on civilians is based on John Laband, "'War Can't Be Made with Kid Gloves': The Impact of the Anglo-Zulu War on the Fabric of Zulu Society," *South African Historical Journal* 43 (November 2000): 179–96. Calculations of population, livestock, casualties, and destroyed dwellings can be found in this article on pp. 184–85, 187, 189, 191–94.

26. Col C. E. Callwell, *Small Wars: Their Principles and Practice*, 3rd ed. (London: His Majesty's Stationary Office, 1906), 37–39, 90–91, 93, 103–4, 106; Laband and Thompson, *Anglo-Zulu War*, 44–46.

27. Lieutenant-General Lord Chelmsford to Brigadier-General H. E. Wood, 25 April 1879, quoted in *Lord Chelmsford's Zululand Campaign 1878–1879*, ed. John Laband (Stroud: Alan Sutton for the Army Records Society, 1994), 160.

28. Chelmsford to Colonel Wood, 16 December 1878, quoted in ibid., 44.

29. Peevaan correspondent, 5 June 1879, *Natal Mercury*, 17 June 1879, quoted in *The Red Book Natal Press Reports, Anglo-Zulu War 1879*, comps. Ron Lock and Peter Quantrill (privately printed, n.d.), 249.

30. Through the practice of *ukusisa* the king pastured his huge herds in the care of subordinate chiefs.

31. Jeff Guy, *The Destruction of the Zulu Kingdom: The Civil War in Zululand, 1879–1884* (London: Longman, 1979), 58–59, 92.

32. Port Durnford correspondent, 20 July 1879, *Natal Witness*, 29 July 1879, quoted in *The War Correspondents: The Anglo-Zulu War*, eds. John Laband and Ian Knight (Stroud: Sutton Publishing, 1996), 150.

33. Lieutenant-Colonel J. N. Crealock to Major-General Sir Archibald Alison, 28 June 1879, quoted in *Zululand at War 1879: The Conduct of the Anglo-Zulu War*, ed. Sonia Clarke (Houghton: The Brenthurst Press, 1984), 229.

34. Chelmsford to Colonel W. Bellairs, 31 December 1878, quoted in *Chelmsford's Zululand Campaign*, ed. Laband, 51.

35. C. L. Norris-Newman, *In Zululand with the British throughout the War of 1879* (London: W. H. Allen, 1880), 47.

36. Ulundi correspondent, 11 August 1879, *Natal Witness*, 23 August 1879, quoted in *War Correspondents*, eds. Laband and Knight, 156.

37. Major W. Ashe and Captain the Hon. E. V. Wyatt-Edgell, *The Story of the Zulu Campaign* (London: Sampson Low, Marston, Searle and Rivington, 1880), 307–8.

38. Krantzkop correspondent, *Natal Mercury*, 27 May 1879, quoted in *The Red Book*, comps. Lock and Quantrill, 215.

39. Ashe and Wyatt-Edgell, *Zulu Campaign*, 305.

40. Correspondent with General Hope Crealock's Division, *Illustrated London News*, 23 August 1879, quoted in *War Correspondents*, eds. Laband and Knight, 147.

SELECT BIBLIOGRAPHY

Bird, John, comp. *The Annals of Natal 1495 to 1845.* 2 vols. Cape Town: C. Struik, facsimile reprint, 1965.
A useful compilation first published in 1888 of rare printed sources relating to early Natal, many of which refer to events in the Zulu kingdom.

Bryant, Rev. A. T. *Olden Times in Zululand and Natal Containing Earlier Political History of the Eastern-Nguni Clans.* London, New York, Toronto: Longmans, Green, 1929.
The missionary and anthropologist Bryant's classic and influential history of the Natal-Zululand region before the coming of white settlers. Once the standard work of reference, it has been critically deconstructed in recent years.

Duminy, Andrew, and Bill Guest, eds. *Natal and Zululand from Earliest Times to 1910: A New History.* Pietermaritzburg: University of Natal Press and Shuter and Shooter, 1989.
A collection of revisionist essays reflecting current scholarship, many specifically on Zululand in the prehistoric, precolonial, and colonial periods.

Fuze, Magema M. *The Black People and Whence They Came: A Zulu View.* Translated by H. C. Lugg and edited by A. T. Cope. Pietermaritzburg and Durban: University of Natal Press and Killie Campbell Africana Library, 1979.
The first history in Zulu of the Zulu people up to 1913, initially published in 1922. It incorporates much oral tradition and conveys a valuable Zulucentric perspective.

Gibson, J. Y. *The Story of the Zulus.* London, New York, Bombay, and Calcutta: Longmans, Green, 1911.
Written by a white magistrate in Zululand at the beginning of the twentieth century, and partially based on interviews with Zulu notables and oral tradition. For its time of writing this classic account is remarkably empathetic.

Hamilton, Carolyn. *Terrific Majesty. The Powers of Shaka Zulu and the Limits of Historical Invention.* Cape Town and Johannesburg: David Philip, 1998.

Through a stimulating analysis of texts Hamilton explores the reasons for the potency of representations of Shaka and examines the ways these have changed over time.

———, ed. *The Mfecane Aftermath. Reconstructive Debates in Southern African History.* Johannesburg and Pietermaritzburg: Witwatersrand University Press and University of Natal Press, 1995.

A collection of conference papers that exhaustively investigates the debate over the nature of the *mfecane* from a wide variety of perspectives. It is essential reading for an understanding of the early Zulu kingdom.

Isaacs, Nathaniel. *Travels and Adventures in Eastern Africa Descriptive of the Zoolus, Their Manners, Customs with a Sketch of Natal.* Edited by Louis Herman and Percival R. Kirby. Cape Town: C. Struik, 1970.

The journal published in 1836, which the youthful Isaacs purported to have kept during the mid-1820s while a trader in Shaka's kingdom. Long esteemed as an eyewitness account, scholars today treat it with caution.

Knight, Ian. *The Anatomy of the Zulu Army from Shaka to Cetshwayo 1818-1879.* London: Greenhill Books, 1995.

A comprehensive and reliable account of how the Zulu army was recruited, trained, and dressed, how it operated in warfare, and how it functioned in society.

Krige, Eileen Jensen. *The Social System of the Zulus.* 6th impression. Pietermaritzburg: Shuter and Shooter, 1974.

First published in 1936 and now somewhat dated, this still remains a standard account of Zulu life and customs.

Laband, John, ed. *Lord Chelmsford's Zululand Campaign 1878-1879.* Stroud: Alan Sutton Publishing for the Army Records Society, 1994.

Selected documents written by Lord Chelmsford while commanding the British forces in the Anglo-Zulu War with explanatory footnotes and an introductory essay.

———. *The Rise and Fall of the Zulu Nation.* London: Arms and Armour Press, 1997.

Authoritative and detailed history of the Zulu kingdom from its earliest beginnings until the end of the nineteenth century.

———, series ed., and Ian Knight, volume ed. *Archives of Zululand: The Anglo-Zulu War 1879.* 6 vols. London: Archival Publications International, 2000.

An extensive compilation of reprinted official publications, rare contemporary articles, pamphlets, and books as well as reproduced manuscripts from archival collections. These volumes are an essential source base for those studying the Anglo-Zulu War.

———, and Ian Knight. *The War Correspondents: The Anglo-Zulu War.* Stroud: Alan Sutton Publishing, 1996.

The Anglo-Zulu War as described by the professional and amateur war correspondents who covered it. Their accounts are placed into context of the campaign.

———, and Paul Thompson. *The Illustrated Guide to the Anglo-Zulu War.* Pietermaritzburg: University of KwaZulu-Natal Press, 2004.

Based on archival research and field work, this definitive work addresses every aspect of the Anglo-Zulu War. It is accompanied by detailed maps and diagrams, as well as by contemporary illustrations and photographs.

Leverton, B.J.T., ed. *Records of Natal, 1823-1839. South African Archival Records: Important Cape Documents.* Vols. 4-7. Pretoria: Government Printer, 1984, 1989, 1990, 1992.

Collection of documents from various South African archives concerning affairs in early nineteenth-century southeast Africa, including those of the Zulu people. There is little other official documentation relating to the Zulu from this period.

Maclean, Charles Rawden. *The Natal Papers of "John Ross": Loss of the Brig* Mary *at Natal with Early Recollections of the Settlement and Among the Caffres.* Edited by Stephen Gray. Durban and Pietermritzburg: Killie Campbell Africana Library and University of Natal Press, 1992.

The experiences, published between 1853 and 1855, of Maclean's boyhood, which he spent in Zulu territory during the mid-1820s. A vivid and sympathetic account of Shaka himself and the Zulu way of life at the time, although the editor's commentary explores difficulties with the text.

Morris, Donald, R. *The Washing of the Spears: A History of the Rise of the Zulu Nation under Shaka and Its Fall in the Zulu War of 1879.* London: Jonathan Cape, 1965.

The very readable and still popular story of the Zulu kingdom, which has been largely superseded by subsequent scholarly work.

Omer-Cooper, J. D. *The Zulu Aftermath: A Nineteenth-Century Revolution in Bantu Africa.* London, Longman, 1966.

The influential book that entrenched the *mfecane* thesis and still deserves to be read.

Shamase, M. Z. *Zulu Potentates from the Earliest to Zwelithini KaBhekuzulu.* Durban: S. M. Publications, 1996.

Intriguing as a recent Zulu nationalist account of Zulu history, making considerable use of oral tradition, and presenting a perspective not to be found in current books by non-Zulu authors.

Stuart, James, and D. McK. Malcolm, comps. and eds. *The Diary of Henry Francis Fynn.* Pietermaritzburg: Shuter and Shooter, 1969.

The heavily edited writings produced by Fynn between 1832 and 1861 relating to his time in Shaka's kingdom in the 1820s. Although one of the very earliest records we have, and commonly treated as a vital eyewitness account, recent scholarship has subjected it to much criticism.

Taylor, Stephen. *Shaka's Children: A History of the Zulu People.* London: HarperCollins, 1994.

A popular general history of the Zulu from earliest times to 1994.

Webb, C. de B., and J. B. Wright, eds. *A Zulu King Speaks: Statements Made by Cetshwayo kaMpande on the History and Customs of His People.* Pietermaritzburg and Durban: University of Natal Press and Killie Campbell Africana Library, 1978.

King Cetshwayo's account of Zulu history and customs given between 1879 and 1881 while held a prisoner at the Cape. Although taken down and translated into English by his interlocutors, this is invaluable testimony by a ruler who had a genuinely informed interest in his kingdom.

———, eds. *The James Stuart Archive of Recorded Oral Evidence Relating to the History of the Zulu and Neighbouring Peoples.* 5 vols. Pietermaritzburg and Durban:

University of Natal Press and Killie Campbell Africana Library, 1976, 1979, 1982, 1986, 2001.

Edited, annotated, and translated notes and transcriptions Stuart made in the early twentieth century of interviews with nearly 200 informants regarding Zulu traditions, customs, and history. A collection of oral evidence that is absolutely essential for anyone involved in Zulu studies.

Wylie, Dan. *Savage Delight: White Myths of Shaka.* Pietermaritzburg: University of Natal Press, 2000.

A sophisticated and challenging analysis of how white writers from the very first encounters with the Zulu to the present have framed our current perceptions of Shaka.

THREE

Civilians in the Anglo-Boer War, 1899–1902

Bill Nasson

WHAT KIND OF WAR?

The Anglo-Boer War or Boer War, also known commonly as the South African War, is no longer viewed, as it once was, as a "white man's war." More than this, it may be seen as not one but many wars. It was a war of imperialist Britons against republican Boers, of pro-British black collaborators against pro-Boer black followers, of pro-British Boers against anti-imperialist Boers, of menacing countryside against besieged towns, of African farm tenants against Boer landowners, of British men against Boer women. This was a colonial conflict never short on complexity.[1]

In popular memory, the war of 1899–1902 also lives on in some simple descriptive and contradictory terms. One image is the myth of the "last of the gentlemen's wars," a phrase coined by J.F.C. Fuller and used as the title of his 1937 account of the South African conflict. In this rosy interpretation, the war had been fought chivalrously on both sides, with decent and dashing Boer commandos fighting clean and courageous engagements with British soldiers. In South Africa, unlike the practice in other white–black African colonial wars, European Christian opponents respected their enemy in battle as fellow human beings, took prisoners, and did not finish off the wounded in the field. The other image is less nostalgic. Invading British forces were not squeamish about doing what was required to conquer the Boer republics. Their scorched-earth policy of farm burnings, the use of concentration camps into which to shovel women and children, and the widespread enactment of martial law

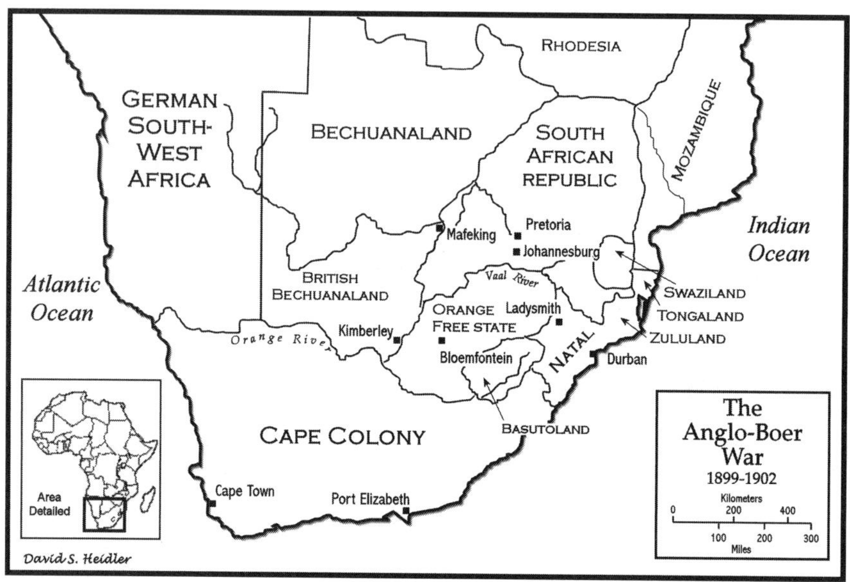

The Anglo-Boer War 1899–1902

led to a war characterized by harshness, civilian suffering, and civilian mortality. Far from the male battlefield, in the concluding words of two of its more recent historians, "in many respects ... the Boer War was a dirty war."[2] Those who ended up most dirtied were overwhelmingly its civilian victims.

FLEEING THE EARLY TIDE OF WAR

As in so many wars, the Anglo-Boer War started by turning groups of civilians into refugees. For men and women whose lives had not prepared them to face danger because they were firmly civilian, war, or even its prospect, induced panic and flight at the end of the 1890s. Once war between Britain and the South African Republic or Transvaal began to loom as a distinct possibility in the early months of 1899, foreigners in Johannesburg and along the gold-mining urban Witwatersrand began to flee for the British coastal colonies of the Cape and Natal. Most white foreigners or Uitlanders had no wish to be caught up in a coming war and were uninterested in its issues. A predominantly male population was also wary of the prospect of being conscripted by the Paul Kruger regime to serve in its Boer commandos, and there were general anxieties about shortages and the disruption of food supplies.

Mainly British miners, artisans, white-collar workers, businessmen, teachers, and their dependants scrambled for trains in a major coastal exodus, egged on by what the *Standard and Diggers' News* of August 25, 1899 called "nameless terror and vague fear," and "whirling rumours" that Boers were set on flattening Johannesburg and destroying its gold mines, and that they would force men to work in trenches, and would desecrate the bodies of their women and children or would use them as captive civilian shields to insulate front-line commandos from British fire. As the English-language press in the Transvaal grew ever more uniformly shrill in its hostility toward the republican state, Boers became portrayed as barbarians and beasts, about to slip the restraining leash of civilization.[3]

Between May and the outbreak of war in October 1899, almost 100,000 whites, as well as several thousand Coloured and Asian inhabitants of the Witwatersrand locality had made their way to the anticipated sanctuary of the British coast, some ferried on free or assisted passages funded by relief organizations. A number of the whites who headed for colonial ports like Durban did so in order to leave Africa altogether, putting shipping companies' berths under pressure.[4] Other prewar refugees found that their identities did not exist in a vacuum: they remained objects of an increasingly racially segregationist political culture. Fleeing Asians were not particularly welcome in Natal, and grumbling colonial authorities agreed to provide refuge only very grudgingly after insistence by Conyngham Greene, the British Agent in Pretoria, that crowds of Britain's Indian subjects could not be left stranded and at peril in the South African Republic.

The rumbling threat of war, and prewar Boer republican mobilization, proved to be a profoundly unsettling predicament for foreign residents. Not only was war mobilization associated with disorder, for the great majority its anti-British imperial cause was not their cause. The widespread urge among swarming, exiting Uitlanders was to cling to peace and order, something they assumed they could count on once they had crossed republican frontiers into an impregnable British colonial bunker. For some refugee train passengers, these expectations were more than confirmed by the experience of being stoned, shot at, and roughed up by sneering Boers as they set off. Such prickly encounters had the desired effect for imperial war rhetoric. In the hysteria over the plight of Uitlander refugees in the count-down to hostilities, particular emphasis was placed upon the hardships of British women, painted graphically as "the helpless victims of repression and brutality."[5]

Meanwhile, rising prewar tension and increasing disruption of Witwatersrand mining operations also gravely affected the African mineworker population, with inhabitants of mine compounds and segregated residential locations growing increasingly discontented and restless. Few mining companies and other urban employers made any provision for repatriating black migrant laborers when works closed. Workers were simply paid off and evicted from properties. Drifting off with their small personal bundles, they took to congregating in large street crowds where some, inflated by drink, took to rioting and looting of goods to haul back to their rural homesteads.

Among blacks, anxieties and stress were especially acute. Vulnerable African workers were fearful of being stuck in Johannesburg and smaller Rand towns such as Krugersdorp and Benoni as their bodies or scrappy possessions might be commandeered by Boer requisitioning units, or they might face petty persecution and the threat of summary police detention for being "idle" and a source of mischief. At the same time, many were equally apprehensive about embarking on an arduous home journey for which there was little if any proper planning and provision, and in which they would be defenseless while crossing borders and potential Anglo-Boer fighting lines.

But, in the surging crisis, they could not but form part of the early refugee momentum. Making heavy weather of it in the teeth of chaos over travel permits, dud rail tickets, and transport blockages, possibly as many as 90,000 Africans joined the immediate prewar exodus. While most were rural migrant workers, the wave included "pimps, prostitutes, criminals and illicit liquor sellers," bent on finding refuge in port towns such as Durban and Cape Town.[6] The majority fleeing the Witwatersrand region by train to Natal and the Cape, as well as to Portuguese Mozambique, did so crammed into coal trucks and cattle cars.

For others, the only option was to walk. Tramping gangs of destitute migrant industrial workers mushroomed, with some ending up racked and cut down by starvation and exhaustion. In one dramatic muscular episode, J. S. Marwick, the Agent of the Natal Native Affairs Department in Johannesburg, led a procession of between 7,000 and 8,000 Zulu laborers back to Natal, marching 30 abreast for over a week, buoyed by the rhythmic ritual of musicians performing classic Zulu songs. Yet, no matter how carefully they trod, they were unable to distance themselves from the first pinch of war. Still en route by mid-October, several hundred men from the column were press-ganged by General Piet Joubert's Natal invasion force into lugging along its heavy guns, while the rest found getting permission from antagonistic republican burgher forces to pass through their lines involved draining and costly negotiations. Nor did arrival in the British zone bring much amelioration of their hazardous position. Itching to be evacuated from the front, migrants had to pay to continue their journey by rail, forfeiting several weeks' wages in a desperate lunge for tickets.

Nearly all black migrant workers squirming through Transvaal frontiers were also subjected to interrogation, arbitrary threats, and continued harassment as wartime mobilization invigorated an underlying mentality of Boer republican rights of appropriation over "savages" or "boys." Thus, responding to the urgent need to conserve money supplies in the South African Republic, Boer officials and commando officers pounced on departing laborers, confiscating wages and anything else of value, including clothing and food. In Cape African territories such as the Ciskei and Transkei, returning migrants were depicted routinely in official reports and press accounts as having limped back destitute and famished. Moreover, in eastern districts of the Cape Colony as well as in Zululand and parts of Natal, rural areas provided little flesh to put on the bones of returning inhabitants. Not only did the dislocation of the migrant labor system at the start of the war trigger an influx of people that squeezed peasant subsistence resources. In addition the coming of hostilities coincided with drought, crop failure, and short harvest yields, which further worsened the crisis of homesteads, now short of food as well as cash earnings to meet colonial hut tax demands. Furthermore, in some parts, crop destruction and the running off of livestock that accompanied early Boer raiding dealt yet another blow to livelihoods.[7]

FRONT-LINE CIVILIANS

Civilian evacuees running ahead of hostilities may have banked on seeing out a hinterland war behind a screen of British coastal safety. Boer first-strike offensive strategy to punch through Natal and the Cape and to nail down a position on enemy territory promptly dashed any such prospect. True enough, at one level republican invasion did not necessarily confront civilians in its path with a particularly intensive brand of warfare. Almost without exception, Boer sieges of the towns of Ladysmith, Mafeking, and Kimberley to try to starve and bombard their populations into surrender were low-key, desultory operations, with sporadic shelling doing more to disrupt commerce and work practices than to slaughter the tens of thousands of black and white townspeople who found themselves hemmed in. If anything, civilians faced besiegers who rarely looked as if they had the energy or the sacrificial will to mount decisive actions to take any of these towns.[8]

In Ladysmith, which was surrounded from October 1899 to February 1900, it took some time for sherry and champagne and accompanying open-air concerts to vanish. During the even longer siege of Mafeking between October and May 1900, Boer attackers consented to Sunday ceasefires and agreed to immunity for a range of civilian targets, including a camp for women and children and a convent. In a rule of engagement for the duration of the siege, the declared honorable duty of republican commanders was neither to orphan children nor to turn men into widowers. Meanwhile, at Kimberley in the same early period, the commander of besieging Orange Free State forces, General Christiaan Wessels, sugared the pill of his opening surrender ultimatum to British defenders. Should they not submit, he would accommodate a period of grace for the orderly evacuation of women and children before the commencement of shelling. In linking the identity and destiny of the most vulnerable civilians to a welfare responsibility or humanitarian social duty, it was "civilized" war, both symbolic and real. And it was also a bit more: a shrewd psychological tactic to sap male nerves.

Yet, this was not exactly the whole story of life in barricaded towns. For inhabitants, the grim load imposed by the war was most visible in the worsening living conditions and corrosion of morale caused by frequent requisitioning, shortages or absence of basic foodstuffs, galloping price increases, rationing, diseases like typhoid, and the suspension of liberties when civil law was supplanted by the martial law of garrison defense, applied with particular severity by the British commander at Mafeking, Colonel Robert Baden-Powell.[9] Nor was this all. Some black workers, who had earlier fled Natal coalfields and outlying diamond diggings in the northern Cape for Ladysmith and Kimberley, found besieged towns a fairly repressive refuge. Garrisons routinely conscripted men to throw up defensive fortifications and to labor on siege supply lines, while outside, for their part, Boer forces commandeered groups of stranded Africans, prodding them into work parties to destroy railway track and to dam up water sources. However much such resentful men were alienated from the war and its sentiment, it was still experienced as something to which they could not but submit.

For African civilians trapped within town perimeters, the greatest threat to well-being was internal starvation and disease rather than Boer shrapnel. After all, for most of those in authority, it was taken for granted that black lives were cheaper and therefore more expendable that those of more politically valuable whites. In Kimberley, for instance, problems with the supply and distribution of food and fuel were resolved by displacing everyday deprivation and suffering onto black backs. When control of the ample fresh food and other stocks of the De Beers' diamond-mining company passed to military authorities, official provisioning concentrated on meeting the needs of white residents. While women and children in thickly-cushioned tunnels and bunkers were kept in milk and remained free of scurvy and malnutrition, dysentery, and other diseases engulfed the adult compounds of mine laborers and also took their toll of African women and children. An African population of about 30,000 suffered a casualty rate of some 1,500 deaths during the siege. By contrast, there were nine civilian deaths in a European settlement of around 13,000 inhabitants.[10]

Here, as elsewhere, there was no entertaining of any notion of equality of sacrifice or any attempt by British town command to enforce fair shares as a means of reducing internal stress and division, sustaining a defense of whole populations on the moral basis of common hardship and sacrifice. The consequence of injustice and incompetence was widespread black mistrust and hostility, whatever the warm-hearted illusions of press opinion, such as that aired by the South African News on February 26, 1900, that "there was very little grumbling" among Kimberley Africans. Feelings among Basotho migrants toward defending British forces can easily be imagined when, following a bungled attempt to expel 3,000 workers from the town, men were first clubbed back by encamped Boers, and a number were then shot accidentally by the Kimberley garrison in the panic and muddle that followed. Later, his hackles raised by dire accounts of siege conditions for Basotho migrants provided by several of his subjects who had managed to flee the town, the Basutoland chief, Jonathan, demanded an inquiry into their rough treatment.

Elsewhere, the dismal siege livelihood story was much the same, if not proportionately worse. During the highly-publicized Mafeking engagement, white civilians were outnumbered by at least four to one by Africans. Europeans were shielded from any serious deprivation, as a conspicuously unequal distribution of siege rations saw blacks reduced to subsisting on forage oats, locusts, stray dogs, and horses. While there is continuing debate among some historians over the degree of Baden-Powell's personal culpability in worsening African mortality by depriving communities of adequate rations or by hounding some inhabitants out of Mafeking to look out for themselves beyond defensive lines, siege death rates from starvation and a lack of medical assistance ran into hundreds.[11]

The question of the meaning of civilian identity and the fate of refugees in this war remains fixed most notoriously by the conditions of internment for Boers in British camps as "the Boer women and children of 1901 became the equivalent of the Belgians of August, 1914," violated by the atrocity of a brutish foreign conquest.[12] In this stark development, rural civilians were not injured as a secondary consequence of battlefield encounters between male combatants. Their homes became direct objects of punitive "pacification" by conquering British forces. The background to this was the grinding, attritional nature of the war in South Africa. In the early stages, the shape of military hostilities had seemed to be conventional enough. There were battlefield reverses and successful counterattacks, fixed siege actions, the growth of various fronts, arduous marches, and great logistical achievements. When, by June 1900, the Boer capitals of Bloemfontein and Pretoria had been taken, the war appeared to be effectively over.

But it was far from finished. The Boers were Europeans in Africa, not Europeans in Europe, and were disinclined to wage their war for independence against Britain in an ordinary or conventional European fashion. In short, they refused to view the fall of their capitals to the enemy or their decisive defeat in frontal battle as the end of their struggle for republican existence. Rather like a mobilized peasantry, an enemy Boer society was as frustrating to the British as the Algerians had been to the French.[13]

By the middle of 1900, Boer forces were down, but by no means out. Reorganizing and crafting more mobile and dispersed counteroffensive tactics, small bands of republican horsemen embarked on a classic guerrilla campaign, harassing and hindering their imperial enemy, severing supply and communications lines, and staging running attacks on camps and smaller units. In its most essential sense, the longer Boer republican objective was to try to make the costs of British imperial occupation and control untenable.

For this, the republicans' quiver was not entirely without arrows. These were expert knowledge of the terrain, accomplished horsemanship and shooting skills, and the social and political infrastructure of a honeycomb home-front territory that could provide guerrillas with the supportive necessities of combat life, and serve as a hole into which they could bolt. For Britain, a crucial and increasingly exasperating part of the military challenge in South Africa was what to do with a Boer civilian infrastructure that was stubbornly oiling a continuing, irregular war effort.

What was required "to prevent commandos from receiving shelter and produce from their own people," was that the rural fabric of Boer civilian life be broken.[14] This entailed the enlargement and intensification of an established punitive tactic of destroying homesteads and confiscating property into a systematic scorched-earth strategy in the two Boer republics, laying waste to crops, gutting livestock, splintering wagons, and torching or dynamiting farmhouses and other buildings. In the Orange Free State, over 5,000 farms were razed, and in a single district, Winburg, one British column was credited with the slaughter of almost 2,000 horses and 60,000 sheep. Shortly after the end of the conflict, the British High Commissioner in South Africa, Alfred, Lord Milner, admitted that at least 30,000 Boer houses had been demolished during the course of hostilities.[15]

Farm-burning, Orange Free State, 1900. H. W. Wilson, *With the Flag to Pretoria* (London: Methuen, 1901).

Tens of thousands of noncombatant Boer women and children, identified as "undesirables" with ties to husbands and fathers who were keeping up the fight as commandos, were forcibly uprooted and displaced from charred farms. They were joined by others as rural clearance grew increasingly indiscriminate. On May 11, 1901, the *Naval and Military Record* carried the satisfied view of the British commander-in-chief, Major-General Lord Kitchener, that ejecting farm women was ending a situation in which, instead of conducting themselves "decently" as neutral civilians, "they give complete intelligence to the Boers of all our movements and feed the commandos in their neighbourhood." To bring the war to a conclusion, he envisaged stripping the countryside of "everything that could possibly help the Boer commandos, especially their families."[16]

For most of 1900, nothing was done to deal with the crisis of families rendered homeless and destitute by the increasingly indiscriminate burning, culling, and pillaging by British columns. For their part, crippled republican authorities lacked the wherewithal to evacuate farm inhabitants from districts that had been overrun by the enemy, or who were stuck in the path of incendiary army sweeps. Some British officers proposed rounding up displaced Boer families and then propelling them into areas known to be infested by guerrilla bands. That would saddle a light and all-too mobile opponent with an unwanted load that they would be obliged to drag along, hampering movement. Field Marshal Lord Roberts had a stab

A British officer trying to communicate with Boer women on the veld. Courtesy of the National Archives, Pretoria.

at this in July 1900, when he shunted around 2,500 women and children into the rump of retreating Boer forces, slowing down their scuttle along the eastern Delagoa Bay line.

This was followed by a draconian decree that all families of active commandos residing in British-occupied districts of the former republics were liable to be evicted and driven off toward enemy commando *laagers* or camps. Such deportation menaced not only drifting Boer civilian "undesirables" with a known or assumed link to Boer fighters, but also the families of republican government officials and agents. Not surprisingly, Boer generals like Louis Botha were incensed by what they considered to be a cruel and un-Christian British tactic, violating customary expectations of immunity and hitting at "wives and children" who would be "chased from this place to that," to try to crush morale and intimidate commandos into submission.[17]

BOER INTERNMENT AND CONCENTRATION CAMP CRISIS

Toward the end of 1900, it had become obvious that the problem of displaced Boer women and children, scratching and foraging their skinny way through the countryside, could not be solved by depositing them with the enemy. As scorched-earth and depopulation drives became increasingly systematic under Kitchener, affecting not only Boer life and resources but also African crop and livestock holdings in the Boer states, something had to be done about mounting chaos in the countryside. That something amounted to securing the affected civilian population in "refugee camps" or "concentration camps," usually bonded to the railway supply spine and close to the core of dispersed military administration in or adjacent to dozens of small towns. Thousands of wives, widows, children, and orphans were spooned into camps, to be joined by old Boer men and others who had surrendered and had declared their neutrality and reversion to a peaceable civilian identity by swearing a Crown subject "oath of allegiance".[18] Along with them came large numbers of refugee African servants, farm tenants, and peasant small-holders, similarly dislocated by British burnings and confiscations, and for whom the army established a racially separate confinement.

The British government response to liberal critics of its treatment of Boer civilians was that the camp provision was nothing if not evidence of its determination to handle civilians in wartime South Africa humanely. With helpless women and children in dire straits and at risk on the veld, merciful British forces were simply accommodating and feeding stricken inhabitants as best they could. As newspapers such as *The Times* suggested repeatedly in 1901 and 1902, it was, after all, Boer combatants who were the real architects of internment camps for their people. By staying out on commando, misguided male breadwinners were callously putting their doomed cause of guerrilla resistance above the crying need of love and

Boer families arriving at a Transvaal concentration camp, 1901. Courtesy of the National Archives, Pretoria.

family togetherness. Indeed, were it not for the eventual protection of camp barbed-wire fencing, women would have been exposed to various blood-curdling dangers from predatory African men. In combining the pull of protective humanitarian sentiment with nightmarish imaginings of what might be done to white women by unrestrained Africans, such propaganda brought together two of the powerful ideological anxieties of imperial Britain in the Victorian era, the assumed weakness or helplessness of women, and the feared "sexual savagery of the black man towards the white woman."[19]

Of course, in a more blunt tactical sense, camp confinement served a clear-cut military intention. Rooted farm families, and women in particular, were never categorized as combatants. Women were not cajoled into swearing neutrality oaths, nor were they forced to surrender any personally owned firearms. Yet, in effect, they were being made prisoners of war through a confinement to British camps. Never one to mince words, for Kitchener it boiled down to putting "an end to all this talk of humanity. We have to aim at the Boers where they are most vulnerable. Their farms must be burnt down, their wives and children separated from the men and put into concentration camps.... all Boers without exception are targets."[20] Whatever the harshness of the language and the ruthless intent it embodied, it remains an important illustration of the fact that in this colonial war, making a routine basic distinction between military and civilian spheres proved tricky for the invading imperial power.

After all, Boer republican societies of the South African Republic and the Orange Free State fought as a nation in arms. Boer men were not regular uniformed soldiers. They were armed citizens who volunteered for battle; could refuse to fight; were inclined to slip away from the front to attend cattle sales, check on crops, or attend to pressing domestic matters; and were sometimes supplied personally in the field by wives or mothers who carted in supplies of meat, biscuits, and clothing.[21] As the war took on the oozing character of a guerrilla conflict, any lingering, threadbare semblance of a clear front more or less evaporated.

The farms of a farming community were a key resupply asset to Boer fighting men, with homestead women a robust reservoir of strident republican, anti-British sentiment. Inevitably, scorched-earth farm clearances deepened the unpopularity of the British, while at the same time not necessarily frightening functioning homesteads from continuing to fortify the republican guerrilla struggle, urging combatants to stiffen themselves and to fight on.[22] And, all the while, the mass dislocation of rural Boer civilians was creating a crisis that would be compounded by its solution, a policy of mass internment.

Commencing in July 1900, when the British erected a "women's laager" or women's camp near Mafeking, an entire improvised network of small temporary settlements was created to provide homeless Boers with shelter, food, medical care, and even education through voluntary English camp schools, which ended up teaching around 13,000 pupils in a forlorn attempt to Anglicize them.[23] The number of Boer camps and their inmates fluctuated but peaked toward the end of 1901, when there were 34 concentration sites holding around 110,000 inhabitants, the majority of them children. Overwhelmingly, then, camps were pools of Boer domesticity, swirling with children and mothers preoccupied by their welfare and needs.

At the same time, fear of poor conditions in the camps prompted numbers of homeless rural families to duck British efforts at rounding them up and to maintain a precarious nomadic existence in the veld, often accompanied by loyal black servants. Always pushing on to avoid being netted by the enemy, bands of fugitive women and children nosed out shelter in mountains, caves, and remote gorges, at times even positioning themselves close to commandos as a fire screen behind which to turn for the next run away from British forces. At the end of the war, there were still over 2,500 families or more than 10,000 women and children roaming the Transvaal countryside, one of this number being Nonnie de la Rey, spouse of the acclaimed Boer general, Koos de la Rey, who for the final year and a half of hostilities criss-crossed the western Transvaal with children, servants, livestock, and carts, not only evading capture and detention but also managing to link up periodically with her husband.[24]

Awareness of civilian suffering and high mortality rates in British camps was well-founded. Morbidity was at its worst during the latter half of 1901, when white camp death rates rose to almost 350 per 1,000 per year. By the end of the war, approximately 28,000 Boers had perished, just over 26,000 of them women and younger children under the age of 16, and some 1,400 aged men who had been too old or medically unfit to ride out on commando service. More than anything, it was conditions in the camps that gave this war its distinctively divided character or dual meaning, a masculine Anglo-Boer military collision on the veld, and a civilian crisis—defined as a female crisis—in the pain and chaos of mass internment. The liberal British social worker, Emily Hobhouse, who first reported on the appalling concentration camp circumstances to a European audience, and established a South African Women and Children Distress Fund to provide food and clothing to inmates, defined it as the outcome of "reviling the Boer mothers," and turning them into "a sick and bereaved womanhood."[25] Although the British government and its pro-war supporters were irritated by her widely-publicized critical views, Hobhouse found common cause with the leader of the Liberal opposition party, Sir Henry Campbell-Bannerman, who in June 1901 memorably denounced his country's war policy in South Africa as a resort to "methods of barbarism."[26]

Still, there is nothing to suggest that the British had some bottom-drawer plan to kill off civilian populations of women, children, and surplus older men in the Boer republics. Concentration camps were, after all, a brutally logical response to the challenge of waging a guerrilla war in which the line between fighting front and civilian rear had become distinctly porous. As the war had become total, so Britain implemented measures of "totality" to deal with an enemy civilian population, even though the underlying function of camp quarantine, control, and intimidation, was obfuscated by claims of Boer consent to a social system of British custody of helpless war refugees. Heavy loss of life here was, in a way, almost inevitable. After all, the British army itself was unable to construct a hygienic institutional environment even for its own troops in South Africa, on balance more likely to succumb to a fecal-oral disease borne by water, dust, or flies than to a Boer bullet.

In addition to being poorly prepared and badly administered by inexperienced officers seconded as general superintendents, there were other factors behind the high mortality rate among concentrated populations. One was the overall environmental impact of the conflict, which was polluting soil and air, spoiling water supplies, disrupting food production, and slashing livestock holdings. A second blight was the poor location of some camps, on wet ground or in spots that furnished little protection against harsh weather. Third, inhabitants were weakened by poor quality food issue and periodic short rations, unhygienic sanitary facilities, and inadequate provision of fuel and water. Fourth, levels of medical staffing and hospital provision were alarmingly patchy, while many Boers themselves resisted modern medical treatment in British hospitals, clinging to therapeutic and other older herbal and animal-based "traditions of healing," part of the integral tissue of "a culture that was being destroyed by British imperialism and that seemed more appropriate to a rural life" than the alien urban, middle-class remedies of British doctors.[27]

Already identified mostly as bitter domestic enemies by camp authorities, Boer women were now also stigmatized as ignorant, backward, and irredeemably superstitious, prone to unhygienic habits and entirely responsible for their serious consequences. In essence, it was persistent adherence to traditional "Dutch" medical remedies and indulgence in backward sanitary practices that were at the bottom of Boer death rates from winnowing epidemics of measles, pneumonia, whooping-cough and the like that bore down heavily on children.

A mounting outcry over camp conditions eventually prodded British authorities to take ameliorative measures, and in November 1901 overall civil control of the network was instituted. This led to a substantial improvement of food, medical, housing, and educational provision, and a continuing drop in mortality rates until the end of the war. But, while official British investigations acknowledged camp maladministration and deficiencies, there was still little sympathy for the civilian dead, and an inclination to blame feckless Boer matriarchs for deaths remained.[28] Other deaths tended to escape explanation or ready branding. In the case of older Boer men and women, the body count may well be seen as a classic symptom of war trauma, as the health of those old or frail was weakened by the shock of rural destruction, a pastoral landowning existence fragmenting into confusion, despair, and a future of bleak uncertainty.[29]

BLACK DISPLACEMENT AND REFUGEE CAMP EXPERIENCE

Any concise account of Boer experience alone does less than justice to the scope and significance of the concentration camp formation for civilian life during the conflict. Containment also applied not only to African house servants and personal farm hands who were deposited in white camps alongside the Boer families to which they were attached, but to black tenant and farm worker families who were flushed off Boer farms as scouring of the countryside destroyed their dwellings, crop stores, and livestock. At first, black refugees swept from the veld by British columns were dumped close to railway terminal sites and left to cope on their own, erecting rough shelter and scrabbling for sustenance from the roots and leaves of surrounding fields. Here, they were joined by more voluntary rural refugees who were simply trying to outrun the war. In August 1900, British military intelligence proposed the systematic removal of Africans from Boer farms and their detention in black concentration camps.

By destroying or confining "every living creature," turning the veld into a "barren and hostile" wasteland, cleared of any kind of succoring

African inmates of a Transvaal concentration camp. H. W. Wilson, *After Pretoria: the Guerrilla War* (London: Methuen, 1902).

or readily exploitable civilian presence, the British sought to provide their forces with "a good fighting environment." [30] Not to be left on their own as onlookers, outside the cockpit of declared Anglo-Boer enmities, entire black families were first shunted into camps and then compelled to remain there under the eventual control of a Native Refugee Department set up in the Transvaal in the middle of 1901. Wartime efforts by African families in larger towns like Bloemfontein and Johannesburg to secure the release of camp inhabitants were mostly rebuffed, even for those who were elderly or sickly, on the grounds that refugees needed to be watched over and controlled.

In its essential outline, the working principle of the black concentration camp system was to augment the noncombatant labor supply for the British war effort and to ensure that the refugee locations were as self-supporting as possible. Camps were laid out close to rail lines to ease communications with, and transport to, bases of military operations and labor depots from which workers were distributed to branches of military employment or to private employers who took on refugees, including children, for domestic, sanitary, agricultural, mining, and other jobs. Paid one shilling per day and rations, camp laborers were enlisted for three-monthly stints to enable them to return periodically to their families.

Rural tenants and sharecroppers who were rounded up with personal loads of grain and other foodstuffs were blocked from bringing supplies into camps to maintain "the dependence of refugees on the camp authorities for food," a begging relationship that could be "exploited in order to encourage men to accept work."[31] In addition, under an agricultural scheme established to ease growing shortages, African men and women were required not only to cultivate food for themselves as well as for army departments, but also to pay for all daily rations. Credit was extended to those short on cash. There was much bitterness among Africans over these onerous charges and deductions, with inmates protesting that Boers were not being forced to pay for food and to undertake cheap labor service, despite being responsible for starting and keeping up a war against Britain.

By 1902, around 70 concentration camps were holding over 18,000 black families that made up a total population of just short of 116,000 refugees. Their assembly in hastily-organized and invariably unsanitary and poorly supplied compounds naturally produced another heavy loss of life. However sparse or hit-and-miss in their impact, Boer camps at least had medical services. In most black camps these were nonexistent. Both the British army and civilian colonial authorities had as a primary concern the health of the military establishment and that of white settler communities. Alleviation of hardship and suffering in African camps was never a priority and certainly took second place to any improvement of conditions in white settlements. Contemporaries paid little attention to the plight of African camp refugees, who remained under the thumb of military control until the end of the conflict, whereas the moral indignation of the anti-war movement in Britain over Boer civilian circumstances helped to nudge the army into relinquishing overall command of camps to civilian authorities and a more nutritious provisioning regime.

Intervention to cut the high mortality rate among black camp populations tended to be restricted to dietary improvement through better milk and vegetable supplies. Cultivation of land by older men, women, and children (so as not to curb the army labor supply) in the close vicinity of camps was also expanded, with the spread of protected arable zones between settlements finally doing something to better dire sanitary conditions and to slow down the increasingly unmanageable spread of diseases such as tuberculosis, chicken-pox, measles, smallpox, and dysentery. But the general well-being of inhabitants really only became a worry in reaction to intermittent scares or panics that dangerous "plagues" or ravaging epidemics might spread to white communities, or else seriously throttle the flow of able-bodied refugees to wartime labor depots. By the end of 1901, the annual death rate had reached 436 per thousand in Orange River Colony camps, and while just over 14,000 Africans are recorded officially as having lost their lives in concentration camps, more recent estimates suggest that at least 18,000 and possibly more than 20,000 black women and children perished.[32]

The scale of the war refugee crisis in black communities was certainly not confined to the grim fate of those huddled under the dubious care of the Native Refugee Department. As daily life became disturbed more and more by military operations, rural tenants and squatters flooded into many municipal and government "native" locations in the annexed Orange River Colony and Transvaal Colony. In the Orange River Colony alone, more than 10,000 refugee civilians settled in locations at Bloemfontein and Kroonstad, while the Thaba Nchu district became a protected haven for African peasant cultivators who were able to sell off their surplus grain and potato production to the British army and to concentration camp administration.

Elsewhere, men who thronged urban municipal locations were regularly conscripted for public works and other general labor service in towns, and in pastoral areas they were often enlisted as cattle guards on stock farms that were supplying meat and milk to British authorities. African territories like Basutoland and Swaziland, which were spared the sometimes devastating costs of intense guerrilla war on their fringes, also temporarily accommodated thousands of black refugees, some herding cattle and horses for safe-keeping, a few with young white children who had been placed in their charge by Boer farming families anxious to get their young away from the horrors of warfare. The Natal government also allowed over 6,000 Africans with livestock from the annexed republics to take refuge on a string of deserted farms, reserves, and locations along the foot of the Drakensberg mountain range.

OTHER LOSSES BUT ALSO OTHER GAINS

Further south, rural black inhabitants of the Cape Colony may be considered to have been comparatively well off. In the opening stage of the conflict, invading republican forces were wary of crossing the prickly frontiers of the Transkeian Territories and thereafter largely continued to skirt the lands of peasant communities here and elsewhere in Eastern Cape districts, doing little to damage the equilibrium of daily existence. Moreover, the Cape region escaped the fiery excesses of Britain's scorched-earth sweeps in the north, which did so much to smash rural livelihoods.

Granted, martial law and treason legislation were severe, but their punitive effect bore down most heavily upon pro-republican Cape rebels who were judged guilty of high treason for having come out against the Empire when they were legally subjects of the British Crown.[33] Still, peaceable civilians did not always get off scot-free when by bad luck or worse judgment they ended up in compromising situations. These included Dutch Reformed Church clergymen who were imprisoned for having held church services for republican commandos during their temporary occupation of smaller towns, and hapless poor white looters who found that their chance theft of the odd sheep or goat from a napping English-speaking landowner had been defined as a war crime by a local British commandant. Other implicating instances involved German and Dutch-speaking missionaries denounced by empire loyalist Coloured

Black and white civilians in the Cape Colony surrendering rifles in 1901 under the provisions of British Martial Law. Courtesy of the Cape Archives Depot.

congregations for being too neutral or ambiguous in their war sympathies, and Boer employers fingered as republican collaborators on trumped-up evidence by disgruntled servants and laborers. Wartime jitters over emergency regulations among Cape Boers opened a door through which blacks with various personal grievances could pursue civil vendettas in the hope of doing in their masters. [34]

At the same time, some sections of the Cape black agrarian population were not left unscathed by the high cost of being in the path of repeated tides of armed republican insurgency. In northern and northeastern districts of the colony, hundreds of dislocated African and Coloured civilians were reduced to tramping the countryside, foraging for food and fuel or else embarking on labor migration to far-distant urban work centers that were sheltered from the worst effects of the war, including Cape Town. Pastoralists and agriculturalists hounded off mission station lands, which were then razed by republican guerrillas, wandered about a mostly arid countryside in desperation, beset by chronic scarcity and high prices for whatever staples could be found. In the northwest, many despondent families abandoned their deep inland existence of flitting about, harried by Boer commandos, and surviving hand-to-mouth. Heading for west coast towns like Port Nolloth and Lambert's Bay, some congregated behind a militia wall erected by British garrisons, while others were shipped down to Cape Town as refugees by the Royal Navy.

Here, as in other parts of the country, pressures on the livelihood of a sharply feminized civilian home front could be crushing. The drift of male providers such as husbands and older sons into British army laboring service brought not only the domestic strain of contract absences of up to 18 months, but privation when the homeward flow of vital wage remittances was disrupted by wartime postal chaos. For other lean, female-headed families, a measure of relief was to be found not in awaiting some grain dole from a charitable Cape or Natal colonial magistrate, but in sucking from the war itself. Battening on to British field columns was eased by their largely arthritic pace, and knots of women, often accompanied by young children, small livestock, and household goods, trailed along, becoming accommodated as camp followers. In addition to rattling empty tins outside mess tents, the labor of black women provided an opportunity for officers to get their laundry done cheaply at camp or to pick up skins, rabbits, and even liquor.[35]

In any longer view, the duration and social reach of the South African conflict suggests that its repercussions upon civilian lives were undoubtedly more far-reaching than those of any other African colonial wars between, say, the Napoleonic and First World Wars. There is good reason to focus on the visibility of refugees as an illustration of what happened to many of those who experienced the risks of the war most directly, and to take account of the consequences for noncombatants of the Boer War's increasingly irregular and steadily deteriorating character from 1900. Becoming casual prey in terrain turned into hunting grounds by Boer and British forces, their fate has been depicted somewhat mildly as "a number of unsavoury incidents" in which "civilians were mistreated and in some cases murdered."[36] We cannot even guess at the numbers of unarmed blacks who fell victim to cross-fire, were summarily shot by Boer commandos on suspicion of conniving with British forces or, on the other hand, were flogged by the British for adhering to a loyal dependency on commando masters.

Equally, these widely injurious effects of the war ought not to overshadow completely some of its other influences on the wartime environment of ordinary civilian life. In more secure, sheltered circumstances, as in larger British colonial port towns, its material impact on leafier white suburbs was probably broadly neutral. For British colonial patriots here, the most important thing brought by war was vicarious excitement, purpose, and companionship with men from the metropole. Schools organized teas for troops, women raffled souvenirs, baked, and knitted for war funds or to provide war comforts, wore martial colors and flag brooches, and in many ways cemented the propaganda bonds of imperial solidarity. During the 1901 Royal Tour by the Duke of Cornwall and York, colonial municipalities forked out lavishly on glittering public festivities, shrugging off the prospect of subsequent rates increases, with the city of Cape Town even arranging for everyone "in hospitals, asylums, homes and other institutions in the city to receive a special meal during the visit."[37]

In Durban, pro-British Indian merchants and traders collected war funds and distributed tobacco, chocolate, pillowcases, and other perks to troops, while in the Cape, African and Coloured businessmen and professionals in war councils and associations rustled up food hampers for army camps near towns such as Port Elizabeth and East London. For that matter, the Boer republics, too, had their sunny moment of a mobilization of civilian imagination. Before their towns were overrun, urban, pro-republican patriots did much the same thing as Cape and Natal British loyalists, such as domesticating their own war effort through the sporting of orange and yellow patriotic plumage. From this perspective, the war was not always entirely a Cinderella affair.

Indeed, it can never be enough to depict civilian wartime life in the South African conflict in simplistic terms as bad. At the same time, given the magnitude of the crisis of refugee survival, it is fairly obvious that there is hardly much of an argument to be made for a positive war experience for noncombatants. What remains to be said, ultimately, is that in its wider effects, the war was adverse or favorable, depending upon the position of particular communities and individual inhabitants. Thus, agrarian upheaval after 1899 intensified the pace of black urbanization and, as a consequence, racial segregation and administrative control of laboring African populations. But with this went feverish, war-related growth in port economies where rising demand for dockers, railway, and other transport workers brought a bonus of better wages. As many contemporary observers noted, at a time when drought, livestock disease, and the disruption of migrant labor hit many rural areas hard, for large numbers of ordinary Africans, "the war meant a boom in employment opportunities, with better pay and better prices paid for agricultural produce, cattle, horses and services of all kinds" by British forces.[38]

COSTS AND CONFUSIONS OF CIVILIAN IDENTITY

A striking feature of the war in South Africa is not so much that the daily routines and survival prospects of civilians cannot be viewed in isolation from the cocoon of military pressures within which they lived. It is more that of a confused, constant interweaving of wartime identities. Boer commandos were not necessarily permanently mobilized, sometimes demobilizing temporarily to be farmers, or surrendering to be left to live in peace, or switching back to their armed cause when laying down arms produced no tangible benefits.[39] The country's black majority was meant to be permanently demobilized, a reassuringly docile "animated geographical background" to the Anglo-Boer confrontation.[40] Black South Africans were never recognized as combatants nor as societies officially on a war footing or parties to the war. Yet, as civilians, possibly as many as 30,000 blacks were enlisted in British forces as armed combatants, and up to 120,000 were engaged in imperial army service as scouts, spies, guards, and other auxiliaries. The Boers, too, were serviced by perhaps as many as 14,000 commando servants, some under arms, providing a kind of pastoral subsidy. In the midst of all this, independent groupings of Africans themselves, set upon exploiting unsettled war conditions, used their dispersed knots of collective power to flare up against Boer authority, lashing out in irregular fashion as civilians gone bad. In a war in which the imperial camp introduced the novelty of using civilians as hostages on trains in an effort to stem Boer commando attacks on the railway, neutrality was mostly in short supply.

TIMELINE

1899 October 11: War commences
October 14: Investment of Mafeking
October 15: Investment of Kimberley
October 30: Investment of Ladysmith
November 3: Durban placed under martial law

1900 February 11: Main British invasion of the Orange Free State and commencement of destruction and confiscation of rural Boer property
February 15: Relief of Kimberley
February 27: Relief of Ladysmith
March 15: British offer terms to Boers who lay down arms
May 17: Relief of Mafeking
June 16: First British proclamation in Transvaal threatening farm-burning
July 4: British authorize burning of all farms identified with enemy guerrillas
September: First Boer refugee camps established
December 20: Martial law proclaimed in northern Cape
December 27: Emily Hobhouse arrives in South Africa to bring supplies to camps and to investigate internment conditions

1901 June: Establishment of the Department of Native Refugees
July: British government appoints commission under Millicent Fawcett to inspect concentration camps and advise on improvement and reform
October 9: Martial law extended in Cape Colony
December 15: British General Staff issues instruction that no further white civilians are to be brought into camps

1902 January–May: Intensification of British practice of arming loyalist African civilians and surrendered Boers
April: Conference of Boer peace delegates cites extent of civilian suffering as a cause of imminent republican capitulation
May 31: Peace Treaty signed

GLOSSARY

Names and Places

Baden-Powell, Major Robert. Commander of the besieged town of Mafeking and, subsequently, founder of the world-wide Scout movement.

Campbell-Bannerman, Sir Henry. Leader of the British Liberal Party from 1898, pro-Boer and fierce critic of the war, especially of its impact upon Boer civilians.

De la Rey, Commandant-General Jacobus Herculaas "Koos." One of the finest and most admired Boer Republican generals, adept at guerrilla warfare.

Dutch Reformed Church. Calvinist Christian church of Boer society. About 80 percent of commando fighters were active adherents.

Hobhouse, Emily. British social worker and pacifist who traveled to South Africa, visiting Boer concentration camps and campaigning over their conditions through speeches, reports, and books.

Joubert, Commandant-General Petrus Jacobus "Piet." The least live-wire of Boer Republican generals, a pessimist who moved at an arthritic pace.

Kitchener, Major-General Sir Horatio Herbert, 1st Baron Kitchener of Khartoum. Enormously energetic and ruthless British general who became Commander-in-Chief of the British war effort in South Africa in December 1900. He achieved popular notoriety as an unsparing persecutor of Boer women and children.

Kruger, S. J. Paulus "Paul." President of the South African Republic (Transvaal) who feared that granting citizenship rights to Uitlanders would bring on foreign domination of his white settler state, and who assumed that the British were set on its annexation, neither view too far from the truth.

Milner, Sir Alfred, 1st Baron Milner. Governor of the Cape Colony and High Commissioner for South Africa. A vigorous British imperialist, he promoted the crisis that led to the Anglo-Boer war in 1899 in order to bring about an amalgamated South Africa under secure British influence.

Terms

berg. Mountain.

Boer. Literally farmer; white person, mainly of Dutch descent, and supporter of republican independence for the Transvaal and Orange Free State.

commando. Boer mounted infantry formation.

commando servants. Trusted personal African servants, known as *agterryers* "after-riders" who accompanied commandos on campaign, cooking, digging trenches, providing medical and other care, and sometimes bearing arms.

laager. Encampment.

squatter. African residing on white farmland.

tenant. African cultivator occupying white-owned land on payment of labor service or share of own crop production.

Transvaal. Common name for South African Republic (officially Zuid-Afrikaansche Republiek).

Uitlander. Literally "outsider" or foreigner in the Witwatersrand goldfields of the Transvaal, particularly from Britain and its Empire.

NOTES

1. Greg Cuthbertson and Alan Jeeves, "The Many-Sided Struggle for Southern Africa 1899–1902," *South African Historical Journal* 41 (1999): 2–21.

2. Denis Judd and Keith Surridge, *The Boer War* (London: John Murray, 2002), 236.

3. Charles Dugmore, "From Pro-Boer to Jingo: An Analysis of Small-Town English-Language Newspapers on the Rand before the Outbreak of War in 1899," *South African Historical Journal 41* (1999): 264–66.

4. Diana Cammack, *The Rand at War 1899–1902: The Witwatersrand and the Anglo-Boer War* (London: James Currey 1990), 42.

5. Elizabeth van Heyningen, "The Voices of Women in the South African War," *South African Historical Journal* 41 (1999): 23.

6. Peter Warwick, *Black People and the South African War 1899–1902* (Cambridge: Cambridge University Press 1983), 127.

7. Bill Nasson, "Black Communities in Natal and the Cape," in *The Impact of the South African War,* eds. David Omissi and Andrew S. Thompson (London: Palgrave, 2002), 50; John Laband, "Zulus and the War," in *The Boer War: Direction, Experience and Image,* ed. John Gooch (London: Frank Cass, 2000), 116.

8. Bill Nasson, *The South African War 1899–1902* (London: Arnold, 1999), 92.

9. Raymond Sibbald, *The War Correspondents: The Boer War* (Johannesburg: Jonathan Ball, 1993), 148–51.

10. Martin Matrix Evans, *Encyclopaedia of the Boer War* (Oxford: ABC-CLIO, 2000), 136.

11. Tim Jeal, *Baden-Powell* (London: Hutchinson, 1989), 245–50; Malcolm Flower Smith and Edmund Yorke, *Mafeking! The Story of a Siege* (Johannesburg: Covos-Day, 2000), 154–60.

12. Bill Nasson, "The War One Hundred Years On," in *Writing a Wider War: Rethinking Gender, Race, and Identity in the South African War, 1899–1902,* ed. Greg Cuthbertson, Albert Grundlingh, and Mary-Lynn Suttie (Athens: Ohio University Press, 2002), 7.

13. Hew Strachan, *European Armies and the Conduct of War* (London: Routledge, 1983), 79.

14. Reviel Netz, *Barbed Wire: An Ecology of Modernity* (Middletown, CT: Wesleyan University Press, 2004), 63.

15. Fransjohan Pretorius, "The Fate of the Boer Women and Children," in *Scorched Earth,* ed. Fransjohan Pretorius (Cape Town: Human and Rousseau, 2001), 40.

16. Alan Krell, *The Devil's Rope: A Social History of Barbed Wire* (London: Reaktion, 2004), 49.

17. M. A. Gronum, *Die Bittereinders, Junie 1901-Mei 1902* (Kaapstad: Nasionale Pers, 1974), 127.

18. S. B. Spies, *Methods of Barbarism? Roberts and Kitchener and Civilians in the Boer Republics: January 1900–May 1902* (Cape Town: Human and Rousseau, 1977), 35.

19. Paula Krebs, "'Last of The Gentleman's Wars': Women in the Boer War Concentration Camp Controversy," *History Workshop Journal* 33 (1992): 45.

20. Philip Bateman, *Generals of the Anglo-Boer War* (Cape Town: Timmins, 1977), 14.

21. Fransjohan Pretorius, *Life on Commando during the Anglo-Boer War 1899–1902* (Cape Town: Human and Rousseau, 1999), 38–39.

22. Helen Bradford, "Gentlemen and Boers: Afrikaner Nationalism, Gender, and Colonial Warfare in the South African War," in *Writing a Wider War,* eds. Cuthbertson, Grundlingh, and Suttie, 45–46.

23. Paul Zietsman, "The Concentration Camp Schools—Beacons of Light in the Darkness," in *Scorched Earth,* ed. Pretorius, 89.

24. Pretorius, "The Fate of the Boer Women and Children," in ibid., 50–54.

25. Owen Coetzer, *Fire in the Sky: The Destruction of the Orange Free State 1899–1902* (Johannesburg: Covos Day, 2000), 121.

26. John Grigg, "Lloyd George and the Boer War," in *Edwardian Radicalism 1900–1914,* ed. A.J.A. Morris (London: Routledge and Kegan Paul, 1974), 19.

27. Elizabeth van Heyningen, "Women and Disease: The Clash of Medical Cultures in the Concentration Camps of the South African War," in *A Wider War,* eds. Cuthbertson, Grundlingh, and Suttie, 205.

28. Spies, *Methods of Barbarism,* 266.

29. Van Heyningen, "Women and Disease," 193.

30. Stowell Kessler, "The Black and Coloured Concentration Camps," in *Scorched Earth,* ed. Pretorius, 134.

31. Warwick, *Black People,* 149–50.

32. Kessler, "Concentration Camps," in *Scorched Earth,* ed. Pretorius, 147–48.

33. Graham Jooste and Roger Webster, *Innocent Blood: Executions during the Anglo- Boer War* (Cape Town: Spearhead, 2002), 217–19.

34. Bill Nasson, *Abraham Esau's War: A Black South African War in the Cape, 1899–1902* (Cambridge: Cambridge University Press, 1991), 142–68.

35. Bill Nasson, "Africans at War," in *Boer War,* ed. Gooch, 136–37.

36. Williamson A. Murray, "Towards World War 1871–1914," in *The Cambridge Illustrated History of Warfare,* ed. Geoffrey Parker (Cambridge: Cambridge University Press, 1995), 251.

37. Phillip Buckner, "The Royal Tour of 1901 and the Construction of an Imperial Identity in South Africa," *South African Historical Journal* 41 (1999): 341.

38. Iain R. Smith, *The Origins of the South African War 1899–1902* (London: Longman, 1996), 9–10.

39. Pretorius, *Life on Commando,* 188–217.

40. Donald Denoon, "Participation in the 'Boer War': People's War, People's Non-War, or Non-People's War," in Bethwell A. Ogot, ed., *War and Society in Africa* (London: Frank Cass, 1972), 11.

SELECT BIBLIOGRAPHY

Cammack, Diana. *The Rand at War 1899–1902: The Witwatersrand and the Anglo-Boer War.* London: James Currey, 1990.

A social history of urban life in the major mining town of Johannesburg that examines the experiences of ordinary white and black inhabitants during the war crisis.

Coetzer, Owen. *Fire in the Sky: The Destruction of the Orange Free State 1899–1902.* Johannesburg: Covos Day, 2000.

Annotated compilation of official British reports and other contemporary depositions, detailing the impact of scorched-earth tactics and documenting life in the concentration camps of the Orange Free State.

Comaroff, John L., ed. *The Boer War Diary of Sol T. Plaatje: An African at Mafeking.* London: Macmillan, 1976.

Fascinating record of the Siege of Mafeking by an educated and intellectual African observer and participant in daily siege life on the British side.

Cuthbertson, Greg, Albert Grundlingh, and Mary-Lynn Suttie, eds. *Writing a Wider War: Rethinking Gender, Race, and Identity in the South African War, 1899–1902.* Athens: Ohio University Press, 2002.

Wide-ranging essay collection on various aspects of the conflict, with important contributions on African experiences, the position of women, and the impact of disease in concentration camps, and on the belligerence of Boer republican women.

Denoon, Donald. "Participation in the Boer War: People's War, People's Non-War, or Non-People's War ?" in *War and Society in Africa.* Edited by B. A. Ogot. London: Frank Cass, 1972): 109–23.

Pioneering early interpretation of the social and political nature of the conflict, examining the relationship between a formal war between white imperial and republican interests, and forms of black involvement and intervention in war affairs.

DuPisani, Kobus, and B. E. Mongalo, "Victims of a White Man's War: Blacks in Concentration Camps of the South African War, 1899–1902." *Historia* 44, no. 1 (May 1999): 148–82.

Article dealing with the establishment of what were termed refugee camps for uprooted African civilians in the Boer states, and illustrating the terrible human consequences of the penny-pinching economy with which they were run.

Evans, Martin Matrix. *Encyclopaedia of the Boer War.* Oxford: ABC-CLIO, 2000.

Comprehensive reference guide with useful entries on civilian themes, including an appendix on refugees and concentration camps. Reprints of original documents include the main portion of the famous report on concentration camps by Emily Hobhouse.

Gooch, John, ed. *The Boer War: Direction, Experience and Image.* London: Frank Cass, 2000.

Although focusing mainly on war-making and military experience, this volume includes useful general assessments of Africans' war experiences and has interesting contributions on the role of the British press in representing war conditions.

Krikler, J. *Revolution from Above, Rebellion from Below: The Agrarian Transvaal at the Turn of the Century.* Oxford: Oxford University Press, 1993.

Detailed interpretation of the disruptive impact of British invasion on Boer-African relations in the Western Transvaal countryside, unlocking buried antagonisms and conflicts between peasant tenants and Boer landowners over resources.

Lee, Emanoel. *To the Bitter End: A Photographic History of the Boer War 1899–1902.* Harmondsworth: Penguin, 1985.

Visually rich and clear narrative account, notable for striking images of rural refugees and camp life.

Lowry, Donal, ed. *The South African War Reappraised.* Manchester: Manchester University Press, 2000.

Concerned with the complex character of British imperialism at the turn of the nineteenth and twentieth centuries, this collection includes chapters on Boer attitudes toward Africans, African views of Britain, and the claims of its war effort, and on the wartime vision and role of Indian observers and inhabitants.

Nasson, Bill. *Abraham Esau's War: A Black South African War in the Cape, 1899–1902.* Cambridge: Cambridge University Press, 1991.

A regional perspective on the impact of warfare across the Cape Colony, assessing the daily involvement and varying fortunes of rural and urban black inhabitants in their relationships with warring imperial and republican camps.

Omissi, David, and Andrew Thompson, eds. *The Impact of the South African War.* London: Palgrave, 2002.

Thematic essays on the impact and consequences of the war for both South African society and Britain and its wider imperial world, with particularly interesting contributions on the civil dimension of religion, philanthropy, and peace activism.

Pakenham, Thomas. *The Boer War.* London: Weidenfeld and Nicholson, 1979.

A fat and exhaustively-detailed military narrative that nonetheless contains good accounts of living conditions during the major sieges of Natal and Cape towns.

Pretorius, Fransjohan. "Caught up in the Cross-fire: A British Citizen in the Orange Free State during the Anglo-Boer War, 1899–1900." *Historia* 43, no. 1 (May 1998): 41–71.

A fascinating view of war affairs in the republican camp from the vantage-point of an inside English observer.

———. *Life on Commando during the Anglo-Boer War 1899–1902.* Cape Town: Human and Rousseau, 1999.

The classic social history of Boer commando experience, with valuable chapters on combatants' relations with women and blacks, and their resilient ties to domestic life.

———, ed. *Scorched Earth.* Cape Town: Human and Rousseau, 2001.

Set of frequently moving essays on the trauma of white and black camps, providing a clear picture of everyday existence and a vivid accompanying record of photographs and other historical documents.

Raal, Sarah. *The Lady Who Fought: A Young Woman's Account of the Anglo-Boer War.* Cape Town: Stormberg, 2000.

Now available in English, this is a poignant memoir of the life of a young Boer woman who accompanied commandos in the field, containing acute observations on the camps and other aspects of civilian life.

Reitz, Deneys. *Commando: A Boer Journal of the Boer War.* London: Faber and Faber, 1931.

The finest war memoir (and still in print), with an atmospheric evocation of the commando world of citizen soldiering, recording regular encounters with ordinary white and black inhabitants caught up in hostilities.

Sibbald, Raymond. *The War Correspondents: The Boer War.* Johannesburg: Jonathan Ball, 1993.

Interesting compilation of reports on various aspects of the war by British newspaper correspondents in the field.

South African Historical Journal 41 (1999): *Special Issue on the South African War 1899–1902: Centennial Perspectives.*

A large thematic issue of this journal, which contains numerous essays on cultural and social facets of the war experience.

Spies, S. B. *Methods of Barbarism? Roberts and Kitchener and Civilians in the Boer Republics, January 1900–May 1902.* Cape Town: Human and Rousseau, 1977.

Densely documented study of the treatment of white and black civilians by occupying British military authorities in the conquered Boer republics, with good photographic illustrations.

Van der Merwe, Chris N., and Michael Rice, eds. *A Century of Anglo-Boer War Stories.* Johannesburg: Jonathan Ball, 1999.

Fine anthology of war fiction and poetry from English and Afrikaans-speaking writers, with prominent authors evoking the imaginative worlds of rural and small-town civilian experience.

Warwick, Peter. *Black People and the South African War, 1899–1902.* Cambridge: Cambridge University Press 1983.

Important and authoritative overview assessment of the varied ways in which the war affected the material circumstances, attitudes, and conduct of all sections of the majority black population.

———, ed. *The South African War: The Anglo-Boer War 1899–1902.* London: Longman, 1980.

This remains an attractive set of illustrated essays, which survey key aspects of the war, including black experience, Boer society, and the position of women.

War Museum of the Boer Republics, Bloemfontein, Free State, South Africa: www.anglo-boer.co.za.

A clear and easily accessible war museum site, with valuable data, including photographs.

FOUR

The Impact of the First World War on African People

Tim Stapleton

Although African people lived far from the scene of the outbreak of the First World War, they were quickly and profoundly affected by this conflict. In 1914, most areas of Africa had been under European colonial rule for less than 20 years. Memories of European colonial invasion and conquest in the 1880s and 1890s were still fresh, and the imposition of taxation and forced labor had caused major rebellions in some places less than 10 years before. Indeed, some areas were just beginning to recover from the ravages of these colonial wars when the global conflict of the First World War was inflicted on them. Germany had at least one colony in each major region of sub-Saharan Africa, while all the other colonial powers were on the Allied side. This meant that in some ways the First World War in Africa was a continuation of the "Scramble for Africa," as all the German colonies were invaded by their colonial neighbors in a bid to expand their territorial empires. Consequently the impact of the Great War would be spread across the continent as each region—west, east, and south—experienced its own local campaign. The impact of the First World War on Africans will be approached through an examination of their role as soldiers and laborers, as well as through the rebellions that broke out during the conflict, the spread of famine and disease, and the political response of the embryonic westernized African elite class.

AFRICAN SOLDIERS AND LABORERS

The First World War was a global war. African servicemen from across their continent were present in every operational theater and were employed by most of the major powers. Melvin Page estimates that around two million Africans saw military service as either soldiers or laborers. Of these, around 250,000, just over 10 percent, lost their lives in Europe, the Middle East, and Africa.[1] It should be remembered that all the colonial powers had used African soldiers and workers during the wars of conquest at the turn of the nineteenth and twentieth centuries and this existing system was simply expanded during the First World War. The colonial armies that had invaded much of Africa during the "Scramble" period usually consisted of an African rank and file, often recruited from older coastal colonies or from African groups allied to the colonial power, led by a few European officers. Once colonial rule was established, Africans were often recruited into local army or police units organized to maintain internal security.[2]

France, which had recruited African soldiers as early as the 1850s, was certainly the most active employer of African soldiers during the First World War and the only major power to send them to the Western Front on a large scale. A decade before the outbreak of war, the French government had made plans to use colonial African troops in the defense of the motherland. When the conflict began, the French brought in over 10,000 North African soldiers to throw into the path of the invading Germans.[3] They spent the first winter of the war in the trenches without proper cold weather clothing. By the end of the conflict, just over 200,000 African soldiers from French West Africa had fought on the Western Front and around 30,000 of them had lost their lives. Although this figure is not much higher than the general casualty rate among French infantry, at times the French high command committed its African units to suicidal attacks with the intention of sparing French lives.[4] For these African men, coming as they did from rural agricultural communities, the horrors of industrialized warfare must have been more than shocking. The first soldiers on the Western Front to experience chemical warfare, during April 1915, were Algerians who abandoned their trenches and fled before giant greenish clouds of poison gas. A few days later a battalion from Senegal was ordered to charge into a gas cloud as part of a diversionary attack. Contact with the gas sent them into such frenzy that they shot their white officers and ran to the rear where they looted supplies and raped nurses at an aid station.[5] However, it seems that the French African soldiers were no more mutinous than their European counterparts, and when another Senegalese battalion rebelled in 1917, it was not in reaction to racism but rather part of the general war-weariness of the French army as a whole.[6] In fact, during the same widespread French mutiny, French commanders used African reserve battalions to restore order in European units. As Page points out, the African units of the French army played a vital role on the Western Front, participating in every major battle of the conflict. Six French West African battalions also participated in the disastrous Gallipoli campaign, where the Allies tried unsuccessfully to take the Ottoman Empire, an ally of Germany, out of the

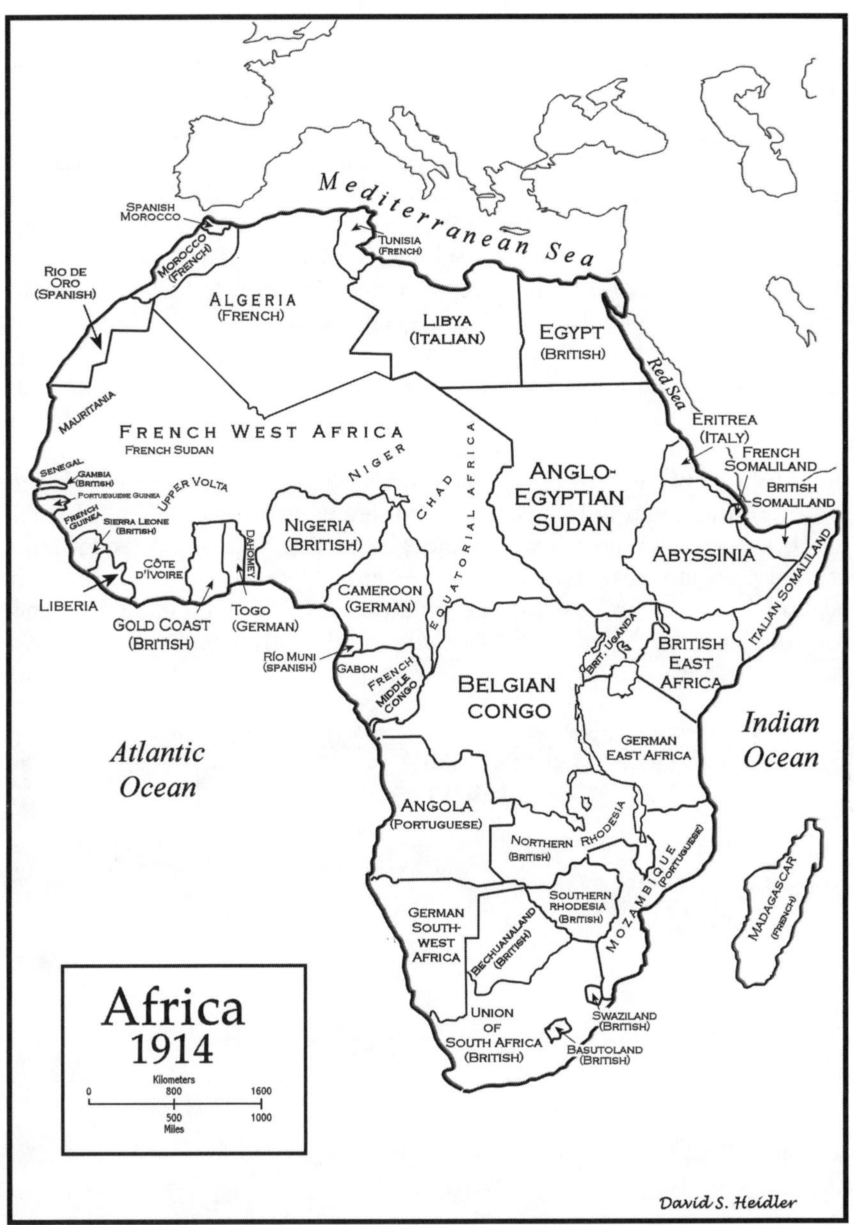
Mediterranean Sea
Spanish Morocco
Tunisia (French)
Rio de Oro (Spanish)
Morocco (French)
Algeria (French)
Libya (Italian)
Egypt (British)
Red Sea
Mauritania
French West Africa
French Sudan
Niger
Chad
Equatorial Africa
Eritrea (Italy)
French Somaliland
British Somaliland
Senegal
Gambia (British)
Portuguese Guinea
Upper Volta
French Guinea
Sierra Leone (British)
Nigeria (British)
Anglo-Egyptian Sudan
Abyssinia
Italian Somaliland
Côte d'Ivoire
Dahomey
Liberia
Gold Coast (British)
Togo (German)
Cameroon (German)
Río Muni (Spanish)
Gabon
French Middle Congo
Belgian Congo
Brit. Uganda
British East Africa
Indian Ocean
Atlantic Ocean
German East Africa
Angola (Portuguese)
Northern Rhodesia (British)
Mozambique (Portuguese)
Madagascar (French)
German South-West Africa
Bechuanaland (British)
Southern Rhodesia (British)
Union of South Africa (British)
Swaziland (British)
Basutoland (British)
Africa 1914
Kilometers
0
800
1600
500
1000
Miles
David S. Heidler

Africa 1914

war.[7] Also present on the Western Front were 21,000 unarmed black South African military workers, the South African Native Labour Contingent [SANLC], who dug trenches and transported supplies.[8]

Although African soldiers and military laborers were present in every theater of the war, most were engaged in the African campaigns. Thousands of African porters kept Allied forces, mostly made up of African soldiers, supplied during the brief invasion of German Togoland in 1914. African servicemen were less involved in the South African invasion of German South West Africa (now Namibia) in 1914 and 1915. The South African government did not recruit armed black soldiers during the conflict as it feared possible rebellion at home, and it had a large enough white population to satisfy military requirements. Similarly, the Germans, who had waged a genocidal counter-insurgency campaign against the Herero and Nama from 1904 to 1907, felt they could not rely on local people. During the two grueling years of bush warfare that characterized the British and French invasion of German Cameroon, all sides relied heavily on African soldiers led by small numbers of European officers. Furthermore, thousands of porters from Nigeria and Cameroon itself kept the fighting forces supplied in rough terrain where there were no roads.

The longest and most costly of the African campaigns occurred in and around German East Africa (now Tanzania, Rwanda, and Burundi). It began with a disastrous British amphibious landing at Tanga in 1914 and dragged on until November 1918 with a relatively small but tenacious

A battalion of *Askaris* (African soldiers who took part in the East African campaign under General von Lettow-Vorbeck) photographed in full marching order on parade at Kigoma on the shore of Lake Tanganyika. *Pictorial History of South Africa* (London: Odhams Press, n.d. [c. 1938. Odhams ceased in 1963]).

German force, composed mostly of black soldiers, tying down thousands of British, South African, Portuguese, and Belgian colonial troops. The British had begun the campaign deploying European and Indian units but, by 1916, when they renewed the invasion of the German colony, they had Africanized their forces and expanded the King's African Rifles, a local colonial regiment, from 3,000 to 30,000 men. Of the one million Africans employed by both sides in this campaign, most served as supply carriers, and it was they who suffered the most casualties from exhaustion and tropical disease. Many were literally worked to death. Although the official figure of total deaths in the campaign was 50,000, 42,000 of whom were porters, G.W.T. Hodges presents credible claims that there were actually 100,000 deaths among British forces alone.[9] The precise number of deaths will probably never be known.

As John R. Morrow relates, "[t]he wartime experience of fighting with and against Europeans, as well as killing them, provided a new experience for African soldiers." Returning from the Western Front, veterans of the French colonial army "considered the war terrible, evil, and futile, and concluded that the French had exploited them."[10] They were now more self-confident, assertive, and conscious of the wider world. But instead of challenging the colonial state they often sought to return to their former lives. In Senegal, veterans' associations did engage in local politics during the 1920s in order to elect Africans to the French government but were often disappointed by continued racial discrimination. In Nyasaland (now Malawi), returning veterans of the British colonial army who had fought in East Africa had lost their fear of Europeans and sometimes openly despised them for failure to acknowledge their wartime sacrifices. Nigerian veterans, many of whom had replaced Europeans in the role of noncommissioned officers, returned home with increased self-confidence and better fluency in English. They became frustrated with lack of back pay and medals, and denial of a place in the London Peace Parade. In the

African porters in British East Africa carrying ammunition through thick bush in the rear of an advancing column. *The Times History of War* (London: The Times, 1914–1921).

mine compounds of Southern Africa black veterans displayed an embryonic workers' consciousness by forming societies that performed military drill during off hours. This worried mine managers, and investigations by Native Department officials in Southern Rhodesia reported that while these groups did not pose a threat to the colonial system, they should be discouraged.[11]

REBELLIONS DURING THE WAR

Not all people in Africa remained loyal to the colonial governments when the First World War broke out. The war seemed to present frustrated Africans with an opportunity to act, and many rebellions broke out during its course. For some, the conflict rekindled hopes of asserting independence by driving out European overlords. In many parts of Africa the rulers of large centralized states had been overthrown by colonial invasion just a decade or so before and had sometimes been replaced by those who were more willing to work under the colonial powers. Decentralized societies were often disrupted by the imposition of colonial appointed chiefs who were usually seen as nothing more than glorified tax collectors and opportunists. In West Africa's Sahel region, the predominantly Muslim faith of the precolonial elites, which had been reinvigorated by holy wars or jihads in the early 1800s, had the potential to mobilize broad resistance against Christian colonial rulers. Samoure Toure, Muslim ruler of the West African Dyula state, had fought against the French for 20 years and had surrendered only in 1898. For many people across the continent, the First World War meant increased colonial demands for manpower, resources, and taxation, which created grievances. At the same time, the departure of soldiers and police for the front lines led to an obvious weakness of colonial administrative and security apparatus, which created an opportunity for violent protest.

The Union of South Africa was only four years old when the war broke out and the Second Anglo-Boer War (1899–1902), which saw the British conquest of the two Boer republics and the deaths of thousands of Boer women and children as well as their African workers in British concentration camps, had ended just 12 years earlier. Although former Boer generals like Louis Botha and Jan Smuts dominated the early Union government, there was a rising tide of Afrikaner (Boer) nationalism that rejected even symbolic British supremacy. There was also considerable sympathy for Germany, which had supported the republics during the Boer War. South Africa, as a British dominion, had no choice but to enter the war on the side of the mother country. The Union forces were mobilized in 1914 and preparations made for the invasion of German South West Africa, which was, to the South African government, an attractive prospective territorial acquisition. Within a few weeks, however, several South African generals who had fought against the British 12 years before, with over a thousand of their soldiers, mutinied and crossed over to the German colony. There was also an uprising of 11,000 Boer farmers in the drought-stricken interior of the country. They were spurred on by extreme poverty and the visions of a seer who foretold Germany's victory and the success of the Boer rebellion. The Union government declared martial law and the uprising was fairly easily crushed by loyalist forces. The rebels discovered that times had changed and their mounted commandos, which had frustrated the British army in the guerrilla phase of the Boer War, were no match for modern motorized vehicles employed by Union forces. Nevertheless, most rebels were treated with clemency as the government was eager to forget this incident and promote national unity.[12]

In Nyasaland, during 1915 an unlikely rebel leader emerged to fight against the British. John Chilembwe was a Baptist minister who had been educated in the United States. He objected strongly to British recruitment of Malawians as soldiers and porters for the East African campaign, and he allegedly sent a message to the Germans seeking assistance. The rebellion broke out when Chilembwe's followers killed a white plantation manager with whom they had a long-standing conflict and mounted his head inside their church. Although the Chilembwe Uprising involved possibly less than 200 people, the wartime emergency atmosphere led to a swift and overwhelming British response. The uprising was quickly put down and Chilembwe was killed while trying to flee. A number of historians have attempted to explain these events and particularly Chilembwe's role in them. For nationalist historians G. Shepperson and T. Price, the Baptist minister had been influenced by the history of John Brown as a martyr in the American abolitionist movement and wanted to strike a blow and die so that future generations would be inspired to reject colonial injustice. On the other hand, Robert Rotberg argues that Chilembwe's actions were not so well thought out and were brought on by mental stress. It is also possible that the rebels had their own personal reasons for striking out against a plantation manager and that the dead Chilembwe became a convenient scapegoat for colonial mismanagement.[13]

The prospect of a similar rebellion caused paranoid British officials in Northern Rhodesia (present day Zambia), who recognized the increased weakness of their own colonial state because of the war, to conduct a virtual reign of terror against African employees of Christian missions. African teachers were conscripted as supervisors for the Carrier Corps in East Africa. Although westernized and Christian African teachers usually saw themselves as loyal British subjects at the time, wartime fears caused the British to suspect the possibility of another Chilembwe in their ranks. Other causes for this suspicion included hostility between the westernized African teachers and local traditional chiefs who worked for the colonial administration, and the general British distrust of the Dutch Reformed Church, to which many of the African teachers belonged, because of its role in the 1914 Afrikaner rebellion against British rule in South Africa.

Wartime oppression, particularly labor conscription and confiscation of food, which created famine, led to the rapid spread in the colony during 1918 of the Watchtower Movement, an African version of the American Jehovah's Witness movement, which preached the imminent second coming of Christ and the end of colonialism. After the war many members of this independent church were arrested and detained by the British.[14] In fact, just after the Chilembwe uprising in 1915, the British in Nyasaland exiled the Watchtower leader Elliot Kamwana to the Indian Ocean island of Mauritius and attempted to ban the movement as its members refused to join the army.[15]

In the northern parts of the Gold Coast (Ghana today) rioting broke out during 1915 and 1916 in the Bongo region. There was popular rejection of British-appointed chiefs and local police, many of whom had a history of abuse and corruption. This was an area, moreover, where resistance to the imposition of colonial rule had continued until 1911 when it had been crushed by a British punitive expedition. Further resentment had been caused when several local shrines associated with past resistance were destroyed by colonial agents. With the outbreak of the First World War the British attempted to recruit young men from this disaffected region for the Gold Coast Regiment, which was bound for the Togoland campaign. Yet at this delicate juncture British control was dangerously weakened when wartime demands led to such a reduction of administrative officials and police officers that many locals believed the British were pulling out. In the so-called Bongo riots that ensued many of the appointed chiefs who collaborated with the British administration were toppled. The British responded to this challenge to their authority with overwhelming force and the appointed chiefs were restored.[16]

At about the same time there were rebellions in parts of Nigeria. In the southeast of the colony, around the Benue Valley, the prophet Ellijah II mobilized Igbo people against the British. The main cause for this uprising seems to have been a dramatic decrease in palm oil prices at the beginning of the First World War, which badly affected the region. Colonial rulers had encouraged West Africans in various areas to specialize in the production of one cash crop, such as palm oil, cocoa, or ground nuts, which tended to create an extremely fragile local economy. When prices rose again, the uprising petered out. In western Nigeria, several rebellions broke out in response to discontent with a new "native authority" system, a form of indirect rule whereby the Europeans governed through appointed local African chiefs, and which threatened traditional power structures among some Yoruba and Egba people. All these uprisings were crushed by colonial regiments consisting of African soldiers led by European officers, and in the Egba case, 500 rebels were killed. Unlike the French, the British had cultivated good relations with Muslim rulers in their territories as part of their system of "Indirect Rule." Consequently, predominantly Muslim areas like Northern Nigeria, where the emirs of the old Sokoto Caliphate ruled under British supervision, remained peaceful throughout the war.[17]

Recruitment of African manpower for the war often led to resistance. In 1914, colonial officials in Southern Rhodesia (now Zimbabwe), which was still administered by the chartered British South Africa Company, told African chiefs and their subjects that the conflict would be a "white man's war," which would only involve the territory's settlers. Of course, the settlers, remembering the Ndebele and Shona rebellions of 1896–1897, were hesitant to arm Africans and saw their own participation in the war as a way to earn exclusively white self-government and nationhood in the future. However, their small numbers, only 30,000 in 1914, meant that they ran out of recruits fairly quickly and by 1915 the administration was making plans to raise an African battalion for the East African campaign. In some African communities, news that colonial officials were asking for African volunteers for the army turned into a rumor that they would impose conscription. This led to an armed stand-off with the Ndebele chief Maduna and his followers. Since experience had taught the Native Department officials that small violent incidents could lead to wider rebellion, they concentrated on isolating Maduna from neighboring chiefs and conflict was avoided.

Around the same time, on the eastern side of the colony, colonial officials arrested some Shona spirit mediums who seemed to be using the news of war as a way of mobilizing their people for renewed resistance. These mediums, even today, are believed to be possessed by important ancestral spirits and several prominent ones had been hanged by the British for their part in the 1896–1897 rebellion.[18] The rebellion that broke out in parts of Portuguese East Africa (Mozambique) in 1917 was similar to many others across the continent as it was stimulated by coercive military recruitment of local labor and a simultaneous weakening of the colonial state in the face of German raids from their territory to the north. Nationalist historians, seeking historical inspiration for more modern independence struggles, often identified this uprising as one part of a long history of resistance to Portuguese colonialism in Mozambique that would ultimately lead to the liberation war of the 1960s and 1970s.[19]

Recruitment of tens of thousands of men in French West Africa led to various forms of resistance. The main problems with French recruiting were that so many men were demanded (thus threatening agricultural production), and that it was usually not voluntary. For example, of the 40,000 men recruited in 1915–1916, it was estimated that only 7 to 8 percent were truly volunteers. Chiefs were given financial incentives for delivering recruits, and the result was that they ordered many men from the traditionally servile classes to enlist. It seems certain that many of the African soldiers who fought for France on the Western Front were actually slaves. Some men tried to escape the army by hiding in the bush, injuring or starving themselves so they would be judged medically unfit, or fleeing across borders into British colonies or independent Liberia. There were widespread and violent uprisings in French territories like Haut-Senegal-Niger, Dahomey, and the Niger Military Territory, where rebel Tuareg people, famous for their dark blue robes and camel caravans, who had dominated much of the trans-Saharan trade, seized the desert town of Agedes in 1916. In addition to the recruitment issue, these actions seem to have been prompted by rumors that the French were losing the war and would be replaced by the Germans (a common rumor in other regions as well), and by the fact that many local French officials had left these areas for military service. The long-standing antagonism between French colonial officials (whose official colonial rhetoric was one of assimilation) and Muslim leaders in these territories, combined with the declaration of a jihad against the Allied powers by the ruler of the Ottoman Empire in 1915, were used by rebel leaders to mobilize their followers. The French, assisted at times by the British in northern Nigeria, had to employ thousands of black and white soldiers, desperately needed on the Western Front, in suppressing these rebellions.[20]

The Volta-Bani War of 1915–1917 in the vast Haut-Senegal-Niger region of French West Africa offers a good example of African resistance to the French during the First World War. The entry of the Ottoman Empire on the German side of the war in 1915 prompted a local French administrator, who already had a violent reputation, to whip and torture a number of Muslim leaders in public. The conscription of local men into the army during 1915, together with the weakening of French security in the area that had a population of around 900,000, caused a league of 11 villages openly to declare war on the French, whom they vowed to expel at all costs. In the initial fighting, the rebels lost around 1,400 people but were able to drive out local French forces from their area. Late in December 1915, the French assembled the largest military expedition they had ever put together in West Africa. A thousand soldiers supported by several artillery pieces confronted 10,000 rebels at the village of Yankaso. After the French had expended all their artillery shells, they were forced to retreat in the face of overwhelming rebel numbers. In February 1916, an even larger French force of 1,500 colonial African soldiers and 2,000 irregular African auxiliaries, supported by artillery and machine guns, invaded the rebel area. They defeated rebel armies on several occasions, destroyed rebel villages and crops, seized women and children as hostages, and executed rebel leaders. In some cases, inhabitants of rebel villages fought against inhabitants of loyalist villages in what became a civil war. By the end of 1917, the Volta-Bani area had been "pacified" in a military campaign that had targeted an entire society and had seen the deaths of 30,000 local people and around 300 black and white French colonial soldiers. The French continued to persecute potential rebels well into 1919 when the area was divided into two new administrative territories that in 1960 became the independent states of Burkina Faso and Mali.[21]

FAMINE AND DISEASE

The First World War was a time of hunger for many African people. The German and Allied armies that pursued each other around the East African bush lived off food produced by the local population, and fighting usually shifted out of areas where food supplies had been exhausted. Although British forces were supposed to acquire food through trade in items like calico, this was not always a voluntary process and looting did occur. The Germans, outnumbered and desperate, simply confiscated what they wanted, forced villagers to act as porters, and summarily shot anyone who objected. When the last remaining German column moved into northern Mozambique in 1918, its purpose was largely to loot the food resources of that region. When these were used up they moved north again with Allied units following close behind.

In the Ugogo area of central German East Africa (Tanzania today), a British official reported that 30,000 out of 150,000 people had died during a wartime famine that locals still call *Mtunya* meaning "the Scramble." It is remembered as the worst famine in the area's long history of drought and war-related famine. Furthermore, it left those without cattle locked in a permanently subordinate position within the colonial economy and vulnerable to future famines. The first impact of the war on the area was felt when German colonial officials, around 1915, ordered appointed African headmen to gather grain from their villages and bring it to depots along the central railway. At first these demands were limited, but when Allied forces invaded German East Africa in late 1915, the Germans also began to demand that the people of Ugogo provide livestock for

A German chain-gang at Kilossa. *The Times History of the War* (London: The Times, 1914–1921).

the soldiers. By 1916, the Germans had taken an estimated 26,000 of the roughly 300,000 cattle in the area. In addition, the Germans conscripted 35,000 men from Ugogo to serve as supply carriers.

When the British occupied the area, they continued the same policy by systematically confiscating food and press-ganging men for labor. Although the British tended to pay for the grain and livestock they acquired, there was an underlying element of coercion and the local people felt they had no choice in the matter. In 1917, the British conscripted 24,000 men from Ugogo into their Carrier Corps. Although British officials knew that lack of rain meant the 1918 harvest would be inadequate to feed the local population, they continued the campaign of acquiring food and labor. Whole villages were abandoned as starving people searched the countryside for food. Hungry mobs often forced those who still had some livestock to slaughter them for food. People collected roots, fruits, and grass from the bush and even boiled their sandals to eat the leather. Even those with money could not buy food as no shops had grain to sell until 1919. Desperate people pawned their children to the wealthy in return for food. It was common to see corpses along paths, and years later one villager remembered that "the people's skulls littered the ground like coconuts." The people of Ugogo remember this famine as a time when all the normal bonds of society broke down and some of the starving even resorted to cannibalism. The advent of the influenza pandemic in 1918 and 1919 had a particularly hard impact as people already weakened by hunger could not resist sickness. When the British (who had formally taken over German East Africa as a mandate of the League of Nations and renamed it Tanganyika) finally brought food relief into the area after the war, they required that it be bought with cash. Even after local food production began to recover in the 1920s and the rains finally came, the result of the great famine was a stark and permanent gap in society between a few rich families who had managed to hold onto their livestock or buy relief grain, and the impoverished masses who had nothing.[22]

Areas that did not see actual fighting also experienced food shortage during the war. The British used their colony of Nyasaland as a logistical base for their forces operating in the southern part of German East Africa and Mozambique. From 1916 onwards, the colonial administration in Nyasaland embarked on a campaign to acquire the colony's whole agricultural surplus. In 1916 and 1917 the government requisitioned Nyasaland's entire rice crop. Villagers were supposed to be paid for their crops but the prices were below market level. In any case, there was little available for the villagers to buy as the war had caused a decline in imports. In some places chiefs and headmen, eager to ingratiate themselves with the administration, made voluntary donations of maize and other produce for the war effort. Unfortunately for the local villagers, these donations were not so voluntary. In addition, by 1917, almost all the cattle of northern Nyasaland had been taken to feed Allied soldiers. Further hampering agricultural production was the absence of so many young men who had enlisted in the army or who were working as supply-carriers in East Africa. More of the heavy agricultural work fell to women. There was even a shortage of hoes to till the land as most iron went to the war effort. These problems, combined with drought in some areas and flooding in others, dangerously reduced the amount of food in the colony. During the war Malawians took to eating wild roots and grass grains to stay alive. Hunger made them vulnerable to disease. Bubonic plague broke out in the northern part of the country and smallpox, previously on the decline in Nyasaland, made a huge comeback in the south. Of course, all of this was but a prelude to the influenza pandemic that hit the entire region at the end of the conflict.[23] The same process happened in other areas bordering German East Africa. In 1916, when the British began an offensive against the Germans from the south, the northeastern region of Northern Rhodesia was swept clean of food and labor. Not only that, the educational and medical activities of missionaries came to a complete halt.[24]

During the First World War, embattled France called upon its West African territories to feed the people of the motherland. In 1917, the French Minister of Production wanted to purchase the entire harvest of his West African territories, particularly sorghum, millet, rice, groundnuts, palm-oil, beans, yams, and manioc. Colonial officials on the ground complained that while they faced demands for greatly increased agricultural production, their efforts were being undermined by the departure of tens of thousands of productive African farmers for the Western Front, by administrative problems created by the departure of many European officials for the war, and by the low prices paid for crops.[25] In contrast to East Africa, these demands for food seem nevertheless not to have caused widespread famine.

AFRICAN ELITES AND THE POLITICS OF LOYALTY

During the First World War the westernized African elite, a product of European missionary schools, was still in its infancy. It represented a tiny minority who had achieved success within the western educational system, mastered the colonial language, converted to Christianity, and usually occupied junior positions within the colonial hierarchy such as clerks, teachers, or clergymen. While members of this elite tended to see themselves as good British subjects or French citizens, in the early twentieth century they began to form embryonic political organizations that used very modest methods to advance their interests within the existing system. While they responded to the outbreak of the Great War with the same patriotic fervor as many Europeans, the wartime experience did profoundly shape their future political development.

When France faced widespread resistance, both violent and nonviolent, to its recruiting efforts in West Africa, it called upon a leading member of the African elite to supply young men for the army. In January 1918, the French Minister of Colonies made the surprising but ingenious decision to appoint Blaise Diagne High Commissioner for the Recruitment of Troops in Black Africa. Diagne was the first black Senegalese deputy ever to be elected to the French Chamber and had championed equal rights for the assimilated Africans of Dakar. As High Commissioner he was accorded equal status with the Governor-General of French West Africa and even given superior powers with regard to recruitment. Diagne only agreed to his appointment because the French government promised him that after the war the harsh system of traditional law applied to nonwesternized people would be relaxed, increased facilities for the acquisition of French citizenship made available, improved medical facilities built, jobs reserved for returning veterans, and development projects undertaken generally to improve the life of people in French West Africa. Diagne proved a brilliantly successful recruiter. He toured the territories in the high style of a governor-general and used African sergeants and officers, covered in medals won on the Western Front, as his recruiting agents. Although his first recruiting drive was meant to enlist 40,000 men, over 63,000 came forward in the first two months. The largest contingent, 21,000 strong, came from the previously rebellious territory of Haut-Senegal-Niger that French recruiters had given up on. After the Armistice, the French broke their agreement with Diagne and the promised reforms never materialized. In some circles Diagne came to be seen as a French puppet who had secured his personal advancement by sending his countrymen to the nightmare of the trenches. However, as Michael Crowder points out, Diagne should be given credit for performing a task that Europeans were unable to accomplish, and for trying to obtain important reforms in exchange for the military service of men who probably would have been conscripted anyway.[26]

When the First World War began, the westernized African elite of South Africa was one of the largest on the continent and already had well-developed political organizations committed to opposing racially discriminatory legislation enacted by the all-white Union government. The South African Native National Congress (the SANNC, later renamed the African National Congress) was formed in 1912 and was the first South African-wide black political organization. When the First World War broke out in August 1914, however, the SANNC suspended its grievances against the 1913 Native Land Act, which prevented Africans from purchasing land outside designated reserves, and resolved to offer the government of General Louis Botha, South Africa's first prime minister, its patriotic assistance. The SANNC delegation, in London seeking the intervention of the imperial government in Union affairs, rushed home so that its members could enlist. African newspapers began to publish articles dreaming about the exchange of African military service abroad for increased rights at home.

Walter Rubusana, who in 1910 had been the first African elected to the Cape provincial legislature, and who was also an SANNC executive member, declared that he could raise a corps of 5,000 African soldiers under his own command for service in the invasion of German South West Africa. His offer was not taken up by the government because of white fears that arming and training Africans for military service would lead to trouble at home. The African Political Organization (APO), a group representing Cape Coloured or mixed race people, mobilized 10,000 men to volunteer for the Cape Corps, which eventually fought in the East African campaign. Faced with continued demands from westernized African leaders that Africans should be allowed to serve their country, the South African Native Labour Contingent (SANLC) was eventually recruited from volunteers mainly from South Africa but also the British Protectorates of Bechuanaland (now Botswana), Basutoland (now Lesotho) and Swaziland. Nearly 21,000 sailed for the Western Front as unarmed laborers and 1,100 lost their lives. According to oral tradition (although not confirmed by any official account), when the troop ship SS *Mendi* sank after a collision in the English Channel in February 1917, 800 doomed SANLC soldiers stripped off their uniforms and sang African war songs as if to challenge the waves that were swamping their vessel. This would become one of South Africa's most enduring public memories of the war. As Bill Nasson concludes, the black political elite saw the war as an opportunity to assert claims of full citizenship in an increasingly segregationist state.[27] However, their hopes were dashed when their cooperation in the war did nothing to improve conditions for blacks in South Africa. As a consequence, the black South African response to the outbreak of the Second World War would be much less "patriotic" at a time when black political movements were becoming increasingly radicalized.

In British Bechuanaland, by contrast, African expressions of loyalty had an important impact on the future of the territory. According to Ashley Jackson, local African chiefs and westernized elites strongly opposed plans for the possible incorporation of Bechuanaland into the settler territories of either South Africa or Southern Rhodesia, both well known for racial discrimination and exploitation. For 30 years, British rule in Bechuanaland had depended on the cooperation of local Tswana chiefs. When these African elites proved their loyalty and contributed significant quantities of money, cattle, and recruits to the British war effort, including over a thousand men who joined the SANLC, it made it politically impossible for their territory to be handed over to neighboring settler states. As a result, Bechuanaland continued as a separate British protectorate and eventually became the independent country of Botswana in 1966.[28] Similar considerations also played some part in Basutoland's and Swaziland's trajectories from protectorate to independent kingdom.

In Southern Rhodesia on the eve of the First World War, the relatively recent history of colonial conquest meant that the westernized African elite was tiny and lacked political organization. The wartime experience changed that and prompted the formation of the first western-style African organizations in that territory. The proliferation of settler patriotic organizations during the war influenced the emergence of similar groups among African elites, although not necessarily with the same objectives. The Loyal Mandebele Patriotic Society (LMPS) was formed by African elites in Bulawayo in 1915 and seemed structurally like a carbon copy of the many similar organizations founded by the colony's settlers. It must be remembered that LMPS members were first-generation African westernized elites who, despite the violent destruction of the Ndebele kingdom in the 1890s and the dispossession of its people, were products of the missionary education system. They held junior positions in the colonial state or church and saw themselves as loyal British subjects. The LMPS portrayed the struggles of the British Empire as its own and appropriated the wartime language of patriotism, albeit with some African symbolism or appeals to African or Ndebele history.

The central aims of the LMPS, however, were different from Rhodesian white patriotic organizations and betrayed the missionary background of its membership. Indeed, the LMPS was far more interested in imposing its Christian patriarchal and puritan views on other Africans than in contributing to the war effort. It embarked on a morality crusade to pressure Native Department officials and police to crack down on prostitution in African parts of the town, which it blamed for the spread of syphilis, and to prevent white men from visiting black women in these neighborhoods since their mixed-race children were often wanted neither by the white nor black community. A far more overtly and specifically political organization than the LMPS founded in Southern Rhodesia during the First World War was the Ndebele National Home Movement. It was formed by members of the Ndebele royal family, who engaged legal assistance in an attempt to redress the results of British conquest in 1893 by restoring the Ndebele monarchy and seeking a return of Ndebele land. These early western-style African political groups might have been small and moderate but they provided the organizational basis for the more radical nationalist movements that emerged after the Second World War.

Throughout the First World War, various Ndebele and Shona chiefs took collections among their people and made cash donations to the colonial administration for the British war effort. It is interesting that this money, unlike settler donations, which went to local patriotic funds, was sent to the Prince of Wales Fund in Britain. Officials claimed that this was so Africans would not be confused about how their donations had been spent, but in reality there was concern that Africans would see wartime sacrifice as a future investment in local political rights.[29]

CONCLUSION

The First World War was the first global event to impact directly on newly colonized Africa and represented the end of the tumultuous conquest period. Hundreds of thousands of Africans served in the colonial armed forces as soldiers or workers, and many lost their lives. The war was also, as Melvin Page points out, the first "national experience" for Malawians as it was for Africans in other colonies, which were, after all, new political and economic entities created less than 20 years before. Colonial conquest had brought diverse African peoples together within arbitrarily imposed boundaries in an entirely novel context, and the degree to which the Great War affected them depended largely on their place in this new order. Those who lived in German territories faced the full brunt of warfare at home and were handed over to new rulers once the war was over because the former German colonies were given to the victorious Allied powers as mandates of the League of Nations. The new colonial authorities were supposed to prepare the mandated territories for self-determination in the very distant future, but in practice they simply treated them as spoils of war. Even in territories where fighting did not actually occur, people not only were expected to supply the colonial power with resources for the war effort, but even to leave home for military service elsewhere. Overall, the most common impact of the war on African communities was lack of food, the consequences of which varied from the simply worrisome to the outright cataclysmic.

African laborers building a blockhouse in German East Africa. *The Times History of the War* (London: The Times, 1914–1921).

At times, regions far away from the main areas of military operations in the German colonies experienced violence and warfare as Africans rose up in rebellion. Some Africans saw in the First World War an opportunity to restore the independence they had enjoyed before European conquest. Others chafed under heavy colonial demands for resources and labor, and all witnessed an obvious weakening of the colonial state brought about by the demands and disruptions of war. The colonial authorities ultimately suppressed all these uprisings and most rebels—and sometimes even those merely suspected of harboring rebel sympathies—experienced harsh reprisals. It should be noted that contrary to the theories of nationalist historians in the 1960s, there is little evidence that these rebellions represented an attempt to expand the scale of resistance or were aimed at creating a new, forward-looking political order. Rebels usually wanted to recover their old way of life or were pushed into violent protest by colonial threats to their very existence. The loyalty of the small westernized African elite was important to colonial governments, but it was usually exploited without the granting of reforms that were anticipated (or sometimes promised) in return.

The war caused the largest movement of Africans from their home continent since the Trans-Atlantic Slave Trade, and many were again taken against their will. Those who returned home would never see the world in the same light again, yet veterans' experiences would not in the main translate into significant new political organizations or action. This can be explained in terms of the postwar direction taken by the colonial state in Africa, where the atmosphere of military occupation that had characterized the previous two decades gave way to one of humdrum bureaucratic administration. Forced labor and confiscation of crops, both previously common causes of violent resistance, became less frequent in many areas. Africans themselves were increasingly absorbed into the growing capitalist economy as wage-earning workers or cash-cropping peasant farmers. During what came to be called the "High Tide" of the colonial era in the 1920s and 1930s, there would be no further unsettling changes in territories controlled by the colonial powers. African rebellions became less frequent as a consequence; protests were less violent and were aimed mostly at improving conditions for Africans within the existing system. Many more Africans converted to Christianity and there was, for a time, a general acceptance of the colonial status quo.

ABBREVIATIONS

APO African Political Organization

LMPS Loyal Mandebele Patriotic Society

SANLC South African Native Labour Contingent

SANNC South African Native National Congress

TIMELINE

1914	Outbreak of First World War Afrikaner (Boer) Rebellion in South Africa Allied invasions of German Togoland (Togo) and Cameroon
1915	Allied invasion of German East Africa South African invasion of German South West Africa (Namibia) Chilembwe Uprising in Nyasaland (Malawi) Formation of Loyal Mandebele Patriotic Organization in Southern Rhodesia (Zimbabwe)
1915–1916	Bongo Riots in Northern Gold Coast (Ghana) Ellijah II Uprising in Eastern Nigeria Egba Uprising in Western Nigeria
1915–1917	Volta-Bani War (Rebellion) in French West Africa
1915	Tuareg rebels capture Agedes in French West Africa Allied Offensive in German East Africa
1916–1917	British requisition entire rice crops in Nyasaland (Malawi)
1916	African Rebellion in Mozambique Sinking of the SS *Mendi* carrying 800 members of the South African Native Labour Corps to the Western Front
1918	German column invades Mozambique from German East Africa Blaise Diagne appointed chief French recruiter in Black Africa
1918–1919	Influenza pandemic
1919	Former German colonies in Africa are given to victorious Allied powers as mandates of the League of Nations

GLOSSARY

Names, Places and Organizations

African Political Organization (APO). A political organization of mixed-race South Africans that mobilized 10,000 volunteers for the South African forces during the First World War.

Bongo Riots. Violent protest in what is now northern Ghana (then the Gold Coast) during 1915 and 1916 against British-appointed chiefs and recruiting of local young men to fight in the First World War.

Botha, Louis. A Boer general who had fought against the British during the South African War of 1899–1902. He became the first prime minister of South Africa in 1910. During the First World War he led South African forces against Boer rebels and directed the invasion of German South West Africa.

Carrier Corps. During the German East Africa campaign of the First World War the British recruited and conscripted several hundred thousand Africans to carry supplies. Between 42,000 and 100,000 of them died from disease, hunger, and exhaustion.

Chilembwe, John. A Malawian Baptist minister who had been educated in the United States. He objected to the British conscription of his people as supply carriers during the First World War and led an unsuccessful rebellion against the British in Malawi (then Nyasaland) in 1915; he was killed while trying to flee.

Diagne, Blaise. The first black West African to be elected to the French government. During the First World War Diagne agreed to take over recruiting in the French African colonies in exchange for promises of colonial reform that would benefit Africans after the conflict. He was a brilliantly successful recruiter but after the war the French failed to deliver on their promises.

Ellijah II. A prophetic leader in South Eastern Nigeria who led a rebellion against the British during the First World War.

Kamwana, Elliot. Leader of the Watchtower Movement (Jehovah's Witnesses) in Malawi during the First World War. The British exiled him to Mauritius as his followers refused to volunteer for military service.

King's African Rifles. A British colonial regiment based in Malawi, Kenya, and Uganda with African rank-in-file and European officers. It was dramatically expanded during the First World War.

Loyal Mandebele Patriotic Society (LMPS). A small organization of African westernized elites in Bulawayo, Zimbabwe (then Southern Rhodesia) formed to support the British during the First World War.

Maduna. An Ndebele chief in Zimbabwe (then Southern Rhodesia) who feared that his men would be conscripted into the army during the First World War.

Rubusana, Walter. In 1910 he was the first and only African to be elected to the Cape legislature in South Africa. During the First World War he offered to raise a special corps of black South African soldiers for the invasion of German South West Africa.

Smuts, Jan. A Boer general who had fought against the British during the South African War of 1899–1902. He took command of British forces fighting in German East Africa during the First World War and later became South Africa's second prime minister.

South African Native Labour Contingent (SANLC). A corps of 21,000 black South Africans who volunteered to serve as unarmed military laborers on the Western Front during the First World War.

South African Native National Congress (SANNC). Formed in 1912, this was the first South Africa-wide political organization of African westernized elites. During the First World War it suspended its protests over discriminatory legislation to provide patriotic support to the South African and British governments. It was later renamed the African National Congress (ANC) and developed into a radical liberation movement after the Second World War. It is the governing party of South Africa today.

Ugogo. A district of German East Africa (Tanzania today) particularly hard hit by famine during the First World War when both German and British forces confiscated food from local people.

Volta-Bani War. From 1915 to 1917, African people in what is now Burkina Faso and Mali rebelled against French oppression and conscription. The French response was brutal, and in the suppression of the rebellion 30,000 local people were killed.

NOTES

1. Melvin Page, ed., *Africa and the First World War* (London: MacMillan, 1987), 14.

2. David Killingray and David Omissi, eds., *Guardians of Empire: The Armed Forces of the Colonial Powers, c. 1700–1964* (Manchester: Manchester University Press, 2000); Timothy H. Parsons, *The African Rank-and-File: Social Implications of Colonial Military Service in the King's African Rifles, 1902–1964* (Oxford: James Currey, 1999).

3. Parsons, *The African Rank-and-File*, 4.

4. Estimates of the number of West African troops employed by France have increased over the years. Hew Strachan, *The First World War.* Vol. I. *To Arms* (Oxford: Oxford University Press, 2001), 497 gives the current figure of 200,000, which he derives from Myron Echenberg, *Colonial Conscripts: The "Tirailleurs Senegalais" in French West Africa 1857–1960* (Portsmouth, NH: Heinemann, 1991), 25–32. John Hargreaves, "French West Africa and the First World War," *Journal of African History* 24 (1983): 288 states that the number was just over 130,000.

5. Winston Groom, *A Storm in Flanders: The Ypres Salient, 1914–1918, Tragedy and Triumph on the Western Front* (New York: Atlantic Monthly Press, 2002), 107–8.

6. Hargreaves, "French West Africa and the First World War," 288.

7. Page, *Africa*, 8.

8. For the South African Native Labour Contingent see Brian Willan, "The South African Native Labour Contingent 1916–1918," *Journal of African History* 19, no. 1 (1978): 61–86; Norman Clothier, *Black Valour: The South African Native Labour Contingent 1916–1918 and the Sinking of the Mendi* (Pietermaritzburg: University of Natal Press, 1987).

9. Page, *Africa*, 14, and Ross Anderson, *The Forgotten Front: The East African Campaign 1914–1918* (Gloucestershire: Tempus Publishing, 2004), 296.

10. John R. Morrow, *The Great War: An Imperial History* (New York: Routledge, 2004), 310.

11. Joe Lunn, *Memories of the Maelstrom: A Senegalese Oral History of the First World War* (Portsmouth, NH: Heinemann, 1999), 187–205, 215, 229–35; Melvin Page, *The Chiwaya War: Malawians and the First World War* (Boulder, CO: Westview Press, 2000), 135–38, 164–66, 203–6, 226; James Mathews, "WW1 and the Rise of African Nationalism: Nigerian Veterans as Catalysts of Political Change," *Journal of Modern African Studies* 20, no. 3 (1982): 493–502; Ian Phimister and Charles van Onselen, "The Labour Movement in Zimbabwe, 1900–1945," in *Keep on Knocking: A History of the Labour Movement in Zimbabwe, 1900–1997*, ed. Brian Raftopoulos and Ian Phimister (Harare: Baobad Books, 1997), 8. National Archives of Zimbabwe N3/21/1–6: Superintendent of Natives, Umtali to Chief Native Commissioner, 1 September 1922.

12. Bill Nasson, "War Opinion in South Africa 1914," *Journal of Imperial and Commonwealth History* 23, no. 2 (1995): 259–65.

13. G. Shepperson and T. Price, *Independent African: John Chilembwe and the Origins, Setting and Significance of the Nyasaland Native Rising of 1915* (Edinburgh:

Edinburgh University Press, 1958); G. Mwase, *Strike a Blow and Die,* ed. R. Rotberg (Cambridge, MA: Harvard University Press, 1967); R. Rotberg, "Psychological Stress and the Question of Identity: Chilembwe's Revolt Reconsidered," in *Protest and Power in Black Africa,* ed. R. Rotberg and A. Mazrui (New York: Oxford University Press, 1970).

14. Edmund Yorke, "The Spectre of a Second Chilembwe: Government, Missions and Social Control in Wartime Northern Rhodesia, 1914–1918," *Journal of African History* 31 (1990): 373–91.

15. P. Curtin, S. Feierman, L. Thompson, and J. Vansina, *African History: From Earliest Times to Independence* (London: Longman, 1995), 515.

16. Roger G. Thomas, "The 1916 Bongo Riots and Their Background: Aspects of Colonial Administrative and African Response in Eastern Upper Ghana," *Journal of African History* 24 (1983): 57–75.

17. Michael Crowder, "The 1914–1918 European War and West Africa," in *History of West Africa,* vol. 2, ed. J . F. Ade Ajayi and M. Crowder (London: Longman, 1974), 508–9.

18. Tim Stapleton, "Views of the First World War in Southern Rhodesia (Zimbabwe) 1914–1918," *War and Society* 20, no. 1 (May 2002): 38–41.

19. Alan Issacman, *The Tradition of Resistance in Mozambique: The Zambesi Valley 1850–1921* (Los Angeles: University of California Press, 1976), 156–58.

20. Crowder, "The 1914–1918 European War and West Africa," 497–500. Jide Osuntokun, "Nigeria's Colonial Government and the Islamic Insurgency in French West Africa, 1914–1918," *Cahiers d'Etudes Africaines* 57, XV-I: 85–93.

21. Mahir Saul and Patrick Royer, *West African Challenge to Empire: Culture and History in the Volta-Bani Anti-Colonial War* (Athens: Ohio University Press, 2001).

22. Gregory Maddox, "Mtunya: Famine in Central Tanzania 1917–1920," *Journal of African History* 31, no. 2 (1990): 181–97.

23. Page, *The Chiwaya War,* 132–39.

24. Yorke, "The Spectre of a Second Chilembwe," 384.

25. Crowder, "The 1914–1918 European War and West Africa," 505.

26. Ibid., 500–503.

27. Nasson, "War Opinion in South Africa," 255–57; Willan, "The South African Native Labour Contingent," 61–86; Clothier, *Black Valour,* 48–73, 150; and Albert Grundlingh, *Fighting Their Own War: South African Blacks and the First World War* (Johannesburg: Ravan Press, 1987).

28. Ashley Jackson, "Bechuanaland, the Caprivi Strip and the First World War," *War and Society* 19, no. 2 (October 2001): 142.

29. For the LMPS and donations by chiefs see Stapleton, "Views of the First World War in Southern Rhodesia," 41–42. For the Ndebele National Home Movement see T. O. Ranger, *The African Voice in Southern Rhodesia* (London: Heinemann, 1970), 55–63.

SELECT BIBLIOGRAPHY

Anderson, Ross. *The Forgotten Front: The East African Campaign 1914–1918.* Gloucestershire: Tempus Publishing, 2004.

Meticulously researched and extremely thorough military history of the German East Africa campaign.

Clothier, Norman. *Black Valour: The South African Native Labour Contingent 1916–1918 and the Sinking of the Mendi.* Pietermaritzburg: University of Natal Press, 1987.

Story of black South African laborers who volunteered to go to the Western Front and the sinking of their troop-ship.

Crowder, Michael. "The 1914–1918 European War and West Africa." pp. 484–513 in *History of West Africa.* Vol. 2. Edited by J. F. Ade Ajayi and M. Crowder. London: Longman, 1974.

This chapter places the First World War in the context of West African history.

Echenberg, Myron. *Colonial Conscripts: The "Tirailleurs Senegalais" in French West Africa 1857–1960.* Portsmouth, NH: Heinemann, 1991.

A comprehensive history of West Africans in French military service.

Grundlingh, Albert. *Fighting Their Own War: South African Blacks and the First World War.* Johannesburg: Ravan Press, 1987.

A thorough examination of how black South Africans responded to the First World War.

Hargreaves, John. "French West Africa and the First World War." *Journal of African History* 24, no. 2 (1983): 285–88.

Analysis of recruitment and rebellion in the French West African territories.

Jackson, Ashley. "Bechuanaland, the Caprivi Strip and the First World War." *War and Society* 19, no. 2 (October 2001): 109–42.

A look at the significance of the First World War for what is now Botswana, then but a small and remote British territory.

Killingray, David. "The War in Africa." pp. 92–103 in *World War I: A History.* Edited by Hew Strachan. Oxford: Oxford University Press, 1998.

A short but comprehensive account of all aspects of the war in Africa.

——— and David Omissi, eds. *Guardians of Empire: The Armed Forces of the Colonial Powers, c. 1700–1964.* Manchester: Manchester University Press, 2000.

A collection of essays on the role of Africans in colonial armies.

Lunn, Joe. *Memories of the Maelstrom: A Senegalese Oral History of the First World War.* Portsmouth, NH: Heinemann, 1999.

The stories of Senegalese veterans of the Great War.

Maddox, Gregory. "Mtunya: Famine in Central Tanzania 1917–1920." *Journal of African History* 31, no. 2 (1990): 181–97.

Detailed study of how the First World War caused a devastating famine in a district of German East Africa (Tanzania) and its long-term impact on the people of that area.

McLaughlin, Peter. *Ragtime Soldiers: The Rhodesian Experience in the First World War.* Bulawayo: Books of Zimbabwe, 1980.

This book concentrates on how participation in the war contributed to the development of a white Rhodesian national identity. It does not focus much on the role of black Zimbabweans in the conflict.

Morrow, John. *The Great War: An Imperial History.* New York: Routledge, 2004.

General history of the First World War with a particularly global focus.

Nasson, Bill. "War Opinion in South Africa 1914." *Journal of Imperial and Commonwealth History* 23, no. 2 (1995): 284–76.

Detailed study of how various groups in South Africa, including Afrikaners and Africans, saw the First World War.

Osuntokun, Jide. "Nigeria's Colonial Government and the Islamic Insurgency in French West Africa, 1914–1918." *Cahiers d'Etudes Africaines* 57, XV-I (1975): 85–93.

Short article on how rebellion in French territories impacted on the British in Northern Nigeria.

Page, Melvin, ed. *Africa and the First World War.* London: Macmillan, 1987.

Collection of essays about aspects of the First World War and various sub-Saharan African countries.

———. *The Chiwaya War: Malawians and the First World War.* Boulder, CO: Westview Press, 2000.

The most comprehensive study of the impact of the First World War on an African country.

Parsons, Timothy H. *The African Rank-And-File: Social Implications of Colonial Military Service in the King's African Rifles, 1902–1964.* Oxford: James Currey, 1999.

Presents a social history of the famous British colonial African regiment.

Ranger, T. O. *The African Voice in Southern Rhodesia.* London: Heinemann, 1970.

This wider work mentions early westernized African elite organizations that emerged in Southern Rhodesia (Zimbabwe) during the First World War.

Rotberg, R. "Psychological Stress and the Question of Identity: Chilembwe's Revolt Reconsidered." pp. 337–73 in *Protest and Power in Black Africa.* Edited by R. Rotberg and A. Mazrui. New York: Oxford University Press, 1970.

This chapter challenges the African nationalist view of John Chilembwe and maintains that mental problems contributed to his leading a rebellion against the British in Nyasaland in 1915.

Saul, Mahir, and Patrick Royer. *West African Challenge to Empire: Culture and History in the Volta-Bani Anti-Colonial War.* Athens: Ohio University Press, 2001.

A comprehensive account of one of the most widespread and violent African rebellions of the First World War period.

Shepperson, G., and T. Price. *Independent African: John Chilembwe and the Origins, Setting and Significance of the Nyasaland Native Rising of 1915.* Edinburgh: Edinburgh University Press, 1958.

An African nationalist portrayal of John Chilembwe that maintains he led a doomed rebellion against the British in Nyasaland in order to become a martyr who would inspire future generations.

Stapleton, Tim. "Views of the First World War in Southern Rhodesia (Zimbabwe) 1914–1918." *War and Society* 20, no. 1 (May 2002): 23–45.

A look at the reaction of British and Afrikaner settlers as well as the African population of Zimbabwe to the outbreak of the First World War.

Strachan, Hew. *The First World War.* Vol. 1. *To Arms.* Oxford: Oxford University Press, 2001.

This mammoth work contains a book-length chapter on the First World War in Africa with detailed sections on each military campaign. With slight revisions this chapter has been issued as a separate book: Hew Strachan. *The First World War in Africa.* Oxford: Oxford University Press, 2004.

Thomas, Roger G. "The 1916 Bongo Riots and Their Background: Aspects of Colonial Administrative and African Response in Eastern Upper Ghana." *Journal of African History* 24, no. 1 (1983): 57–75.

An examination of an African rebellion in a British West African territory during the First World War.

Willan, Brian. "The South African Native Labour Contingent 1916–1918." *Journal of African History* 19, no. 1 (1978): 61–86.

Black South African laborers who went to the Western Front.

Yorke, Edmund. "The Spectre of a Second Chilembwe: Government, Missions and Social Control in Wartime Northern Rhodesia, 1914–1918." *Journal of African History* 31, no. 3 (1990): 373–91.

The impact of the First World War on colonial administration in northern Zambia.

FIVE

African Civilians in the Era of the Second World War, c. 1935–1950

David Killingray

Civilians always suffer in wars. Women and children bear the burden of absent men and mourn their loss; armies plunder and destroy homes and farms; villagers flee to avoid military and labor recruiters; and the tentacles of war dislocate livelihoods and distort economies distant from campaigns. War is destructive and disruptive of lives and economies. As a doctor with the German forces in East Africa recorded in his diary in September 1918:

> Behind us we leave destroyed fields, ransacked magazines and, for the immediate future, starvation. We are no longer the agents of culture; our track is marked by death, plundering and evacuated villages. Just like the progress of our own and enemy armies in the Thirty Years War.[1]

In the Second World War, as with the earlier Great War of 1914–1918, Africa was sucked into the conflict because European imperial powers controlled most of the continent as colonies. The result was that serious damage was inflicted on areas of north and northeast Africa where military campaigns were fought. A total and global war, such as the conflict of 1939–1945, touched all African territories, even the colonies of neutral powers. But the Second World War was also a catalyst for social, economic, and political change by providing new perspectives on the past and the future and opportunities to implement social and political reform.[2] The war was thus of seminal importance for the future of Africa; after 1945 there was a new world order and the colonial relationship had been severely shaken. It is therefore important to see the impact of the war on civil society as spreading over a period longer than the years of actual hostilities. A reasonable periodization would be *c.*1935–1950. For Ethiopia the war began in 1935 when the Italian fascist state invaded that country; and the impact of the changes brought by the war can be seen there and in other parts of Africa long after 1945. For example, wartime inflation and shortages of consumer goods continued having a profound influence on colonial economies and the lives of African producers and consumers well after the war. Although the war in many ways helped to weaken colonial control, the needs of postwar reconstruction made the resources of the African colonies more valuable than ever before. Great powers such as France, that had initially been defeated, and Britain, severely challenged and forced into fiscal reliance upon the United States, were not about to lose their great power status if the possession and exploitation of empire might help sustain it.

By the early 1930s most of colonial Africa had been "pacified." Colonial rule was based on European power and the idea of white racial superiority over black subjects. However, European control was often very thinly spread; there were many people throughout Africa, especially north of the Zambezi, who rarely if ever saw a European and who were effectively ruled by African chiefs and headmen. The economic depression of the 1930s led to a reduction in the number of European administrators and also in economic investment in Africa. Economic investment had always been highly selective and skewed toward exploiting Africa's raw materials; thus railways connected mines and plantations to ports so that their products could be exported to the metropoles. Most Africans lived in rural areas, were engaged in subsistence agriculture, were illiterate, and had little or no contact with the products of modern manufacturing industry. Most African towns were small, except for those in northern and southern Africa where there had been some industrial development. Many Africans lived precarious lives; they endured frequent shortages of food and water and suffered from diseases and malnutrition. Among Europeans, modern ideas of "economic development" were little discussed and notions of welfare were only just beginning to be noted. The modern African educated elite were few in number, mainly confined to the towns, and their political ambitions were largely directed toward reforms that would advance their own positions and interests.

In October 1935 the Italians invaded Ethiopia with a modern army and air force. The war and the continuing resistance to Italian occupation were very destructive. Large numbers of civilians were killed in bombing or were murdered by the Italians and by Ethiopian "patriots." A new political order was imposed on Ethiopia and property in towns and rural areas confiscated for use by administrators and Italian and Eritrean settlers. The long and not very successful attempts to pacify the country dislocated the economy; the Italians built new roads and introduced some industries but at great cost. When the Second World War broke out in September 1939, Italy did not immediately become involved. Only when France was about to fall in June 1940, and it looked as if Britain would follow, did Mussolini enter the war in support of Germany. This brought war to north and east Africa.

France agreed to an armistice with Germany and a new pro-German French government was established at Vichy. French resistance continued with anti-German and anti-Vichy elements associated with General de Gaulle. More or less overnight French colonial territory in Africa, formerly allied to Britain, now became potentially hostile, thus further extending the possibility of war in the African continent. Fighting occurred in North Africa from Suez to Morocco, most destructively in Tunisia, from mid-1940 to May 1943, and in East Africa and southern Sudan from 1940 to 1941. There was an unsuccessful British–Free French naval assault on Vichy-held Dakar in September 1940, and a British and South African invasion that cleared the Vichy French from Madagascar in 1942. In addition there was war in the seas around Africa and a British naval blockade of Vichy African ports. Freetown, Cape Town, Durban, and Mombasa were key ports on strategic sea lanes; Kenya became a major British military base connected with a northern supply road to Egypt, while another vital route was developed with United States support through Takoradi in west Africa via Kano to the Middle East.

Little has been written about the immediate consequences of the fighting in Africa. African casualties were relatively few, although it is difficult to assess the pain and suffering inflicted on soldiers and their wives and families. The detritus of war littered the landscape, particularly in north Africa, and lethal landmines and abandoned ammunition continued to kill and maim civilians including children, long after the war had ended. Drought and famine continued to plague Africa in the war years, their relief taking secondary place to the prosecution of the war. Although Africa did not suffer the kind of death rates of Bengal in the famine of 1943–1944, nevertheless serious drought in central Tanganyika in 1942–1943, and in the southern sahelian region in 1943–1944 resulted in increased deaths as crops failed; in the Cape Verde Islands 25,000 people died in the long drought of 1940–1943; in Rwanda wartime exactions and drought are estimated to have killed some 300,000 during and immediately after the war. North Africa experienced harsh droughts in the years 1942–1945, resulting in disastrous harvests; half of Morocco's sheep died and three-quarters of those in Algeria. France's defeat and the resulting deterioration of Algeria's economy meant greater suffering, especially for the poor. Belgium was also defeated and occupied by the Germans in mid-1940. The vast colony of Belgian Congo, separated from the metropole, now became effectively autonomous. The colonial administration took greater control of the economy, and this was to have a profound impact upon the civilian population of the colony.

THE IMMEDIATE IMPACT OF THE WAR

When war broke out in autumn 1939 there was little idea how long the conflict would last. Early indications were that it might be a continuation of the static confrontational trench warfare fought in Western Europe in 1914–1918. Germany had lost her colonies in 1919 and there was less chance of direct conflict in Africa; colonies would be involved but mainly to supply resources for the war effort. This situation was dramatically changed by Italy's entry on the Axis side in early June 1940, and the collapse of France and Belgium. Vichy France held on to the African colonies with the exception of Chad, where the black governor declared his support for General de Gaulle, the Free French leader in Britain who was determined to continue the war with Germany. For the British the war now became a total war, with all resources from home and overseas mobilized in fighting the Axis powers. Total war in Africa required new bureaucratic structures, which had to rely to a large extent upon Africans. To ensure supplies of raw materials the state also penetrated colonial economies and brought them increasingly under central direction.

Most Africans were loyal to their colonial masters. The French, British, and Belgians had little difficulty on the outbreak of war in securing sufficient soldiers for their expanding colonial armies from the traditional recruiting grounds. The elites, whether the indigenous rulers who often owed their enhanced position to colonial rule or the small number of formally educated people who lived mainly in the urban centers and had occasionally criticized colonial policies, all supported the war effort. African chiefs and headmen assisted in recruiting troops and labor. In British West Africa local legislative councils with the support of African members raised substantial sums of money from local communities. The Gold Coast had a "pitfire Fund," while Nigeria had a "Win the War Fund."[3] Altogether Africans in British colonies donated several million pounds to support the war effort. However, not all colonial "subjects" were regarded as loyal. A handful of African nationalists or suspected dissidents were detained under emergency regulations by the French and British. The French executed or imprisoned some Africans who opposed the Vichy regime, while the British detained some they thought had leftist sympathies. Wartime censorship and surveillance were fairly effective in discouraging any who actively opposed the colonial state. Government propaganda sought to promote official views, although there were bigger and seminal forces at work during the war that were slowly but surely changing African perceptions of European empire and white rulers.

The declaration of war disrupted African exports and the importing of manufactured goods as shipping was diverted to the war effort and the volume of trade fell. In various colonies trucks were requisitioned by the army to move soldiers, which damaged local trade, for example in Uganda where the disruption of the sale and distribution of bananas pushed up prices.[4] The closure of frontiers disrupted trade routes, particularly in west and equatorial Africa after June 1940 as the French colonies now became potentially hostile territory. The terms of trade for Africans involved in the export business were already poor as a result of the Depression years of the 1930s; they worsened for most Africans during the 1940s. The British blockade of the Vichy colonies reduced colonial exports of foodstuffs such as groundnuts, cocoa, and rice to France. Loss of cash income drove peasant producers back into subsistence farming. At the same time the reduction in imported manufactured goods offered opportunities to local weavers and blacksmiths to produce cloth and ironware for local markets.

Migrant labor was vital for many colonies, and international frontiers meant little to those accustomed to moving from one colony to another. Many mines and plantations relied heavily on seasonal migrant workers. Military recruiting put a premium on the continuation of labor flows, although there were fewer officials and necessary resources available to regulate the movement, employment, and settlement of labor. For example, over 100,000 migrant workers annually entered Uganda from neighboring Ruanda-Urundi, mainly to work in the production of cotton and sugar. The war increased Uganda's reliance on immigrant labor, but the colonial state was unable to regulate the flow and employment.[5] South Africa's mines and farms relied heavily on migrant labor both from within South Africa and from colonies north of the Limpopo. The war put conflicting demands on labor, and colonies faced with a potential shortage were unwilling to see men crossing the border in the direction of South Africa.

The immediate shortage of imported goods caused by the outbreak of war led to price inflation. For example, in Lagos, the capital of Nigeria, cement, bicycles, corrugated iron, sewing machines, and bedsteads all increased steeply in price within a month. The government did not immediately respond, and it was not until January 1940 that there was an attempt to control import prices and to fix the price of goods.[6] Similar price rises took place all over colonial Africa, which led to a black market in scarce goods. Gasoline and tires were in short supply, which hindered the transport system and the distribution of important staple foods and items such as salt, sugar, and flour. In West Africa in particular many coastal peoples had come to rely on imported canned foods to supplement home-grown foods and also on imported kerosene for cooking and lighting, goods that the war put in short supply. Rationing was gradually introduced as the war progressed. This took time to implement as the colonial administration lacked adequate resources not least officers. In Tanganyika race relations were dented when some urban Africans claimed that Indian storekeepers were hoarding goods and profiteering. In the Belgian Congo, cut off from Europe after Belgium had been occupied, rationing was introduced and the colonial government set about mobilizing the economy to serve the Allied war effort in Africa.

When war broke out many Europeans in official and commercial employ enlisted for military service. The retrenched colonial administrative service initially shrank in size and thus effectiveness. The withdrawal of Europeans meant that many rural areas, subject to forms of indirect rule by African chiefs, were increasingly governed by Africans. The withdrawal of Europeans for war service provided new opportunities for Africans in government service, in commercial firms, and also in missions, where catechists took the place of white missionary clergy. Increasingly Africans were to be encountered behind official desks, and running shops, trading companies, and schools. As the war continued many more Europeans came to Africa as soldiers and minor officials—perhaps as many as 100,000 in west Africa alone—so that Africans came into contact with more white men who were very different in background and attitude from those formerly found in peacetime administration and commerce. Among the whites were American contractors and soldiers, who from late 1940 onwards were in the Gold Coast developing the American-funded supply route to the Middle East. African American troops were in Liberia but for the most part purposely excluded from British and French colonies for fear that their presence might disturb the racial patterns of colonial rule. The war inevitably helped to change African attitudes to whites. Africans could not work alongside, fight against, and guard white prisoners of war without beginning to perceive white dominance in a different way. In French Africa the turmoil of changed regimes, to Vichy and then to Free French, diminished in many African eyes the idea that white men were superior and to be respected and obeyed.

Another group of Europeans coming into sub-Saharan Africa during the war were refugees, Jews and Poles, other displaced peoples, and prisoners-of-war. Jewish refugees escaping from defeated France to North Africa found that, along with the 400,000 Jews in the three French territories, they were subjected to anti-Semitic laws passed by the Vichy regime. Several hundred Jews were placed in Saharan prison camps. Some 11,000 Polish refugees were given shelter in Kenya and Uganda; Italian prisoners, captured in the East African campaign, were put in camps in Kenya and Southern Rhodesia and employed in various public works such as road building. White men engaged in hard manual work would have been a new sight for most Africans, yet another indication to them that the world was changing.

MOBILIZING AFRICAN RESOURCES FOR THE WAR EFFORT

It was clear to the British by late 1940 that they were in for a long war. The Americans thought so too and increasingly provided the British with material aid "short of actual war." The European-African war was turned into a global conflict by two decisive events in 1941: the German attack on the Soviet Union in June, and Japan's attack on Pearl Harbor in early December. Britain's defeat at the hands of the Japanese and the loss of the oil, tin, and rubber of the southeast Asian colonies in early 1942 were highly significant for the African colonies as they now had to fill the gap by producing war materials. With total war the economies of all the African colonies of the belligerents were centrally managed and directed. As the official report of the Belgian Congo stated: "Since 1940 the Administration has had above all the economic aim of production: it has adapted economic programmes to the circumstances of war and has provoked the growth of native resources to the maximum." A Roman Catholic priest recorded that "all the black population has been mobilized to produce the maximum possible as fast as possible."[7]

For Britain increased African primary production would help reduce dependence upon the United States, uphold the international value of sterling, and enable the country to earn dollars. For wartime planners winning the war was vital but so also was Britain's postwar status. The wartime controls imposed on the African colonies involved bulk-purchase, marketing monopolies, fixed prices, rigid exchange controls, import licensing schemes, and shipping management, all organized through a variety of newly created councils and boards. The result was a degree of control by government over civilian production and livelihood never before experienced in colonial Africa.[8] Under Vichy rule a new and harsher racial order was imposed on the French African colonies that demanded heavier production from peasants. This did not change when the colonies came under Free French control in 1942; in many respects life for Africans became more severe with larger exactions demanded for the war effort. The Italians had also exploited the labor and resources of their East African empire, although under the British administration from 1941 the regime was less harsh. Wartime economics brought a significant change to ideas of future colonial finance. Before 1940 there was little talk of economic development, and each colony was meant to be economically self-sufficient. This was changed in 1940 with the Colonial Development and Welfare Act, and subsequent similar acts that committed Britain to invest in the colonies. France introduced similar measures in 1946. These changes were important for people in postwar Africa as they heralded a new metropolitan approach to colonial economic development and also to investment in welfare provision.

MILITARY RECRUITMENT

Most colonial armies were relatively small and used primarily to maintain internal security. The French, in contrast, were concerned about Germany's demographic advantage and conscripted a colonial army in West Africa and Madagascar that was employed in overseas garrisons and for use, as in the First World War, in a European war. In 1940 Africans constituted about nine percent of the total French army in France. The intent of the British and Belgians was to confine African soldiers to Africa and not involve them in a war against Europeans troops. However, manpower shortages and the valuable role of African troops in the war against the Italians in East Africa changed British thinking. From 1941 onwards Africans were recruited for employment in North Africa and the Levant and eventually for use against the Japanese in Burma. Many of these men were noncombatants employed as laborers in uniform. The South African government was opposed to arming black men, although in combat zones some Africans did carry arms; altogether 123,000 blacks served in the Union Defence Force out of a total of 390,000 men and women enlisted. Between September 1939 and the collapse of France some 100,000 men were mobilized in French West Africa alone. North Africa and Madagascar provided further troops. The British recruited soldiers from all their African colonies, with nearly 500,000 men being enlisted or conscripted for war service.[9] Italy trumpeted its large black army of 250,000 men, but desertion and absenteeism reduced its effectiveness in 1940–1941.

Military recruitment impinged upon civilians. Men deemed idle were swept off town streets, for example in Bagomoya, Tanganyika, and in Bathurst the capital of the Gambia. Conscription drives in the countryside, conducted in nearly all colonies, caused fear and led to flight into the bush or across nearby borders.[10] Men impressed by army recruiters left behind women, children, and the elderly upon whose shoulders fell the burden of maintaining the family and of rural production. In peacetime soldiers' wives lived in the communal "lines"; wartime armies were different, with men housed in barracks and women left in the villages. Women now headed households. And, of course, women waited anxiously at home for news of their men and mourned their death or their long absence. Remittances did come but colonial welfare structures were faulty and slow moving. As a result of military service many African women began to think and act independently, finding it increasingly difficult to accommodate to the rigors of indigenous society or the demands of a returning soldier who expected a subservient wife. It is hardly surprising that family breakdown increased, that men sued for divorce, and women carved out for themselves autonomous lives. For some men military service, with its opportunities to become numerate and literate, was a catalyst for social change. Many men returned with their social horizons broadened by overseas service, new ideas of modernity and hygiene, and also an expectation that the welfare services provided by the military would somehow continue. Given the exposure of soldiers to so many new experiences it is surprising that the vast majority settled relatively easily back into civilian life. Most soldiers came from the traditional recruiting areas, often from peripheral areas of the colony or even from a foreign colony, and that was where the majority returned on demobilization.

Military conscription turned civilians into reluctant soldiers; labor conscription subjected many civilians to military-like conditions of work. Colonial rule was characterized by various forms of forced labor: customary labor and communal labor exacted by chiefs for a specific number of days each year in building and maintaining roads. This had attracted considerable criticism from humanitarian bodies, and in 1930 the League of Nations banned forced labor except in emergencies. However, various forms of customary and communal labor continued, particularly in the Belgian and Portuguese colonies and in the Italian East African Empire. In the Portuguese island colonies of São Tomé and Principe women and children were also forced to work. Forced labor was not formally ended in French colonial Africa until 1946. War resulted in the intensification of the use of forced labor. In Europe civilians were conscripted for the armed forces and also for essential services, and the thinking was that a similar system should apply in the colonies.

FORCED LABOR

Tropical Africa had a primarily peasant-based economy, which meant that wage labor was invariably in short supply for government and commercial undertakings. Wartime required increased labor to produce vital goods and to build and maintain infrastructures for the war effort. For example, the Public Works Department in Nigeria expanded from 10,000 in 1940 to 55,000 in 1942, while wage labor in Freetown increased from 10,000 in 1939 to 45,000 in 1943. Over 10,000 men were employed building the bases for the United States air-ferry service on the Takoradi-Kano-Khartoum route in 1941–1942, and a work force that reached 13,000 in October 1943 built the new road and rail system in order to exploit the vital bauxite supplies of the southern Gold Coast. In the Sudan large road-building gangs, relying mainly on conscripted labor, built and maintained the vital north-south supply road until the end of the North African campaign in 1943.[11] Wages could persuade some men to work but the only way to get labor for less popular forms of employment was by force. Higher wages attracted some Africans into the mainly urban wage-labor market, but wartime inflation and the acute shortage of goods also impelled others.

As wartime labor shortages increased, colonial governments abandoned *laissez-faire* policies and resorted to conscription. Inevitably there was conflict between the demands of the military, which also required labor, and those of the civilian sectors. In many colonies men were conscripted to meet agricultural shortages, especially after the loss of the southeast Asian colonies in early 1942. Forty-five thousand *navétanes* (seasonal workers) from Soudan and Guiné were conscripted to maintain the work force for groundnut production in Senegal in 1943.[12] In British colonies in east and central Africa forced labor was used on European-owned farms. In Southern Rhodesia people and their cattle were evicted from lands to make way for aerodromes needed for the Empire Air Training Scheme, and thousands of men were then conscripted to build them. Later the white settler government introduced the Compulsory Native Labour Act, which had the prime purpose of directing wage workers to white-owned farmers, legislation which continued after the war had ended.[13] Kenya began conscripting agricultural labor in October 1941. An Essential Undertakings Board decided which industries were eligible for forced labor. Conscripts were taken from their homes and often housed in conscript camps to produce sisal, sugar, lime-burning, rubber, and flax. Nearly 3,000 conscripts worked on the railways and in irrigation schemes. The majority of forced laborers were in private employ.[14]

The result was that large areas were denuded of able-bodied men, so that food production fell and extra burdens were placed on women and the elderly. Sisal from Tanganyika, a high dollar earner, was produced with conscript labor after 1941. An official report from southern Tanganyika in 1943 indicates African hostility to and flight from this kind of work:

> Conscription has had to develop into a cunning procedure on the part of both the hunter and the hunted. A date is fixed with the Liwalis and any signs of the impending action, such as the ordering of lorries for the transport of recruits to Lindi and preparation of notices of selection, must be kept secret.... Then in the day preceding the fatal day a swoop is made and a few of the weak, meek, and slow are gathered.[15]

By the end of the war more than 84,000 Africans in Tanganyika had been conscripted for work on sisal estates. White settlers wanted the system continued, but the Labour Government in London ended conscription in 1946. Predictably Africans had resisted conscription by deserting, so that guards were placed on labor compounds and camps. Some of the worst suffering as a result of forced labor occurred in Nigeria, where between April 1942 and April 1944 over one hundred thousand men from Northern Nigeria were conscripted to work in the tin mines on the Jos Plateau. The loss of Malaya in late 1941 turned Nigeria into Britain's main tin supplier. Forced labor was introduced suddenly and at the start of the farming season. Peasants clung to their land and attempted to resist recruiters and the efforts of chiefs to supply men. The climate of the Jos Plateau was colder than the savanna lands of the north, and inadequate provision had been made to house and feed migrant workers and their families. Death rates were high, reaching 10 percent of the Tiv migrants working on the Tenti Dam. Laborers deserted in large numbers, as many as 60 percent being absent in April–June 1942. Output was low, reinforcing the view of critics that forced labor was inefficient compared to free labor. Attempts to improve working and welfare conditions of laborers did not lead to increased production. Forced labor in Nigeria had little impact on output and diverted workers away from food production.[16]

The Belgian authorities in the Congo during wartime, and with greater intensity from 1942 onwards, increased pressure on peasants to produce for the war effort. Obligatory labor, which included road building, was doubled in 1944 to a maximum of 120 days a year and, with the support of the police, that was the exaction demanded of Africans in agricultural production and the collection of wild rubber. Each administrator was judged on the productivity of his territory. While Africans worked harder, the wartime value of the Congo franc fell. In many respects this was what Africans in central Africa called *chibaro*—work that is without value. The French system of forced labor, *prestation,* was a tax paid by a specific amount of work. Under the Vichy regime, forced labor was increased in order to maintain the export economy. While there was a nascent system of corporatist planning, colonial officials debated how best to guard African peasant productivity and also to develop a modern economy. For African men and women forced to work, their experiences differed little with regime change. Forced labor demands by the French resulted in Africans fleeing across borders, for example 20,000 to 30,000 Mossi farm laborers from Upper Volta went to the Gold Coast rather than to the Ivory Coast in 1944. Africans were directed into obligatory labor to produce agricultural export crops such as bananas, groundnuts, and cotton. In the Ivory Coast 35,000 people were conscripted in 1939; this had risen to 41,000 in 1942 and to 55,000 in 1943. Some 90 percent of this labor "recruited by administrative decree" was directed to private enterprises, mainly cocoa and coffee plantations. For African peasants it spelled misery and the disruption of their lives, and work with little return. African wage laborers, who formed part of the mainly urban stable labor force, were also coerced. In Dakar, as the economy contracted following the fall of France in 1940, people deemed to be "unemployed" were sent back to the countryside. Later as the wage labor force resumed its natural competitiveness, legislation was introduced to prevent workers leaving one employment for another in search of higher wages. Thus, African workers were caught in a low-wage system from which it was difficult to escape.[17]

WARTIME ECONOMIC PRODUCTIVITY

The war disrupted but also stimulated the economy of Africa. First, wartime demands for strategic military commodities helped Africa to climb out of the Depression and recession years of the 1930s. Government control over pricing and marketing, along with bulk buying schemes, provided a monopoly system that ensured some degree of economic stability. Second, the loss of the southeast Asian colonies in early 1942 increased the significance of African resources such as tin, tungsten, rubber, and rice. Third, for the French, Belgians, and British the dollar-earning potential of African resources became vital in a global economy increasingly dominated by the United States. Fourth, the United States' economic interest in sub-Saharan Africa increased after 1940–1941, especially in strategic minerals. Cobalt and uranium produced by the Belgian Congo and South Africa were essential to the production of the U.S. atomic bomb. U.S. trade with Africa increased. Exports of machinery and capital goods were partly paid for by the import of minerals and agricultural products. The result of this growth in economic activity was that more Africans became wage earners; for example, in the Belgian Congo the number nearly doubled in the war years to 800,000 by 1945.

Although the focus here is mainly on the war years it is important to see 1939–1945 in the context of the prewar decade. As we will see, this was especially so with agricultural production in certain colonies, where the challenge for colonial administrators was how to encourage more peasant farmers to produce for export or to work for farmers who grew cash crops. African-initiated cash-crop farming had developed in the Gold Coast, Northern Nigeria, and Senegal where cocoa and groundnuts were grown and exported on a large scale, but most farmers throughout Africa were tied to subsistence production for the household and the local market. Force was used to increase rural production, more successfully where there were plantations of sisal, sugar, coffee, cotton, and tobacco. Competition for the limited supply of labor meant that in a colony such as Kenya by 1945 there were more people working in nonagrarian employment than in agriculture. Even neutral colonial states used forced labor to meet wartime induced shortages, the Portuguese in Mozambique enforcing people to grow rice and cotton.

In parts of Africa agricultural producers derived little if any benefit from wartime demands. Egypt was predominantly agrarian, but land ownership was the main source of income for the wealthy few. During the war the number of peasant farmers increased, but inflation and shortages reduced their ability to function profitably as they were cut off from essential imports such as fertilizers, farm implements, and irrigation machinery. In the Sudan, however, cotton production in the Gezira was profitable, with the value of exports rising from £E8.8 million in 1941 to £E62.1 million in 1951. But for the most part peasant real incomes were eroded; in Uganda cotton-producing peasants in 1940 received 50 percent of the export price of the crop and in 1942–1943 only 28 percent. Inflation and increased taxes, plus the cost of clothing and school fees, all hit peasant incomes; the price received for cotton in wartime fell well below that of the free market years of the 1920s. In British West Africa the marketing boards handling peasant cash crops used European mercantile companies as agents, monopolies over which African producers had little influence.

The Depression of the 1930s hit many white settler farmers in Kenya and Southern Rhodesia hard. In Kenya, where whites enjoyed a privileged position, Africans were prevented from growing certain cash crops such as coffee, while the fiscal base of the colony rested heavily on taxes paid by Africans. The stimulus of war to agrarian production rescued white and also some African farmers. Government-guaranteed minimum prices strengthened the economic and political position of white farmers, who were able to increase mechanization. European maize farmers in 1940–1945 secured a monopoly of the Kenyan market with prices above world market prices. They also benefited as the British Army in the Middle East bought their maize, wheat, and vegetables to feed the troops. Some African peasant producers were able to exploit the black market in maize to their own economic advantage. With expanding demand, and despite mechanization, white farmers required labor, and thus they encouraged African squatters to settle on lands designated for white use. African farmers were able to compete with white producers, and by the end of the war these "proto-capitalists" posed a serious challenge to the future of the white-dominated settler state. Wartime changes, with their roots in the 1930s, and postwar ecological issues that questioned peasant farming methods, all pointed to a serious crisis between black and white rural producers.[18]

Besides the minerals urgently needed by the Allies after the Japanese victories in Asia in 1941–1942, Africa also provided four other vital products: industrial diamonds, cobalt, uranium, and gold. During the peak years of the war Africa supplied 50 percent of the world's gold, 19 percent of magnesium, 39 percent of chromite, 24 percent of vanadium, 17 percent of copper, nearly 90 percent of cobalt, and 98 percent of industrial diamonds. Increased mineral output required more labor. For example, nonwhite workers in the South African mining industry increased by nearly 20 percent during the war years, to 404,000. In the Northern Rhodesian copper industry the labor force grew from 26,600 in 1939 to 39,400 in 1943. A sizeable part of most mine labor forces consisted of migrant workers employed on contract terms. This was systematically organized in South Africa, in the two Rhodesian colonies, and in the Belgian Congo. Migrant labor to the mines of South Africa came from rural areas within the country, but a very large percentage came from outside the Union, increasingly from Mozambique during the war years. Rural poverty and the desire for cash incomes, sometimes to meet tax demands, drove men to leave their homes and become migrant laborers. It was low-paid work in labor-intensive industries. Despite the increased wartime demand there were few advantages for unskilled migrant workers, who continued to receive low wages that were eroded by inflation.

Migrant workers came from impoverished backgrounds, and those from tropical areas suffered grievously from respiratory diseases, particularly tuberculosis, in the South African gold mines.[19] The whole migrant labor system was criticized in a report by the Social and Economic Planning Council in 1946 as a threat to "the stability of Native family life which constitutes a danger to the whole nation—black and white alike—in the spheres of health, of morality and of a general social structure, peace, order, reasonable contentment, goodwill, and a sense of national solidarity.... The nation as a whole must fight for its family life and sound and sane tradition."[20] Much of the literature on South African migrant labor is concerned with gold and diamond mining, but migrants also came to work in coal mines. South Africa has vast reserves of coal, and this was the base of South African industrial expansion during the Second World War. Output doubled between 1935 and 1950 and, unlike the gold mines, as much as 60 percent of the labor force was stable, living with their families close to the mines. A more stable labor force grew in wartime South Africa, both in the mining and manufacturing industries, as labor was in short supply and racial restrictions on urban settlement were relaxed. In the Belgian Congo and Northern Rhodesia the copper mining companies, before and during the war, adopted a policy of "controlled mobility" of African labor designed to keep men on the mines until the end of their working life when they would then return to their rural homes. Needless to say such policies to prevent African urbanization were only partially successful.

African labor was also required in towns for manufacturing industries stimulated by the war. The reduction in shipping and the decline in the import of manufactured goods promoted the growth of small-scale secondary industries throughout Africa producing soap, clothing, household goods, and processed foods. Many of these import substitution industries created in Algeria in the years 1940–1942 in response to the blockade were forced to close down when the colony was reintegrated into the world market after 1945. In South Africa there was rapid industrialization in wartime that built on the foundations laid by the mining and transport industries and government promotion through the Iron and Steel Industrial Corporation founded in 1928. War industries required mass production in place of the craft production of small-scale industry. South African manufacturing employment increased by 60 percent in the years 1939–1945, with African workers outnumbering whites in most sectors. While African workers increased by 43 percent, white labor fell in every sector but for metal, engineering, and machinery. To a much lesser extent a similar process occurred in Southern Rhodesia, where the gross output value from factories grew from £5.1 million in 1938 to £25.8 million in 1948. As a result Africans had increased opportunities to acquire new skills, to live with their families as permanent urban dwellers, and to gain access to a range of new urban welfare benefits.

POPULATION CHANGE AND URBAN GROWTH

In the 1940s large areas of Africa were not closely administered and were inadequately mapped (although wartime aerial photographs would help that process after 1945), and the population was only crudely enumerated. The lack of accurate data makes it difficult to study population change with great accuracy. Into the 1940s certain areas of tropical Africa continued to face a demographic crisis because of low levels of fertility, largely as a result of disease, malnutrition, and the migrant labor system. The areas of most rapid growth in the 1920s to 1940s "were chiefly the well-populated areas of cash-crop farming, intensive missionary work, and widespread primary schooling."[21] By 1940–1945 Africa's population growth was about one percent a year and growth became the established pattern. The probable reason for the increase, argues John Iliffe, was a decline in the death rate, especially a fall in the infant mortality rate.[22]

The war reduced to a trickle the small-scale immigration of Europeans to the white settler colonies of Southern Rhodesia and Kenya. After 1945 white immigration resumed, most rapidly to Rhodesia where the settler population grew from 82,380 in 1946 to 136,000 in 1951. White settlers to the Belgian Congo more than doubled to 69,000 in the years 1945–1951, and Salazar's New State encouraged Portuguese settlers to go to Angola and to Mozambique, where numbers nearly doubled in the 1940s, to 78,800 in Mozambique and 48,200 in Angola. The arrival in settler-dominated societies of yet more whites escaping from a war-ravaged Europe and in search of a better life added greatly to the racial tensions that developed in these territories in the postwar years.

During the war years there was an increased movement of Africans from rural areas to the towns. War industries and services needed workers, and African men were attracted by the prospect of wages needed to pay taxes, for bride-price payments, and to buy consumer goods that were unobtainable in rural areas. Both push and pull factors were at work, sometimes starkly as in Morocco, where rural famine in 1943 drove people to the towns in search of food. During the war years both black and white rural dwellers continued to move to the towns and cities. In the colonies paternalist authorities did not wish to see Africans becoming urbanized. They thought Africans were better suited to rural pursuits and that for them towns were unnatural places of instability and vice. The South African government for many decades had attempted to control African permanent settlement in towns by a system of passes and influx control, and to segregate people by race in towns. In wartime influx control broke down, segregation laws were ignored, and the pass system was relaxed, allowing Africans to work in urban industry and also to take their families with them.

The result was growing urbanization during the war, which continued more rapidly after 1945. In Africa in 1939 less than five percent of the population lived in sub-Saharan towns, most of which were small; by 1950 this had increased to nine percent. During the 1940s Brazzaville grew from 30,000 (1938) to 60,000 (1948); Lagos in 1939 was home to 75,000 people, in 1950 to 230,000; between 1939 and 1946 the population of Dar es Salaam doubled to over 50,000 people. In the ten years from 1936 to 1946 South African towns grew rapidly; the number of black people living in South African towns increased by 1.8 million, from 17.3 percent to 23.7 percent. As towns grew so also did house rents and land prices, and there were parallel increases in the costs of construction and building materials, especially cement. New arrivals set up home in unsanitary and overcrowded shanty towns. By 1942 there were 10,000 Africans in slums on the Cape Flats south east of Cape Town; six years later there were 150,000 squatters around the city. Despite official attempts at slum clearance in Johannesburg, new squatter camps grew.[23] Diseases such as malaria, and especially tuberculosis in South Africa, were endemic. There were problems feeding the growing towns and many people suffered from malnutrition.

Traditionally most urban migrants were young men. This pattern changed more rapidly in the war years as increasing numbers of women moved to towns. Married women joined their husbands. Many women escaped to towns from the traditional demands placed on them by male-dominated village life. The urban environment offered a new start, a degree of anonymity, and the opportunity to earn money in domestic service, in a factory, or by brewing beer. By 1946 women formed 36 percent of the African population of Johannesburg, and around 50 percent of the population of East London, Port Elizabeth, and Durban. Poverty was one reason, but not the sole one, why many women in towns became prostitutes. In towns with large numbers of men, and in places with substantial garrisons, such as Nairobi and North African cities from Cairo to Algiers, prostitution flourished.[24] Venereal disease was widespread among soldiers and civilians. Family life was threatened not only by disease, slum living, and marital infidelity, but also in the cities of South Africa by the authorities, who sought to uphold segregation and to send Africans back to the rural areas. The Fagan Commission in South Africa, reporting in 1948, argued that African urbanization should be accepted, but by then the National Party had taken power with a mandate to introduce apartheid. Slum conditions and urban poverty also helped to breed crime and juvenile delinquency.

Slums were also places of hope, a first step for many rural Africans into the cash economy. However, as people entered the money economy they became captive to the authorities, who fixed wages, and also to inflation, which eroded their buying power.[25] Shortages of most goods were met by spiraling prices of both imported consumer goods and locally produced basic foods.[26] Real incomes fell steeply and continued to decline through the war years and after. In Cairo industrial wages fell by 41 percent in the war years; in Duala the purchasing power of the official minimum wage was halved; and in Accra real income for skilled workers declined by one-third in the same period. But in addition to work and cash the town also offered a great deal that might be absent in the countryside. Modern labor required learning and observing industrial time. There were also new skills that migrants learned; they entered into new forms of association such as welfare and ethnic groups, acquired consumer goods, dressed differently, wore shoes, bought furniture, and had access to a new diet with tinned foods, wheaten bread, and commercially brewed beer. And there was communal and often improvised entertainment: dance, music, films, and football. Africans were in towns to stay.

INFLATION, AND URBAN AND RURAL PROTEST

Labor unions received a fillip during the war. Railwaymen, stevedores, miners, and clerks were not only skilled workers in essential services (more so in wartime) but their mode of work and places of employment enabled them to form unions to bargain with employers. African unions had a long history in South Africa; elsewhere in the continent they were small bodies, but by the mid- and late 1930s they were displaying a growing militancy as real wages were reduced during the Depression. The British tried to guide and tame labor unions by establishing labor departments in each colony from 1938 onward. But labor officers' efforts could do little to stem the effects of wartime shortages and price inflation, which led to union demands for higher wages and improved working conditions. A growing sense of class consciousness and resentment against wage differentials based on race also spurred unions to go on strike, although most unionists struck for improved industrial conditions rather than for political ends.

The strikes by gold miners in the Gold Coast and by miners on the Northern Rhodesian "Copperbelt" provide examples of continuities of action since the 1930s. Between 1938 and 1944 there were 17 stoppages by workers in the gold mines of the Gold Coast, most of which involved demands for higher wages. Declining real income was the major cause; miners' real wages fell in the 1930s and continued downward in the war years. On the "Copperbelt" the miners' strike of 1935 showed the potential of African labor power. In 1940 white labor unions went on strike for higher wages, and this encouraged African miners to do likewise, led mainly by "boss-boys" who resented the higher wages paid to Europeans for similar work. The week-long strike ended in violence and some increase in wages.[27] A principal cause of wartime strikes was inflation with rising prices and falling real pay, which severely hit workers in urban areas who were reliant upon cash incomes. This was the case with the two dock workers' strikes in 1943 and again in 1947, although the latter was directed against government rather than employers.[28] In most colonies the government was the largest employer of wage labor. Dock workers in Mombasa struck eight times between 1939 and 1945.[29] Industrial action was also taken by stevedores in Durban and at other ports in Africa.

The number of labor unions increased rapidly in wartime as workers sought to improve wages and working conditions. For example, in Nigeria unions increased from 5 to 70, although by 1945 less than 20 percent of workers were unionized. Unions also grew in number and militancy in South Africa, although government refused to give them official recognition and introduced emergency War Measures to prevent industrial action and to prosecute union organizers.[30] The African Mine Workers' Union, founded in 1941, rapidly increased in size and muscle. When 70,000 miners on the Rand struck over low wages and food shortages in August 1946, the police were used against them. Nine miners were killed, 1,200 injured, and over 1,000 arrested.[31] The strike failed largely, argues Alexander, "because it posed a fundamental threat to South Africa's political economy and the state was prepared to use massive force to ensure its defeat."[32]

The problems caused by wartime prices outstripping wages, coupled with the growth of organized labor, were demonstrated in a series of general strikes that occurred throughout colonial Africa in the years 1945–1948. The month-long and often violent action in Uganda in early 1945 was officially interpreted as a political conspiracy, but firmer evidence indicates that "economic grievances in towns and among laborers on plantations lay at the heart of the strikers' interests and largely explain the origin, the spread and settlement of the strike movement."[33] Cost of living grievances also lay at the heart of the Nigerian general strike, which brought out over 30,000 workers from the railways, public works department, and civil service from June to August 1945. A general strike also occurred in the Kenyan port of Mombasa in January 1947 involving 15,000 workers demanding higher wages. A similar strike in Dar es Salaam, begun by stevedores in September 1947, spread to railway workers and thus inland.[34] Railway workers were a wage-earning elite, many employed in workshops and operating in a good communications system, circumstances ideal for union organization and activity. Trapped by continuing inflation, railway workers brought the Gold Coast system to a halt in October 1947. A much longer strike paralyzed the railways of French West Africa from October 1947 to March 1948.[35]

Inflation and the effects of wartime demands and controls reached far into the African countryside, compounding existing grievances and leading to further unrest. War brought new grievances: demands for labor and tax, further alienation of land, the requisitioning of crops and cattle, and the removal of squatters.[36] In addition there were the ongoing and postwar measures to address local ecological crises caused by increasing population and the overstocking of land and soil degradation, the latter encouraged in East Africa by the demand for higher wartime production. Official policies for land betterment and soil conservation, long established in South Africa, but introduced in Kenya and Tanganyika late in the war and immediately after, were promoted by force where necessary. This involved culling of stock and new methods of farming such as ridge plowing and terracing. All were met by peasant resistance.[37] In South Africa land conservation and coercion was closely tied to official policies of racial segregation; in East Africa it arose out of local policy makers' misperceptions of African rural society, genuine concern over land degradation, and the promotion of the interests of white settler farmers as opposed to those of emerging African capitalists and their political allies.[38]

HEALTH, WELFARE, AND EDUCATION

African health, welfare, and nutritional levels suffered during wartime. Not that these were at a high level in the 1930s when limited budgets went mainly to public health programs. Men who entered the armed forces did well; most soldiers returned well-fed and healthy, while African civilians bore the marks of wartime shortages. With war the meager medical services provided by government and Christian missions were reduced, and many drugs became scarce. Even in relatively prosperous colonies such as the Gold Coast, medical services in the 1930s to the 1940s largely marked time, coping with inadequate revenue, reduced staff, and overcrowded hospitals with deteriorating sanitary conditions. The war increased African expectations of welfare provision of hospitals, housing, and schools. Postwar colonial budgets were constrained, and despite the new metropolitan-led investment that brought technical experts to Africa, health and welfare development could not keep pace with the demands of growing populations. In South Africa economic growth and social change stimulated ideas of social welfare reforms with old age pensions for all racial groups, and also of health centers. One historian has summed up some "notable examples of the impetus towards planning and social reform." They include:

> the creation in 1942 of the Social and Economic Planning Council, the establishment of a Council for Scientific and Industrial Research, the 1940 Van Eck (industrial and agricultural requirements), 1942 Smit (social conditions of urban Africans), 1944 Lansdown (wages and working conditions of black miners) and 1948 Fagan (black urban societies and "influx control") Commissions of Enquiry, and the investing of an ambitious scheme for a national health system by Henry Gluckman (1944 National Health Services Commission).[39]

Sadly for South Africa, the wartime changes were opposed by white minority voters who were anxious to safeguard their privileged position and who could only see the country's future in terms of racial division. The result was the reinforcing of racial segregation under the policies of apartheid after 1948. South Africa marched in the opposite direction to the rest of the continent and directed health and welfare benefits into its white population, partly paid for from cheap black labor.

The relatively few government and mission schools in colonial Africa in 1939 taught basic literacy and numeracy. As white teachers left for the war their places were taken by African teachers. There were few secondary schools and teachers' training colleges, but several were taken over for wartime military use in Nigeria, Kenya, and the Gold Coast, thus displacing students. Encouraging literacy was a major concern of missions, and the supply of reading materials probably increased as a result of the war, partly for propaganda purposes. Government propaganda also used the radio and films so that many Africans gained a wider global picture of the war. The African-owned press was also active but subject to censorship and government controls over the supply of newsprint. Further investment in education after 1945 increased literacy, although the number of educated Africans exceeded the available jobs.

AFTER 1945

Most authorities agree that the war was a watershed for Africa. War changed the global balance of power, and the European colonial powers had lost much of their former status. The world was dominated by two new superpowers, the United States and the Soviet Union, both avowedly anticolonial. Globally attitudes to empire were gradually changing and did so more rapidly with the loss of Asian empire after 1945. European politicians and officials in 1950 did not think that African colonies would be ready for many decades to follow India and Pakistan to independence, although those views were to change markedly over the next 10 years. At the Brazzaville conference in 1944, de Gaulle had no intention of leaving Africa; indeed, the French aim was to tie the colonies closer to the metropole, although the reforms of two years later that ended forced labor, introduced new ideas of citizenship, and elected territorial assemblies all helped pave the way to future independence. The British, French, and Belgians, their economies severely weakened and heavily dependent upon the United States, also saw great economic advantage in empire. Colonial products would earn dollars and, for Britain, help plug the sterling gap, and thus contribute toward the costs of reconstruction. After 1945 many of the state-directed wartime economic controls in Africa were maintained and extended, for example the abortive Groundnut Scheme in Tanganyika in 1947–1949 that was planned to help with Britain's oils and fats crisis. The great increase in postwar technical and welfare aid to the African colonies—the "second colonial occupation" as it has been called, was in part a response to African demands, but also to show in a Cold War world that European colonial rule was beneficial and not exploitative. However, a major purpose was to tie African resources closer to the metropole.

The war had been fought in part against German racialist ideas. Yet empire in Africa, with white superiors and black subjects, was intrinsically racist, and this pervaded most colonial economic, social, and political relationships. This slowly changed with ideas of African inclusion, although to a much lesser extent in the white settler colonies, and certainly not in South Africa where race became even more a defining idea. War stimulated white nationalisms in South Africa and the settler colonies where whites used state power enhanced by the war to curb their African economic and political rivals. In the British colonies notions of trusteeship were replaced by the idea of partnership; in French Africa the distinction of citizen and subject was abandoned and political assimilation was briefly adopted. Britain's system of indirect rule through traditional authorities was slowly replaced by elected local governments. West African political parties contested territorial elections. By contrast in Kenya and Southern Rhodesia, ideas of multiracialism were proposed but were at odds with the ideas of white settlers who were determined to retain political and economic dominance. Thus West African territories advanced to independence constitutionally, whereas conflict marked the slower transition to independence of the two tropical settler colonies and Algeria.

The experience of war and the resulting new world order helped to promote African nationalism. Most of the elite leaders of the prewar small urban political parties in sub-Saharan Africa failed to read the signs of change brought by war. Pressure for change came from Africans whose horizons had been widened during the war as they moved to burgeoning towns where their expectations were disappointed by inflation and acute shortages. Political groups, trade unions, welfare associations, and farmers' organizations all became more radical. Youth groups in parties such as the African National Congress, in South Africa, and in the small political parties of West Africa, demanded more vigorous action to bring about economic and political change. The new assertive postwar African nationalist parties, such as the Convention People's Party in the Gold Coast, and the Rassemblement Démocratique Africain in French West Africa, gained support from discontented urban workers and peasant producers who felt that they had been disadvantaged by the war. Electoral politics offered but did not guarantee a peaceful way of negotiating change. Transition was meant to be slow and guided by white paternalistic hands that would also dispense new development and welfare funds. Constitutional reform for the most part was peacefully implemented and where it was not offered, as in South Africa, the white settler colonies, and Algeria, violent confrontation with European domination was merely postponed. In Algeria the war ended with tragedy. Police fired on a demonstration waving a red flag during the peace celebrations at Sétif on May 8, 1945. Muslims turned on French *colons* and the authorities responded with repression and reprisals in which several thousand Muslims died. Two years later an insurrection broke out in Madagascar led by young radicals intent on breaking with France. Wartime exactions probably helped stir popular resistance, particularly in the east of the island. The rebellion was crushed with great severity and the death of at least 60,000 Malagasy.

The war brought important economic and political change to Africa and to the colonial powers. For many Africans the war enlarged their perceptions of the world and helped change their attitudes to European rule. The European colonial powers had change thrust on them by their economic vulnerability in a greatly altered postwar global world order. By the early 1950s empire was increasingly seen as a costly burden to be disposed of as far as possible, albeit in a politically wise and orderly way.[40] By 1960 most colonial territories were either independent or on their way to independence. Ironically for the European imperial powers, the war made empire more valuable but it also sowed the seeds for its demise.

TIMELINE

1935 October: Italian forces invade Abyssinia (modern Ethiopia)

1936 August: Abyssinia defeated but guerrilla resistance continues against Italian invaders

1939 September 3: Britain and France declare war on Germany in support of Poland

1940 March–April: White and black miners strike on Northern Rhodesia Copperbelt for higher pay
May 10: Germany invades Belgium, which is defeated by May 28. Belgian Congo now cut off from Belgium
June 4: British and some French troops encircled at Dunkirk evacuated across the Channel to Britain.
June 10: Italy enters the war against France and Britain. Start of war in North and East Africa
June 22: France signs armistice with Germany. Vichy puppet regime created
July 17: Britain passes the Colonial Development and Welfare Act to provide investment for the colonies; a further Act follows in 1945
July: Félix Éboué, governor of Chad, declares his support for de Gaulle and Free France. Most of the French Empire remains loyal to Vichy
September 23–25: British and Free French abortive attack on the Vichy-held West African port of Dakar
December: With United States assistance, the West African Reinforcement Route, via Takoradi, Kano, and Khartoum to the Middle East is fully operational by end of 1940, providing U.S. supplies to the British forces in North Africa

1941 January: British Commonwealth forces defeat Italians in Libya and prepare to advance into Tripolitania (western Libya)
February: German Afrika Korps under Rommel begin to reinforce the Italians in North Africa
March: United States introduces Lend-Lease, which supplies Britain to continue the war against Germany and Italy
April: Afrika Korps pushes British troops out of Libya and threatens Egypt
May: Italians defeated in Ethiopia and East Africa
June 22: Germany attacks the Soviet Union
August: Roosevelt and Churchill produce the Atlantic Charter
December 7: Japan attacks Pearl Harbor and the European colonies in east and southeast Asia; Germany and Italy declare war on the United States

1942 February 15: fall of British colony of Singapore to Japan
May: British, South African, and Free French forces seize Vichy-held Madagascar
October: defeat of Rommel's Afrika Korps at El Alamein in North Africa
November 8–11: Operation Torch: United States troops land in Morocco; Vichy forces surrender within a few days

November: German troops occupy Vichy France. French colonies in Africa now switch support to Free French

1943 May: Axis troops surrender in Tunisia

1944 January 30–February 8: Brazzaville conference in French Equatorial Africa proposes colonial reform
June 6 : D-Day. Allied forces invade France and begin the liberation of Europe
August 25: Paris liberated from German occupation

1945 May 7: Germany defeated and occupied by British, French, Soviet, and U.S. forces June–August: general strike in Nigeria

1946 January: French colonial reforms introduced; colonies become Overseas Territories and humiliating status of French subjects abolished
April: *Fonds pour l'Investissement pour le Développement Economique et Social* introduced to provide new investment in the French African colonies
August: 70,000 miners go on strike over low pay and food shortages on the South African Rand

1947 January: General strike in Mombasa September: General strike in Dar es Salaam spread inland by railway workers
October: Strike by railway workers in the Gold Coast. Strike by railway workers in French West Africa, which lasts until March 1948

1948 February 28: Gold Coast ex-servicemen's demonstration in Accra fired on by police and followed by riots
May 26: National Party wins white-only general election in South Africa and then begins to implement the policy of apartheid

GLOSSARY

Names, Places, and Organizations

Atlantic Charter. Propaganda declaration made by President Roosevelt and Prime Minister Churchill in August 1941, which included the right of people to choose their own government. Many African nationalists argued that this applied to Africa, but Churchill, an ardent imperialist, said it was concerned only with European countries under foreign occupation.

Axis. Originally the German-Italian alliance of 1939, but came to identify all those powers allied to Germany during the Second World War.

Depression. The economic slump of 1929 and the years of the 1930s when international trade declined and there was a loss of confidence in the international economy.

Félix Éboué (1884–1944). Black governor of Chad in 1940 who sided with the Free French; he became governor-general of French Equatorial Africa.

Free French. French forces that continued the war after mid-1940 when the French government agreed to an armistice with Germany.

General Charles de Gaulle (1890–1970). French army officer who led the Free French in the war against Germany after 1940. President of France 1958–1969.

Gezira. Area of the Sudan, irrigated by waters from the River Nile, that became a major cotton producing region.

Vichy regime. Following the armistice with Germany, northern and western France was occupied by German forces. A French puppet government established itself at the small town of Vichy in southeast France.

Terms

apartheid. Legally enforced system of racial segregation introduced into South Africa after 1948.

assimilation. Idea that people in the French overseas empire could, by adopting the French language and customs, become French citizens. Political assimilation was a policy to tie the French colonies closer to France.

bauxite. Mineral that contains alumina from which aluminum is manufactured.

cash crops. Crops grown for sale rather than for personal use as food or materials.

chibaro. Word widely used in central and southern Africa to describe slavery, and forced and contract labor.

customary labor. Labor provided by indigenous rulers under colonial rule to build roads and other public works. When wages were paid the chief or ruler could take a portion, so that the work was a form of tax on laborers.

indirect rule. System of "native administration" under colonial rule, in which indigenous chiefs were permitted to govern their own societies or polities, but were subject to control by European officials.

industrial time. Pace of work and output determined by the demands of a factory, machine, plantation, and so on.

influx control. Laws and measures restricting Africans from moving to urban areas and becoming permanent settlers there; mainly applied in South Africa.

migrant laborers. Workers, usually younger men from rural areas, who travel long distances to find paid work; in southern and central Africa mine and plantation workers were seasonal migrants employed on contract terms.

navétanes. Migratory workers in French West Africa who came from the Sudan to work in the peanut (groundnut) fields of Senegal.

prestation. Liability of people in French colonies for a certain number of days' labor each year, often to build and maintain roads.

primary products. Minerals, crops, and basic materials required by manufacturing industry.

real wages/income. The *actual* purchasing value of money wages relative to the price of goods.

self-sufficiency. Ability of peasant producers to provide by their own labor all that is required to maintain the lives of their families and communities.

squatters. People who settle or squat on land to which they have no legal claim. In many settler colonies peasants were encouraged by white farmers to become squatters because they provided a ready source of cheap labor.

sterling. British currency. The sterling area was formed from countries whose currencies were tied to the British pound and whose reserves were mainly kept in sterling rather than in gold or dollars.

subsistence agriculture. System of *self-sufficient* farming in which almost all produce is consumed by the farmer and the household.

terms of trade. Ratio between prices paid for imports and received for exports.

total war. Modern warfare in which all the human and physical resources of the state, at home and overseas, are mobilized to prosecute the war.

NOTES

1. Ludwig Deppe, *Mit Lettow-Vorbeck Durch Afrika* (Berlin: 1919), 393, quoted in Hew Strachan, *The First World War.* Vol. 1. *To Arms* (London: Oxford University Press, 2001), 571.

2. See the introductory comments in Joanna Lewis, *Empire State-Building: War and Welfare in Kenya 1925–52* (Oxford and Athens: James Currey and Ohio University Press, 2000), 5–6.

3. Michael Crowder, "The 1939–45 War in West Africa," in *History of West Africa,* vol. 2, ed. J. F. Ade Ajayi and Michael Crowder (London: Longman, 1974), 609–10.

4. Gardner Thompson, *Governing Uganda: British Colonial Rule and its Legacy* (Kampala: Fountain Publishers, 2003), 193.

5. Ibid., 181ff.

6. Ayodeji Olukojo, "The Cost of Living in Lagos 1914–45," in *Africa's Urban Past,* ed. David M. Anderson and Richard Rathbone (Oxford: James Currey, 2000), 134ff.

7. Both quoted by Roger Anstey, *King Leopold's Legacy: The Congo under Belgian Rule 1908–1960* (London: Oxford University Press, 1966), 145.

8. David Killingray and Richard Rathbone, "Introduction," 11; Michael Cowen and Nicholas Westcott, "British Imperial Economic Policy During the War," chap. 2; and Westcott, "The Impact of the War on Tanganyika, 1939–49," chap. 5, in *Africa and the Second World War,* eds. D. Killingray and R. Rathbone (Basingstoke: Macmillan, 1986).

9. For one west African colony see David Killingray, "Military and Labour Recruitment in the Gold Coast During the Second World War," *Journal of African History* 23, no. 1 (1982): 83–95.

10. John Iliffe, *A Modern History of Tanganyika* (Cambridge: Cambridge University Press, 1979), 370–71.

11. David Killingray, "Labour Mobilization in British Colonial Africa for the War Effort, 1939–46," in *Africa and the Second World War,* eds. Killingray and Rathbone, 69–70.

12. Crowder, "War in West Africa," 607.

13. David Johnson, *World War II and the Scramble for Labour in Colonial Zimbabwe, 1939–1948* (Harare: University of Zimbabwe Publications, 2000).

14. See Anthony Clayton and Donald C. Savage, *Government and Labour in Kenya 1895–1963* (London: Frank Cass, 1974), chap. 7.

15. J. Gus Liebenow, *Colonial Rule and Political Development in Tanzania: The Case of the Makonde* (Nairobi: East African Publishing House, 1971), 161.

16. Bill Freund, *Capital and Labour in the Nigerian Tin Mines* (London: Longman, 1981), 6.

17. Frederick Cooper, *Decolonization and African Society: The Labor Question in French and British Africa* (Cambridge: Cambridge University Press, 1996), 141ff.

18. David Anderson and David Throup, "Africans and Agricultural Production in Colonial Kenya: The Myth of the War as a Watershed," *Journal of African History* 26, no. 4 (1985): 327–45; John Lonsdale, "The Depression and the Second World War in the Transformation of Kenya," in *Africa and the Second World War*, eds. Killingray and Rathbone, 97–142.

19. Jonathan Crush, Alan Jeeves, and David Yudelman, *South Africa's Labor Empire: A History of Black Migrancy to the Gold Mines* (Boulder, CO: Westview Press, 1991), 41ff.

20. Quoted by Charles H. Feinstein, *An Economic History of South Africa: Conquest, Discrimination and Development* (Cambridge: Cambridge University Press, 2005), 152.

21. John Iliffe, *Africans: The History of a Continent* (Cambridge: Cambridge University Press, Cambridge, 1995), 240.

22. Ibid.

23. A. W. Stadler, "Birds in the Cornfield: Squatter Movements in Johannesburg, 1944–1947," *Journal of Southern African Studies* 6, no. 1 (1979): 93–127.

24. Luise White, *The Comforts of Home: Prostitution in Colonial Nairobi* (Chicago: Chicago University Press, 1990).

25. Iliffe, *Modern History of Tanganyika,* 353–54.

26. Olukoju, "Cost of Living in Lagos," 135–38.

27. Jeff Crisp, *The Story of an African Working Class. Ghanaian Miners' Struggles, 1870–1980* (London: Zed Books, 1984), 77; Charles Perrings, *Black Mineworkers in Central Africa* (London: Heinemann, 1979), 217ff.

28. Iliffe, *History of Modern Tanganyika,* 401–4.

29. Frederick Cooper, *On the African Waterfront: Urban Disorder and the Transformation of Work in Colonial Mombasa* (New Haven, CT: Yale University Press, 1987), chap. 3.

30. Baruch Hirson, *Yours for the Union: Class and Community Struggles in South Africa* (London: Zed Books, 1990), chap. 9; Edward Roux, *Time Longer Than Rope: The Black Man's Struggle for Freedom in South Africa* (Madison: University of Wisconsin Press, 1964), 331ff.; Peter Alexander, *Workers, War and the Origins of Apartheid: Labour and Politics in South Africa 1939–48* (Oxford: James Currey, 2000).

31. Alexander, *Workers, War and Apartheid,* 102–6; Hirson, *Yours for the Union,* ch. 14. Roux, *Time Longer than Rope,* 337ff.

32. Alexander, *Workers, War and Apartheid,* 104.

33. Thompson, *Governing Uganda,* chap. 12.

34. Iliffe, *Modern History of Tanganyika,* 402–4.

35. Cooper, *Decolonization and African Society,* chaps. 4 and 6.

36. On the removal of squatters in Kenya see Tabitha Kanogo, *Squatters and the Roots of Mau Mau* (London: James Currey, 1987), chap. 4.

37. Colin Bundy, "Land and Liberation: Popular Rural Protest and National Liberation," in *The Politics of Race, Class and Nationalism in Twentieth Century South Africa*, eds. Shula Marks and Stanley Trapido (London: Longman, 1987), 254–83; Tom Lodge, *Black Politics in South Africa Since 1945* (London: Longman, 1983), chap. 11; Hirson, *Yours for the Union*, chap. 10.

38. David Throup, *Economic and Social Origins of Mau Mau* (London: James Currey, 1987), chaps. 1, 4–7.

39. Alan Jeeves, "South Africa in the 1940s: Post-War Reconstruction and the Onset of Apartheid," introduction to a special issue of the *South African Historical Journal* 50 (2004): 3.

40. See Cooper, *Decolonization and African Society*, chap. 10, "The Burden of Declining Empire."

SELECT BIBLIOGRAPHY

Alexander, Peter. *Workers, War and the Origins of Apartheid: Labour and Politics in South Africa 1939–1948*. Oxford: James Currey, 2000.

Shows that widespread inter-racial worker unity existed in South Africa during the war years; deals with state relations with organized labor, strikes, and political activity.

Le Congo Belge durant la Seconde Guerre Mondiale: Recueil d'Etudes. Bijdragen over Belgisch-Congo Tijdens de Tweede Wereldoorlog. Brussels: Académie Royale des Sciences D'Outre-Mer, 1983.

Wide-ranging essays on the Belgian Congo in wartime, including two in English on strategic minerals and Belgian-French relations.

Cooper, Frederick. *Decolonization and African Society: The Labor Question in French and British Africa*. Cambridge: Cambridge University Press, 1996.

A provocative comparative study of French and British colonial policy on the recruitment and organization of labor; Parts I and II deal with the war years.

Crowder, Michael. "The 1939–45 War and West Africa." In *History of West Africa*. Vol. 2. Edited by J.F.I. Ajayi and Crowder, 596–621. London: Longman, 1974.

Provides a useful introduction to all aspects of the war in the whole of West Africa.

Daly, M. W. *Imperial Sudan: The Anglo-Egyptian Condominium 1934–1956*. Cambridge: Cambridge University Press, 1991.

Chapter 6 examines the Sudan at war and the responses of nationalists; chapter 7 is on economic and social developments.

Davenport, T.R.H., and Christopher Saunders. *South Africa: A Modern History*. Basingstoke: Macmillan, 2004.

Chapter 13 is a comprehensive introduction to the effects of the war on South African politics, economy, and society.

Iliffe, John. *A Modern History of Tanganyika*. Cambridge: Cambridge University Press, 1979.

A brilliant study that has a great many perceptive and wise things to say on the war years.

Jackson, Ashley. *Botswana 1939–1945: An African Country at War*. Oxford: Clarendon Press, 1999.

A full and detailed study of the economic, social, and cultural impact of the war on the peoples of a southern African British protectorate.

———. *War and Empire in Mauritius and the Indian Ocean.* Basingstoke: Palgrave, 2001.

Looks at the Indian Ocean island colony of Mauritius, its strategic position, the war at sea, defense, recruitment of soldiers and labor, mutiny, and the effects of war on the home front.

Johnson, David. *World War II and the Scramble for Labour in Colonial Zimbabwe, 1939–1948.* Harare: University of Zimbabwe Publications, 2000.

Describes the wartime competition for wage and forced labor, and African responses, in the white settler colony of Southern Rhodesia.

Journal of African History 26, 4 (1985): special issue on "World War II and Africa."

Contains essays on Moroccan nationalism, the neutral powers, agriculture in Kenya, propaganda, French African soldiers in France, and strategic minerals.

Killingray, David, and Richard Rathbone, eds. *Africa and the Second World War.* Basingstoke: Macmillan, 1986.

The "Introduction" provides a good outline of the topic. Other essays deal with imperial economic policy, labor mobilization, military recruitment, Kenya, Tanganyika, Botswana, Cameroon, Sierra Leone, and Algeria.

Lawler, Nancy. *Soldiers, Airmen, Spies and Whisperers: The Gold Coast in World War II.* Athens: Ohio University Press, 2002.

Account of the Gold Coast at war that deals with the United States' supply line via Takoradi, the covert world of spying and smuggling, and the relations of the British with the Vichy regime and the Free French.

Lewis, Joanna. *Empire State-Building: War and Welfare in Kenya 1925–52.* Oxford and Athens: James Currey and Ohio University Press, 2000.

A study of the impact of war and British administrative attempts to engineer social change by development and welfare among the Kikuyu of Kenya.

Mazrui, Ali, ed. *UNESCO General History of Africa.* Vol. 8. *Africa Since 1935.* Berkeley and London: University of California Press and Heinemann, 1993.

Section 1 contains three useful chapters that focus on north and tropical Africa, 1935–1945; there is relatively little on the impact of the war on southern Africa.

Roux, Edward. *Time Longer Than Rope: The Black Man's Struggle for Freedom in South Africa.* Madison: University of Wisconsin Press, 1964.

Classic study of African struggle against segregation by a veteran left-wing opponent of apartheid. Chapters 24–28 deal with the war years.

Shuckburgh, John. "Colonial Civil History of the War." 4 vols. Typescript, 1949.

British official civil history of the impact of the war on the Empire that was never published; copies are in The National Archives, Kew, the library of the Institute of Commonwealth Studies, University of London, and the Royal Commonwealth Society Collection, University Library, Cambridge.

Thomas, Martin. *The French Empire at War 1940–45.* Manchester and New York: Manchester University Press and St. Martin's Press, 1998.

Best single volume on the twists and turns of French imperial policy under Vichy and Free France, with some useful sections on the impact on civilians.

Thompson, Gardiner. *Governing Uganda: British Colonial Rule and its Legacy.* Kampala: Fountain Publishers, 2003.
Focuses on the business of governing in the war years; points up British administrative weaknesses and the role of Africans in shaping the colony.

UNESCO. *The General History of Africa, Studies and Documents.* Vol. 10. *World War, 1939–1945.* Paris: UNESCO, 1985.
A collection of papers, some dealing with civilians in wartime, contributed to the *UNESCO General History of Africa,* edited by Mazrui (see above).

SIX

Angolan Civilians in Wartime, 1961–2002

Inge Brinkman

In 1961 war broke out in Angola. With some intervals, the country continued to be plagued by violence for the next 40 years. Violence was initially directed against the Portuguese colonial regime in Angola in an anticolonial war, but already before Angola's Independence Day on November 11, 1975 the various nationalist parties were fighting each other over the leadership of the country. The socialist MPLA, led initially by Agostinho Neto and later by Eduardo dos Santos, gained control over the capital, Luanda. This did not stop the war because the rival groups, FNLA and UNITA, did not recognize the newly installed government. While the FNLA was defeated soon after independence, the war between the MPLA and UNITA only ended in 2002 with the death in combat of the long-time UNITA leader, Jonas Savimbi.

Most analyses of the war have focused on high politics, international structures, and macroeconomic systems. There is some reason for this: many international factors were indeed crucial to an understanding of the war. Yet this focus was also born out of necessity. In many regions of Angola research and prolonged fieldwork became next to impossible because of the war and researchers in the arts and humanities hardly wrote about Angola at all. The consequence of the prevailing macro-factor focus is that the actual people of Angola hardly appear in what scant and unreliable literature there is about the country. In any case, most statistics with sociological data are mere guesses since they are not based on empirical investigation. We know very little from available studies about ordinary Angolans' perspectives on the war, nor the ways in which they have interpreted the history of their country. Yet an understanding is essential because it is ordinary people who both wage the war and suffer from it, and in wartime people's actions can have mortal as well as lifesaving consequences. The most adequate answer to the question: "Why does Angola matter?" is, as the British-based Angolan student Teresa Santana pointed out, "because there are people there."[1]

Angola

OVERVIEW OF EVENTS

In order to describe the experiences of Angolan civilians during the war, we need some understanding of the background to the conflict. After the Second World War, many countries in Africa and Asia became independent. In most African countries this happened in the early 1960s. Portugal, however, hung on to its colonies and in Guinea Bissau, Mozambique, and Angola nationalist groups started fighting for independence. In the case of Angola, 1961 proved a turning point. The Portuguese army suppressed a rebellion in the Malanje district east of Luanda, the capital. In February large-scale violence occurred in Luanda itself, and in March war broke out in the north of the country. Although the various nationalist groups did not succeed in taking control over the country, they continued to carry out guerrilla actions. The FNLA fought from its bases in the Congo, later called Zaire. Most of its support came from the Baptist Bakongo people of northern Angola. The Mbundu people of Methodist and Catholic background from Luanda and surrounding areas were prominent in the MPLA. The MPLA, operating from the neighboring independent countries of Zambia and Congo-Brazzaville, was especially active in the Cabinda enclave and in eastern Angola. As of 1966 the smaller UNITA (the core of its leadership consisting of Congregationalist Southerners) occupied an area near the Lungue-Bungo River in eastern Angola. UNITA did not pose a challenge to the colonial regime, and ample proof exists that UNITA cooperated for a number of years with the Portuguese to oust the rival MPLA. All attempts to unite the Angolan liberation movements failed, and from the start relations between them were marked by suspicion, tension, and violence.

The Portuguese spent enormous sums prosecuting the counterinsurgency war in their Angolan colony but never quite managed to wipe out the nationalist groups. Since the Portuguese saw the Roman Catholic Church as the state church, and since the Protestant churches in Angola were associated with the nationalist movements, the Portuguese singled them out for repression and persecution, and some saw their entire infrastructure destroyed. The Portuguese government attempted to keep the public at home from knowing how many soldiers were dying in the war in the colonies, but over the years resentment grew among the Portuguese population against military conscription. Especially in Mozambique, where the nationalist group Frelimo gained a number of successes against the colonial army, Portuguese losses were relatively high.

On April 25, 1974, war-worn soldiers and commanders of the Portuguese Armed Forces Movement staged a coup in Lisbon and overthrew Dr. Caetano's dictatorial regime. Not long after, a cease-fire was negotiated in Angola. Within a year, most Portuguese settlers had packed their belongings and left the country. However, Independence Day in 1975 was not a festive occasion. Although an accord had been signed between Portugal and the three nationalist groups, fighting over the spoils had already begun. The FNLA invaded northern Angola with the support of Zairian troops, while UNITA, with the help of South African forces, occupied southern and central Angola and advanced to within less than 300 km of Luanda. The MPLA clung on to the capital and formed a government, later recognized by most foreign states. During the Cold War era Angola, with its rich natural resources, was perceived to be of strategic significance, and an understanding of the war in the country requires some grasp of the context of international politics. The South Africans backed up UNITA as the United States' surrogate, and the Cubans intervened for the Russians to support the leftist MPLA. As the MPLA government supported SWAPO, the liberation movement struggling to establish South West Africa (now Namibia) as an independent state free of South African control, regional politics and the wider international context became inextricably linked.

Initially, it seemed that the FNLA would prove the strongest of the three rival nationalist groups, but a series of military blunders turned the tide, and in 1976 the FNLA was defeated. The MPLA and UNITA continued to fight each other for another 26 years with fluctuating success and several short pauses. The international community made only a few, half-hearted attempts to bring the war to an end. After the fall of the Berlin Wall in 1989, Cold War strategic interests in Angola diminished, but by then the struggle for control of Angolan oil and diamonds had become such a dominant concern that Tony Hodges has labeled the conflict "a resource war." As he puts it, "Angola presents a terrible, shocking paradox. One of the best resource endowments in Africa has been associated not with development and relative prosperity, but with years of conflict, economic decline and human misery on a massive scale."[2]

The Angolan pattern was replicated in Mozambique, where the South Africans supported Renamo against Frelimo. During the war of independence against Portugal Frelimo had been the only major nationalist group, but soon after independence Renamo started a bush war that destabilized the entire country. As in Angola, the regional political context intersected with Cold War strategies. The leftist Frelimo government of Mozambique hosted ZANU and the ANC, movements that aimed at freeing Rhodesia (now Zimbabwe) and South Africa, respectively, from white minority rule. Rhodesian forces not only invaded Mozambique several times to strike at ZANU, but also helped to create the rebel organization, Renamo. When in 1980 white rule came to an end in Rhodesia, South Africa continued to subsidize Renamo in order to weaken the liberation forces based in Mozambique. Because Mozambique was much closer to South Africa than Angola, South African military intervention was more sustained there than in Angola. All the same, South African forces were heavily engaged in Angola, and South African intervention was its most intensive in the first half of the 1980s. In 1988 the MPLA managed to hold on to the strategically important town of Cuito Cuanavale in southeastern Angola and force the South African and UNITA troops to withdraw. This event marked the beginning of a series of negotiations, culminating in 1991 with the signing of the Bicesse Accords. The battle of Cuito Cuanavale, as it came to be called, coincided with the changing international environment that accompanied the end of the Cold War era. This factor proved decisive in Mozambique where a lasting peace was negotiated because the contending parties were prepared to work with a United Nations' peacekeeping mission. This mission was brought to a successful end in January 1995.

In Angola, by contrast, the process worked less well. In terms of the Bicesse Accord, the first Angolan general election was held in September 1992. The MPLA government party of dos Santos received 46 percent of the vote, while Jonas Savimbi's UNITA garnered 40 percent. The United Nations declared the elections "generally free and fair," but Savimbi refused to accept the results and renewed the war. The next year saw the worst fighting ever in Angola. The central Angolan town of Kuito, for example, was besieged for nine months. At least 30,000 people were killed and the town almost completely destroyed. Although several other attempts were made to end the fighting, violence continued for years. Only in 1996 and 1997 were there periods of relative quiet, although both the warring parties exploited the respite to rebuild their forces. In 1998 full-blown war broke out once more, financed by the exploitation of Angola's diamond and oil riches. Following the MPLA's successful 1998 offensive, serious disagreements in UNITA led to the fracturing of the movement into three groups. In 2002 UNITA's long-time and charismatic leader, Jonas Savimbi, was killed in combat. UNITA was effectively finished, and some months later UNITA and MPLA leaders signed a cease-fire agreement. Since then, the country has known relative peace. People who had been displaced as a consequence of the war have returned in massive numbers to their areas of origin. It is planned to hold general elections late in 2006.

AN "AREA OF SILENCE": THE ANTICOLONIAL WAR

With the end of the war, interest in Angola has slowly burgeoned in developmental, scholarly, and journalistic circles, as well as in the business and tourist sectors. However, the marginality of Angola in scholarly, journalistic, and general informative literature dates back to before the war. During the colonial period Angola could already be classified as an "area of silence."[3] Many foreign scholars were discouraged from carrying out research by the linguistic requirements and the sharp censorship exercised by Salazar's right-wing regime in Portugal. Nor did the political and economic situation in Portugal favor any open debate about Portuguese colonial policies, particularly since censorship rules made it risky to criticize the regime openly. Research was permitted only so long as it dealt with subjects deemed innocuous, and access to recent literature from other countries was limited. The colonial regime had created some transport routes in Angola to make trade attractive for Portuguese immigrants, but many regions within the vast colony remained next to inaccessible. Thus, as late as the 1940s, it took two months to cover the distance between Luiana and Cangamba in southeastern Angola, a stretch of some 600 km.[4] Not surprisingly, very few researchers, writers, or journalists made their way to such regions.

After the war began in 1961 matters did not improve. For military purposes, the road network was rapidly improved, but access to the colony for foreigners was tightly restricted and closely monitored when permitted. Teams of journalists were allowed into the country only for propaganda purposes. They traveled under strict Portuguese supervision and were not allowed to speak with local people on an independent basis. Other information on the Angolan situation was provided by outside observers who entered the country by illegally crossing the border with one or another of the nationalist insurgent groups. They were under constant surveillance by the nationalists and usually depended on interpreters from the party that hosted them. In short, news about what happened during these first phases of the war was based on selective information provided by the various warring parties eager to present their version of events. We have been taught that "truth is the first casualty of war," and what went on in Angola may be an extreme case in point. Many authors have pointed out, for example, that the figures provided in war communiqués by the nationalist groupings might well be nothing but falsifications citing impossible claims and unrealistic figures.[5] The same holds for the Portuguese who attempted to centralize their war reports through a single channel. Frequently, however, the various departments of the Portuguese army and government contradicted each other. In order to give a more positive impression of the army's performance, death rates of Portuguese soldiers were systematically lowered in the statistics, while the figures concerning the population under colonial control were deliberately inflated.

In general, we learn very little through any of these various official channels about civilian life during the anticolonial war in Angola. The war reports we have focused on the results of the fighting and mostly presented figures and statistics. More usefully, the journalists visiting Angola during this phase of the conflict paid some attention to the context in which the Angolan population in the war zones survived and made reference to general conditions and to the living standards of the civilians. Their focus, however, remained on the Portuguese army or the nationalist groups. To them, civilians were only important insofar as their "popular support" might, or might not, have strengthened the position of one or the other of the warring parties. The views and evaluations of civilians themselves were hardly ever considered in the literature of the anticolonial war.

"THE FORGOTTEN TRAGEDY": THE POSTCOLONIAL WAR

Despite international political and economic interests, the conflict in Angola has been called a "forgotten tragedy."[6] Few people elsewhere really cared about what was happening in this "lost corner of the world," and neither the international media nor the world's leading politicians did much to alter that. Little attention is paid in the existing literature to Angolan civilians who experienced the interminable postcolonial war. If there is any reference to civilians at all, they usually figure as statistics. Thus, Angola is known for its high infant mortality (at least one in four children dies before its fifth birthday); it has the world's highest rate of amputees because of landmine accidents; only 42 per cent of the population is literate; its low life expectancy ranges from an estimated 36 to 42 years. Statistics such as these might be most revealing, yet they tell us little about how Angolans cope with the realities of their situation. The few journalists who stayed in Angola during the postcolonial war usually described their encounters with Angolan people, but as a rule did not offer an interpretation of the civilians' perspective on the war.

"FROM WHENCE COMETH MY HELP?": FOREIGN AID

Given the critical situation in Angola, one would expect a long record of foreign aid. Yet, until the end of the 1980s Angola received the lowest amount of assistance per capita in the whole of southern Africa. The first international donor conference on Angola was held only in 1985 when it called for food assistance to an estimated 0.5 million war-affected people. Only three years later, during a second donor conference, the estimated figure of war-affected Angolans had risen to 1.5 million. Yet the international response remained "half-hearted and uninterested."[7] As Inge Tvedten has pointed out, several factors played a role in this neglect. Angola did not belong to the Western bloc during the Cold War, so the western world was reluctant to provide any assistance to the country. Furthermore, the MPLA government failed to present the case of the Angolan people to donor institutes. In any case, circumstances often did not allow for donor intervention. It was impossible in many areas to set up an aid program because the security of personnel could not be guaranteed. The 1990s saw a sharp increase in foreign aid, but most of it took the form of emergency relief since coordination of the various programmes was difficult given Angola's weak administrative structure. For example, in 1994 the World Food Programme distributed 80 percent of Angola's food aid by air and maintained only a limited presence on the ground among its marginalized people.[8]

Over the years the most active agents aiding the Angolan population have been the Christian churches. Thus the Catholic nongovernmental organization (NGO), Caritas, and a host of Protestant NGOs have distributed enormous amounts of medicine, clothes, and blankets in Angola, mainly to internally displaced civilians. Apart from general relief programs, the Christian NGOs have also developed programs for diseases, such as sleeping sickness, and for specific groups of people, such as landmine victims, orphans, and the displaced. In general, the churches in Angola have assumed responsibilities far beyond the narrowly religious. Many Angolans, in their extreme poverty and hunger, have depended on the churches for survival. Most churches organize basic education, adult literacy classes, and courses of various kinds, as well as leisure activities that form the core of social life for many Angolans. A combination of hope and despair has led many to find support and solace in new churches, often in the Pentecostal sphere. The churches also played a crucial role in the Angolan peace process and continue as the most important pressure group in the Angolan political landscape.[9]

Now that the war has ended, programs have been set up to assist returning refugees and internally displaced persons (IDPs). Yet, even now, donor assistance is not adequately forthcoming. The current Angolan government refuses to live up to the criteria for good governance and transparency, so its calls for an international donor conference have yet to be heeded. Besides, the working circumstances for development organizations remain extremely difficult. And since little reliable information is available, it is hard even to know the people's needs and wishes. Consequently, it has proved difficult to make the shift from emergency relief to postwar reconstruction.

GATHERING PEOPLE

The few references made by commentators to civilian life during the war usually focus on "the situation" in which Angolans lived. Descriptions are given of living conditions, usually in terms of housing and sanitation, and the general humanitarian situation. Angolan civilians, on the other hand, pay a lot more attention to "mobility." In their accounts of the war they do not present a static description of a situation, but describe the circumstances and conditions of movement, as well as the restrictions in this realm. This importance given to mobility is related to many other spheres of life: food security, agriculture, social contacts, marriage, and so on. Angolan civilians choose to describe their lives not so much through a situation in any given location, as through the conditions related to movement and containment.[10]

These issues not only played a role in civilian accounts; the fighting parties were equally concerned about mobility. When the war started, the guerrillas were in no position to seize their main strategic goals in Angola from the Portuguese. The guerrillas of the UPA (as of 1962 called the FNLA) and later of the MPLA and UNITA only operated in the north and the east of the country and never managed to reach the western parts of Angola, a region vital both economically and politically. Port cities such as Luanda and Benguela did not fall within the guerrilla action radius either. Nor was it a wise strategic option to attack the Benguela railway, which went through the Moxico District bordering on Zambia, because that land-locked country, which supported the Angolan guerrilla movements against the Portuguese, heavily depended on imports by rail. Considerations such as these meant that standard strategic goals never came to play an important role in the guerrilla war, and conquering territory for itself was not given priority by the fighting parties. Instead, the struggle became, as Basil Davidson put it, "a war for people."[11]

Both the Portuguese and the Angolan nationalist groups tried to assemble as many people as possible under their control. They sought to do this mainly by abducting people from their homes and taking them either to concentrated settlements built by the colonial regime, or to the bush, where the guerrillas were in charge. Before the war, most people in the fighting zones had lived as villagers, practicing small-scale agriculture. After the war started, the villages in the war areas were destroyed and farming on an independent basis became impossible. An opposition was created between people in "town," that is, under Portuguese control, and people in "the bush," those under guerrilla control. Contact between these two groups became increasingly difficult. The Portuguese regarded everybody in the bush as "bandits," while the guerrillas saw those who went to stay in the Portuguese settlements as "traitors." As a result of these new categories of identity, people from "town" and people from "the bush" forged a new kind of connection through violence.

The Portuguese-concentrated settlements were surrounded by barbed wire and guard-towers, and a watch was set in the evening to prevent people from leaving the town. The guerrillas, whether UNITA, MPLA, or FNLA, took stern measures against all persons who tried to flee from the bush in an attempt to place themselves under the protection of the colonial authorities. In the east, the MPLA also tried to prevent people from fleeing into exile in Zambia. It was different in northern Angola, where soon after the war started in 1961 civilians were encouraged to join the UPA in exile in Congo-Léopoldville (later Zaïre).

REFUGEES AND IDPS

It is impossible to give precise statistics regarding the people who fled Angola during the war. In June 1961 over 100,000 people fled to Congo/Zaire, and by 1972 their number had reached 500,000. Some 20,000 to 40,000 people fled from southeast Angola to neighboring Zambia and South-West Africa (later Namibia).[12] People who fled Angola often found themselves under guerrilla control. In Congo/Zaire, for example, a popular saying went: "Whether you like it or not, it is FNLA here." People without a membership card of the FNLA-dominated government in exile (GRAE) did not have access to food rations distributed by the Baptist missionaries, and any initiative taken by non-FNLA Angolan refugees was likely to encounter serious opposition. For most refugees the wish to return to Angola remained very strong throughout their stay in exile. Even youngsters who had been born after their parents had fled to Congo/Zaire (and who therefore often had an education in French rather than Portuguese), still felt strong ties with their parents' country of origin. After a cease-fire had been agreed upon in 1974, many refugees in Zaire returned to Angola.

For a brief spell in 1974 it was hoped that decolonization would bring peace to Angola. People returned from exile, while those who had lived in "town" or in "the bush" also returned to the countryside. Mobility was not contained as it had been during the war between the Portuguese and the nationalist groups, and people attempted to resume village life. It did not take long, however, before the fighting began again. The dream of the returnees was shattered, and once more they had to flee and live in exile. As the war waxed and waned, the number of Angolan refugees abroad fluctuated. In most years it totaled about 500,000 people living mostly in Zaire, Zambia, and South-West Africa/Namibia. Some of these people stayed in refugee camps, while others took up residence among the host population. The latter group in particular depended heavily on their ties with the host community. Access to arable land often proved difficult, as the example of Namibia showed:

> That is why we say that we will go back if there is peace in our country. It is such a nice place. We can go and plant crops, eat good food and possess our own farms. Here we are suffering from hunger. In the bush the owner of the land plants, but when we want to start farming, we are told: "No, this is our place. Don't plant here!"[13]

In the host countries land shortages, poverty, and hunger already posed problems, problems that the refugee groups were believed to exacerbate. It was also feared that Angolans crossing the border would bring war upon their hosts. In Zaire as well as in Namibia negative labels were used to refer to the Angolan refugees.

Not all people who were displaced went abroad. In fact, the majority of those who fled their homes remained within Angola's borders, becoming even more difficult for international donors to reach than the international refugees. According to the United Nations, in 2001 4.1 million people were displaced within Angola.[14] Many of these IDPs made their way to Luanda, and the capital's population soared to 2.8 million, well over 20 percent of the country's inhabitants.

During the pause in the fighting in the early 1990s, many people once again attempted to return to the countryside; but once again their hopes were dashed when fighting flared up soon after the 1992 elections. Many of the returnees were trapped in the towns besieged by UNITA forces and large numbers died. It is therefore all the more astonishing that, now that the war is over, so many people have once again dared to return to Angola's countryside. In some cases the return has not been voluntary. It is known that people have been forcibly put on transports to Angola from the refugee camps in neighboring countries. Yet, in the majority of cases, people are eager to make a new start in their place of origin, despite the difficult circumstances they know they will confront:

> UNHCR [United Nations High Commission for Refugees] explained that there would be no food, houses or schools, and they also told us there would be a lot of mines. But even if we don't have houses, we don't have food, we don't have schools, we wanted to return to our country because it's our country.[15]

Throughout its history, the MPLA government has focused more on Angola's towns than on the countryside, assuming that everybody who lived out of town was a UNITA supporter. There are still today widespread complaints that government support for the returnees is entirely lacking, and that the people are left to fend for themselves. International organizations, such as Human Rights Watch, are calling upon the government to assist the returnees.

TOWN AND BUSH

The MPLA's lack of support for the countryside can be explained by Angola's complex postcolonial history. After the Portuguese had left, Angola's nationalist groups attempted to take their place and move into the towns they had abandoned. Shortly after the fighting started, the MPLA succeeded in securing control over most of the urban centers. UNITA mainly operated from the bush. As they had during the colonial war phase, the parties attempted to increase the numbers under their control by abducting people from their enemies' territory. The MPLA took civilians from UNITA areas and brought them into town, while the UNITA soldiers caught townspeople and led them into the bush.

In most cases, abducted individuals did not want to have anything to do with the fighting but were forced to take part. Party allegiance hardly played a role since most people merely wanted the war to stop. Residence determined which party one belonged to: everybody staying in town was considered MPLA, while all people in the bush were considered UNITA. In order to make life more difficult for their opponents, both parties also aimed at starving the opposing population. It has been estimated that in 1990 only 25 percent of the land once cultivated in 1975 was still in use as farmland.[16] Whenever any food was available it was likely to be stolen or claimed by the equally hungry troops of the rival MPLA or UNITA. The MPLA saw all agricultural plots in the bush as war targets, because the crops from these fields were used to feed UNITA troops. Often the fields were destroyed or the population in the bush forced to flee before they could be harvested. MPLA troops burned down their huts, tortured and killed them if they were caught, and drove away their livestock. Bereft of all their possessions, many UNITA civilians were reduced for considerable stretches of time to living on what they could gather from the bush. They tried to avoid the government soldiers by using camouflage tactics, moving at night only, and following paths they hoped were not known by the soldiers.

Townspeople in MPLA areas also regularly went hungry. UNITA attempted to bring all agricultural activities in MPLA areas to a standstill and to prevent all food distribution to the people in the regional towns. As there was not enough agricultural space within the towns' limits to produce food, townspeople were forced to create small farming plots on the outskirts. This was very risky indeed, for UNITA regarded all territory outside the towns as their domain. When civilians left town to look for food, firewood, and other necessities, they trod paths to the fields on which UNITA soldiers had planted mines and were in constant danger of being abducted or killed. As a woman trying to survive in Menongue in southern Angola explained:

> There were no vehicles, nothing moved. It were terrible things we saw. We went outside of town and stole food from the UNITA, as our food was finished. But if you go there, you may be killed. It was like signing: "If I must die, then I will die." Some would come back, some would be killed. That was the problem we had in Menongue.[17]

Townspeople were reportedly often tortured before being killed. UNITA soldiers would brutally toy with them, ordering them to "shit" salt, soap, sugar, or any other product that was only available in town. When the civilians pleaded they could not do this, they would be killed with a blunt axe or with their own agricultural tools. Through such actions UNITA made it clear that they would not allow townspeople to venture outside the urban centers and would regard any person from town as an MPLA supporter. Of course, this policy could prove counterproductive. As one woman expressed it: "They kill them, because they are MPLA. They are the cause that MPLA has so many people."[18] In the 1970s and 1980s people who remained within the towns were relatively safe from UNITA. However, during the fighting in the 1990s, when UNITA besieged many regional towns in central and southern Angola, a great many civilians were trapped inside and died in the shelling.

Once in the bush or in town, it was difficult for people to switch allegiance. If an area was conquered by the other side the civilians living there would then automatically belong to the victorious group. Either that, or they were taken along with the fleeing troops or killed by the incoming army. People could not move themselves and attempts to flee were punished severely. No one was allowed to leave the bush and move to town. Merely mentioning the word "town" or complaining about life in the bush could result in severe punishment.

FORCED SOLDIERING

Some people who were abducted by the fighting parties continued to be considered as civilians. They merely switched sides and went from town to bush or from bush to town. Although this often constituted a drastic change in their lives, and although the measures to contain these people were often rigorous, they nevertheless felt they were better off than people who were forced to fight. Strictly speaking, forced soldiering (being made part of a fighting force against one's will) falls outside the scope of an analysis of civilian life during wartime. Even so, it is important for several reasons to pay attention to the impact of forced soldiering. First, the fear of being taken captive and forced to fight is frequently mentioned as a reason for fleeing the country. One young man explained that, since he had turned 16 years old, the fear that the MPLA would call him up for military service became too strong and he fled abroad. Some boys he knew had already been called up when as young as 14.[19] Another reason for considering forced soldiering is that at the moment of their abduction people are still civilians, and they are often held captive for a considerable time before being sent to the battlefront. The pattern described for controlling civilians—forcibly increasing one's own numbers while violently attempting to reduce those controlled by the enemy—is also followed in the case of forced soldiering. In the Angolan highlands, people were abducted from their homes and marched to UNITA strongholds in southeast Angola to receive training and fight. One young man wrote an account of his experiences:

> My life has a lot of history ... In 1985 I was captured and forcibly moved to Cuando-Cubango [a province in southeast Angola] to train and serve in the troops ... To make this journey we needed 5 months. Our column was bombed by the government so as to prevent us from arriving. Some died on the way. Some of hunger, of exhaustion and yet others died because of the bombardments. It was in September that we left between Usoke and Kasonge. These municipalities are half-way between Benguela and Huambo, and we arrived in Jamba [UNITA's long-time capital] in January the following year.[20]

Often the people abducted by UNITA were very young. Children of 10 years old have been known to have been taken away to carry out tasks for the troops, and some were only 11 when they were sent to the war front. While it was mostly boys who were trained to fight, girls and women were also abducted in large numbers by UNITA. They were required to farm and cook for the troops, to carry out administrative and logistical tasks, to act as animators who energized UNITA meetings, to carry supplies, and/or to become the sex slaves of UNITA superiors. Women who refused to "marry" UNITA men were in some instances threatened with death. Reportedly, a group of women from southeast Angola who were captured by UNITA initially refused to accept their new "husbands." But one evening they overheard the soldiers saying that at the break of day they would torture to death all those women who would not cooperate. The women thereupon decided to give in and explained to the UNITA women's leader: "We all have accepted the men, otherwise they will kill us in the morning."[21]

When UNITA soldiers were demobilized after 2002, they were normally entitled to receive identity papers, travel documents, five months' wages, and US$100 travel money. The process did not necessarily go smoothly: some soldiers were not given these items; transport from the demobilization camps was often not available; and ex-combatants sometimes received a chilly reception in their home area. All the same, by the end of 2004 some 300,000 soldiers had been demobilized and had returned to their areas of origin. In contrast, the benefits meted out to adult soldiers were extended neither to child soldiers nor women and girls who had taken no part in the actual fighting. As Cristina M. explained in 2003 to a Human Rights Watch delegation at a demobilization camp:

> We don't have food or money. We stayed in the bush for too long. Now, nobody recognizes us anymore. In the bush, I had a man to protect me. He died and now I don't have anyone. We were taken to the bush and it was bad. Now we are taken to the camps and things are worse.[22]

Several initiatives have been taken to assist women and children who were forced to support UNITA troops during the war, but these measures remain by and large inadequate.

LANDMINES AND FEAR

Throughout the war, the fighting parties engaged in planting antipersonnel mines. This means that people were—and still are—not confined in their movements only by the physical presence of armed groups. UNITA planted mines primarily to prevent people from leaving the towns, while MPLA government troops also laid mines extensively. Both sides were using landmines as a strategy to prevent people from building up a well-functioning society. Normal tasks, such as drawing water, going to the fields, herding cattle, and gathering firewood were all rendered life-endangering activities. As Julia Kissanga explained in 1992 to a Human Rights Watch delegation:

> Here in Massango we are surrounded by mines: all the fields around our town are mined. A friend of mine died by a mine a while ago. I spend much more time

getting water from the river, as the old path is too dangerous ... These mines make this no safe place for children. They cannot play safely and our fields are far away. They are safer in the cities.[23]

Landmines created fear. In order to assess the consequences, it is not enough to mention the number of mines and the number of casualties. During the war, the fear of the mines often made agriculture impossible and resulted in shortages of water and firewood, which in turn led to hunger and disease. The social fabric of communities was destroyed as people no longer dared visit each other. Victims of mine incidents often could not be treated, for lack of medical services, and those who could no longer work were forced to rely on the support of their families. The fear of mines thus seriously impaired people's mobility. Even if people knew the whereabouts of mine-fields, hunger often drove them to take risks. Augusto Jocinto, for example, was looking for some manioc when a mine exploded taking away his entire left leg. When asked by journalist Karl Maier whether he had not known that there were mines around, he answered: "Yes, but I had no choice. I have a wife and baby son and we had no food. We knew there were mines, but our stomachs were empty."[24] Angola has the highest number of amputees in the world.

In Angola there are now more landmines than people. In this sense, the war is far from over. De-mining is a costly and time-consuming affair. Many areas in Angola remain inaccessible because of the mines and accidents frequently occur after heavy rains have washed mines onto roads or into areas that were mine-free before. As the fighting parties did not always trouble to map their mine-fields, in many areas it is not even clear where the mines are located. Since the end of the war incidents with anti-personnel mines have actually risen since many people returning to the countryside are not familiar with the landmine situation.

BULLETS DON'T CHOOSE

The human costs of the war have been dramatic. It has been estimated that the war left a million people dead, the majority of them noncombatants. As we have seen, half a million people fled abroad, while over four million were forced to move within the country. Nearly all Angolans have been directly affected by the war and have lost family members. Numerous people have come to form part of one or more war-affected group: widows and orphans; disrupted families; amputees from landmine incidents; former soldiers with psychological problems; children with war traumas; women who were raped by the soldiers.

Because of the relative youth of Angola's population the majority of people have known nothing but a state of war. Angolans refer to the war as an agent, a thing that acts and moves on its own. People may state: "We were at home in our village, when the war found us;" or when asked who killed their relative, they may reply with "the war." Survival was regarded as a matter of chance or of God's will. "Bullets don't choose," Angolans often say. This is not to suggest that they accept violence as a normal state of affairs. The civilians interviewed were outraged by the violence and suffering inflicted on the non-fighting population.

The war has discontinued many cultural and religious practices. At the same time, especially in the war zones, people have attempted to find new ways to address the critical situation. Religious rituals and ceremonies have been especially important in this. People gave their children amulets to wear to prevent them being forced into the army during round-ups; soldiers tried strictly to follow all the procedures to make magic potions effective against bullets; and malign spirits were exorcised, especially in newly established independent churches. Many people, civilians and soldiers alike, suffer from war traumas and traditional healers are often called in to treat them. In many Angolan societies, the funeral is an extremely important event and mourning rituals were—and often still are—regarded as essential for the peace of the deceased's soul. During the war, there was often no opportunity to carry out the appropriate rituals for the dead. Many people went missing and, in some cases, people had no option but to leave the bodies of their relatives unburied when they fled. Apart from the personal traumas this might involve, many people fear that restless spirits will further disrupt social life. In an attempt to address this threat, symbolic mourning rituals and funerals were held.[25]

In nearly every family people are known to have died or to have gone missing during the war. The search for the missing was often extremely difficult or even impossible since the warring parties prevented any contact between groups of civilians. It is important in all Angolan cultures to know one's relatives well, and it is customary to pay regular visits to members of the extended family. However, during the war these contacts often could not be established. People who were in town could not visit those in the bush or vice versa. Some families had relatives on both sides, but they were forced to live isolated from each other. The many stories told about incestuous marriages between people who did not realize that they were relatives indicate that this was perceived as a real problem.

A DIFFICULT LIFE

Although Angola is rich in diamonds, oil, and other natural resources, only a tiny upper class has been able to profit from the revenues from these products. These few live in extraordinary luxury, which is in stark contrast to the circumstances of average Angolans. For most of the Angolan population life during the war was extremely hard. Many people cite the politics of containment that was imposed by the armies as the most important reason for their problems. All knew that a sound economy depended on exchange. In time of peace farmers would normally sell their surplus production on the urban markets, enabling them to buy soap, clothes, salt, and other items only available in town. People would only start living in town when they had a job with a paid salary so they could buy the food offered on the market and not have to depend on the limited space within town to grow their own. During the war, however, normal agricultural production ceased almost entirely at a time when town and the bush were isolated from each other by the warring factions. This led to a food crisis and many civilians, both in town and in the bush, went hungry. Nor was this an incidental consequence of the war: the fighting forces used hunger as a deliberate strategy. People were forced to leave their villages and, since the security situation in the countryside was poor, to flee to Angola's towns in large numbers. As it was very risky to leave town, the urban population—especially in Luanda—increased rapidly. This in turn led to severe problems with housing, sanitation, and sewerage. Diseases, such as measles and tuberculosis, quickly spread in the overcrowded Luandan slums. Death rates, especially from malaria, were (and are) high among children and adults alike. The many difficulties that stemmed from overpopulation in the towns were not generally duplicated in the areas controlled by UNITA. There, living mainly in the bush, civilians faced hardships related to food, income, health, and education. In many areas, there was literally nothing available. People had to use bark for clothing, and plants as substitutes for soap and salt. Large areas had no schools, no hospitals, no doctors, no electricity, no shops, no soap, no salt, no cars, no clothes, nothing.

Medical services in Angola are still few and far between. In the bush areas controlled by UNITA, there were hardly any medical or educational facilities. Near Jamba, the long-time UNITA capital in southeast Angola, some schools and hospitals had been built, but most of these were destroyed when MPLA troops took over in 1999. By the end of the 1980s, only 46 out of Angola's 146 districts had a doctor. In 2003 there was only one doctor for every 13,000 people. Only 35 percent of the personnel working in the medical sector had even adequate training.[26] The few existing private hospitals and doctors are far too expensive for the average Angolan.

Educational facilities are equally lacking. Under Portuguese rule the schooling system did not allow for a high degree of literacy among the population. After independence the situation only became worse. Between 1980 and 1992, for example, half of the 20,000 available classrooms were destroyed. Another 1,500 classrooms fell into ruin between 1992 and 1996. Only slightly over half the children of school-going age actually attend class.[27] Schooling still poses enormous problems. People who return to their home areas often find that there is no possibility whatsoever for sending their children to school. Returnees who gained their education in French or English while in exile in the Congo, Zambia, or Namibia find they are excluded from government service and other jobs.

During the war, women headed many households since so many men had been killed or were away fighting in one or another of the armies. Those women most in danger of destitution were those with children but without any relatives in the place where they were living. As there were so few formal economic activities available in Angola, most women tried to eke out a living through petty trade in the informal markets. The same held for most of the non-fighting male population. They worked as traders and artisans in the informal sector, often recycling waste material. In the diamond-rich Lunda-speaking provinces of northern Angola, many tried their luck as diamond diggers (*garimpeiros*), an insecure and often dangerous undertaking. The largest profits of the diamond trade did not go to the local populations, but to the UNITA and MPLA leadership. Government officials and UNITA troops have been known to extort bribes from the diamond diggers. In general, corruption remains widespread in Angola. The word *gasosa* (soda) is used as a euphemism to denote such practices. Policemen, soldiers, government officials, but also private company mangers, may ask for "a soda" (bribe) in return for a service provided. Especially in Luanda the combination of poverty and the ready availability of firearms rendered criminality—theft, armed violence, rape—rife. The large number of demobilized soldiers without any prospects for making a living is calculated to make this problem even worse.

FINAL REMARKS

This chapter has shown that words such as "marginality" and "suffering" call for an explanation and a qualification. In many instances they function as self-evident descriptions of the situation and no further elaboration is required. Yet such words have a history and require an interpretation. Instead of taking them for granted, we may learn by assessing what people mean when they use such words.

In Angola, the fighting parties lost all credit in the eyes of the population. During the earlier war for independence, the behavior of the nationalist groups was frequently criticized, but most people agreed on the evils of colonialism and the need to live in a free Angola. Yet, after independence, Angolans did not become free. All too often they had no other option but to flee, or were forcibly moved from one place to the other. The anger and resentment shows, for example, in the widespread saying: "MPLA steals, UNITA kills." For many Angolans peace means that they can remain in, or move freely to, locations of their own choice. "I want my country to be free and people to move wherever they want," one young man stated.[28] Neither mobility nor containment are deplored or praised as such; it is the freedom of choice that matters. People want to be able to visit their relatives, create farms where they wish, engage in trading activities, and look for water and firewood without fear. Farming is regarded as primordial. As Ambrosio Pimentel explained to the Dutch visitor Bob van der Winden:

My brother and I would like to go back to Piri, to reactivate the coffee plantation, but also to plant bananas and the like. But this is only possible in peacetime. With a little bit of finance we could produce a lot of coffee, the farm is several hundred acres. Even if we produce a few hundred bags we could start exporting and build up the farm, little by little. I wouldn't even mind if UNITA governs the province there, as long as they leave us in peace. We are farmers, we just want to be able to work, we're sure to stick to the law.[29]

The focus on marginality and mobility in this chapter has excluded many other subjects. More attention could have paid to the role of oil and diamonds; to the media in Angola; to the human rights situation and the condition of war-related special groups such as widows, orphans, and handicapped people; to civil organizations that have called for peace. Nevertheless, the focus on mobility was intended to bring new links and insights to light. When asked about their experiences, many Angolan civilians mention the issue of mobility as the most crucial factor in their existence and the one most disrupted by the 40 years of war. Indeed, in this regard, Angola may be an extreme case in point. Nearly the entire population was affected in terms of mobility. Most people were moved, had to flee, or were forced to stay put in a particular place. Yet, in their emphasis on mobility, the Angolan people may not have stood alone. David Birmingham describes very similar conditions for civilians during the second phase of the war in Mozambique:

Village women going to the stream for water were still liable to be captured by terrorists and taken away to serve as porters and to provide sexual services for the soldiers. Young men were still press-ganged into the opposition's regiments of irregulars. Barn-yards were still raided nightly for food. Refugees streamed across the borders into Malawi and Zimbabwe where they received a bleak welcome from host populations themselves suffering from drought, food shortage and underemployment.[30]

In other words, the significance of mobility has been stressed in other war contexts.[31] The perspective taken here may thus open up possibilities for comparison and offer research directions outside the Angolan context.

ABBREVIATIONS

Frelimo Frente da Libertação de Moçambique (Front for the Liberation of Mozambique)

FNLA Frente Nacional de Libertação de Angola (National Front for the Liberation of Angola)

GRAE Govêrno Revolucionário de Angola no Exílio (Revolutionary Government of Angola in Exile)

GURN	Govêrno de Unidade e Reconciliação Nacional (Government of Unity and National Reconciliation)
IDP	Internally Displaced Person
MPLA	Movimento Popular de Libertação de Angola (Popular Movement for the Liberation of Angola)
NGO	Nongovernmental Organization
PIDE	Polícia Internacional e de Defesa do Estado (International and State Defence Police)
PDA	Partido Democrático de Angola (Democratic Party of Angola)
Renamo	Resistência Nacional Moçambicana (Mozambican National Resistance)
UNHCR	United Nations High Commission for Refugees
UNITA	União Nacional para a Independência Total de Angola (National Union for the Total Independence of Angola)
UPA	União das Populações de Angola (Union of the Peoples of Angola)
UPNA	União das Populações do Norte de Angola (Union of the Peoples of Northern Angola)

TIMELINE

1956	MPLA founded
1957	UPNA founded
1959	UPNA becomes UPA
1961	February 4: Riots in Luanda March 15: War starts in northern Angola
1962	UPA (together with the PDA) becomes FNLA
1966	UNITA founded
1974	April 25: Bloodless coup in Portugal overthrows the dictatorship
1975	January 15: Alvor Agreements signed by Portugal and the nationalist parties of Angola setting a date for Angolan independence. Soon after, however, fighting starts between the three nationalist groups November 11: Independence Day of Angola August–December: South African troops, together with UNITA and FNLA, open an offensive and occupy large parts of southern Angola. In northern Angola, Zairian troops support the FNLA
1976	January–March: Aided by Cuban troops, the MPLA regains the initiative and reoccupies much terrain. The FNLA is defeated and most South African troops withdraw
1977	May: Attempted coup, led by Nito Alves, against the central government. A period of repression follows
1979	September: Agostinho Neto dies of cancer. He is succeeded as president of Angola by José Eduardo dos Santos

1984	February: South Africa and the MPLA sign the Lusaka Accords, stipulating the withdrawal of South African troops. Fighting between UNITA and MPLA continues
1987	The MPLA opens a major offensive but does not succeed in its mission
1988	March: battle of Cuito Cuanavale, South Africa and UNITA are forced to withdraw. Peace negotiations start
1989	June 22: Cease-fire agreement is reached by Savimbi and dos Santos in Gbadolite (Zaire)
1991	May 1: Bicesse Accords signed in Portugal aimed at disarmament, unification of the two MPLA and UNITA armies, and general elections
1992	September: General elections held in Angola. Although declared "generally free and fair" by the United Nations, UNITA does not accept the results and takes up arms again October–November: Fierce fighting between UNITA and the MPLA in Luanda. Nearly the entire UNITA leadership in Luanda is killed. Over the next years Angola experiences heavy fighting and enormous destruction
1993	January 22: "Bloody Friday." People from Zaire and northern Angola are attacked in Luanda
1994	November 15: Protocol of Lusaka signed. Aimed at reinforcing the Bicesse Accords and ending the war, but violence continues
1995–1997	Protocol of Lusaka partly implemented; period of relative peace in Angola
1997	April: GURN is formed, including ministers from UNITA as well as MPLA backgrounds. Jonas Savimbi, however, is not present
1998	Fighting resumes
1999	April: UNITA launches an offensive to occupy the entire country October: The MPLA opens a major offensive and expels UNITA from some of its traditional strongholds. UNITA continues to occupy the diamond-rich eastern provinces
2002	February 22: Death of Savimbi in combat April: Peace accords signed between the MPLA and UNITA. Although fighting in the northern Cabinda enclave continues to this day, in the rest of the country the peace has held up. UNITA forces have been largely demobilized, and UNITA leaders have taken up ministerial posts in the government. Many IDPs and refugees have returned to their former homes

GLOSSARY

Neto, Agostinho (September 17, 1922–September 10, 1979). After studying medicine in Lisbon (Portugal), Neto returned to Angola, where he was imprisoned on suspicion of political activism. He escaped from prison and became the first President of the MPLA. After Angolan independence he became the first president of Angola.

Roberto, Holden (January 12, 1923–). Became the president of UPA, later FNLA. When the military and political influence of the FNLA diminished, he resided for some time in Paris, but later returned to Angola.

Savimbi, Jonas Malheiros (August 3, 1934–February 22, 2002). Joined the UPA in 1961 but resigned in 1964 to form his own party, UNITA. Until his death in combat in 2002, Savimbi remained a rebel leader, fighting against the MPLA.

Santos, Eduardo dos (August 28, 1942–). An active member of MPLA, dos Santos became a prominent politician after independence. After Neto's death in 1979 he became Angola's president and was reelected in 1992.

NOTES

1. Keith Hart and Joanna Lewis, eds., *Why Angola Matters: Report of a Conference Held at Pembroke College, Cambridge, March 21–22, 1994* (Cambridge and London: African Studies Centre in association with James Currey, 1995), 114.

2. Tony Hodges, *Angola from Afro-Stalinism to Petro-Diamond Capitalism* (Lysaker, Oxford and Bloomington: Fridtjof Nansen Institute and International African Institute, in association with James Currey and Indiana University Press, 2001), 1.

3. Basil Davidson, *The Search for Africa: A History in the Making* (London: James Currey, 1994), 179.

4. *Mensageiro de São Bento* 10, no. 3 (1941): 88, and 10, no. 6 (1941): 181.

5. As René Pélissier wrote: "An MPLA communiqué of June 18, 1966, announced that one of its units had destroyed two jeeps and five *carrinhas* (light 'pick-up' vehicles), killed seventy-five Portuguese soldiers and captured important supplies, with no loss to itself. This is the kind of exaggerated claim that amuses the experts." Douglas L. Wheeler and René Pélissier, *Angola* (New York, Washington and London: Praeger, 1971), 269.

6. See Margaret Anstee, "Angola. The Forgotten Tragedy: A Test Case for UN Peace-Keeping," *International Relations* 9, no. 6 (1993): 495–511.

7. Nicole Ball and Kathleen F. Campbell, *Complex Crisis and Complex Peace: Humanitarian Coordination in Angola* (New York: OCHA, 1998), http://www.reliefweb.int/ocha_ol/pub/angola/index.html.

8. Inge Tvedten, *Angola: Struggle for Peace and Reconstruction* (Boulder, CO and Oxford: Westview Press, 1997), 93–100.

9. Inge Brinkman, "Angola," in *Worldmark Encyclopedia of Religious Practices,* Vol. 2, ed. Thomas Riggs (Detroit: Thomson Gale Group, 2006), 22–29.

10. Interviews held by the author in 1996, 1997, and 1999 with refugees from southeast Angola living in Namibia, and then in 2002 and 2003 with people from the north of Angola, alert us to their overriding concern with the ability and freedom to move.

11. Basil Davidson, *In the Eye of the Storm: Angola's People* (London: Longman, 1972), 27.

12. Wheeler and Pélissier, *Angola,* 187; René Pélissier, *Le naufrage des caravelles: Études sur le fin de l'Empire portugais 1961–1975* (Orgeval: Éditions Pélissier, 1979), 53.

13. A woman born in Mavinga, Kaisosi, Namibia, interviewed on August 26, 1996.

14. OCHA Reliefweb, "The Humanitarian Situation in Angola Special Report," 7 March 2002, http://www.reliefweb.int/rw/rwb.nsf/AllDocsByUNID/e7f00a821ed5274b85256b750060248.

15. Interview with João N., cited in Human Rights Watch, *Coming Home: Return and Reintegration in Angola* 17, no. 2 (A) (2005): 11.

16. Tvedten, *Angola,* 111.

17. Young woman born in Luengue, Kaisosi, Namibia, interviewed on August 1, 1996.

18. Woman aged 28 years, interviewed in Kehemu, Namibia, on September 2, 1996.

19. Pedro R., interviewed on June 19, 2003.

20. Author's name withheld on request. Manuscript given to Inge Brinkman at Kehemu, Namibia, on July 2, 1999.

21. Woman aged 28 years, interviewed in Kehemu, Namibia, on September 2, 1996.

22. Human Rights Watch, *Struggling through Peace: Return and Resettlement in Angola* 15, no. 16 (A) (2003): 25.

23. Human Rights Watch, *Landmines in Angola* (New York, Washington and London: Human Rights Watch, 1993), 10.

24. Karl Maier, *Angola: Promises and Lies* (Rivonia: William Waterman Publications, 1996), 144.

25. Ibid., 13.

26. Tvedten, *Angola,* 130; Zoe Eisenstein, "Angola Health System in Tatters after War," *Reuters Alertnet* 26 (February 2004).

27. Tvedten, *Angola,* 110; UNICEF, http://www.unicef.org/angola/education.html.

28. Young man, interviewed at Kaisosi, Namibia, on August 26, 1996.

29. Bob van der Winden, ed., *A Family of the Musseque: Survival and Development in Postwar Angola* (London: One World Action, in association with World View Publishing, 1996), 147.

30. David Birmingham, *Frontier Nationalism in Angola and Mozambique* (London: James Currey and Africa World Press, 1992), 72.

31. See, for example, Liisa H. Malkki, *Purity and Exile: Violence, Memory and National Cosmology among Hutu Refugees in Tanzania* (Chicago: University of Chicago Press, 1995).

SELECT BIBLIOGRAPHY

Accord 15 (2004): Guus Meijer, ed., *Da paz military à justiça social ? O processo de paz angolano.*

Portuguese-language issue of this review on the peace process in Angola. Contains references to other titles in Portuguese.

Anstee, Margaret. "Angola: The Forgotten Tragedy: A Test Case for UN Peace-Keeping," *International Relations* 9, no. 6 (1993): 495–511.

Article on the role of the United Nations in Angola, written by the former head of the UN peace-keeping commission in Angola.

———. *Orphan of the Cold War: The Inside Story of the Angolan Peace Process, 1992–1993.* New York and London: Macmillan, 1996.

The collapse of the Angolan peace process after the elections of 1992.

Ball, Nicole, and Kathleen F. Campbell. *Complex Crisis and Complex Peace: Humanitarian Coordination in Angola.* New York: OCHA, 1998. http://www.reliefweb.int/ocha_ol/pub/angola/index.html.

Report assessing the role of the United Nations Office for the Coordination of Humanitarian Affairs (OCHA).

Birmingham, David. *Frontline Nationalism in Angola and Mozambique.* London: James Currey and Africa World Press, 1992.

Sound analysis of nationalism in Angola and Mozambique.

Bridgland, Fred. *Jonas Savimbi: A Key to Africa.* New York: Paragon House Publishers, 1986.

Partial biography of Jonas Savimbi.

Brinkman, Inge. *"A War for People": Civilians, Mobility, and Legitimacy in South-East Angola during MPLA's War for Independence.* Cologne: Rüdiger Köppe Verlag, forthcoming 2005.

Interpretation of civilian perspectives on the war for independence on the MPLA's eastern front, based on accounts from Angolan immigrants in Namibia.

Brittain, Victoria. *Death of Dignity: Angola's Civil War.* London: Pluto Press, 1998.

Partial account based on conversations with Angolan civilians and MPLA leaders during visits to Angola, explaining foreign intervention.

Davidson, Basil. *In the Eye of the Storm: Angola's People.* London: Longman, 1972.

Report of a journalist's visit to the MPLA's eastern front during the fight for Angola's independence.

Guimarães, Fernando Andresen. *The Origins of the Angolan Civil War: Foreign Intervention and Domestic Political Conflict.* London: Macmillan, 1998.

The author brings together external and internal factors of the war. Written by a Portuguese diplomat, but not much is said about the role of Portugal.

Hare, Paul. *Angola's Last Best Chance for Peace: An Insider's Account of the Peace Process.* Washington, DC: United States Institute of Peace Process, 1998.

An account by the U.S. special representative of the peace negotiations during the Lusaka Protocol.

Hart, Keith, and Joanna Lewis, eds. *Why Angola Matters: Report of a Conference Held at Pembroke College, Cambridge, March 21–22, 1994.* Cambridge and London: African Studies Centre in association with James Currey, 1995.

Conference report with papers of varying quality.

Heywood, Linda. *Contested Power in Angola: 1840s to the Present.* Rochester, NY: University of Rochester Press, 2000.

Monograph offering an interpretation of the history of Ovimbundu ethnicity.

Hodges, Tony. *Angola from Afro-Stalinism to Petro-Diamond Capitalism.* Lysaker, Oxford, and Bloomington, IN: Fridtjof Nansen Institute and International African Institute, in association with James Currey and Indiana University Press, 2001.

Offers an explanation of the war that focuses on crude economic interests.

Human Rights Watch, *Landmines in Angola.* (New York, Washington, DC, and London: Human Rights watch, 1993.

Report on anti-person mines in Angola.

———. *Struggling through Peace. Return and Resettlement in Angola* 15, 16(A) (2003).

———. *Coming Home. Return and Reintegration in Angola* 17, 2(A) (2005).

Two reports on Angola after the peace agreement between UNITA and MPLA, indicating the lack of government support for the returnees. See also other reports on the HRW Web site: http://hrw.org/doc/?t=africa&c=angola.

Kapuscinski, Ryszard. *Another Day of Life.* New York: Penguin, 1988 (1st edition 1976).

English translation of the account by a Polish journalist who spent three months in Luanda in the summer of 1975.

Maier, Karl. *Angola: Promises and Lies.* Rivonia: William Waterman Publications, 1996.

Journalist's personal account of his encounters with Angolan people.

Malkki, Liisa H. *Purity and Exile: Violence, Memory, and National Cosmology among Hutu Refugees in Tanzania.* Chicago: University of Chicago Press, 1995.

Monograph on the way in which Hutu refugees from Burundi remember the violence in their home country.

Marcum, John A. *The Angolan Revolution*. Vol. 1. *The Anatomy of an Explosion (1950-1962);* and Vol. 2. *Exile Politics and Guerrilla Warfare (1962–1976).* Cambridge and London: MIT Press, 1969 and 1978.

Extensive discussion of good quality on the war against Portuguese colonialism and its aftermath.

Médecins sans frontiers. Various reports and articles are available that describe the situation of Angola's people: http://www.msf.org/.

Mendes, Pedro Rosa. *Bay of Tigers: An Odyssey through War-Torn Angola.* London: Granta Books, 2003.

Fascinating novel written by a Portuguese journalist about his journey through Angola.

Messiant, Christine. "Angola, les voies de l'ethnisation et de la décomposition." *Lusotopie* 1, no. 2 (1994) : 155–210; and 2, no. 2 (1995): 181–212.

Extensive, well-argued analysis of the political processes in Angola in the first half of the 1990s.

Pélissier, René. *Le naufrage des caravelles: Études sur la fin de l'Empire portugais (1961–1975).* Orgeval: Éditions Pélissier, 1979.

Analysis of demographic data on the former Portuguese colonies.

Sogge, David. *Sustainable Peace: Angola's Recovery.* Harare: Southern African Research and Documentation Centre, 1992.

Over-optimistic title, but detailed account of Angola in the 1990s.

Somerville, Keith. *Angola: Politics, Economics and Society.* London: Frances Pinter, 1986.

Exhaustive and critical analysis of the MPLA's policies.

Tvedten, Inge. *Angola: Struggle for Peace and Reconstruction.* Boulder, CO and Oxford: Westview Press, 1997.

Accessible introduction to Angola's geography, history, and politics with an emphasis on the postcolonial period.

Wheeler, Douglas L., and René Pélissier. *Angola.* New York, Washington, DC, and London: Praeger Publishers, 1971.

Dated, but in most respects a sound survey of Angola's history and the events during the first years of the anticolonial war.

Winden, Bob van der, ed. *A Family of the Musseque: Survival and Development in Postwar Angola.* London: One World Action in association with World View Publishing, 1996.

Describes the impact of the war through an account of the life of a civilian family in Luanda in the 1995.

Wolfers Michael, and Jane Bergerol. *Angola in the Front Line.* London: Zed Books, 1983.

Describes the conflict from a leftist perspective.

SEVEN

Liberia and Sierra Leone: Civil Wars, 1989–2004

Lansana Gberie

In the late nineteenth century, the West Indian-born Pan Africanist Edward Blyden wrote of Liberia and Sierra Leone as twins whose destiny, for good or ill, will remain inextricably linked.[1] In their modern forms the two countries were founded—Sierra Leone first in 1787 and then Liberia in 1822—as places for resettlement of freed slaves from North America. While Sierra Leone was formally colonized by the British in 1808, Liberia maintained its independence but was effectively a client state of the United States throughout the nineteenth and much of the twentieth centuries. The presence of these Europeanized ex-slaves, who maintained a charmed, elite status in situations where they were clear minorities among the indigenous population, set the two countries apart from their neighbors. Blyden, who lived and worked in both countries, advocated a more intimate relationship between the two and wanted greater integration of all their people. This never happened; and events at the close of the twentieth century revealed, in bold relief, the explosive nature of the inherent deformities and incoherence that grew mainly from the foundational principles and structures of the two states.

Throughout the 1990s and almost half a decade into the twenty-first century, warfare in the two countries, beginning as an armed incursion by dissidents into Liberia on Christmas Eve in 1989, became a tragedy of major humanitarian, political, and historical proportions. A force of about 150 fighters had advanced over the border from Côte d'Ivoire and attacked the Liberian border town of Butuo, in Nimba County. The incursions quickly morphed into a devastating civil war in Liberia—Africa's oldest republic—which subsequently spawned no less than five armed factions and tens of thousands of combatants and almost completely destroyed the country's already very limited infrastructure. In less than eight years, the war killed an estimated 200,000 people, the vast majority civilians, in a country with a population of just over two million—a proportion higher than that of Poles killed during the Second World War.[2] In less than two years after the Liberian war started, and following intervention by a West African mediation force called ECOMOG (Economic Community of West African States Military Observation Group), groups of armed men operating in rebel-held Liberia invaded Sierra Leone (March 1991). Like the Liberian war, the Sierra Leonean variety, spearheaded by a previously unknown group called the Revolutionary United Front (RUF), was characterized by banditry and horrific brutality, wreaked primarily on civilians. Between 1991 and 1999, the war took over 75,000 lives, caused half a million Sierra Leoneans to become refugees, and displaced more than half of the country's 4.5 million people.[3]

LIBERIA: FROM TYRANNY TO ANARCHY

At the time of the incursions into Liberia, there was a pervasive sense of gloomy anticipation among Liberians, who had been traumatized by violent upheavals and regime brutality for a long time. The 1980s was a decade of unprecedented political violence in Liberia, beginning with the bloody coup that overthrew President William Tolbert (whose father was American-born) and the long-reigning True Whig Party (TWP). The TWP, which had governed Liberia since the mid-nineteenth century, was simply an alliance of wealthy Americo-Liberians or Congos, as the ex-slaves were called. Mildly brutal and clannish, successive TWP governments were deeply resented by the vast majority of Liberians, the indigenes, who were shut out, by accident of birth, from the charmed circle. The coup leaders, led by Master Sergeant Samuel Doe, an illiterate NCO from the indigenous Krahn ethnic group, shot Tolbert to death in his bedroom. They had already gunned down 27 members of Tolbert's presidential guard. Later, after a show trial, they executed a dozen government officials on the beach.[4] The coup effectively ended the corrupt Americo-Liberian oligarchy.

What it did not do, however, was signal any genuine popular or indigenous mobilization. Amos Sawyer, Liberia's best-known intellectual and politician, has reflected that although the coup-makers "were all from indigenous ethnic backgrounds, only a few had lived and grown up in their communal areas and been socialized in indigenous values." As a result,

> many of them partook of the subculture of the urban unemployed and reflected the characteristic suspicion and opportunism typical of that group.... Two impulses seemed to dominate [the coup-makers'] behaviour. The first was the impulse to

Liberia

rule in a brutal and tyrannical manner with the liberal use of the machine gun; the second was to satisfy personal greed by raids not only on the public treasury but, with the use of the gun, on people in the society.[5]

Doe, an inexperienced Master Sergeant when he took over the affairs of state, was deeply insecure and even more brutal than the effete elite he had so dramatically destroyed. His near-psychotic regime starkly demonstrated a depressing feature of much of Third World politics: the congruent corruptions of oppressor and oppressed. Liberia under Doe was a place of morbid fear and sustained terror. Gun-toting soldiers roamed the streets of Monrovia, the seedy, often violent capital, and perceived political opponents were jailed or murdered. In 1985, under pressure from both within and without the country, Doe organized elections, which, after massive rigging, he won. The opposition cried foul. The United States, Liberia's most influential supporter, thought otherwise, however. Visiting Liberia shortly after the elections, President Ronald Reagan's secretary of state, George Shultz, endorsed the polls, saying that they "were quite open, and the only questions that I have heard are about the vote-counting process." These, Shultz said, could be accounted for by the fact that "something like three-quarters of the people involved are not literate."[6] Blindly applauded by Liberia's most important foreign backer, the elections would thus become almost as emblematic as the 1980 coup: they convinced opponents of the regime that only a violent assault against it would free the nation of Doe's depredations.

Shortly after the elections, one of Doe's former aides, General Thomas Qwiwonpka, who was said to have been the mastermind of the 1980 coup, led a group of ex-soldiers and dissidents in an attempted coup, which nearly succeeded. The coup was foiled largely by Doe's Israeli security advisers—the Liberian president was a loud and opportunistic supporter of the state of Israel.[7] The aftermath was all too predictable. Doe, of the minority Krahn ethnic group, mobilized his largely Krahn army under the command of a fellow Krahn, the notoriously brutal General Charles Julu. After murdering and mutilating Quiwonkpa, who was captured after the abortive coup (the ex-General's decapitated body was displayed in a public square in Monrovia), Julu was sent to pacify Nimba County, ancestral home of Quiwonkpa. The result has been well-documented by Bill Berkeley in *Liberia: A Promise Betrayed,* a report prepared for the New York-based Lawyers Committee for Human Rights. Julu's army carried out brutalities unprecedented in even Doe's violent Liberia, killing thousands of defenseless peasants, destroying homes, pillaging businesses and farms, and raping women.[8]

Memories of these atrocities were still fresh in the minds of Nimba residents when, on Christmas eve of 1989, Charles Taylor launched his incursion into Liberia at the head of the rag-tag forces of the National Patriotic Front of Liberia (NPFL).The flamboyant and articulate Taylor astutely exploited the anti-Doe grievances to win recruits and other forms of support in the area in a manner that would plunge the country into a horrific state of pogroms and destruction. In radio broadcasts, particularly on the BBC, Taylor declared his war to be a "continuation" of the failed Quiwonkpa coup, an unmistakable appeal to the ethnic Gio and Mano who dominated Nimba County and who were brutally massacred by Doe for allegedly supporting Quiwonkpa's abortive coup in 1985. In reaction, the hysterical Doe once again sent Charles Julu to deal with the situation in Nimba.

General Julu's forces could probably have had little difficulty containing Taylor's lightly armed guerrillas, but this was not the aim of his "counter-insurgency" operations. He wanted to teach Nimba residents a hard lesson once and for all. It was a repeat of the 1985 massacres, only this time it was more intense. Julu's almost entirely Krahn soldiers killed and raped with reckless abandon and rounded up opposition figures and had them beheaded, their remains left unburied. The result, as Berkeley has informed us in a powerful book on contemporary warfare in Africa,

> was exactly what Taylor might have hoped for. Gios and Manos by the thousands rushed to join up with Taylor's forces and he welcomed them. "As the National Patriotic Front of Liberia (NPFL) came in," Taylor told me, "We didn't even have to act. People came to us and said, 'Give me a gun. How can I kill the man who killed my mother?'"[9]

The war quickly took on an ethnic character, with the Gio and Mano peoples rallying to Taylor's NPFL (even though Taylor himself was a member of the Americo-Liberian elite), and the Krahn and Mandingo peoples rallying to Doe. Ethnic violence and massacres became widespread, and by the mid-1990s, the war had killed tens of thousands of Liberians, almost all of them civilians targeted largely because of their ethnicity. Doe's regime was on the verge of collapse, and the NPFL forces were investing the coastal capital of Monrovia. By this time, Taylor's NPFL had itself split into two, with the breakaway faction led by his former forces commander Prince Yormie Johnson, who called his group the Independent National Patriotic Front of Liberia (INPFL).

The conflict inevitably unleashed a humanitarian catastrophe on a massive scale. In the first year of the war, as many as 700,000 Liberians fled the country, many of them to Côte d'Ivoire, Guinea, and Sierra Leone. Tens of thousands more fled to Ghana and Nigeria. In the words of Amos Sawyer, the conflict was characterized by the

> pervasiveness and intensity of looting, pillage, and plunder ... the lack of a stable and systematically organized structure of command and control among the armed bands, the criminal misuse of children, the employment of strategies of confidence artistry, the opportunistic use of a variety of cultural symbols, the orchestration of state anarchy....[10]

Warfare of this sort defies easy characterization. It lacked an ideological motivation or direction and was delineated by sordid opportunism. Sawyer rejects the term "warlordism" as too limited to capture its essence, preferring to describe the mode of operation of Taylor's NPFL and the other factions as "constitutive of the behaviour of *gangsters who use terror* as their ultimate instruments of control." Sawyer's analysis of Taylor's insurgency can hardly be bettered:

> Right from the start, Taylor's armed band consisted of individuals drawn from many West African countries. Several of his commanders were Sierra Leoneans, and Gambians. They and their cohorts joined this group at the Libyan Mathabat

[Libyan revolutionary school] where their training was sponsored by a Libyan government organization.... Whatever discipline and revolutionary principles instilled by such training seemed to have been undermined by the NPFL's leadership's exhortation to "capture what you can" and "keep what you capture." Thus, banditry was the ideology of the NPFL right from the start.... In the absence of political ideology, terror, use of drugs and opportunity for booty served to drive the group and underpin personal loyalty to its leader. Children were the most vulnerable victims of this form of brutal control. NPFL commanders became their surrogate uncles and the papay[11] became their father. Far from seeking to establish a social order, educate or indoctrinate villagers and thereby win their support—behaviour typical of the guerrilla movements of the 1970s—the NPFL and its cohorts in plunder so terrorized local populations that they fled in the rainforest and to refugee camps in Sierra Leone, Guinea and Ivory Coast.[12]

By August 1990, there were officially 80,000 Liberian refugees in Sierra Leone, which included Liberia's most politically active leaders, like Doe's vice president Harry Moniba. Thousands more were in Côte d'Ivoire, Guinea, Ghana, and Nigeria. The near-bankrupt government of Sierra Leone announced that month that it was spending 80 million Leones (over a million U.S. dollars) a month to maintain the refugees and to fund peace talks that were being held in Freetown.[13] These talks initially involved the setting up, on May 30, 1990, of a five-member consultative group of mainly Anglophone West African states. The committee comprised representatives of Nigeria, Ghana, Sierra Leone, The Gambia, and Guinea and was charged with the responsibility of maintaining peace and security in the region. The group, known as the Standing Mediation Committee (SMC), initiated talks between Doe's disintegrating government and the NPFL in Freetown in July 1990.

The NPFL was represented by the blustering and flamboyant Tom Woewiyu, who announced at a press conference shortly after the initial meetings that his group would not be accepting any cease-fire proposition. Nor, he declared, would it accept any ECOWAS (Economic Community of West African States) peacekeeping mission, a possibility he described as an "invasion."[14] The talks, it seemed, were getting nowhere. But the West Africans leaders pressed on. On August 6, leaders of the SMC convened in Banjul, The Gambia, and for two days discussed plans to resolve the humanitarian disaster in Liberia. The SMC agreed on a peace plan that called for an immediate cease-fire in Liberia, the creation of a cease-fire monitoring group to be known as ECOMOG, the formation of a broad-based interim government for Liberia, the appointment of a special representative of ECOWAS who was to work closely with the ECOMOG commander in Liberia, and ultimately the conduct of free and fair elections in the country. This plan was approved by the Authority of ECOWAS Heads of State and Government on August 25, 1990. That same month ECOMOG was set up to stem the tide of the carnage in Monrovia and reestablish normative order. The NPFL condemned the move and vowed to resist any "invasion force."

At that time, the remnants of Doe's defeated but heavily equipped Armed Forces of Liberia (AFL) were trapped in the enclave around the Executive Mansion, the presidential palace, where Doe and his remaining officials were holed up. A deadly battle for control was sustained between these forces and Taylor's forces on the one hand, and between Taylor's forces and Johnson's on the other.

In quick order, nearly 4,000 troops from five West African states (Nigeria, Ghana, Guinea, Sierra Leone, and The Gambia) were dispatched to Monrovia from their forward base in Freetown, under the command of Ghanaian Lieutenant-General Arnold Quainoo. Sierra Leone's President Joseph Momoh seemed to have spoken for many of the West African leaders when he defended the action as a disinterested and necessary humanitarian intervention:

> We view such an initiative as both timely and appropriate and we hope that all the warring factions in Liberia will see reason and agree with us.... Sierra Leone being one of the next door neighbours of Liberia is in a position to appreciate the seriousness of the Liberian situation as we are directly feeling the heat. The massive influx of refugees into our country with its attendant economic and social consequences is just one of the many grave responsibilities we are now called upon to shoulder ... it is our duty as leaders to re-affirm to the world and all those involved in the Liberian conflict that the ECOWAS is a genuine effort aimed at bringing peace and happiness to war-torn Liberia.[15]

These fine sentiments notwithstanding, controversy was guaranteed right from the start. Unlike previous peacekeeping missions, ECOMOG intervened in the Liberian crisis before any cease-fire agreement and, indeed, against the expressed wishes of the country's most important warring faction, Taylor's NPFL. For this reason, Taylor promised to attack the West African troops if they ventured into Liberia, a threat he carried out on the very first day that the troops landed in Monrovia (at a base provided them by another, less powerful factional army of the INPFL). Regional rivalries and differences, promoted mainly by France, a longstanding hegemonic rival of Anglophone Nigeria, the dominant state in West Africa, also complicated the mission. The only Francophone state to contribute troops to ECOMOG was Guinea (Conakry), long at odds with other Francophone states in the region. Outside perception of the force was also affected negatively by the fact that almost all the leaders contributing troops (with the exception of tiny Gambia's President Dauda Jawara) were nondemocratic military men who had taken power in coups or in suspect circumstances.

This controversial beginning ignited a debate among African scholars about the role and mandate of the interventionist force. Was it a bold attempt at peacekeeping, offering strong lessons in regional conflict management in a world in which the international community was progressively disengaging from Africa?[16] or was it, as Sesay characterized it, an ill-conceived and regionally divisive intervention exercise by autocratic leaders with disastrous consequences for regional cohesion and sustainable democracy?[17] This debate reflected, in part, the mixed reviews that ECOMOG operations were earning.

Many West African militaries lacked capabilities—weapons, equipment, logistics, and so on—for planning and conducting sustained campaigns outside their own countries. Only Nigeria had an air force and navy of any significance. In Liberia, the quality of ECOMOG's joint multinational military leadership was spotty. While some commanders, like the Nigerian General Joshua Dongonyaro, were astute and decisive, maintaining sustained pressure on the rampaging NPFL fighters; others, like the force's first commander General Arnold Quainoo (from Ghana) were perceived to be less aggressive. It was under Quainoo's leadership that one of the faction leaders, Prince Yormie Johnson, captured the beleaguered Doe, and executed him along with 70 of his bodyguards.[18] Looting was so common among the troops—with stolen cars and household furniture and other goods being routinely shipped to Nigeria and elsewhere—that Liberians corrupted the acronym, ECOMOG, to stand for "Every Car Or Moving Object Gone." The force was also hampered by what Herb Howe has called "an incoherent logistical tail."[19] ECOMOG's air power, for example, was so limited that by 1995 the only serviceable helicopter was used by the force commander as his personal taxi. Other logistical constraints have been listed by Aboagye in his excellent study of the early ECOMOG intervention, *ECOMOG: A Sub-Regional Experience in Conflict Resolution, Management and Peacekeeping in Liberia* (1999). These included the lack of maps (recalling Graham Greene's journey through the country in the 1930s, described in *Journey without Maps: A Travel Book*),[20] poor roads, old vehicles, and inadequate supply of fuel and food, not to mention an uncertain and often hostile political climate.

President Doe was captured on September 9, 1990 by Johnson's faction when Doe ventured, unannounced, to ECOMOG headquarters in Monrovia's Freeport, in an area that had been secured by Johnson's INPFL. According to Stephen Ellis, who has provided the most comprehensive and perceptive account of the Liberian war, "ECOMOG's peacekeepers looked on as Johnson's men pushed Doe downstairs, bound him and drove off to Prince Johnson's Caldwell Base, a few minutes drive away.... There he was stripped of his five-star general's uniform and shown to a crowd of bystanders." He was then tortured in the most brutal fashion: he was beaten mercilessly, his ears were cold-bloodedly sliced off, and he was left to bleed to death. The torture and murder were filmed by a Palestinian correspondent of a Middle Eastern news agency, who was only too eager to capture the graphic details of the humiliation and end of a president who had been an outspoken supporter of Israel against the Arab world.[21]

The event severely undermined the credibility of the West African intervention force, because serious questions were asked as to why the peacekeepers did not act to save Doe, who was nabbed by Johnson while on a visit to their headquarters. Quainoo was promptly recalled and replaced by the highly competent Nigerian General Joshua Dongonyaro, who proved a more effective commander. However, contrary to initial expectations, the removal of Doe did not bring the factions closer to an agreement; indeed, it compounded the crisis as the most powerful factional leader, Taylor, feeling robbed of the symbolic price of victory—the capture of the sitting president—through the machinations of ECOMOG, became even more bellicose and determined to fight to the finish. ECOMOG, however, was able to secure Monrovia sufficiently to install the Interim Government of National Unity (IGNU) for Liberia, which in August 1990 had been elected in Banjul, The Gambia, under the auspices of ECOWAS. However, the interim government, which was headed by Amos Sawyer, a famed political scientist, was rejected by Taylor and so beleaguered that it had to rely entirely on ECOMOG for protection. As a result of this, it could barely function, even in Monrovia.[22]

SIERRA LEONE: THE CONFLICT SPILLS OVER

On November 1, 1990, Taylor broadcast a statement on the BBC threatening to attack and destroy Sierra Leone's international airport, arguing that by allowing its territory to be used as an operational base for ECOMOG, Sierra Leone had made itself a legitimate target. President Momoh responded by naively describing Taylor as "ungrateful." "Of all people," the self-adoring Momoh said, "Charles Taylor should appreciate the problems he has created for us here with his war in Liberia. We are overstretching our resources to care for his people, our social amenities have been over-tasked and even our economy dislodged. A man like that should not think of making such a statement." An "Army spokesman" then added his, more bellicose, voice to his commander-in-chief's desperately uninspiring one: "Sierra Leone has a trained army, with World War II experience and success. We need not remind Charles Taylor of our performance at the Somalia Drive in Monrovia to make our point."[23] In March 1991, attacks by armed groups from Liberia on parts of eastern and southern Sierra Leone led to serious fighting and bloodshed in Sierra Leone. The fighting soon after escalated into a civil war in which a group calling itself the Revolutionary United Front (RUF) emerged out of the initial fighters from Liberia who had attacked the Sierra Leonean border areas. It was led by Foday Saybanah Sankoh, an aging former Sierra Leonean soldier who had hitherto been fighting in Taylor's NPFL. The group claimed that it aimed to overthrow Sierra Leone's President Momoh and his "corrupt and despotic" one-party state.

Sierra Leone gained independence from the British in 1961. Founded by British abolitionists and ex-North American slaves in 1787, the country is arguably sub-Saharan Africa's first modern state. It is home of West Africa's first western-style university, Fourah Bay College. For most of the period under colonial rule, the descendants of the ex-slaves—known as Creoles—constituted, like the Americo-Liberians, an elite class, and saw themselves as partners of the British in the "civilizing" of West Africa. For much of the nineteenth century, the British encouraged this feeling of hauteur in the Creoles. As educated Africans began to emerge from among the indigenous population, however, the colonial authorities, who had always in any case preferred the "true natives" to the westernized or "trousered blacks." began to sideline the Creoles.

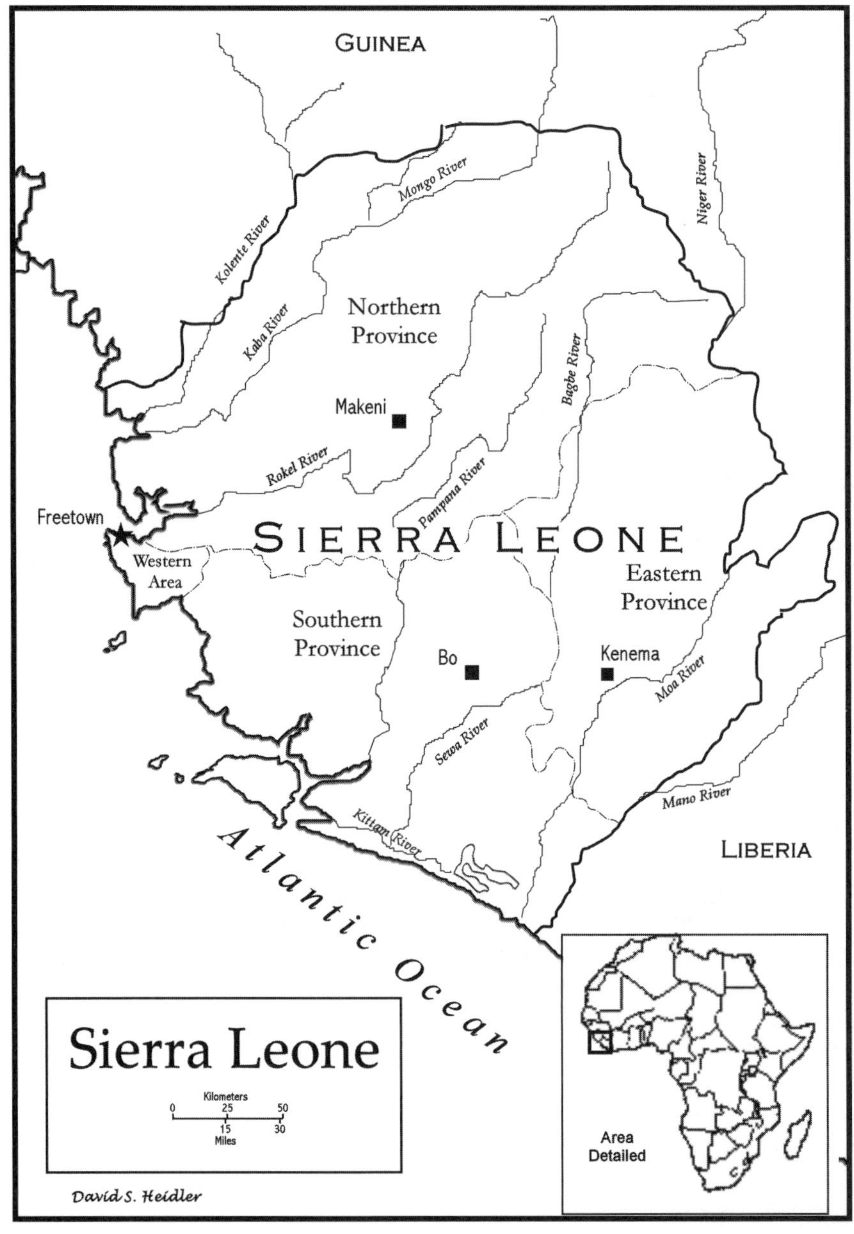

Sierra Leone

Two factors continued, however, to set the Creoles apart from the indigenous population, ensuring that they still held primacy in the affairs of the country. The first was that Sierra Leone was divided into Colony and Protectorate, with the Colony constituting the core and the Protectorate the periphery. The Colony, being the original home of the Creoles, was dominated by them in all practical terms. The second factor was that the Creoles were far and away more educated than anyone else in the rest of the country.

The first attempt to bring all of Sierra Leone—the Protectorate and the Colony—together in a political unit was the 1924 constitution. It made provision for a unicameral legislature with the Colony and the Protectorate represented in the same chamber. The Colony was allocated five seats in the chamber, three representatives to be elected and two nominated from professional and other groups. The three representatives from the Protectorate, which was beginning to produce its own western-educated elites, were uneducated chiefs.[24] It is reasonable to argue that the preference for chiefs over western-educated people from the Protectorate was intended to prevent the forging of a united front between the two groups. The colonial authorities argued, however, that chiefs were preferred because "under the tribal system no others would have adequate title to speak."[25] Development between the two groups was markedly uneven. The 1931 census showed that of the 17,606 children in school in the entire country—or about just one percent of the population—9,349 were enrolled in the Colony.[26] This is a puny figure overall; just about half of the proportion of that of the Gold Coast at the same time. It goes without saying that the vast majority of the students in the Colony were Creoles. This lopsided advantage assured the Creoles great prominence in the future development of the country, even though politically the British tried hard to have them marginalized. It also helped to reinforce Creole self-image as a group apart, different from every other in the country.[27]

By 1960, however, educated people from the Protectorate had organized themselves in such a politically active way that they could no longer be ignored. Under Sir Milton Margai and his Sierra Leone Peoples Party (SLPP), the Protectorate people had forced the British to introduce a new constitution in 1951 that effectively guaranteed them majority control. In 1961, after elections that confirmed this dominance, the British granted independence to Sierra Leone, with Sir Milton Margai (now named prime minister) and his SLPP in control. Shortly after this, feeling snubbed, a group of conservative Creoles sued in an English court to have the Constitutional Order in Council, under which independence was granted, declared invalid on the grounds that the Colony and the Protectorate were "separate countries," citing the Protectorate Declaration Act of 1896, which declared the Protectorate to be "foreign countries adjoining the Colony." The case was summarily thrown out of court by Justice William Wilberforce, a descendant of the philanthropist who had assisted in having the Sierra Leone settlement established, as "legally hopeless" since it concerned the sovereignty of an independent nation, well above the court's writ.[28]

The first five years of independence were marked by steady growth. Then in 1966, the country experienced its first coup. Led by Brigadier David Lansana, this coup was shortly after overturned by NCOs and junior officers, who in quick order handed over power to the opposition All Peoples Congress party (APC), led by a former trade unionist, Siaka Stevens. Vigorously incompetent and corrupt, the APC ruled the country for a remarkable 25 years through a combination of raw violence and legal chicanery. In 1978, the APC banned all formal opposition and declared a one-party state, based on a pseudo-Stalinist model. Corruption and nepotism became rampant, the state began to recede, and there was widespread disillusionment. Stevens, himself a Protectorate man, initially drew support largely from the Creoles and people in the north of the country, many of them then feeling marginalized by the southern-dominated SLPP.

Stevens handed over the bankrupt state to Major General Joseph Momoh, his pliable army commander, in 1985. The country continued its downward spiral. It was in 1991 under Momoh that the RUF (Revolutionary United Front) declared its insurgency. That year, with the country's diamond exports (its most significant foreign exchange earner) reduced to almost nothing as a result of smuggling and official theft, the United Nations Development Programme (UNDP) had announced that Sierra Leone was last on its Human Development Index, an announcement that caused widespread angst among the country's educated classes.

The RUF declared that it aimed to overthrow the corrupt and autocratic APC, and to reinstitute multiparty democracy and social justice. This was not stated in a printed manifesto but through public pronouncements (mainly on the BBC) by the group's leader Foday Sankoh, who was then nothing more than a shrill, disembodied voice. It was only in 1996, five years after the insurgency started, that the RUF issued what might be construed (for want of a better name) a manifesto, *Footpaths to Democracy.* This document was nothing more than a crude hodgepodge of antiestablishment rhetoric, environmental romance, and crude socialist piety, but it appealed directly to the rural peasantry, who it claimed had been reduced to "hewers of wood" by the corrupt Freetown-based elite and its "exploitative foreign backers." If read without knowledge of what had actually transpired in the previous five years, its wide appeal might be understood. But since 1991 the RUF, completely bereft of ethnic or regional support—and made up largely of foreign mercenaries and rootless young people—had targeted mainly these very rural peasants to whom its manifesto was addressed, destroying their villages, driving them off their farms (which they then looted), and chopping off hands and limbs. Their leader, Sankoh, had trained in Libya with Liberia's Charles Taylor, and it was soon clear that it was the better educated and equipped Taylor who was actually manipulating the RUF. Taylor's aim was both to destabilize Sierra Leone and ECOMOG, and, for good measure, to loot Sierra Leone's diamond reserves for himself, just as he was comprehensively looting Liberia's hardwood timber reserves. The war, then, had become little more than mercenary and violent predation without political purpose.

Momoh's corrupt and inept army nearly collapsed in the first few months of rebel advance, which was spectacular. By May 1991, the rebels, who made a two-pronged advance into eastern and southern Sierra Leone, had taken over the districts of Kailahun (in the east) and Pujehun (in the south), and were moving toward Bo and Kenema, two important regional centers. In desperation, Momoh invoked a bilateral defense pact that the APC had signed with Guinea in 1971. Guinean troops promptly intervened on the side of the beleaguered Sierra Leonean troops. This temporarily checked the advance of the RUF, but the war continued.

The destruction associated with the war was immense. By 1995, 70 percent of the country's schools, already troubled by the time the war started, had been destroyed in the fighting, and only 80 of the 500 health centers in the country were still functioning, most of them in and around Freetown, which was then untouched by the fighting. The United Nations estimated in March 1996 that 330,000 Sierra Leonean refugees had crossed into war-ravaged Liberia and Guinea, and Freetown held an estimated 750,000 displaced people. A further million or more internally displaced people (IDPs) had moved to the bigger provincial towns like Bo, Kenema, and Makeni, and 900,000 had registered for food aid. In all, nearly half of the population—2.1 million people—had been driven from their homes by the fighting.[29]

By this time, the APC government was already history: it was overthrown by junior officers in 1992. Calling themselves the National Provisional Ruling Council (NPRC), the new military rulers, who declared aims identical with the RUF's but with a new twist—ending the war, reviving the economy, and returning the country to multiparty democracy—turned out to be as corrupt and predatory as the APC, and indeed as the RUF. The war escalated under the new junta's watch, with many of its members substituting illegal diamond mining for governance. In 1995 the junta sensed that its own survival was at stake. The RUF was becoming stronger and stronger, and the NPRC ever more reluctant to engage in talks with rebels, whom the junta's head, youthful Captain Valentine Strasser, dismissed (not without some justice) as "bandits sent by Charles Taylor." The NPRC hired a South African mercenary outfit, Executive Outcomes (EO), to fight on its behalf. Deploying superior firepower, training, and helicopter gunships, the EO launched attacks against the RUF in the country's premiere diamond district, Kono, which the rebels had captured. The mercenaries cleared the district of the rebels within weeks. The RUF soon after began to send out tentative feelers for peace. Sierra Leonean civil society capitalized on this to pressure the junta to organize elections and begin peace talks. Elections were held in March 1996 and won by a revamped SLPP under Ahmed Tejan Kabbah, a former UN bureaucrat, who took over as president.

The new president accelerated talks with the RUF, which had been tentatively started by the NPRC. In November 1996, a peace agreement was signed between the government and the RUF in Abidjan, Côte d'Ivoire, declaring an immediate ceasefire, and setting out a program of disarmament and reintegration that would see the RUF transformed into a political party. The agreement collapsed in May 1997 after rogue government soldiers overthrew Kabbah and invited the RUF to join a power-sharing agreement under what they chose to call the Armed Forces Ruling Council, AFRC. That arrangement turned out to be nothing less than bloody chaos, and the AFRC was unseated in 1998 by West African troops led by Nigeria. Kabbah was reinstated, but the war continued. It climaxed in a devastating attack on Freetown by the rebels in January 1999. Over 5,000 people were killed and nearly a thousand survivors suffered crude amputations. A large part of the city was destroyed. These atrocities finally led to a massive UN and British intervention, and, after a program of disarmament and elections, Sierra Leone's war was declared over in 2002.

LIBERIA: THE FESTERING CHAOS

Meanwhile, Liberia's war had continued almost unabated. Shortly after the interim government was set up, in September 1991 another Liberian factional army emerged. The United Liberation Movement for Democracy in Liberia (ULIMO) was formed in Sierra Leone out of the remnants of Doe's disintegrated army. Vowing to rid the country of Taylor and his rebels, the group that month launched attacks from eastern Sierra Leone against Taylor's "Greater Liberia." In October 1991, ECOWAS's mediation led to yet another accord, signed in Yamoussoukro, Côte d'Ivoire. It called for the encampment and disarmament of all factions in the country, to be followed by national elections.

In fact, Taylor's forces and ULIMO continued fighting, and in October 1992, Taylor launched the highly destructive "Operation Octopus" on Monrovia. ECOMOG repulsed the attacks after heavy fighting and destruction of lives and property, and the UN Security Council imposed an arms embargo on Taylor and the other factions. The Security Council also appointed a special envoy to Liberia. He was Trevor Gordon-Somers, a Jamaican diplomat. The Liberian conflict was now beginning to receive high-level UN attention, but Gordon-Somers's relationship with ECOMOG and the interim government was far from cordial.[30]

Characteristically, Liberia's opportunistic factions tended to splinter whenever there was hope of a resolution of the crisis. In March 1994 ULIMO split into Krahn and Mandingo factions, respectively ULIMO-J (headed by Roosevelt Johnson) and ULIMO-K (headed by Alhaji Kromah).

It was in that same month that the new Council of State was inaugurated, with a little known lawyer, David Kpomakpor, as chairman, while Sawyer quietly left the political scene. Violence continued in the country, however, with the different factions fighting for dominance. In September 1994, the Akosombo Agreement was signed by leaders of the three main factions—NPFL, AFL, and ULIMO-K—calling for an immediate cessation of hostilities and a reconstituted Council of State, which would reflect a better balance of factional forces in the country. Disputes inevitably broke out over this latter point, and the agreement collapsed over matters of power sharing, with Taylor insisting that he should dominate any such arrangement. Three months later, in December, Akosombo II Agreement was signed. The new agreement appeared to satisfy the various factions, and a cease-fire came into effect, along with a commitment to conduct elections in late 1995.

In early 1995 ECOWAS, now chaired by Nigeria's General Sani Abacha, once again brought all the factions together in Abuja. Here, an agreement confirming the cease-fire was hammered out, and in September the Council of State, which included leaders from the three major factions, was established, with Wilton Sankawulo, an aging academic, as chairman. The Abuja Accord scheduled elections for August 1996, and it provided for the comprehensive deployment of ECOMOG troops throughout Liberia to oversee a planned disarmament and reintegration process. However, in April 1996, barely four months before the scheduled elections, heavy fighting broke out in Monrovia between Taylor's troops and fighters loyal to Roosevelt Johnson. The fighting began after Taylor, in a characteristically rash move, announced that he was sending troops to arrest and detain Johnson. The intense fighting, which raged for over two months, left hundreds of people dead. Large parts of Monrovia were also destroyed. As a result, another peace agreement, known as Abuja II, had to be signed. In accordance with its provisions, the Council of State was reconstituted in September 1996 with Ruth Perry, Liberia's first woman head of state, in the chair.... .It also provided for elections to be held in May 1997.

ECOMOG ordered the warring factions to dismantle their military wings and scheduled disarmament to be completed by January 1997. The process, however, was extremely flawed, and Taylor's faction remained virtually intact, while less powerful factions were encamped and disarmed. At the end of the disarmament process, a total of 28,819 fighters out of the estimated 33,000 had been disarmed, and a paltry 13,167 small arms, 1,628,584 rounds of ammunition, 6 field guns, and 4,145 bombs/explosive ordnance taken from all factions.

On July 19, 1997, Liberians went to the polls to elect a new government. Only 750,000 out of an estimated population of over two million were registered to vote. Taylor, the richest and still the most powerful man in the country, used his ill-acquired wealth to bribe voters, while his rebel-thugs (a large number of whom were not disarmed, because of the shabby way in which the process had been conducted) intimidated those he could not bribe. A large part of the country, probably 80 percent of it, was still controlled by Taylor's militias, and they staunchly prevented opposing candidates from campaigning in these areas. The elections were largely a farcical affair and the results were never really in doubt. Many voters, fearful that Taylor would resort to war if he lost, decided to vote for him. One of the election slogans in favor of Taylor was: "He killed my ma, he killed my pa, but I'll vote for him." Taylor sent busses to refugee camps in Guinea, from where traumatized Liberian refugees and some Sierra Leonean ones, bribed with food and the promise that the war would finally end if Taylor was elected, were bussed to Liberia to vote for him.[31]

Taylor's most active challenger at the polls was Ellen Johnson-Sirleaf, a prominent politician and long-time Liberian figure, who had supported Taylor in the early stages of the war. Johnson-Sirleaf found herself simply out of her element. Her supporters were intimidated and she herself faced death threats. Taylor emerged the overwhelming winner.

Now both the *de facto* and *de jure* leader of Liberia, Taylor did little, however, to improve the conditions of the war-torn nation. Illiteracy and unemployment remained above 75 percent throughout his presidency. Moreover, even after being in office as president for five years, he continued to function in a foraging mode, operating the quintessentially warlord economy. He actively refused to rebuild formal state institutions that had been destroyed during the war he had started, and he destroyed those still existing. In the words of a Human Rights Watch report in 2002:

> After five years in office, President Charles Taylor's government continues to function without accountability, exacerbating the divisions and resentments fuelled by the war. Taylor has steadily consolidated and centralized power by rewarding loyalists and intimidating critics. State power is regularly misused by high-ranking officials to further the political objectives of the executive branch, to avoid accountability, and for personal enrichment. State institutions that could provide an independent check on the Taylor administration … remain weak and cowed.[32]

Liberia's transition from war to peace under Taylor's leadership was, in other words, a complete failure. In 2001 the country imploded into destructive factional fighting, mainly as a result of Taylor's lack of commitment to reconciliation and state building. That year, a new grouping emerged called the Liberians United for Reconciliation and Democracy (LURD). LURD was created from remnants of die-hard anti-Taylor factions, and its core comprised ex-ULIMO fighters, many of whom had been disarmed just before the elections. Finding Taylor's misrule and predatory violence insufferable, in 1998 they had regrouped in the forest regions of Guinea (Conakry) bordering Liberia to renew the struggle. There other Liberian dissidents joined them and eventually formed LURD.[33] LURD received active support from Guinea (Conakry), which in 2000 had repelled Taylor-supported armed incursions into the country's diamond-rich southeastern forest regions.

Peacekeeping troops of the United Nations Mission in Liberia disarming Liberian militias. Courtesy of UNMIL'S Community Outreach and Public Information Section.

In September 2002 widespread violence broke out in Côte d'Ivoire after a failed coup attempt, and three rebel factions emerged soon after. Two of them, operating in western parts of the country bordering Liberia, comprised mainly ex-RUF and Liberian soldiers. In reaction, the Ivorian authorities armed and supported a faction of LURD called the Movement for Democracy in Liberia (MODEL). Both LURD and MODEL rapidly gained strength, and by July 2003 both rebel forces were besieging Monrovia.

On August 18, 2003, in Accra, Ghana, the Liberian government signed a Comprehensive Peace Agreement with the rebels, political parties, and civil society actors. Taylor relinquished power on August 11 and went into exile in Nigeria. A two-year National Transitional Government of Liberia (NTGL), under the presidency of businessman Gyude Bryant, was established. The NTGL was to be responsible for the administration of the country until formal elections were held in October 2005. In September 2003 the UN Security Council adopted Resolution 1509, establishing the United Nations Mission in Liberia (UNMIL) and calling for the deployment of 15,000 United Nations peacekeeping troops. The UN mission was mandated to disarm the armed militias, and to conduct the elections in October 2005. By the end of October 2004, the United Nations had disarmed 100,000 militias. Tellingly, only 26,000 weapons were collected from the "disarmed."[34] The elections were held on schedule. There were over 20 presidential candidates, including former leaders of militia factions, a popular soccer star, and a Harvard-trained economist and veteran politician. The campaigns demonstrated the still-pervasive hold that the traumatic era of Taylor had over Liberians. In an interesting twist, one of the slogans for one of the leading candidates, the soccer star George Weah, was a variation on that which brought Taylor to power in 1997. Weah's mostly youthful supporters would chant in Monrovia "Did he kill your ma? No! Did he kill your pa? No! Vote for George Weah!"[35] Weah's chief challenger was Ellen Johnson-Sirleaf, who had been Taylor's main opponent in the 1997 elections.

UNDERSTANDING WARFARE IN LIBERIA AND SIERRA LEONE

The linked Liberian and Sierra Leonean wars were among the first post–Cold War conflicts in Africa. Because they completely lacked Big Power involvement—which is to say, the once-ubiquitous Cold War antecedents—and clear ideological, religious, and ethnic dimensions, they posed a major challenge to analysts and policy makers alike. The first influential (if feverishly journalistic) attempt to understand the conflicts was Robert Kaplan's widely cited article, "The Coming Anarchy," in the American magazine *Atlantic Monthly,* which appeared in February 1994.[36] Kaplan, who visited the region briefly, depicted the wars as anarchic, rather than political, suggesting that they presaged an era of Hobbesian chaos that would engulf the continent. What was happening in the region, he wrote, was a new phenomenon of states succumbing to harsh demographics and environment, the unchecked spread of disease, the pervasiveness of criminal violence, and the rise of tribal domains. There was no other rational explanation for the violent conflicts themselves: they were an atavistic throwback to an ancient, deeply primitive past.

The British anthropologist Paul Richards was the first to challenge Kaplan's thesis in an extended scholarly discussion of the wars, focusing on Sierra Leone's conflict. In *Fighting for the Rainforest: War, Resources and Youth* (1996),[37] Richards rejected Kaplan's environmental and cultural prognosis, depicting a conflict that was starkly modern in its manifestations, and rational in motivation. Richards portrayed Sierra Leone's war as a crisis of modernity, caused by the failed patrimonial system of successive postcolonial governments. He argued that three decades of bad government blighted the hopes of most young people for a meaningful life, and that RUF terror techniques—conditioned in part by repeated viewing of Rambo and other "lone warrior" videos—are compensation for a lack of opportunity. Richards described the RUF as being headed by a highly educated "excluded intellectual" leadership and depicted the rebel group as one with a political agenda within an understandable—even reasonable—anthropological and environmental context.

This argument was broadly and systematically rejected by Sierra Leonean scholars on several grounds. There was clearly no "excluded intellectual" element in the RUF, nor did the group articulate any coherent political ideas beyond its fulminations against the ever-changing leadership of Sierra Leone. While it is true that the RUF was made up of disaffected young men, many of them did not join the group of their own volition, and clearly the external dimension of the war—in the form of its connection to the Liberian one—was very important in the growth of the RUF. Many combatants were children who were kidnapped, drugged, and forced to commit atrocities. The "radical intellectual" roots of the RUF, where they existed, were extinguished in murderous internal purges during the RUF's first year of operation. And its brutal attacks on civilians stand in sharp contradiction to its ostensible aim of creating a "revolutionary egalitarian system."[38]

One argument that soon gained prominence over all others was that encapsulated in a study of the war by a group of Canadian researchers, *The Heart of the Matter: Sierra Leone, Diamonds and Human Security* (2000).[39] The study argued that while there is no doubt about widespread public disenchantment in Sierra Leone with their failing country, similar corruption and lack of opportunity elsewhere in Africa during the late 1980s and early 1990s did not lead to years of brutality by forces devoid of ideology, political support, and ethnic identity. Only the economic opportunity presented by a breakdown in law and order, it argued, could sustain violence at the levels that plagued Sierra Leone after 1991. Successive investigations by the United Nations amplified this analysis. A similar argument had earlier been made about the Liberian war by William Reno, a political scientist. Reno argued that what kept Taylor's insurgency (he preferred the term "warlordism") going was Taylor's continuing looting of Liberia's hardwood timber, and his access to Sierra Leone's diamond reserves. Warfare in this view was simply profitable theft: pillage, rather than politics, was the key driver of the conflicts.[40] No doubt arguments about motives and underlying causes can never be satisfactorily resolved, but in the case of the conflicts in Liberia and Sierra Leone, the key manifestations are self-explanatory:

First, although the corruptions and deformities of Liberia and Sierra Leone clearly helped set the stage for their unraveling—they never grew into solid, integral or functioning entities—the violent insurgents who caused their near-total destruction were not motivated by any evident desire for social justice, or any wish to reconfigure the states in ways that would make them more responsive to their overall citizenry. In other words, governance and democracy, although sometimes harped upon by the insurgents, were not the motivating factors. Clearly, the spread of the violence and its perpetuation had more to do with the weaknesses and failure of the states the insurgents took on than with any mass appeal or intrinsic strength enjoyed by the insurgents. The grievances of the majority of the people against the estranged elites of the capital city were real, but there is no evidence that the insurgents represented those grievances in any meaningful sense. Where ethnicity was evident in the campaigns of the insurgents—as in the case of the Liberian war—it was being instrumentally used—merely as a means to divide and control. It was never the end in itself.

Secondly, both the NPFL (Liberia) and the RUF (Sierra Leone) were from the start desperate to latch on to and exploit the primary resources of their countries (timber in the case of Liberia, and diamonds in the case of Sierra Leone). This desperation became an obsession. In the end, whatever high ideals some of the insurgents might have held, the control and exploitation of their respective countries' natural wealth clearly became their primary motivation. Both groups made millions of dollars out of the illegal exploitation of these commodities, money that served mainly to enrich the rebel leaders.

Perhaps most importantly, the insurgents in the two wars targeted mainly civilians, rather than armed opponents, and there was little or no attempt to win over the general populace. There was no systematic political program that would appeal to the general citizenry, nor any coherent ideology that would serve to give an insight into what the insurgents would do once they gained power. When they temporarily took power, in both cases the result was continuing pillage, violence, and destruction, and an inability to set up any stabilized form of governance.

Predatory violence of this sort is not new in West Africa. In the era of the slave trade, armed groups, known as the *Ceddos,* ran amok, pillaging villages and enslaving civilians, who were then sold to European slave traders. This may seem like an easy parallel, but the operations of the likes of Taylor and Sankoh were painfully reminiscent of such criminal and violent groups.

THE JUSTICE TRIBUNAL AND THE TRUTH AND RECONCILIATION COMMISSION (TRC)

The setting up of Truth and Reconciliation Commissions, sometimes accompanied by a tribunal for prosecuting war crimes, has now become almost a ritual element in UN-sponsored peacemaking efforts. In the case of Sierra Leone, the UN-sponsored Lomé Accord of July 7, 1999, which was the definitive document that ended the war, made provision for the setting up of a TRC but not a war crimes tribunal. Article XXVI of the accord states that a TRC was to be established to "address impunity, break the cycle of violence, provide a forum for both parties and perpetrators of human rights violations, to tell their story, get a clear picture of the past in order to facilitate genuine healing and reconciliation."[41]

Following the signing of the accord, the UN High Commission for Human Rights (UNCHR) worked intensely with the Sierra Leonean government to prepare the way for the TRC, and on February 10, 2000, the Sierra Leonean Parliament passed an act legally setting it up. The act described the TRC as an instrument designed to create "an impartial body of historical record" of the war and to "help restore the human dignity of victims and promote reconciliation." The TRC was required to conduct a year-long nationwide process of collecting testimonies, and to undertake to foster "inter-change(s) between victims and perpetrators."[42] The act also made provisions to compel persons to appear before the TRC when commissioners were convinced that this would be necessary to obtain important statements. At the end of the year, the TRC was to present a report to the Sierra Leonean government, which would then share the findings with the UN Security Council. A budget for the exercise was initially set at US$10 million, but this was reduced toUS$6.5 million after potential donors complained that the earlier figure was too high. The cash-strapped Sierra Leonean government was to contribute only a small fraction of this cost. All seemed set for work to start, with commissioners already earmarked, but then suddenly in May 2000 the RUF abducted UN peacekeepers, forcing the government and the donor community to suspend the process indefinitely.

The May 2000 events forced the government and the architects of the Lomé Accord to rethink the amnesty provisions. President Kabbah wrote to the UN secretary-general on June 6, 2000 requesting the organization's assistance in setting up a "Special Court" which would specifically "try Foday Sankoh and other senior members of the RUF" for "crimes against the people of Sierra Leone and for the taking of United Nations peacekeepers as hostages."[43] The UN Security Council responded by adopting Kabbah's proposal as its own, and Secretary-General Kofi Annan promptly sent out a mission, followed by a team of experts, to liaise with the Sierra Leonean government. Finally, on January 16, 2002, the Statute for the Special Court for Sierra Leone and the Agreement between the United Nations and the Sierra Leonean government on the Establishment of the Court were issued.[44]

Meanwhile, work on the setting up of the TRC had resumed with a series of workshops, seminars, and meetings involving civil society activists and human rights monitors, thus underlining how relevant their involvement was for the longer-term stability of the country. Finally, on July 5, 2002 the TRC was inaugurated in Freetown and was headed by Sierra Leonean Anglican Bishop, Joseph Humper. Its budget was limited, for by the end of its first year of work only US$3.5 million of the US$6.5 million pledged by donors had arrived. Nevertheless, by December 2002 it had begun to work vigorously, touring the country on a "sensitization" mission.

In July 2002 the Special Court also officially began work, with the arrival in Freetown of a prosecutor, David Crane (a former U.S. army lawyer) and a registrar, Robin Vincent (a former judicial official in Manchester, England). With a budget of well over US$80 million, the Special Court was mandated to act against persons who, since the signing of the Abidjan Accord in 1996, were most responsible for breaking international and Sierra Leonean law and for undermining the peace process, and who had "planned, instigated, ordered, committed or otherwise aided and abetted in the planning, preparation or execution" of war crimes. As part of the global effort to combat impunity—even in once-forgotten and marginalized corners of the world—the court was to focus especially on "crimes against humanity." These were defined as crimes constituting a pattern of "widespread and systematic attack against any civilian population," including offenses like murder, enslavement, extermination of whole populations, sexual slavery, child recruitment for combat purposes, forced deportations or displacements, torture, rape, and enforced prostitution.[45]

In March 2003 the Special Court indicted an initial batch of perpetrators in terms of its mandate, including Foday Sankoh, a popular member of Kabbah's government; Hinga Norman, the putative head of the Civil Defence Force (CDF) and the former Deputy Minister of Defence; a former military leader, Johnny Paul Koroma; the RUF's Sam Bockarie; and several others. Koroma and Bockarie were out of the country at the time, reportedly fighting for Taylor's beleaguered regime in Liberia. The Special Court asked that President Taylor hand both of them over. Instead, Bockarie was murdered and Koroma simply vanished a few weeks later.

In early June 2003, shortly after Taylor arrived in Accra, Ghana, for peace talks to end Liberia's ever-widening and never-ending civil war, the Special Court unveiled a long-sealed indictment accusing Taylor of bearing "the greatest responsibility" for the decade-long war in Sierra Leone. It called on the Ghanaian authorities to have him arrested and sent to Sierra Leone to stand trial. However, the Ghanaian government, embarrassed by this request, ignored the indictment and sent Taylor back to Monrovia in a Ghanaian government plane. But the indictment clearly unsettled Taylor and helped destabilize his regime. He quickly offered to resign if he were an obstacle to peace. The Nigerian president, Olusegun Obasanjo, offered him asylum, and in August 2003 Taylor flew to Nigeria in self-exile. Until March 2006 Nigeria staunchly refused to hand Taylor over to the court, thus stalling this experiment in international justice.[46]

The TRC, meanwhile, produced a 5,000-page report in October 2004 meticulously detailing the causes of the war in Sierra Leone and the atrocities that marked it. It also made wide-ranging recommendations, including a ban on capital punishment, and called for more judicious use of Sierra Leone's mineral resources. The report was widely praised in Sierra Leone for its even-handedness. While it noted that the RUF was responsible for the vast majority of the atrocities committed during the war (about 70%), the report also cited cases of serious abuses by the Sierra Leonean army, as well as by the pro-government Civil Defence Force and ECOMOG.[47]

Perhaps influenced by the work of the TRC in Sierra Leone, in June 2005 Liberia's interim government (which was headed by President Guyde Bryant) passed a TRC act of its own. It called for a similar commission to look into Liberia's decade and more of carnage. By September 2005 commissioners were being sought to carry out the work of the TRC. The government, however, resisted calls by civil society activists to set up a war crimes tribunal, claiming than this would be divisive, and an unnecessary waste of money.[48]

If the experience of Sierra Leone with these two instruments of postconflict justice and reconciliation is any guide, then there are serious questions about their effectiveness. The Sierra Leonean government received the TRC report coldly, perhaps because it was unsparing in criticizing the government's conduct of the war. The government initially even refused to acknowledge the recommendations set out in the report. Only after serious pressure from civil society groups did it publish a hastily written and noncommittal *White Paper* that rejected some of the report's core recommendations, such as an end to capital punishment.[49] Although the local media gave coverage to the report, with some even serializing its findings and recommendations, the lack of serious government commitment to the dissemination of the report meant that public discussion was reduced to the level of fringe agitation. The Special Court has fared even worse. Many Sierra Leoneans regard the court as a foreign imposition, led and dominated by westerners who, without any experience of the war, are pursuing an agenda of their own. In particular, the indictment of the popular leader of the CDF, Hinga Norman, has been condemned widely in Sierra Leone and is regarded as a threat to the country's longer-term stability. It was all very well for UN Human Rights Commissioner, Mary Robinson, to pronounce glibly in 2000 that "there must be no selectivity, no sanctuary, no impunity for those guilty of gross human rights violations."[50] The reality of war and peace in West Africa demonstrates that such a comfortably optimistic view can all too often be wide of the mark.

ABBREVIATIONS

AFRC Armed Forces Ruling Council
APC All Peoples Congress
CDF Civil Defence Force
ECOMOG Economic Community of West African States Military Observation Group
ECOWAS Economic Community of West Africa States
FBC Fourah Bay College
IMF International Monetary Fund
INPFL Independent National Patriotic Front of Liberia
LURD Liberians United for Reconciliation and Democracy
MODEL Movement for Democracy in Liberia
NPFL National Patriotic Front of Liberia
NPRC National Provisional Ruling Council
NRC National Reformation Council
OAU Organisation of African Unity
PAC Partnership Africa Canada
RUF Revolutionary United Front
SLA Sierra Leone Army
SCSL Special Court for Sierra Leone
TRC Truth and Reconciliation Commission
ULIMO United Liberation Movement of Liberia for Democracy
UNDP United Nations Development Programme
UNAMSIL UN Mission in Sierra Leone
UNMIL UN Mission in Liberia

TIMELINE

1787 More than 300 destitute black and white colonists from Britain land in Sierra Leone; most die within two years

1792 1200 "free Negroes" or "Black Loyalists" sail from Nova Scotia to Sierra Leone where they establish the settlement of Freetown

1799 Royal Charter gives legal status to the colony of Sierra Leone

1808 Establishment of the British Crown Colony of Sierra Leone

1822 Hundreds of free blacks from the U.S. South are resettled in Liberia

1827 Establishment of Fourah Bay College, the first university in sub-Saharan Africa

1847 Liberia is declared an independent republic with Jenkins Roberts as the first president, heading the True Whig Party

1896 Establishment of a Protectorate over territories of the interior of Sierra Leone

1961 Sierra Leone gains independence from Britain, with Sir Milton Margai as prime minister

1967 Army seizes power in Sierra Leone as the "National Reformation Council"

1968 Noncommissioned officers seize power in Sierra Leone and invite Siaka Stevens, apparent winner of the 1967 election, to take power. Elections reconfirm him in office

1970s Stevens consolidates power through violence, corruption, and intimidation, creating an Internal Security Unit with Cuban assistance. 1977 elections are rigged and marred by violence, after which Stevens declares a one-party state in Sierra Leone

1980 Bloody coup in Liberia brings Master-Sergeant Samuel Kanyon Doe to power

1985 With Sierra Leone's economy in ruins, Stevens (now 80 years old) hands over power to former army chief, Joseph Momoh. Doe rigs elections that confirm him as civilian president of Liberia
Dissidents led by Gen. Thomas Qwiwonpka, a former Doe aide, attempt a coup but fail
Doe organizes mass killings in Qwuiwonpka's home county and the regime's brutality intensifies throughout the country

1990 Charles Taylor begins his insurgency in Liberia
80,000 Liberian refugees flee to Sierra Leone
ECOMOG is established with Freetown as its rear base
Doe is killed by Johnson's INPFL
In Sierra Leone Momoh moves to reintroduce multiparty democracy
UNDP *Human Development Report* places Sierra Leone last out of 160 countries

1991 Bloody stalemate in Liberian conflict as ECOMOG intervenes
Former army corporal Foday Sankoh leads the Revolutionary United Front (RUF) attacks on Sierra Leone border towns from Liberia; attacks continue, marked by brutality against civilians; children are kidnapped and inducted into RUF

Momoh doubles the army, recruiting "hooligans, drug addicts and thieves" as well as children

1992 April: a mutiny by unpaid soldiers in Sierra Leone becomes a coup. Momoh flees
National Provisional Ruling Council (NPRC) assumes power under Capt. Valentine Strasser (age 27)
Brutal war continues

1996 Palace coup in January in Sierra Leone in which Julius Maada Bio replaces Strasser in power
Peace talks with RUF begin in Abidjan
March: Elections marred by RUF violence are otherwise reported free and fair by international observers
Ahmed Tejan Kabbah becomes President of Sierra Leone
November: President Kabbah and Foday Sankoh of RUF sign a peace accord. A tentative peace agreement in Liberia leads to selection of Ruth Perry as interim president

1997 Charles Taylor wins elections in Liberia with his supporters singing, on elections day, "He kill my ma; he kill my pa; but I'll vote for him"
In Sierra Leone soldiers release 600 prison inmates and seize power in a very bloody coup, forming the Armed Forces Ruling Council (AFRC)
Kabbah flees and Major Johnny Paul Koroma, a former coup plotter, becomes chairman of the AFRC and invites RUF to join the government

1998 In Sierra Leone ECOMOG launches offensive on Freetown, driving the AFRC/RUF out
President Kabbah returns
Sierra Leone armed forces disbanded
UN Security Council creates UN peacekeeping operation for Sierra Leone, UNOMSIL, and sends 40 military observers and later human rights observers.
Rebel attacks continue

1999 In Sierra Leone rebel elements attack and enter Freetown resulting in two weeks of arson, terror, murder, and atrocities; cabinet ministers, journalists and civil servants are tortured and killed; parts of the city are razed and over 6 000 civilians are killed before ECOMOG pushes rebels back; 2,000 children are reported missing
The government of Sierra Leone concludes a negotiated peace agreement with RUF, giving Foday Sankoh and several other RUF and AFRC leaders cabinet positions
All RUF and AFRC leaders are given amnesty
UN Security Council approves a 6,000-member peacekeeping force for Sierra Leone with authority to use "deadly force" if required

2000 February: Truth and Reconciliation Commission set up in Sierra Leone
RUF abducts UN peacekeepers and TRC process suspended

2001 Liberia implodes into violence once again after attacks by Liberians United for Reconciliation and Democracy (LURD); violence spreads

2002 Special Court for Sierra Leone established and TRC resumes work
Sierra Leonean government and the United Nations announce that disarmament is completed
Elections organized with Kabbah reelected by a landslide

2003 Charles Taylor forced into exile in Nigeria after peace accord in Ghana
UN troops move into Liberia

2004 Liberian disarmament announced complete. 100,000 (mostly teenage) fighters pass through UN-supervised disarmament process

2005 Liberia sets up TRC and holds nationwide elections

2006 Taylor put on trial by the Special Court

GLOSSARY

Doe, Samuel Kanyon (1950/1951–1990). Staged a military coup in Liberia in 1980 and remained president through rigged elections until 1990 when he was captured and executed by INFPL rebels under Prince Johnson.

Johnson, Prince Yormie (or Yeomi) (b. 1952). Liberian warlord who broke away from the NPFL in 1990 and formed a faction called the INPFL. He contended with Charles Taylor for control of Liberia. In the Liberian elections of October 2005 he won a senate seat despite his reputation for gross human rights abuses.

Johnson, Roosevelt. Liberian rebel who split from ULIMO in 1994 to form ULIMO-J. He was dismissed from the ULIMO-J leadership in 1996 and fled Liberia in 1998. In 1999 he was convicted in absentia of treason.

Kabbah, Ahmad Tejan (b. 1932). President of Sierra Leone from 1996 to 1997 when he was ousted by rebels under Foday Sankoh. He was reinstated as president in 1998 by ECOWAS forces, and was reelected in 2002 at the conclusion of the civil war.

Kromah, Alhaji. Liberian rebel who split from ULIMO in 1994 to form ULIMO-K. Since the end of the civil war he has twice run for elected office most unsuccessfully.

Momoh, Joseph Saidu (1937–2003). Army general and president of Sierra Leone from 1985 to 1992, when he was overthrown in a military coup by Captain Valentine Strasser.

Sankoh, Foday (1937–2003). Rebel leader of RUF in Sierra Leone who initiated his vicious insurrection in 1991. He was arrested in 2000 and died in detention while facing trial on charges of war crimes and crimes against humanity including rape, sexual slavery, and extermination.

Stevens, Siaka (1905–1988). President of Sierra Leone from 1971 to his retirement in 1985. In 1978 he created a one-party state in Sierra Leone and survived several coup and assassination attempts.

Taylor, Charles (b. 1948). Liberian warlord and commander of the NPFL who launched an armed uprising in 1989. Served as president of Liberia from 1997 to 2003 during an endemic civil war. He faces trial in 2006 on 654 counts of war crimes and crimes against humanity.

Tolbert, William R., Jr. (1913–1980). Succeeded William Tubman as leader of the True Whig party and president of Liberia in 1971. In 1980 he was brutally killed in a military coup led by Master Sergeant Samuel Doe.

NOTES

1. Edward Blyden, *Christianity, Islam and the Negro Race* (London: W. B. Whittingham and Co., 1887). Blyden was, in fact, highly optimistic about the salutary effects the two countries would have on the continent of Africa. "There is no part of West Africa where the openings and opportunities for introducing civilisation and Christianity into this continent are greater than these contiguous states present," he wrote. "The attractions which they offer to the efforts of the philanthropist and African Colonisationist (in the American sense of that phrase) are not without just grounds.... [I]t is not difficult to predict the effects [of these two countries] upon the general interests of civilisation, upon the welfare of the Negro race, and upon the great cause of humanity" (275–76).

2. I am grateful to William Reno, a professor of political science at Northwestern University, for this observation.

3. See Ian Smillie, Lansana Gberie, and Ralph Hazleton, *The Heart of the Matter: Sierra Leone, Diamonds and Human Security* (Ottawa: Partnership Africa Canada, 2000); found at http://www.pacweb.org/documents.

4. For an interesting, if self-pitying, account of the coup, see Victoria Tolbert, *Lifted Up: Victoria Tolbert's Story* (Minneapolis, MN: Macalester Park Publishing Company, 1989). The author was Tolbert's wife, and witnessed the assassination of her husband. She describes a ritual of horror that would become all too familiar to observers of the Liberian scene in the 1990s: "...six virtually naked and horrifyingly masked men rushed by me. Their bodies were painted for war, in tribal fashion—like the warriors of Cape Palmas during Liberia's tribal wars. Only jagged and weathered scraps of fabric hung securely about their loins. I could see that their gruesome masks, designed to terrify, disguise and intimidate, were painted on.... Suddenly, a deafening explosion blasted our ears. One of the men had shot Bill [Tolbert]. He sank to the chair, his walking stick dropped to the floor, and I knew he was dead." (138).

5. Amos Sawyer, *The Emergence of Autocracy in Liberia: Tragedy and Challenge* (San Francisco, CA: IGS, 1992), 293–94.

6. Quoted in James Youboty, *A Nation in Terror: The True Story of the Liberian Civil War* (Philadelphia, PA: Parkside Impressions Enterprises, 2004), 84. The author is a former Liberian journalist.

7. According to Aboagye, Israel's Mossad helped trained Doe's Special Anti-Terrorist Unit (SATU) as the Presidential Guard "besides the construction of a modern Defence Ministry Complex." See Festus Aboagye, *ECOMOG: A Sub-Regional Experience in Conflict Resolution, Management and Peacekeeping in Liberia* (Accra: SEDCO, 1999), 25.

8. Bill Berkeley, *Liberia: A Promise Betrayed* (New York: Lawyers Committee on Human Rights, 1986).

9. Bill Berkeley, *The Graves Are Not Yet Full: Race, Tribe and Power in the Heart of Africa* (New York: Basic Books, 2001), 48.

10. Amos Sawyer, "Violent Conflicts and Governance Challenges in West Africa: The Case of the Mano River Basin Area," *Journal of Modern African Studies* 42, no. 3 (2004): 437–63.

11. Papay is literally Liberian for father but is often used to refer to a father-figure.

12. Sawyer, "Violent Conflicts," 441.

13. "Le. 80 million spent on war," *New Citizen* (Freetown), 11 August 1990.

14. See Aboagye, *ECOMOG,* 59.

15. *New Citizen,* 8 November 1990.

16. Margaret Vogt, ed., *The Liberian Crisis and ECOMOG: A Bold Attempt at Regional Peacekeeping* (Lagos: Gabumo Publishing Co., 1992).

17. Max Ahmadu Sesay, "Civil War and Collective Intervention in Liberia: A Strange Case of Peacekeeping in West Africa," *Review of African Political Economy,* 67 (March 1996).

18. Barely three months after the force landed, the commander of the Sierra Leonean contingent, Lieutenant-Colonel Modu Hanciles, was withdrawn for cowardice and dereliction of duty.

19. Herb Howe, "Self-Help African Style: Nigerian Intervention in Sierra Leone Highlights New Trends in African Security," *Global Watch,* June 1998.

20. Graham Greene, *Journey without Maps: A Travel Book* (Garden City, NY: Doubleday Doran, 1936).

21. Stephen Ellis, *The Mask of Anarchy: The Destruction of Liberia and the Religious Dimension of an African Civil War* (London: Hurst and Co., 1999), 9.

22. One of the best accounts of the early years of ECOMOG's intervention can be found in Aboagye, *ECOMOG.*

23. See Lansana Gberie, "War and State Collapse: The Case of Sierra Leone" (MA thesis, Wilfrid Laurier University, 1998), and Lansana Gberie, *A Dirty War in West Africa: The RUF and the Destruction of Sierra Leone* (London and Indianopolis: Hurst and Co. and University of Indiana Press, 2005).

24. Gershon Collier, *Sierra Leone: Experiment in Democracy in an African State* (New York: New York University Press, 1970), 82.

25. Quoted in John Cartwright, *Politics in Sierra Leone 1947–67* (Toronto: University of Toronto Press, 1970), 19.

26. Ibid., 22.

27. The Colony area constitutes far less than one-tenth of the total land area of Sierra Leone, and at the time of independence Creoles constituted only 2 percent of the population. They, however, had a literacy rate at the time of independence of 80 percent, compared with 6 percent for the rest of the country. See Roy Lewis, "Sierra Leone: Independence without Pains," *Africa Report* 6, no. 4 (April 1961): 11.

28. "Creoles Case Thrown Out," *West Africa,* 16 May 1964.

29. Ian Smillie and Larry Minear, *The Charity of Nations: Humanitarianism in a Calculating World* (Bloomfield, CT: Kumarian Press, 2004), 26.

30. There were times when the relationship between Gordon-Somers and the West African force was openly hostile. The two groups were mutually suspicious of each other, with ECOMOG officers believing that the UN envoy was partial toward Taylor. See James Jonah, "The United Nations," in *West Africa's Security*

Challenges: Building Peace in a Troubled Region, eds. Adekeye Adebajo and Ismail Rashid (London: Lynne Rienner Publishers, 2004), 319–48.

31. Author's interviews with Liberian refugees in Guinea (Conakry) and with Commany Wesseh, a prominent Liberian civil society activist (Abidjan, 2001).

32. Human Rights Watch, *Back to the Brink: War Crimes by the Liberian Government and Rebels* (New York: Human Rights Watch, 2002).

33. Author's interview with J. Laveli Supuwood, a prominent LURD member (Abidjan, April 2001).

34. Mike Crawley, "Fewer Guns, but Tensions Persist in Liberia," *Christian Science Monitor,* 28 October 2004.

35. Lydia Polgreen, "For Liberians, an Election Is Also a Vote for Confidence," *New York Times,* 10 October 2005.

36. Robert Kaplan, "The Coming Anarchy: How Scarcity, Crime, Over-Population and Diseases are Rapidly Destroying our Planet," *Atlantic Monthly,* February 1994.

37. Paul Richards, *Fighting for the Rainforest: War, Resources and Youth in Sierra Leone* (London: James Currey, 1996).

38. See Ibrahim Abdullah, ed., *Democracy and Terror: The Sierra Leone Civil War* (Dakar: Codesria, 2004); also Lansana Gberie, *Dirty War in West Africa.* My own MA thesis, "War and State Collapse: The Case of Sierra Leone" (Wilfred Laurier University, Waterloo, Ontario, Canada) rejected both Kaplan's sweeping and impressionist views and Richards's more subtle but no less unhelpful arguments.

39. Smillie, Gberie, and Hazleton, *Heart of the Matter.*

40. William Reno, *Warlord Politics and the African States* (Boulder, CO: Lynne Rienner Publishers, 1998).

41. Quoted in Gberie, *Dirty War in West Africa,* 208.

42. Sierra Leone Government, *The Truth and Reconciliation Act 2000* (Freetown: Government of Sierra Leone Publications, 2000).

43. United Nations, *Fifth Report of the Secretary General on the United Nations Mission in Sierra Leone,* UN document S/2000/751, 31 July 2000, para. 9.

44. Both the statute and the agreement regarding the Special Court of Sierra Leone can be found at: http:/www.sierra-leone.org/specialcourt/html.

45. See ibid.

46. See Gberie, *Dirty War in West Africa,* 213–14. The Special Court has received permission to carry out Taylor's trial at the International Criminal Court in The Hague.

47. Witness to Truth: Report of Sierra Leone's Truth and Reconciliation Commission (Accra: Graphics Packaging Ltd., 2004).

48. Author's interviews in Liberia with journalists and civil society leaders, June 2005.

49. Sierra Leone Government, *White Paper on the TRC Report* (in author's possession).

50. Quoted in Chernor Jalloh and Alhaji Marong, "Ending Impunity: The Case for War Crimes Trials in Liberia," in *A Tortuous Road to Peace: The Dynamics of Regional, UN and International Humanitarian Interventions in Liberia,* eds. Festus Aboagye and Alhaji M. S. Bah (Pretoria: ISS publications, 2005), 218.

SELECT BIBLIOGRAPHY

Abdullah, Ibrahim, ed., *Democracy and Terror: The Sierra Leone Civil War.* Dakar: CODESRIA, 2003.

Brief but comprehensive collection of essays by leading Sierra Leonean scholars on the country's decade-long civil war, which covers various facets of the conflict, with a particular focus on the role of marginalized, or "lumpen," youth.

Adekeye, Adebajo, and Ismail Rashid, eds. *West Africa's Security Challenges: Building Peace in a Troubled Region.* London: Lynne Rienner Publishers, 2004.

Invaluable collection of 16 essays on issues related to conflicts and international mediation efforts in the troubled region of West Africa. The authors, most of whom are from the region and are intellectual and political heavyweights, focus particularly on the role of the West African regional body, ECOWAS.

Berkeley, Bill. *The Graves Are Not Yet Full: Race, Tribe and Power in the Heart of Africa.* New York: Basic Books, 2001.

One of the most incisive and sympathetic journalistic accounts available concerning violent conflicts in Africa. Includes invaluable insights into the Rwandan genocide, the implosion of the Congo under Mobutu, and Charles Taylor's insurgency in Liberia.

Ellis, Stephen. *The Mask of Anarchy: The Destruction of Liberia and the Religious Dimension of an African Civil War.* London: Hurst and Co., 1999.

The most trenchant and comprehensive book yet on Liberia's civil war. Ellis, who was editor of the authoritative *African Confidential* newsletter, explains Liberia's decline from dictatorship to criminal violence and analyses the depravities and recklessness of the insurgent forces in terms of Liberia's material culture.

French, Howard W. *A Continent for the Taking: The Tragedy and Hope of Africa.* New York: Random House, 2004.

Serious journalistic account by a former *New York Times* Africa correspondent of the violent conflicts and criminal predation in Africa, particularly the Congo. French's reflections on Charles Taylor's depredations in Liberia are among the most insightful available.

Gberie, Lansana. *A Dirty War in West Africa: The RUF and the Destruction of Sierra Leone.* London and Indianapolis: Hurst and Co. and University of Indiana Press, 2005.

First-hand account of Sierra Leone's civil war, 1991–2002, describing the key protagonists. Presented both as a journalist account and an historical analysis, it is the most comprehensive account to date of Sierra Leone's implosion into violence and terror.

Mgbeoji, Ikechi. *The Liberian Crisis, Unilateralism, and Global Order.* Vancouver: UBC Press, 2003.

Analysis of the legal issues involved in the flawed but necessary intervention of ECOMOG in the Liberian civil war.

Reno, William. *Warlord Politics and the African States.* Boulder, CO: Lynne Rienner Publishers, 1998.

Very useful critique of conventional thinking about violent conflicts in Africa, including the Liberian and Sierra Leonean civil wars. Reno rejects notions of tribalism or primeval nihilism and instead focuses on the political economy and criminal predation both by insurgents and state actors. He sketches a bleak picture of failing states succumbing not so much to tyranny as to calculated criminality and violence.

Richards, Paul. *Fighting for the Rainforest: War, Resources and Youth in Sierra Leone.* London: James Currey, 1996.

First book-length study of Sierra Leone's civil war, which is seen in largely anthropological terms. Richards depicts the war as a "crisis of modernity," fueled by a failed "patrimonial" state, rather than as an anarchic and criminal conflict.

Sawyer, Amos. *The Emergence of Autocracy in Liberia: Tragedy and Challenge.* San Francisco, CA: IGS, 1992.

Written by Liberia's foremost scholar and a former politician, this book provides important background to the more than decade-long civil war. Sawyer trenchantly analyses the failings of the Americo-Liberian elite and shows how they paved the way for Samuel Doe's bloodthirsty regime and eventual civil war.

Smillie, Ian, Lansana Gberie, and Ralph Hazleton. *The Heart of the Matter: Sierra Leone, Diamonds and Human Security.* Ottawa: Partnership Africa Canada, 2000.

Report that analyses the secretive and corrupt world diamond trade. Most of its recommendations, including sanctions on Liberian diamonds and a more vigorous control of Sierra Leone's diamond fields by the United Nations, were subsequently implemented, and are partly credited for helping end the war.

Tolbert, Victoria. *Lifted Up: Victoria Tolbert's Story.* Minneapolis, MN: Macalester Park Publishing Company, 1989.

Moving personal account of the last days of True Whig Party rule in Liberia, and particularly of the bloody coup of 1980 and its aftermath. The author was the wife of the murdered President William Tolbert.

Youboty, James. *A Nation in Terror: The True Story of the Liberian Civil War.* Philadelphia, PA: Parkside Impressions Enterprises, 2004.

Valuable first-hand account of the Liberian war. Weak on analysis, it nevertheless provides important details concerning the conduct of the war, the various players involved, and the sufferings of ordinary Liberians.

EIGHT

The Consequences of Sudan's Civil Wars for the Civilian Population

Jane Kani Edward and Amir Idris

For over four decades since its independence in 1956, violent and continuous civil wars have been raging in postcolonial Sudan. Arguably, these have created the largest number of refugees and displaced persons in Africa. Besides the great human suffering involved, the consequences of this interminable strife have been tragic for social, economic, and political development. Indeed, the civil conflicts and political violence that have spread from the southern Sudan to the western region of Darfur are currently threatening to dismantle the postcolonial state in the Sudan.

The first phase of the north-south civil war in Sudan started in 1955 and ended with the signing in 1972 of the Addis Ababa Agreement between the Government of Sudan (GOS) and the Southern Sudan Liberation Movement (SSLM). The second phase of this civil war began in 1983 and concluded with the signing in Kenya on January 9, 2005 of the Niavash Peace Agreement between the GOS and the Sudan People's Liberation Movement/Army (SPLM/A). The untimely death in July 2005 of Dr. John Garang, the charismatic chairman of the SPLM/A, will doubtless have a serious impact on the future of the peace agreement. There are no established statistical data specifying how many Sudanese people have either died or been displaced by the civil wars in Sudan. Nevertheless, various estimates put the figure of those who have died in the north-south conflict at about 2 million, mainly from southern Sudan;[1] while there are an estimated 5.5 million (mainly southerners) who have been displaced, 4 million of them internally. The United Nations (UN) and other human

Sudan

rights organizations have estimated that the conflict in Darfur has led thus far to the death of an estimated 300,000 people and the displacement of more than 2.4 million others. The United Nations has described the situation in Darfur as "the world's worst humanitarian crisis"; the United States Congress and the State Department have described it as "genocide."

This chapter seeks to rethink the underlying causes of Sudan's civil wars and highlight some of their consequences for the civilian population. In the first section of the chapter, different perspectives on the root causes of the north-south conflict will be reviewed, and then an attempt will be made to rethink the underlying causes of this civil war in the context of the subsequent conflict in Darfur. Root causes will be seen to include a complex of social, economic, historical, religious, and racial identity issues. Sudan's official discourse on national identity, which is based on Arabism and Islamism, will be analyzed to reveal the dynamics that have contributed to the outbreak and persistence of war in Sudan. This section will also deal with persistent economic, political, and gender injustices that have persuaded some groups in Sudan to embrace the option of violence as a way of voicing their concerns. The second section of the chapter will consider the consequences of the civil war, characterized by massive displacement of people, loss of lives, violation of human rights, destruction of infrastructures, disruption of social institutions, and environmental degradation. In particular, the spread of gender-based violence will be highlighted.

PERSPECTIVES ON SUDAN'S NORTH-SOUTH CONFLICT

Literature on Sudan's north-south conflict clearly indicates that scholars differ somewhat in the emphasis and priority they put on the various factors that can be identified as leading to political instability and war. Many Sudanese scholars tend to emphasize identity issues around race, ethnicity, religion, economic deprivation, unequal distribution of natural resources, and political power.[2] Others prefer to blame cultural factors, as well as British colonial policies toward the south, for contributing to the unfriendly relations between the north and the south.[3] Still others focus on the racialized and ethnicized nature of the state in Sudan, which they believe has led to ongoing conflict.[4] Western scholars writing about Sudan tend to emphasize religion, the unequal distribution of resources and political power, and the underdevelopment of the south as major factors behind the Sudanese conflict.[5]

According to Dunstan Wai,[6] north-south conflict in the Sudan dates back to precolonial days and has its roots in cultural, racial, and economic antagonisms that have led to mutual distrust between the two groups and to a desire for southern secession. For him, the southern people's bitter experiences with Arab Muslim slave traders and raiders, and also with Egyptians and northern Sudanese during the period of Turko-Egyptian rule in Sudan (1821–1885), followed by that of the Mahadist state (1885–1898) and then the Anglo-Egyptian Condominium in Sudan (1898–1956), combined with the brutal ways in which Islam and the Arabic language were imposed, all represent the bases for continuous conflict in the Sudan. For Oliver Albino, on the other hand, "[r]acial differences constitute the root of the problems which beset the Sudan."[7] Francis Deng emphasized the contentious issue of identity, particularly in relation to constructing a narrative of Sudanese national identity. In this quest he saw the most controversial issues revolving around the questions of language, religion, and ethnicity. As he put it:

> northern Sudanese see themselves as Arabs and deny the strongly African element in their skin color and physical features. This denial of the African element is grounded on their perception and association of these features with the Negroid race and they see it as the mother race of slaves, inferior and demeaned.[8]

On the other hand, southern Sudanese, who view themselves as Africans with strong cultural and moral values, perceive the northerners as a confused people with no proper origins. Identity within such a context is viewed as

> a function of how people identify themselves and are identified in race, ethnicity, culture, language and religion and how such identification determines or influences their participation in the political, economic, social and cultural life of their country.[9]

Gamal M. Hamid attributes the root cause of the conflict to the following four factors:

> (i) Weak national sentiments between heterogeneous peoples who share the same territory, yet have little in common in terms of a common culture or history; (ii) bitter memories of a distant past marred by human enslavement in which various people from the north, the south and from outside the Sudan participated; (iii) a series of mistrustful acts, unkept promises, and dishonored agreements between the North and the South which have precipitated a deep sense of mistrust between southerners and northerners; and (iv) colonial policies and other historical forces that facilitated domination of the economy and the state apparatus by northern elites, who used it to perpetuate the subordinate position of the South vis-à-vis the North. The end result of this situation has been lack of socio-economic development in the south.[10]

Other Sudanese scholars single out the British colonial administration's policy of "divide and rule" during the period of Anglo-Egyptian Condominium (1898–1956) as a contributing factor to the separation and worsening of relationships between the north and the south, as well as to the underdevelopment of the south.[11] The most criticized aspect of British rule is the "Southern Policy" of 1930–1947, which permitted the south to be administered separately from the north. The intention was to keep the south from being influenced by Arab culture and religion, while at the same time allowing the British to spread Christianity in a region where most people followed traditional African religious practices. Northern Sudanese were not free to travel or live in the south without obtaining a special permit from the British authority. English, rather than Arabic, was taught in southern schools. However, with pressure from the northern nationalists and Egypt, as well as from the postwar Labour government in Britain, in 1947 the British officials in the Sudan abandoned their "Southern Policy." In its stead they merged southern Sudan with the north by creating a unified administrative system for the whole country.[12] It should be noted that scholars who concentrate on the responsibility of British colonial policies for widening the gap between the northern and southern Sudan conveniently ignore the role of successive northern-dominated postcolonial governments in also oppressing and marginalizing the south.

RETHINKING THE UNDERLYING CAUSES OF THE CONFLICT

Darfur: Upsetting Prevailing Perceptions of Civil Strife in the Sudan

The Darfur conflict in the western Sudan began in 2003 when two armed movements, the Sudan Liberation Army/Movement (SLA/M) and the Justice and Equality Movement (JEM), raised a rebellion against government policies in Khartoum that they believed have marginalized the Darfur region. In response to the rebellion, the Islamized and Arabized government in Khartoum mobilized its army and air force and armed a militia group, known as *Janjaweed* (meaning "evil horsemen"). These forces follow a strategy of scorched earth, massacre, and starvation in an attempt to defeat the rebel groups.

The Darfur conflict represents a turning point in the history of the Sudanese conflict because it disrupts the prevailing, but simplistic, perceptions of civil strife there as a struggle between the north and south in which Arabs are pitted against Africans, or Muslims are ranged against Christians and "animists." In other words, the Darfur conflict marks the fragmentation of the north's supposedly unified Arab and Islamic identity. It further disrupts the dominant Sudanese national discourse, which presents the people of Sudan's northern, western, and eastern regions as a single, homogeneous group bound by Islamic religion and Arab culture, while the people of the south are portrayed as non-Arabs and non-Muslims who need to be Islamized. Unlike the earlier and long-standing "north-south" conflict, which has been perceived in essentially racial and religious terms, the conflict in Darfur is complicated by the fact that those who are fighting each other—though ethnically differentiated—are all Muslims.

Some scholars divide the people of Darfur into several ethnic groups. According to Suliman Mohamed, the population of Darfur can be separated into the nomadic camel and cattle herders who identify themselves as Arabs, and the rural-based sedentary farmers and small-scale cultivators who are mainly non-Arabs and belong predominantly to the Fur people (Darfur means "The Land of the Fur").[13] Others draw attention to migration, linguistic, and occupational factors when identifying the ethnic structure of Darfur. Those who stress the ethnic and tribal elements of the region tend to argue that the conflict is a result of both ecological and

A Fur village called Shoba on the northern slopes of Jabal Marra after an attack launched by Sudanese government forces in May 2002. Courtesy of Gamal Adam.

social factors. Struggle over scarce natural resources was the main reason for earlier conflicts from the 1950s to the 1970s between the nomads and the settled farmers. However, over time—and particularly in the 1980s—the conflict took a political character, with GOS policies of divide and rule continuing to be a major cause of the conflict. Dawud Ibrahim Salih argues that the real reason that violence has torn apart the lives of so many people in western Sudan in the 1990s lies in GOS policy. By arming and financing local Arab paramilitary groups, the GOS has quite intentionally created ethnic (and in fact racial) conflicts across western Sudan. GOS has disarmed non-Arab groups, making them virtually defenceless against the well-armed government militias. The GOS has instigated nothing short of a racial war against the non-Arab inhabitants of western Sudan.[14]

The political and economic marginalization of the region is also cited as leading to war in Darfur. The two armed groups in Darfur, SLM and JEM, demand the end of the marginalization of Darfur and more protection for the settled population. They also insist on full political representation and a share in power in Khartoum.[15]

The Economic Exploitation of the Southern Sudan

Underdevelopment, wide regional economic disparities, and the unequal sharing of political power certainly all contribute to the continuing conflict in the Sudan. Economic as well as political power continues to be concentrated in the center, while the rest of the country is marginalized.[16] As far as the south is concerned, successive regimes in the Sudan since the eighteenth century have not been interested in the development of the region. Instead, they have concentrated on exploiting its natural and human resources. For example, its Turko-Egyptian rulers (1821–1885) extracted its gold, ivory, and slaves. The Anglo-Egyptian Condominium (1898–1956) was determined to hold onto the south to secure the Nile that flows through the region and, incidentally, to carry out their "civilizing mission" among its animist peoples. However, it saw no immediate economic benefits accruing from the region itself and neglected to develop it.[17]

The consequence for the southern Sudan of this neglect—coupled with the Islamization and Arabization policies pursued by the successive northern-dominated government after independence in 1956—is that it has remained far behind the north in terms of social infrastructure, trade, industry, and the development of economic and financial institutions. Moreover, the exploitation of southern Sudan's natural resources and economic potential has not ceased with the departure of the colonial power. Successive governments in independent Sudan have established a mechanism for controlling the southern economy. Although the south was given regional self-government after the Addis Ababa agreement in 1972, southern political leaders were stripped of their previous power to decide on important economic issues affecting their own region. Decisions regarding planning and budgeting of economic projects still remain the responsibility of the central government. The situation is further aggravated by the discovery and exploitation of oil in the south in the 1980s and the 1990s. Since the government controls oil production as well as benefiting from its profits, the southerners are denied its benefits and are displaced from their homelands to make way for the further exploitation of oil and the construction of related infrastructure.

Centralized Government

Besides maintaining a tight grip on the country's economy and the exploitation of its natural resources, the northern-dominated governments of the independent Sudan have continued to exercise firm political control over the country. For instance, decisions pertaining to "defence, foreign affairs, currency, inter-regional communications, and the broad functions of economic, social and educational planning" are the responsibility of the central government in Khartoum, and not of individual provinces like Southern Sudan or Darfur.[18] In other words, the central government decides for the whole country who should be in charge of education, planning and administration, and who should set and distribute the national budget. Thus the southern Sudanese, the people of Darfur, and other marginalized groups in Sudan are either excluded from decision-making or are relegated to noninfluential positions in the political and economic structures of the country. It makes no difference that, for example, the marginalized people of Darfur constitute the backbone of the Sudanese national army, are devoted Muslims, and have been traditionally loyal to the ruling Umma Party in Khartoum. It is against this background of economic and political deprivation that the southern Sudanese, and later the Darfur people, have resisted and continue to resist Khartoum's political domination and economic exploitation.

Cultural and Political Identities

According to Amir Idris, the customary, facile perception of the north-south conflict as an ethnic and religious one between the "Arab" Muslim north and "African" Christian or animist south is misleading. Instead, he suggests that in the context of the Sudan the concepts of "African" and "Arab" have one crucial thing in common: both denote political identities that have produced particular historical forms of power, self-identity, and exclusion. He therefore argues that neither culture nor race is at the heart of the conflict. Rather, he concludes that it is the racialized state that has transformed these cultural identities into political identities through the practice of slavery in the precolonial period, indirect rule during the colonial period, and the state-sponsored Islamization and Arabization in the postcolonial period.[19]

A Crisis in National Identity

The civil war in the Sudan is thus more than a matter of the Arab Muslim north pitted against the African Christian south. The crisis in Darfur has shown the complexity of the conflict and the inadequacy of the north-south perspective in explaining the historical and political causes of the Sudan's civil wars. In the context of a north-south conflict, for instance, the people of Darfur are commonly considered Muslims and northerners. Yet, like the people of the Southern Sudan, they have been politically oppressed and relentlessly deprived economically under both colonial and independent rule. The recent violent attacks against some non-Arab Muslim groups such as the Fur, the Zaghawa, and the Massaleit in Darfur prove that in present-day Sudan conversion to Islam cannot fully compensate for the absence of an Arab origin.[20]

The conflict in Darfur is in fact the latest manifestation of the national crisis that has ravaged the country since the first stage of the civil war broke out in Southern Sudan in 1955. Neither of the two wars in the south, nor the current conflict in Darfur, are aberrations. Instead, these wars should be seen as the logical consequence for a state dominated from its inception by the interest of an Islamized and Arabized ruling group. Indeed, the question of the national identity of the Sudan is at the center of the crisis. The Sudanese state was long in forming, and the nature of the state that was created during the precolonial period, and which consolidated and institutionalized its policies during the colonial and the postcolonial periods, laid the seeds of the current political violence. The legacies of slavery and colonialism have contributed to the invention of two categories of people with different entitlements. Those who are considered "Arab" by the racialized state are treated as citizens, and those who are perceived as "non-Arabs" are treated as subjects.[21]

EXCLUSIVE NATIONAL IDENTITY AND CONFLICT

In the context of Sudan, any discussion on the nature and the meaning of the national identity should grapple with a series of questions. How is the Sudanese nation "narrated" or, in other words, how is its story manipulated and presented? What cultural, social, ethnic, and racial aspects are evoked in the process of "narrating the nation"? How do the Sudanese people identify themselves, and how are they identified by others? What measures have been taken to ensure the promotion and sustainability of the emerging national identity? In an attempt to address these questions we focus on the Sudan's nationalist discourse with respect to the complex national identity issue.

Edward Said, in his analysis of nationalism and its relation to exile, defined nationalism as "an assertion of belonging in and to a place, a people, a heritage. It affirms the home created by a community of language, culture and customs."[22] However, this "assertion of belonging" does not emerge from a vacuum. Rather, it is informed and shaped by a particular interpretation of history, culture, and the myth of origin. As Benedict Anderson suggested, "nationalism has to be understood by aligning it not with self-consciously held political ideologies, but with the large cultural system that preceded it."[23] Anderson went on to argue that:

nationality, or ... nationness, as well as nationalism, are cultural artefacts of a particular kind. To understand them properly we need to consider carefully how they have come into historical being, in what ways their meanings have changed over time, and why today, they command such profound emotional legitimacy.[24]

Following Anderson's analysis, and bearing in mind that in the process of imagining the nation, nationalists usually draw on a particular history, culture, origin, and ideology, it becomes clear that the forging of a national identity tends to be exclusionary in nature. For example, given the heterogeneity of the people who inhabit a territory such as the Sudan, the interpretation of nationalism solely from a particular viewpoint of its history, culture, and ideology might not appeal to all. Therefore, those who feel they do not belong might opt to assert their own sense of belonging, which in turn is informed by their own particular understanding of history, value systems, and experiences.

Nationalism in the Sudan was and is closely linked to the pan-Arab and the Arab nationalist movements of the first half of the twentieth century. As Amir Idris notes, in the early 1920s "the question of race and descent became very significant in determining the course of Sudanese nationalism."[25] Idris went further to argue that:

[t]he nationalist narrative of the 1930s had created for itself a genealogy that stretches far into the Islamic Arab past. It suggested a primordial and essential identity shared by all those who lived in the north regardless of their particular historical experiences and cultural orientations.[26]

As a result, the successive northern-dominated governments in Sudan have insisted on Arabism and Islamism as the defining elements of Sudan's national identity. In fact, the northern-dominated ideology of nationalism has long been shaped by the legacy of slavery and the slave trade. Southern or western Sudanese who became Muslims were stigmatized by their slave status or origins. Islam and the claim of Arab origin in turn have provided the ideological justification for the practice of racism and the use of violence against non-Arab groups. Thus color and religion are irrelevant in the context of Darfur, where it is descent that matters. As in the case of southern Sudanese, those who converted to Islam have never been fully accepted into society and have not been treated by the Arabized and Islamized state as citizens with social and political rights.

In the process of forging a unified national identity, several measures have been deployed to insure its success. These range from exclusionary practices to the integration or assimilation of the other; from suppression of forms of knowledge and history that are deemed incompatible with the idea of the national culture and identity to coercion to conform, or the elimination of those who resist. For instance, the northern Sudanese continue to assume that southern Sudan is a "cultural vacuum" that needs to be filled by Arab culture under an Islamic revival. The measures employed to effect this considerably predate independence and go back to the period of the Mahadist state (1885–1898) in Sudan, which was "an Islamic state fashioned to revive the concept and practice of the early Islamic community of [the prophet] Muhammad and his companions."[27]

Between the 1950s and the 1970s the northern-based nationalists targeted the educational system as a structure through which Islamization and Arabization of the south could take place. During this period an integrated educational policy was designed for the whole Sudan, replacing the separate educational and administrative systems originally constituted under the British administration.[28] This new educational policy was accelerated during General Ibrahim Abboud's military regime (1958–1964) through the enforced spread of Islamic education, conversion, and the promotion of the Arabic language as the national language. Christian missionary schools were nationalized, and foreign missionaries were expelled from the south to make way for Arabization and Islamization. All these interventions triggered resistance from the southerners and partly contributed to the southern uprising and Sudan's first civil war (1955–1972). In some parts of southern Sudan, particularly in urban areas, school-age children, to enable them to enroll in school, were given new Arabic names in compliance with the policies of Arabization. It is consequently common among southern Sudanese for one person to have three different names: traditional, Arabic, and Christian. The latter baptismal name can either be a European one or might commemorate a biblical figure.

Similarly, the imposition of *Shari'a* (the religious law of Islam) has become a prerequisite for imagining the Sudanese nation. During the military regime of General Jaafer M. Nimeiri (1969–1985) further steps were taken to reconsolidate the Islamic *Shari'a* in the Sudan. Several Islamic-oriented projects aimed at accelerating the spread of Islam and Arab culture in the South were designed and implemented, including Arab-funded projects such as the Islamic African Center and the Islamic African Relief Agency, which were designed to help African Muslims.[29]

In 1980 Nimeiri's regime made a more radical move to enforce the Islamic *Shari'a* by amalgamating the formally autonomous civil and *Shari'a* court systems into a single judicial hierarchy.[30] Subsequently, in September 1983 President Nimeiri proclaimed the Islamic *Shari'a* to be the sole guiding force behind the laws of the Sudan. Measures were introduced to ensure that punishment for crimes conformed accordingly, and included "amputation for proven theft ... the death penalty for adultery ... and the Islamic punishment of flogging for drinking, or for the possession, sale or transport or manufacture of alcoholic beverages."[31] Although in theory the Islamic *Shari'a* should have applied only to Muslims in Sudan, in real life it has affected non-Muslims as well, especially those living in Khartoum and other northern cities.

The measures taken to Arabize and Islamize non-Muslim and non-Arab Sudanese have become increasingly aggressive, particularly since 1989 when the National Islamic Front (NIF) military regime came to power in a military coup. The main agenda of the new government is to establish a single Islamic identity for the whole Sudanese nation, whereby both the constitution and the law would be based solely on the *Qura'n* and the *Sunna.* Like its predecessors in power, the NIF regime has targeted the educational system at all levels to accelerate the Arabization and Islamization of the country. Between 1990 and 1991 Arabic became the medium of instruction in almost all universities in the country, replacing English, which had been in use since the period of British colonial rule. Similarly, instruction in all primary, junior, and senior secondary schools was changed from English to Arabic. In addition, the NIF regime requires new students enrolled in universities and other higher institutions of learning to undergo militia training as members of the Popular Defence Forces (PDF) before starting their studies.[32] The registration of students for universities has consequently been moved from the campuses to the militia camps. This requirement remains crucial for the government in its efforts to perpetuate the war in the south since the militia are deployed to reinforce government forces in the civil war. And, not unintentionally, these processes have further reduced the presence of southern Sudanese students and faculty in Sudan's institutions of higher learning. Clearly, the enforcement of all these measures of Islamization and Arabization have sought to suppress the different languages, cultures, histories, and religious practices of the non-Arab and non-Muslim groups in the Sudan.

On another level, the histories, experiences, voices, and the intellectual contributions of the non-Arab and non-Muslim people in Sudan have been excluded from the official national discourse. This exclusion is evident in their absence from the educational curriculum and public media. For instance, southern Sudanese children are taught about Arab history and literature, the desert, and animals such as the camel, none of which are relevant to their experiences, the local situation in the south, or its environment. Nothing is taught about such animals as the goat, the buffalo or the elephant, which are common in the south. This exclusion is necessary if successive northern-based governments are to justify their assertion that the Sudan has a unified Arab and Islamic identity. As Edward Said has clearly pointed out, "the power to narrate, or to block other narratives from forming or emerging is a crucial method by which imperialists impose their powerful all conquering value system."[33] To retain control and disseminate Arabism and Islamism, and to ensure national cohesion, unity, and stability on their own terms, the northern nationalists and the successive northern-dominated governments have pursued a deliberate strategy of controlling or otherwise eliminating the narratives and voices of non-Muslims and non-Arabs.

NATIONAL IDENTITY AND THE STATUS OF WOMEN

The dominant northern Sudanese nationalist discourse has not only eliminated the voices of the non-Musim and non-Arab groups, but it has also impacted on the role and status of women in the Sudan. Gender-based violence, particularly rape (as will be shown below), has become widespread in southern Sudan and more recently in Darfur. In the Sudan, the position of women in the nationalist project continues to be shaped by the ideology of a nationally unified culture and identity that finds its unifying principles in Arab culture and the Islamic religion. The *al mara'h al Sudaniyah* (or the "Sudanese woman") is constructed in opposition to the non-Muslim and non-Arab woman. Adherence to Islamic teachings, proper "modesty," and compliance with the Islamic *Shari'a* in all aspects of people's lives represent the social and moral principles through which women are located within the nationalist discourse.

During the period the NIF military regime has been in power, such moral principles have been rigorously applied in Sudan. Laws governing women's conduct and behavior, both within the family and within the larger society, are formulated specifically to regulate the lives of women and the roles they play. For example, laws such as the *Law Governing Public Conduct for the Central State* (1992) and the *Law Governing Public Order for El-Khartoum State* (1991)[34] were formulated with the prime intention of regulating women's as well as men's conduct and behavior, particularly in public spaces. One of the provisions of these laws concerns conformity to an Islamic dress code, or *'al ziyy al-Islami'*, to be followed by all working women and all women who happen to be in public places like the market or the park, or on public transport. In such spaces, women are required to express in their conduct and appearance the spiritual qualities that are regarded as characteristics of an Islamic people and state. For example, section 5 (1) of the *Law Governing Public Conduct for the Central State* (1992:3) stipulates that "[a]ny Muslim woman walking in the street or appearing in a work place or any public place without an Islamic dress will be punished by flogging and the payment of the sum of five hundred Sudanese pounds."[35]

As indicated above, these laws, although intended for Muslim women only, affect non-Muslim women who live in Khartoum and other northern cities as well. Thus, non-Muslim female students, as well as women from the south displaced by the war who work in public offices in the north, continue to be forced to wear Islamic dress on the grounds of "modesty." As indicated in reports published by *Africa Watch* in 1993 and *Amnesty International Focus* in 1995, women are flogged or threatened with dismissal from their jobs for not conforming to the government's idea of what constitutes decent dress.[36] In other words, the nationalist discourse on women places a particular group of them, namely, those who are Arab and Islamic, in a privileged position. This, in turn, tends to exclude or marginalize those women who are racially, ethnically, culturally, and religiously different from these Arab and Islamic women and has contributed to the marginalization of indigenous identities and to the denial of their development and recognition.

THE CONSEQUENCES OF CIVIL WARS FOR CIVILIANS

The two civil wars of 1955–1972 and 1983–2005 in southern Sudan and the current conflict in Darfur have had devastating consequences in Sudan in general, and particularly in the two regions most directly affected. These wars have led to massive displacement and to the death of millions of people, besides the destruction of the infrastructure and the social, cultural, and economic fabric of the southern and western Sudanese societies.

The revolt of 1955 triggered the first phase of a civil war that lasted for 17 years. In 1958 Abboud's military regime put an end to civilian politics after only two years of Sudanese independence. The military regime's approach to "national unity" was aimed at the assimilation of southerners into the northern Sudanese cultural fabric. The cycle of violence and terror was intensified during the civilian government of Mohammed Ahmed Mahjoub (1966–1968), who was known for his open racism toward the people of southern Sudan. He claimed that the "only language southerners understand is force."[37] Mahjoub's period of rule witnessed one of the bloodiest campaigns of terror in the south. Villages were burned and thousands of people fled to neighboring countries. One of the most ruthless single massacres took place at Juba on July 8–9, 1965 when an estimated 1,400 people were slaughtered. The total number of southerners killed between 1963 and 1966 by the government's forces was estimated at more than 500,000. The acts of terror and racial discrimination toward the people of southern Sudan increased when the Nimeiri government (1969–1985) unilaterally divided the south into three regions and implemented Islamic law in 1983.

The state-sponsored terror and violence against the south has been given increasingly religious justification with the implementation of the Islamic *Shari'a* in 1983. For instance, the period of Sadiq el-Mahdi's rule (1986–1989) witnessed the increased use of Arab militia against the people of southern Sudan. Like the Janjaweed later in Darfur, these forces attacked mainly civilians and looted their cattle. As an example of the consequences of Sadiq's militia policy, southern civilians were massacred in Al-Da'ein in southern Kordofan on March 27–28, 1987, when local militias killed more than 1,000 Dinka civilians.[38] Since 1989 the government of the National Islamic Front has pursued a *jihad* against the south and the civil war has escalated. The government has systematically encouraged slavery and the slave trade. Militias organized by the government have sold people (including children) from many non-Muslim groups living in southern Sudan and the Nuba mountains into slavery. Government discrimination in the north against several million internally displaced southerners has been common.

As a consequence of the war, the existing infrastructure in southern and western Sudan has been destroyed, leading to economic crisis and the spread of disease. Lack of medical facilities and medicine, poor sanitation, and malnutrition have further led to the spread of diseases and the loss of

Southern Sudanese women refugees in 1997 preparing food and tea for sale along the road in Alere refugee camp in northern Uganda. Photograph by Jane K. Edward, 10 July 1997.

lives. Furthermore, the prevalence of land mines, particularly in the south, has claimed the lives of many civilians. In Juba, for example, where people depend largely on firewood as a source of cooking fuel, many women have been killed by land mines planted by the government forces around the city with the intention of preventing rebel forces from penetrating the city.

The war has also negatively affected the educational system in the affected regions. For example, from the late 1980s through the 1990s as the war intensified, many schools and other institutions of higher learning in the south ceased to function. This was particularly true of the rural areas. In towns, where many displaced people had taken refuge, refugees temporarily occupied many schools before they were relocated to displaced people's camps constructed by international agencies operating in the south. Similarly, because of this insecurity, the only university in the south was transferred in 1987 from Juba to Khartoum. The Juba university campus, as well as the faculty and student residences, was then occupied by the Sudan government's army and the PDF. Ever since the war broke out in Darfur, the people of the western Sudan have faced similar conditions as they struggle to survive.

The war has negatively affected the system of production and the means of livelihood in the affected regions, leading to famines and economic difficulties. Those who practice agriculture, for example, are unable to work the land effectively because of the constant movement of people from one

Southern Sudanese refugee children in 1997 attending school under the trees in Alere refugee camp. Photograph by Jane K. Edward, 8 July 1997.

Southern Sudanese refugee children in 2001 eating their lunch in their classroom in one of the church-sponsored refugee schools in Cairo, Egypt. Photograph by Jane K. Edward, 24 November 2001.

village to another to avoid the fighting, because of the number of land mines on their lands, or because their villages have been burned down. Besides its impact on economic, social, cultural, and educational aspects of the affected regions, the war has further contributed to environmental degradation and the depletion of natural resources, particularly in the south. The continuing war has degraded the soil, grazing land, and natural vegetation upon which the majority of the Sudanese depend for their rural livelihood. Over-grazing, and the cutting down of trees both by the government and the rebel forces, and by some residents of the south, have contributed to deforestation on a massive scale, land erosion, and ecological degradation. Many government soldiers deployed in the south, particularly in garrison towns, were engaged in trade in lumber, shipping great quantities north for economic development. Earlier reports from the SPLM/A-controlled areas alleged that some SPLM/A commanders were involved in a similar trade, mainly between the liberated areas and the neighboring countries of Uganda and Kenya.[39] Since wood has become the only source of fuel for cooking in the south, many residents were (and still are) engaged in the firewood trade, supplying households, local bakeries, and other small-scale business facilities. The degradation of the vegetation in the bush country of the south where the war was mainly fought has also had devastating consequences for the wildlife, leading to the local extirpation of some species and the movement away by others into neighboring countries.

WOMEN, CIVIL WAR, AND GENDER VIOLENCE

As we have seen, the regulation of women's conduct and behavior through prescribed laws and through gender-based violence is embedded in the Sudanese government's policy toward non-Muslims and non-Arabs. The consequences for the physical and psychological well-being of Sudanese women have been devastating. Gender-based violence was first manifested in the southern Sudan as a strategy of Islamization, Arabization, marginalization, and humiliation. During the north-south conflict southern Sudanese women and girls have been subjected to all forms of sexual violence including rape, torture, killing, early or forced marriage, and compelled prostitution. For example, while one of the authors was staying in Juba, an increasing number of young southern Sudanese women were observed who have become wives of, or have born children to, northern Sudanese soldiers stationed in the area. It should be noted that many of these relationships between these women and the soldiers had been initiated neither in a peaceful manner nor in accordance with the culturally accepted way in which marriage is conducted in the south. In fact, these women were either forced into the relationship, or were raped.

Given the general situation in the south (and in Juba in particular), which was characterized by insecurity, economic hardships, and military rule, the parents or members of the extended families of these women were unable to prevent violence against them out of fear for their own lives. Worse still, some of these soldiers, upon completion of their mission in the south, returned to the north, leaving behind these unfortunate women and their children to fend for themselves. Government soldiers are not solely at fault, however. Many young women in the SPLM/A-controlled areas have fallen victim to forced relationships with rebel soldiers. With the breakdown of society brought about by war and dislocation, it is perhaps not surprising to learn that some married women have experienced domestic violence and abuse at the hands of their husbands. In his study of the experience of women in the western Dinka area, Jok M. Jok noted that "nearly 80% of the sample women [he interviewed] reported having been battered several times throughout their marriage life for reasons related to refusal of sexual services. Many cases of domestic abuse which took place at night were witnessed."[40]

The war has consequently affected marriage and the institution of the family in southern Sudan. In particular, it has led to changes in the family structure, and to an increase in the number of teenage single parents, both inside Sudan and in the refugee camps in neighboring countries. An increasing number of children are being cared for either by a teenage mother or a grandmother. The father is either at the front, has been killed, or has simply left, and this has led to an increase in the number of female-headed households.[41] With so many adults killed in the fighting, many children have been left orphans and are cared for by other women in the community. Many southern Sudanese women and girls have also been abducted and subjected to sexual slavery and forced labor, while destitute women have had resort to prostitution in order to support themselves and their children.

According to the 1992 Human Rights Report of the U.S. State Department, the Sudanese Army was "identified with numerous human rights abuses, including many civilian deaths … extra-judicial executions, forced conscription, rape and pillage."[42] Pointing out the actions of the government forces and militia does not imply that rebel forces fighting in the southern Sudan were themselves free from human rights violations. On the contrary, both warring parties in the southern Sudan have engaged in various human rights abuses against the civilian population and against women in particular. Girma Kebbede has outlined how both government and rebel forces have shown "little or no concern for the rights of civilians" and have contributed to their suffering in the south through the forced conscription of young boys (especially by the SPLA), and the ruthless destruction of people's livelihoods.[43] Women, as has been shown earlier, have suffered particular abuse.

Gender-based violence similar to that in the southern Sudan is being repeated in Darfur. According to Amnesty International Human Rights Report on Darfur (2004),[44] the Janjaweed militia have used rape as a weapon of war to intimidate and humiliate the people of Darfur. Other human rights violations, which have specifically targeted women and girls, include abductions, sexual slavery, torture, killing, and forced displacement. Torture and killing, for example, are directed at those women who either resisted rape or (in the case of married women) at those who initially refused to reveal the whereabouts of their husbands who might have been with the resistance fighters. Women's everyday responsibilities put them at further risk of rape and death. As is the case in most African societies, women in Sudan have the sole responsibility for feeding and caring for their children and other members of the extended family, regardless of the perils of the situation. They have to produce and prepare food, fetch water, collect firewood, and perform other family necessities. As a result, in conflict situations they are always in the front line, exposed to all kinds of threats. In the south, women's lives continue to be put at risk when they go gathering firewood because of the ubiquity of landmines. Likewise, in Darfur, women are usually at risk of rape by armed militias lurking in the vicinity of their villages or refugee camps when they venture out to collect the firewood upon which their families depend for survival. A recent study of sexual violence in Darfur documented the impossible choice women have to make daily:

> The hundreds of thousands who fled the destroyed villages have now sought refuge in makeshift camps with little but rags and sticks as shelter. But they have found no safety there. In spite of high-profile visits of the world's leaders, people still face persecution and intimidation inside the camps. Rape, a feature of the attacks on their villages, has now followed them insidiously into their places of refuge. Families, in order to sustain themselves, have to continue collecting wood, fetching water or working their fields. In doing so, women have to make a terrible choice, putting themselves or their children at risk of rape, beatings or death as soon as they are outside the camps, towns or villages.[45]

The report also cited the testimony of three women, aged 23, 30, and 40, who were raped in October 2004 in west Darfur by the Janjaweed:

> We saw five Arab men who came to us and asked where our husbands were. Then they told us that we should have sex with them. We said no. So they beat and raped us. After they abused us they told us that now we would have Arab babies; and if they would find any Fur [one of the non-Arab or African tribal groups of Darfur], they would rape them again to change the colour of their children.[46]

Of course, the Khartoum government backing the militias has systematically used sexual violence against the women of Darfur as an instrument of counter-insurgency. Rape in the context of war serves to create fear, shame, and demoralization among the victimized group and the individual who has been directly assaulted. Given the fact that rape is regarded as a taboo subject and a matter of great shame in the Sudan, social stigma attaches to the victim and the associated social ostracism that follows negatively affects the lives of rape survivors. Rape victims are consequently reluctant to report the incident either to their families or to medical personnel, whether those in local health facilities or refugee camps. As in the southern Sudan, so in Darfur rape has deliberately been used as a state-sponsored instrument of terror for the cultural and ethnic destruction of those whom the dominant ruling group considers to be non-Arab.[47]

CONCLUSION

Identity issues revolving around race, ethnicity, and religion, expressed through the official national discourse in the Sudan, arguably represent the main factors that led to the outbreak of civil war and to its perpetuation. Nevertheless, struggles over natural resources and political power also constitute a major source of conflict.

Non-Arab and non-Muslim groups such as the people of southern Sudan, and those from the Nuba Mountains, as well as the Fur of the western Sudan, have all been subjected to state terror in the Sudan. In the existing Arabized and Islamized state they have long been treated as subjects, rather than as citizens, and assigned inferior racial identities. Yet neither culture nor race is at the center of the bloody conflict in the Sudan; rather it is the nature of the state itself. Since political independence in 1956 successive military and civilian regimes have exercised power with the notion that only a Muslim state can legitimately exercise power over a Muslim majority. In the process of implementing this single vision of nation and state, acts of terror and brutal violence have become the driving force of the nation-making project in the Sudan. The dreadful implications of this single vision are being acted out in the present civil war in Darfur, as for many years they have also in southern Sudan. The consequences of decades of civil wars in the Sudan are naturally severe for the victims, particularly women. Many civilians from the targeted regions perish, while many more are harassed, humiliated, terrorized, tortured, raped, dehumanized, and, being left without protection, become desperate refugees with little hope for the future.

ABBREVIATIONS

GOS Government of Sudan
IGAD Inter-Governmental Authority on Development
JEM Justice and Equality Movement
NIF National Islamic Front
PDF Popular Defence Forces
SSLM Southern Sudan Liberation Movement
SLM/A Sudan Liberation Movement/Army

SPLM/A Sudan People's Liberation Movement/Army

UN United Nations

TIMELINE

1821–1885 Turko-Egyptian rule in Sudan

1885–1898 The Mahdist state

1898–1955 Anglo-Egyptian Condominium in Sudan

1947 Juba Conference

1956 January 1: Independence of Sudan from Anglo-Egyptian colonial rule

1955–1972 First north-south civil war

1972 Addis Ababa Peace Agreement between the Southern Sudan Liberation Movement and the Government of Sudan

1983–2005 Second north-south civil war

1983 September: Implementation of the *Shari'a* laws in Sudan (which came to be known as "the September Laws") during the regime of General Jaafar Mohamed Nimeiri (1969–1984)

1989 June 30: Military coup by the National Islamic Front overthrows the democratically elected government of Sadiq al-Mahdi (1985–1989)

2003 February: War in Darfur begins

2005 January 9: Signing of the Comprehensive Peace Agreement between the Sudan People's Liberation Movement and the Government of Sudan in Niavasha, Kenya

GLOSSARY

Names

Abbod, General Ibrahim (1900–1983). Educated at Gordon Memorial College and the Khartoum Military College. Joined the Sudan Defence Force in 1925, and after the military coup of November 1958 became president of the Supreme Council of the Armed Forces and prime minister. Forced into retirement by the October Revolution of 1964.

Garang, Dr. John (1947–2005). Born into the South Dinka group. Studied in southern Sudan, Tanzania, and the United States, where in 1977 he earned a Ph.D. in agricultural economics from Iowa State University. In 1983 founded and became the leader of the SPLM/A. Advocated the vision of "New Sudan," which called for a united democratic Sudan that would respect the rights of all its citizens. Considered the champion of the marginalized peoples of the Sudan. Following the signing of the 2005 Comprehensive Peace Agreement he was appointed first vice-president, a position he held for only three weeks before he was killed in a helicopter crash on July 30, 2005.

el-Mahdi, Sadiq (1936–). A political and religious leader and member of the influential al-Mahdi family. Educated at the Universities of Khartoum and Oxford. Became the head of the Umma Party in 1961 and was prime minister in 1960–1967 and again in 1986–1989. Was overthrown in June 1989 by an Islamic military coup led by the National Islamic Front (NIF).

Mahjoub, Mohammed Ahmed (1908–1976). Political and intellectual leader who graduated from Gordon Memorial College and the Khartoum School of Law. In 1953 he was elected to parliament as an independent. Became associated with the Umma Party. Served as Minister of Foreign Affairs 1956–1958, and he was prime minister in 1965–1966 and 1967–1969.

Nimeiri, General Jaafer M. (1930–). Graduated from the Sudan Military College in 1952 and received military training in Germany and the United States. Leader of the May Revolution in 1969 and became the chairman of the Council of the Revolution and minister of defence in the new military government. Overthrown on April 6, 1985 and spent 14 years in exile in Egypt. Returned to Sudan in 1999.

Terms

Janjaweed. Term used to refer to a militia group armed by the government of the Sudan to fight two armed opposition groups in Darfur.

Jihad. Holy War.

Al Mara'h al Sudaniyah. A Sudanese woman.

Qura'n. The Muslim Holy Book.

Shari'a. The religious law of Islam.

Sunna. A normative custom of the Prophet or of the early Muslim community, as set forth in the hadith; or an account of what the Prophet said or did. Second in authority to the Qura'n.

Umma. Nation.

Al ziyy al–Islami. Muslim women's dress code.

NOTES

1. See Grime Kebbede, "Southern Sudan: A War-Torn and Divided Region," in *Sudan Predicament: Civil War, Displacement and Ecological Degradation,* ed. Grime Kebbede (Aldershot: Ashgate, 1999), 44–61.

2. See Oliver Albino, *The Sudan: Southern Viewpoint* (London: Oxford University Press, 1970; Dunstan Wai, *The African-Arab Conflict in the Sudan* (New York: African Publishing Company, 1981); Francis Deng, *War of Visions: Conflict of Identities in the Sudan* (Washington, DC: Brookings Institution, 1995); Simon E. Kulusika, *Southern Sudan: Political and Economic Power Dilemmas and Options* (London: Minerva Press, 1998).

3. Muddathir Abdel Al-Rahim, "Arabism, Africanism, and Self-identification in the Sudan," in *The Southern Sudan: The Problem of National Integration,* ed. Dunstan Wai (London: Frank Cass, 1973), 29–45; Mohammed Omer Bashir,

Educational Development in the Sudan: 1898–1956 (Oxford: Oxford University Press, 1969); Gamal Hamid, *Population Displacement in the Sudan* (New York: Center for Migration Studies, 1996).

4. Amir Idris, *Sudan's Civil War: Slavery, Race and Formational Identities* (Lewiston: The Edwin Mellen Press, 2001).

5. Ann Lesch, *The Sudan: Contested National Identities* (Bloomington and Oxford: Indiana University Press and James Currey, 1998); Gabriel Warburg, *Historical Discord in the Nile Valley* (London: Hurst and Co., 1992).

6. See Wai, *African-Arab Conflict in the Sudan.*

7. See Albino, *The Sudan,* 3.

8. See Deng, *War of Visions,* 14.

9. Ibid.

10. See Hamid, *Population Displacement,* 56.

11. See Mohamed Omer Bashir, *The Southern Sudan: Background to Conflict* (London: C. Hurst, 1968).

12. See P. M. Holt and W. M. Daly, eds., *A History of the Sudan: From the Coming of Islam to the Present* Day (New York: Longman, 2000).

13. Suliman Mohamed, "Ethnicity from Perception to Cause of Violent Conflicts: The Case of the Fur and Nuba Conflicts in Western Sudan," paper presented at a CONTCI International Workshop, Bern, July 6-11, 1997, online article, 5. Available from http://www.ifaanet.org/ifaapr/ethnicity_inversion.html.

14. Dawud Ibrahim Salih, Muhammad Adam Yahya, Abdul Hafiz, Omar Sharief, and Osman Abbakorah, "Not Ready-for-Prime-Time Genocide: Despite the Hype, Slaughter and Ethnic Cleansing Go Unnoticed in Western Sudan," *Toward Freedom Magazine* (September/October 1999): 2.

15. Amnesty International, "Darfur: Rape as a Weapon of War: Sexual Violence and its Consequences," online article, pp. 1–27. http://web.amnesty.org/library/print/ENGAFR5407622004.

16. See B Bure Yongo, "The Underdevelopment of the Southern Sudan since Independence," in *Civil War in the Sudan,* eds. M. W. Daly and Ahmed A. Sikainga (London: British Academics Press, 1993), 51–77.

17. Ibid.

18. See P. M. Holt and M. W. Daly, *A History of the Sudan: From the Coming of Islam to the Present Day,* 5th ed. (New York: Longman, 2000), 170.

19. See Idris, *Sudan's Civil War.*

20. See Amir Idris, *Conflict and Politics of Identity in Sudan* (New York: Palgrave/Macmillan, 2005).

21. Ibid.

22. Edward Said, "Reflections on Exile," in *Out There: Marginalization and Contemporary Cultures,* eds. Russell Perguson, Martha Gever, Trinh T. Minh-ha, and Cornel West (New York: The New Museum of Contemporary Art, 1990), 357–66.

23. Benedict Anderson, *Imagined Communities: Reflections on the Origin and the Spread of Nationalism* (London: Verso, 1983), 19.

24. Ibid., 14.

25. Idris, *Sudan's Civil War,* 81.

26. See Amir Idris, "The Racialized and Islamicised Sudanese State and the Question of Southern Sudan," in *State Crises, Globalization and National Movements in North-East Africa,* ed. Asafa Jalata (London and New York: Routledge, 2004), 40.

27. For more on the Mahadist State, see Gabriel R. Warburg, *Historical Discord in the Nile Valley* (London: C. Hurst and Co., 1992); Holt and Daly, *History of the Sudan.*

28. During British colonial rule in the Sudan, separate administrative and educational systems were established. Thus, the southern Sudan was administered by British administrators and its education system by the missionaries. The English language was used as a medium of instruction instead of Arabic. English was also the official language. For more on the separate system during the British rule see Dunstan Wai, *The African-Arab Conflict in the Sudan* (New York: African Publishing Company, 1981); and Bashir, *Southern Sudan.*

29. Abdelwahab Al-Affendi, *Turabi's Revolution: Islam and Power in Sudan* (London: Grey Seal, 1991), 149.

30. Abdulahi Ahmed An-na'im, *Toward an Islamic Reformation: Civil Liberties, Human Rights, and International Law* (Syracuse, NY: Syracuse University Press, 1990); also see Carolyn Fluehr-Lobban, *Islamic Law and Society in Sudan* (London: Frank Cass, 1987), 280.

31. Fluehr-Lobban, *Islamic Law and Society in Sudan,* 281.

32. The Popular Defence Forces (PDF) is a militia, organized along the lines of the Iranian Revolutionary Guards, who help train its members. For more details, see *Near East Report* (May 24, 1993), 96.

33. See Edward Said, *Culture and Imperialism* (New York: Vintage Books, 1993), xiii.

34. M. A'wad Alhasan, *Laws Governing Public Conduct for the Central State* (Khartoum, Sudan: n.p., 1992), 2–6. See also Mohammed O. Said, *Laws Governing Public Order for El-Khartoum State* (Sudan: n.p., 1991), 1–3. (Arabic sources, author's translation.)

35. Author's translation.

36. See "Sudan: Refugees in Their Own Country," *Africa Watch* 4, no. 8 (1992): 3. See also "Living in a State of Fear," *Amnesty International Focus* 25, no. 2 (1995).

37. Cited in Albino, *The Sudan,* 40.

38. See Ushari Ahmed Mahmud and Suliman Ali Baldo, *Diein Massacre: Slavery in the Sudan* (Khartoum: n.p., 1987).

39. Personal interview with Mr. Sebit Abe in Yei town in southern Sudan, 1997.

40. Jok Madut Jok, *Militarization, Gender and Reproductive Heath in South Sudan* (Lewiston: The Edwin Mellen Press, 1998), 138.

41. Jane Kani Edward, "Understanding Socio-Cultural Change: Transformation and Future Imagining among Southern Sudanese Women Refugees" (Ph.D. diss., University of Toronto, 2004).

42. Cited in Dantaf Oliver and Joel Himetfarb, "The Sudan: Another Case of Ethnic Cleansing?" *Near East Report* (March 1993): 51–52.

43. See Kebbede, "Southern Sudan," 55.

44. See "Sudan: Darfur—Rape as a Weapon of War: Sexual Violence and its Consequences," *Amnesty International Report* (19 July 2004).

45. Cited in Eric Reeves, " Rape as a Strategic Weapon of War in Darfur," 5. Posted by Eric Reeves, June 25, 2005 on www.sudanreeves.org.

46. Ibid., p. 4.

47. See Ibid.

SELECT BIBLIOGRAPHY

Abdel Rahim, Muddathir. "Arabism, Africansim, and Self-Identification in the Sudan." In *Sudan in Africa*. Edited by Y. F. Hassan. Khartoum: KUP, 1970.

Gives the history of the word Sudan, the coming of the Arabs, and the spread of Islam.

Africa Watch. *"Denying the Honor of Living": Sudan: A Human Rights Disaster.* New York: Africa Watch and Human Rights Watch, 1990.

Reports on violations of human rights in the Sudan in the period 1988–1990 and places them in the historical context.

Al Effendi, Abdel Wahab. "Discovering the South: Sudanese Dilemmas for Islam in Africa." *African Affairs* 89 (1990): 371–389.

Argues that the second civil war in the South had very little impact on the rise of Islamic political activism in the Sudan, and that the Sudanese Islamic movement only recently discovered the south.

Alier, Abel. *Too Many Agreements Dishonoured.* Exeter: Ithaca Press, 1990.

Outlines the agreements that have been dishonored by the Sudanese central government.

Bashir, Mohamed Omer. *The Southern Sudan: Background to Conflict.* London: C. Hurst & Co., 1968.

Provides background to the early contact between the north and the south, starting with the first explorers and traders, the Turko-Egyptian government, and the Mahdiya.

Daly, M. W., and Ahmad Alawad Sikainga, eds. *Civil War in the Sudan.* London: British Academic Press, 1993.

Seeks to provide basic information about the war in the Sudan, the issues at stake, and the course of events up until June 1989.

Deng, Francis M. *War of Visions: Conflict of Identities in the Sudan.* Washington, DC: Brookings Institution, 1995.

Argues that the concept of identity in the Sudan is the result of a historical process that is the outcome of a division between the Arab-Islamic north and the African south, and that it is based more on myth than the realities of the situation.

Edward, Jane Kani. "South Sudanese Refugee Women: Questioning the Past and Imagining a Future." In *Women's Rights and Human Rights: International Historical Perspectives.* Edited by Patricia Grimshaw, Katie Holmes, and Marilyn Lake. New York: Palgrave, 2001, 273–389.

Explores the experiences of southern Sudanese women refugees in Egypt and northern Uganda and the implication of the changes for their lives.

———. "Understanding Socio-Cultural Change: Transformation and Future Imagining among Southern Sudanese Women Refugees," Ph.D. diss., University of Toronto, 2004.

Examines the experiences of Sudanese women refugees during exile, and shows how these women use their newly acquired roles, skills and knowledge to reevaluate their past and challenge the image of victimized and dependent women refugees in the refugee literature.

Human Rights Watch. *War in South Sudan: The Civilian Too.* New York: Human Rights Watch, 1993.

Documents the abuses and their consequences in the early 1990s of the civil war on the civilian population of the Sudan.

Idris, Amir H. *Conflict and Politics of Identity in Sudan.* New York: Palgrave/Macmillan, 2005.

Discusses the relationship between the process of state formation and political identities in the context of Sudan's civil wars.

———. *Sudan's Civil War: Slavery, Race and Formational Identities.* Lewiston: The Edwin Mellen Press, 2001.

Examines how "African" and "Arab," as competing racial identities, have been produced in the Sudan, and interprets the roles of various actors with different interests in creating these identities.

Jok, Jok Madut. *Militarization, Gender and Reproductive Health in South Sudan.* Lewiston: The Edwin Mellen Press, 1998.

Investigates the effects of armed conflict on gender and reproductive health among women in southern Sudan, and traces women's reaction to gender differentials that affect their health.

Lesch, A. M. *The Sudan—Contested National Identities.* Bloomington and Oxford: Indiana University Press and James Currey, 1998.

Addresses the difficulty of achieving a consensus concerning national identity in the Sudan, and the consequences this has for the structuring of a constitutional system in a diverse society.

Mahmud, Ushari Ahmed, and Suliman Ali Baldo. *Diein Massacre: Slavery in the Sudan.* Khartoum: n.p., 1987.

A documentation of the massacre of 1,500 Dinka in al Diein (Daein) in southern Kordofan in 1987 and the subsequent enslavement of surviving Dinka refugees from the civil war in the south.

Rone, J., J. Prendergast, and K. Sorensen. *Civilian Devastation: Abuses by All Parties in the War in Southern Sudan.* New York: Human Rights Watch, 1994.

Documents serious, extensive, and lasting human rights violations by all the parties involved in the war.

Salih, M.A.M., and S. Harir. "Tribal Militias: The Genesis of National Disintegration." In *Short-Cut to Decay: the Case of the Sudan.* Edited by S. Harir and T. Tvedt. Uppsala: The Scandinavian Institute of African Studies, 1994: 187–203.

Discusses the emergence of tribal militias in the beginning of the second civil war in the Sudan and how the warring parties used them.

Wai, Dunstan M., ed. *The Southern Sudan: the Problem of National Integration.* London; Frank Cass, 1973.

Contains essays on the nature of the north-south conflict and civil war and the resulting political problems and obstacles to economic and social integration of the two regions of the Sudan.

NINE

The Making of the Rwandan Genocide and the Future Protection of Civilians in Africa

Alhaji M. S. Bah

> The bitter lesson we have to learn from the Rwanda situation is that Africa should be ready to take its destiny into its own hands.
>
> —Salim Ahmed Salim[1]

The violent civil conflicts that gripped the Great Lakes region of Africa[2] in the post–Cold War caused the unprecedented suffering of the civilian population. The crisis in this central African region left millions dead and millions more displaced and led to one of the most complex humanitarian emergencies of our time. The genocide in Rwanda between April and June 1994, which was central to the crisis of the region, was one of the most gruesome massacres of civilians since the Holocaust during the Second World War. Furthermore, the mass exodus of civilians during that three-month period was arguably the largest forced movement of civilians in recent history. Those responsible for driving them out of Rwanda into the eastern provinces of neighboring Zaire (since 1996 the eastern Democratic Republic of the Congo) were the Armed Forces of Rwanda (AFR) and the *Interahamwe* militia of the ruling party, the same groups responsible for carrying out the genocide.

Several factors were behind the expulsion of these predominantly Hutu civilians from Rwanda. First, it was meant to "protect" the Hutu population against the advancing Tutsi-led Rwandan Patriotic Front (RPF), which had launched its armed incursion into Rwanda from Uganda in October

1990. Second, since the Hutu constitute about 80 percent of the Rwandan population, their flight was deliberately designed to "empty" the country, thereby depriving the victorious RPF of a significant part of Rwanda's productive population. Third, the retreating AFR and the *Interahamwe* militia viewed the civilians as convenient human shields between them and the advancing RPF. Fourth, the genocidal soldiers and militias calculated that they could pin responsibility for the massive displacement of the Hutu civilian population on the RPF, thus deflecting attention away from the terrible atrocities they had themselves recently committed. Consequently, the extensive refugee camps that sprang up in the eastern provinces of Zaire contained not only genuine refugees but scores of armed soldiers and militias. These armed groups immediately took over control of the camps and ensured that no refugees returned to Rwanda, killing hundreds who attempted to escape from what had essentially become "military garrisons." This mixture of armed forces and civilians in the camps presented the international community, especially the humanitarian agencies, with a serious dilemma since the soldiers and militias could always hijack relief support and manipulate its distribution as a means of dominating the civilian refugees.

That the Rwandan genocide unfolded unhindered for three months was a serious indictment of the international community, including that of Africa. International indifference toward the approximately 800,000 civilians slaughtered under the helpless eyes of the United Nations Assistance Mission in Rwanda (UNAMIR) confirmed the perception that Africa had become marginalized in the post–Cold War world and rendered the post-Holocaust cliché "never again" meaningless. These terrible events further buttressed what some observers have described as international "disengagement" from Africa, which was first clearly signaled by the humiliating withdrawal early in 1994 of the United Nations Mission in Somalia (UNOSOM). (The withdrawal of UNOSOM was precipitated by the killing on October 3, 1993 of 18 U.S. Rangers in a firefight south of Mogadishu that led, under public pressure, to rapid American disengagement.) For their part, Africans saw in the Rwandan genocide a need to develop homegrown mechanisms to deal with future conflicts and to confront some of the principles that guided inter-state relations in the postindependence era: namely, those of sovereignty and nonintervention.

For the purpose of this study, analysis of the conundrum of the conflict in the Great Lakes region will, for two reasons, be centered on Rwanda. The first is that the polarized ethnic dynamics in Rwanda, which pit Hutu against Tutsi, are viewed by most observers as having formed the core of the strife in the region, especially in the post–Cold War era. The second is that the genocide in Rwanda has propelled Africa into exploring ways and means of dealing with conflicts in their own backyards—in other words, into finding African solutions to African problems. The chapter will accordingly be divided in three sections. The first section will focus on the background to the ethnic antagonism in Rwanda leading to the 1994 genocide. The second section will look at the role of the international community during the genocide. The final section will briefly highlight some of the responses and initiatives by the African Union (AU) aimed at protecting civilians in the future.

THE DEADLY COCKTAIL OF ETHNICITY, RELIGION, AND POLITICS IN THE MAKING OF A GENOCIDE

The Construction of Ethnic Divisions

Rwanda has become synonymous with the violent civil conflicts that erupted across Africa in the immediate aftermath of the Cold War. This tiny landlocked and mountainous country in central Africa (often referred to as the "Land of a Thousand Hills") is bordered by the Democratic Republic of the Congo, Tanzania, Burundi, and Uganda. It is now notorious for exporting its domestic political problems through the massive flow of refugees into neighboring countries. With a population of approximately 8 million, Rwanda is one of the most densely populated countries in the world, and this is perhaps one explanation for the constant ethnic strife it has experienced. Rwandans are divided into three ethnic groups: Hutu (84 percent); Tutsi (15 percent); and Twa (1 percent). Unlike most other African countries with their diverse and distinct linguistic differences, the three ethnic groups in Rwanda speak the same language, *Kinyarwanda.* In addition to a common language, these groups—especially the Hutu and Tutsi—share similar cultural practices and values. Perhaps the major difference between the Hutu and Tutsi is that the former are sedentary and practice subsistence agriculture, while the latter are nomadic and pastoralist. One should hasten to caution, however, that there are some overlaps in the economic activities of the two groups. In other words, although cattle-rearing is perceived as the major preoccupation of the Tutsi minority, it is not its sole preserve, as has been projected by some missionaries and anthropologists. Years of coexistence and intermarriage have meant that some Hutu own cattle while some Tutsi till the land.

With the advent of colonialism in the late nineteenth century and its preoccupation with racial categories, the physical differences between Hutu and Tutsi were fatally invoked and accorded precedence over the linguistic homogeneity of the two groups. The Tutsi are indeed generally thinner and taller than the Hutu and have angular features, while the Hutu are relatively shorter and more muscular with strong Bantu features. The Twa are pygmies who live by hunting and gathering. There is no consensus on what explains the physical differences between the Tutsi and Hutu. Historians and anthropologists have long argued that the Twa are the original inhabitants of Rwanda, while the Hutu, a predominantly Bantu group, moved in from the neighboring countries while the Tutsi

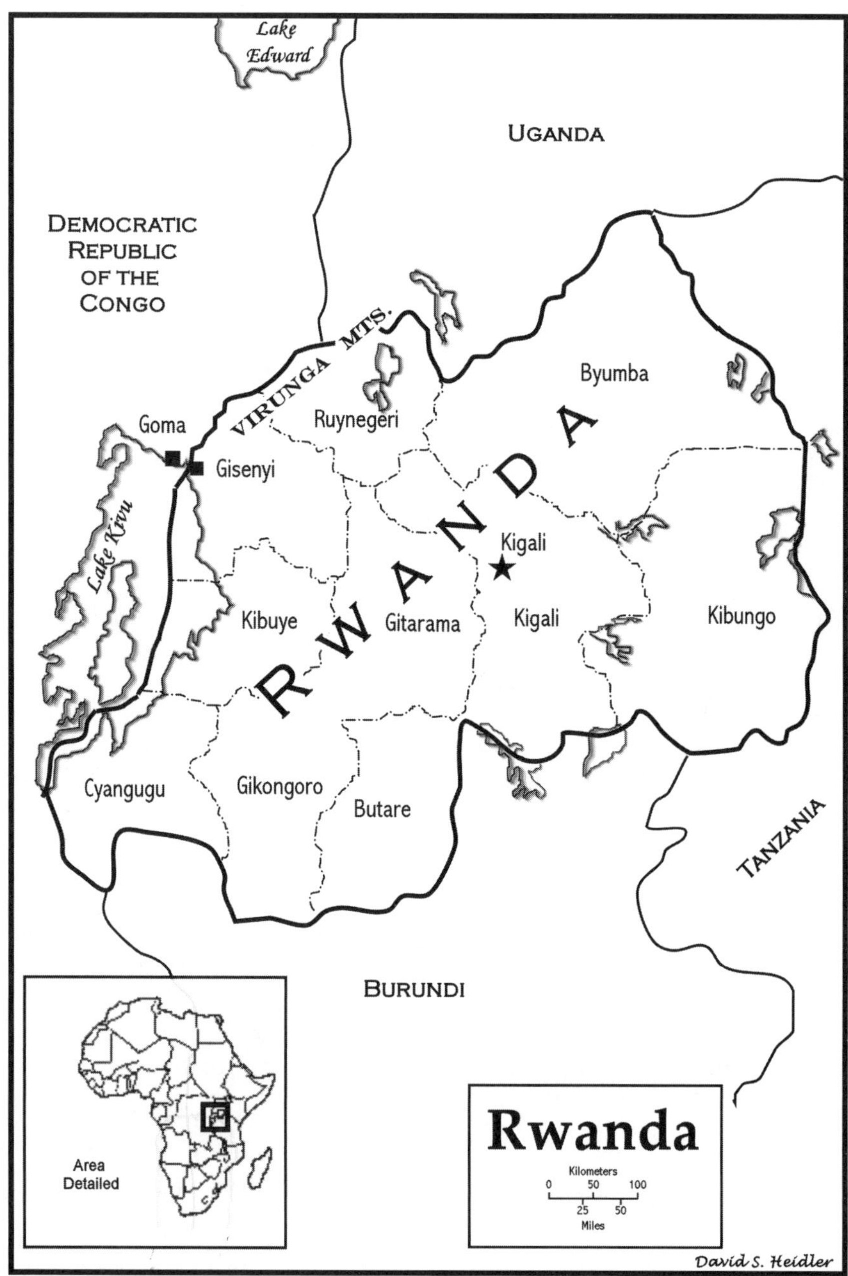
Lake Edward
UGANDA
DEMOCRATIC REPUBLIC OF THE CONGO
VIRUNGA MTS.
Byumba
Ruynegeri
Goma
Gisenyi
RWANDA
Lake Kivu
Kigali
Kibuye
Gitarama
Kigali
Kibungo
Cyangugu
Gikongoro
Butare
TANZANIA
BURUNDI
Area Detailed
Rwanda
Kilometers
0 50 100
25 50
Miles
David S. Heidler

Rwanda

migrated from the distant southern plains of Ethiopia. According to Linda Melvern, the concept of Hutu and Tutsi as distinct ethnic groups can be traced back to the English explorer John Speke, the first European to set foot at the source of the Nile. Blinded by his ill-informed and biased view of Africans, Speke propagated the idea of the existence of a superior race in the region. In his view, the social and political systems that existed in central Africa in 1859 were too advanced for the "negro." He therefore concluded that the Tutsi, who constituted the political elite in Rwanda during that period, must have originated from further north and were even possibly related to the "noble Europeans." He asserted that the Tutsi, who were taller and had thinner noses than the Hutu, were "superior and too fine to be 'common negroes.'" Speke further believed they possessed an intelligence and refinement of feelings that were "rare among primitive people."[3] Developing these racist ideas, some nineteenth-century missionaries, for example, suggested that the Tutsi could be traced to ancient Egypt, positing that "their ... delicate appearance, their love for money, their capacity to adapt to situations seem to indicate a Semitic origin."[4] Unhappily, prejudice such as this set the stage for protracted and conflicting theorizing on the origins of the Tutsi and would prove fatal for Rwanda in the postindependence era.

In more modern times two polarized views have emerged concerning the origins of the Tutsi and their relations with the Hutu. The first group of theorists, commonly associated with the Tutsi, and particularly with propagandists of the RPF, argues that there are no differences between the two groups. It holds that what apparent differences do exist should in fact be viewed as a class difference between rich and poor, or as a "division of labor" between agriculturists and pastoralists, and that such class and occupational differences are bound to be found in all societies. This school further contends that any physical differences are a result of "normal" differences that derive from different lifestyles such as access to food and the like. However, those who advance the view that differences really do exist invoke biological and social factors to explain what they see as two distinct and unrelated groups. This second view is often associated with the Hutu, who strongly feel that the Tutsi migrated from the north, conquered Hutu territories, and imposed their rule on them.[5] In his book on the Rwanda genocide, the renowned African scholar Professor Mahmood Mamdani stressed that the two accounts of the origins of Hutu and Tutsi "need not be seen as incompatible," and that "they can be seen as complementary rather than alternative accounts, each highlighting a different aspect of history. While neither is able to account for the history underlined by the other, each is incomplete without the other."[6] Regardless of which side of the debate one finds oneself, the racial theorizing that was reinforced and consolidated during the colonial and postcolonial eras has without doubt played a large part in poisoning inter-ethnic relations in modern-day Rwanda.

The Precolonial Social and Political Hierarchy

Precolonial Rwanda was organized into an intricate social and political hierarchy with the *Mwami,* or king, at its summit. Administratively, the Kingdom of Ruanda (Rwanda) was divided into four units: province, district, hill, and neighborhood. The *Mwami* appointed all the chiefs, subchiefs and leaders of the hills and neighborhoods. These were responsible in their respective communities for collecting taxes, dealing with grazing rights, and with other similar issues. The administrators of the various units in the kingdom reported to their immediate superiors, who in turn reported to the central authority, the *Mwami,* in the capital. According to Linda Melvern, "each layer of the hierarchy was linked in a relationship of mutual dependence based on reciprocal arrangements regarding goods and services. This was known as *ubuhake* and it referred to a contractual service in which a more powerful person could provide protection in exchange for work."[7] In this patron-client relationship the Tutsi were the patrons, although there were a few exceptions. It is believed that the patron-client relationship based on *ubuhake* contributed to sowing the seeds of hatred between the predominantly Tutsi patrons and their Hutu clients. Exploitation of the existing discord between the two groups by both the German and Belgian colonial authorities and later by postindependence governments further exacerbated the Hutu-Tutsi divide.

The Era of German Indirect Colonial Rule (1897–1916)

At the Berlin Conference of 1884–1885, during which the African continent was carved up between the interested European powers to avoid future open conflict over the spoils, the tiny kingdoms of Urundi (Burundi) and Ruanda (Rwanda) were allotted to Germany without the knowledge or consent of the people living there. So, when in the 1890s the *Mwami* welcomed to his court Count von Gotzen, the first German colonial official, he certainly was not aware of the long-term consequences of this relationship. For their part, the Germans, impressed by the advanced level of political and social organization in Rwanda and lacking sufficient administrative manpower of their own, opted to rule through the *Mwami* and his network of local chiefs. Through this system of indirect rule the traditional, social, and political system in Rwanda was kept intact for as long as the *Mwami* remained loyal to the colonial authorities. The *Mwami* was comfortable with indirect rule because it allowed him to continue the patron-client relationship (*ubuhake*) that had characterized his rule before the advent of colonialism. In addition, the support he received from the German colonial officials assisted him in expanding his kingdom by forcefully bringing under his control territories that had hitherto been free of his rule. Thus, the early period of German colonial rule witnessed the annexation of several Hutu principalities, thereby increasing the *Mwami's* power through taxation and the much detested *ubuhake* system.

The arrival of the Germans coincided with a period of upheaval in the kingdom following the sudden death of the *Mwami* Kigeli IV Rwabugiri in 1895. His immediate successor did not rule for long, as he was deposed in a *coup d'etat* organized by the Queen Mother, who was traditionally seen as the custodian of the kingship. There followed intense competition for the succession characterized by purges and assassinations of rival claimants. Ignorant of the intricate and complex political dynamics of Rwanda, the German colonial authorities were manipulated by the various groups locked in the struggle for the *Mwamiship.* However, it does seem that the Germans were not unaware that they were being used. As Gerard Prunier put it, "since the Germans maintained only a very light presence in Rwanda (in 1914 there were only 96 Europeans there, including missionaries) they were ready to overlook the exploitation of their interventions by the central state since they hoped to use it as a tool of colonialism."[8] There was therefore a convergence of interest between the *Mwami,* who saw the presence of the Germans as an opportunity to consolidate and expand his kingdom, and the Germans, who saw in the king an opportunity to control Rwanda with the limited manpower at its disposal. Although German rule did not last for long, its collaboration with the *Mwami* meant that Tutsi rule was consolidated, which was to have lasting effects on Rwandan society. Following the end of the First World War, Germany lost all its colonial territories as part of the postwar peace settlement. Through a mandate of the League of Nations all former German colonial territories in Africa were transferred in 1919 to other colonial powers. Rwanda and Burundi fell into the hands of Belgium, which was the colonial power in the neighboring Belgian Congo (now the Democratic Republic of the Congo) whose history is closely intertwined with its tiny neighbors to the east.

The Era of Belgian Direct Rule (1916–1959)

Unlike German colonialism in Rwanda, which lasted for less than two decades, Belgian rule endured from the conquest of the country from the Germans in 1916, through the Second World War, and up to independence in 1961. Belgium (which was notorious for the inhumane treatment of its subjects in the neighboring Congo) did not rush into dismantling the foundations of German colonial rule. Only after seven years of "wait and see" in Rwanda between 1919 and 1926 did it radically depart from the German policy of indirect rule and begin deploying a coterie of administrators and soldiers to enforce its rule directly.

A feature of Belgian colonialism was the close link between colonial administrators and the Roman Catholic missionaries in Rwanda. As in most parts of Africa, colonialism in Rwanda had been preceded by the arrival of Christian missionaries, and nowhere else did the relationship between the Catholic Church and the colonial administration remain closer, nor the Church's central role in politics appear more obvious.

As a consequence, adherence to Roman Catholicism was viewed as a test of loyalty to the colonial authorities—besides being seen as the one true path to salvation. During the period of "wait and see," when Belgian administrators were exploring the contours of the complex Rwandan social structures and the political system of indirect rule they had inherited from the Germans, they relied heavily on the advice of missionaries. This advice was ambivalent and often contradictory, as was manifested by Monseigneur Classe, a Belgian bishop who had lived in Rwanda since the turn of the nineteenth century and who was highly respected by the colonial authorities. In 1927 Mgr. Classe wrote that although the "Mututsi youth was an incomparable element of progress," one should not forget that the Rwandese kings of old "elevated to high dignity Bahutus and even Batwa lineages, giving them rank in the landholding class, them and their descendants."[9] However, three years later, in an about-face, Mgr. Classe cautioned the Belgian authorities against a radical reorganization of the society, saying that:

> The greatest mistake this government could make would be to suppress the Mututsi caste. Such a revolution would lead the country directly to anarchy and to hateful anti-European communism.... [W]e will have no better, more active and more intelligent chiefs than the Batutsi. They are the ones best suited to understand progress and the ones the population likes best. The government must work mainly with them.[10]

Mgr. Classe's bewildering ambivalence was reflected in the early Belgian colonial policies, which showed themselves largely undecided on which would be the best type of sociopolitical reforms to undertake without at the same time undermining Belgian rule. The indecision of the Belgian authorities did not last long, however, since even during the period of "wait and see," Belgian civil servants were appointed to "assist" the *Mwami* directly. The *Mwami* was no longer allowed to appoint regional chiefs, which limited his powers. In a further move aimed at stamping their authority on Rwanda, in 1931 the Belgian officials deposed *Mwami* Musinga, who was resistant to colonial rule, and replaced him with his more "amenable" son, Mutara Rudahigwa, who became known as *Mwami w'abazungu*, or the King of the Whites. Henceforth, Belgian colonial officials were directly involved in the administration of the country through the newly created bureaucracy, their control of education, and the monetization of the local economy.[11]

In a significant boost to Belgian colonial rule, the new *Mwami* converted to Christianity in 1943. At the height of his newfound spirituality, *Mwami* Mutara consecrated his country to Christ the King in October 1946, a measure (in the words of Gerard Prunier) "which put him in the rather bizarre company of General Franco and the quasi-fascist prime minister of Quebec, Maurice Duplessis."[12] In a major victory for the Belgian authorities, who were trying to impose their rule without destroying the hierarchical order that had existed in Rwanda before their arrival, the king's conversion was followed by the mass conversion to Christianity of most of the Tutsi, who had previously been reluctant to embrace the new religion brought by the Europeans. For the Tutsi elite conversion became a cardinal requirement for membership in the political class and was driven by a realization that Belgian policy was remodeling Rwandan society with the Church as its central institution. They reasoned that it was better for them to convert and become part of Belgium's new Rwanda than risk being marginalized. For their part, the Catholic priests were delighted to see the Tutsi elite flock to the Church instead of the lower classes and social outcasts who in the past had constituted the bulk of their converts. As a result of this shift the Catholic Church became a central pillar in Rwandan society. Unfortunately, its monopoly of education further reinforced the ethnic divisions within Rwandan society because, as the ruling class, the Tutsi were given priority over their Hutu counterparts and were taught subjects appropriate for a future career in the administration. As a result of this favoritism, most of the Hutu who wanted postsecondary education had no choice but to study theology. Even after graduating from the theological schools, Hutu often struggled to find employment. This left them disappointed and embittered since they often had to settle for low-paying clerical jobs.

In addition to difficulties faced in entering postsecondary learning institutions and finding employment afterward, the Hutu felt further subjugated by the Belgian policy of individualized forced labor. Under Belgian rule, the *ubuletwa,* or the hated forced labor system, was extended to areas where it had previously not existed. Moreover, the new policy introduced the notion of "individual" obligation. In other words, every able-bodied member of society, whether male or female, was expected to participate in the *ubuletwa* system. This policy was characterized by abuse, which often took the form of public flogging. Many Rwandans, especially Hutu, fled to British-controlled Uganda where they could find employment without experiencing humiliation and abuse at the hands of the Belgian colonial officials and their agents.[13]

Perhaps the most destructive policy the Belgians instituted in Rwanda was the classification of the entire population either as Hutu, Tutsi, or Twa. In 1933 the Belgian colonial authorities held a census in which all inhabitants of Rwanda were not only counted but classified. Mahmood Mamdani has described this as "racializing the Hutu/Tutsi difference" and has taken this as proof that "the Belgian authority considered Tutsi and Hutu as two distinct races."[14] In order to establish the racial identity of the inhabitants of Rwanda, the colonial administrators measured their height, the length of their noses, and the shape of their eyes. In terms of the classification they employed, the Tutsi were tall and slim with Caucasian features such as pointed noses, while the Hutu were short and stocky, often with broad noses. A major problem with these criteria was the failure to take into account those who were products of intermarriage between Hutu and Tutsi. In addition to physical appearance, the number of cattle possessed by an individual was also used to determine their "racial" group. This was based on the false assumption that all cattle owners were Tutsi, ignoring the fact that some Hutu also owned cattle.

In spite of the flaws in the criteria used to classify people as Hutu, Tutsi, or Twa, after the census the Belgian authorities issued identity cards to all adults in Rwanda bearing their ethnic identities. This policy of issuing identity cards indicating ethnic identity was continued by the postindependence governments of Rwanda and was later to serve as a convenient but deadly indicator of "race" during the genocide in 1994. In Mamdani's view, one of the long-term consequences of classification was the consolidation of the belief that the Hutu were Rwanda's indigenous inhabitants, while the Tutsi were seen as alien. He therefore contends that "through the distinction between alien and indigenous, the Tutsi came to be defined as a race—the Hamite race—different from the Hutu, who were constructed as indigenous Bantu."[15] With the codification of Hutu and Tutsi as two distinct "racial" groups, it was no longer possible for an individual either to rise to the status of Tutsi or be demoted to the servile position of Hutu. In the past this kind of social mobility had been feasible, and it is believed that a good number of cattle-owning Hutu were assimilated into the ranks of the Tutsi. Now, all forms of social mobility were frozen and two distinct "racial" groups artificially created: the one Hutu, indigenous and inferior; the other Tutsi and alien, but the superior master race, destined to rule.

The Catholic missionaries justified the superiority of the Tutsi and even introduced "apartheid-style" segregationist policies in the schools. For instance, in schools controlled by the "White Fathers" and other missionaries, while "the Tutsi were given milk and meat-based meals, the Hutu had to eat maize porridge and beans."[16] Inevitably, the preferential treatment enjoyed by the Tutsi under Belgian colonial rule widened the rift between the Tutsi and Hutu. By the end of the Second World War, the Hutu were openly questioning their servile situation in Rwanda, even though they were greatly numerically superior to the Tutsi. Years of suppression and abuse by the precolonial Tutsi elites and their continuation under colonial rule eventually led to the first bloody uprising against the *status quo*, in what is known as the "social revolution" of 1959.

The "Social Revolution" of 1959

By the mid-1950s, the relationship between the Belgian colonial authorities and their Tutsi protégés was seriously deteriorating for several reasons. First, the Catholic missionaries were concerned that they were losing control of the Church because, by this time, there were more Tutsi priests than Belgian. Second, there was a significant shift in the background of the Belgian priests who were being sent to Rwanda. While the earlier group of missionaries had been drawn from the middle to upper classes of society in Belgium, in the post–Second World War period there were more priests from "humble" backgrounds. This new cadre of priests readily identified and sympathized with the Hutu, whose second-class status reminded them of the divisions in Belgium between the dominant Walloons and the Flemish. Third, the Belgian authorities were disappointed by the Tutsi elite's demand for immediate independence, which, it is believed, was aimed at forestalling efforts by the new Belgian missionaries to reorganize Rwandan society in favor of the Hutu.[17] Besides, the support that the pro-independence Tutsi groups received from the anticolonial Communist bloc annoyed the Belgians, who felt betrayed by the very group they had elevated to superior status. The disenchantment of the Belgian authorities was aptly captured by the last vice-governor general when in the late 1950s he stated that:

> From then on, the unspoken agreement which the administration had made in the 1920s with the Tutsi ruling caste in order to further economic development ... was allowed to collapse, also tacitly. The Tutsi wanted independence and were trying to get it as quickly as possible by sabotaging Belgian actions, whether technical or political.... The administration was forced to toughen its attitude when faced with such obstruction and hostility coming from chiefs and sub-chiefs with whom we had collaborated for so many years.[18]

Apparently betrayed by their former allies, the Belgian authorities embarked on creating a Hutu counter-elite and throwing their weight behind it. The decision coincided with the rise to prominence of a group of Hutu intellectuals agitating for liberation from the yoke of Tutsi domination. One of the first major steps the Belgian authorities took was the establishment of a church periodical, *Kinyamateka*. The editor was Gregoire Kayibanda, one of the rising Hutu nationalists who had developed a close relationship with the Catholic Church. Published in the Kinyarwanda language, the periodical had a wide readership and served as an inspiration to the nascent Hutu elite. In 1957 a group of Hutu intellectuals published what was perhaps their most powerful message to the international community about their plight. The action was aimed at coinciding with the visit to Rwanda of a UN trusteeship mission. The document, *Notes on the Social Aspect of the Racial Native Problem in Rwanda*, commonly known as the *Hutu Manifesto*, explained the polarized ethnic situation in their country as

> basically that of the political monopoly of one race [sic], the Mututsi. In the present circumstances, this political monopoly is turned into an economic and social monopoly.... And given the *de facto* selection in school, the political, economic and social monopolies turn into cultural monopoly which condemns the desperate

Bahutu to be for ever subaltern workers, even after an independence that they will have contributed to gain without even realizing what is in store for them. The *ubuhake* has been legislated away, but these monopolies have replaced it with an even stronger oppression.[19]

The publication of the *Hutu Manifesto* marked the beginning of a protracted and often violent political struggle between Hutu and Tutsi, culminating in the 1994 genocide. Several political parties, each one of them either predominantly Hutu or Tutsi, were established as the two sides intensified their contest over the control of the Rwandan state. The two most prominent parties were the pro-monarchist and anti-Belgian Tutsi party called the Union National Rwandaise (UNAR), and the predominantly Hutu Rwandese Democratic Party or the Party of the Movement and of Hutu Emancipation (MDR or PARMEHUTU).

The mysterious death in July 1959 of King Mutara III Rudahigwa after he had received an injection from Belgian doctors added to the growing tensions in Rwanda. By now, there were frequent clashes between supporters of the UNAR and MDR or PARMEHUTU, which fostered a tense and unpredictable political atmosphere that could be ignited by the smallest spark. The powder keg exploded when a group of UNAR supporters attacked the PARMEHUTU leader, Dominique Mbonyumutwa, in the town of Gitarama. As rumors of the attack spread across Rwanda, the Hutu set out to avenge the killing. Violence spread like wildfire as scores of PARMEHUTU supporters attacked their Tutsi neighbors, deliberately targeting the Tutsi chiefs and subchiefs whom the Hutu regarded as the particular symbols of oppression. According to official estimates in 1964, the Hutu killed approximately 3,000 Tutsi in the course of the pogrom, destroyed their homes, and drove more than 336,000 into exile.[20] This was the fateful moment that marked the beginning of large concentrations of Tutsi refugees in the neighboring countries of Burundi, Uganda, and what are now Tanzania and the Democratic Republic of the Congo. The refugees disputed the official estimates and put their own numbers as high as 500,000, arguing that the official figures failed to take into account the many refugees who did not live in camps. Whatever their numbers really were (and there were certainly hundreds of thousands), the refugees shared a burning, common desire to return to Rwanda.

Having switched sides to support the Hutu, the Belgian authorities downplayed the killings, dismissing them "as a problem of race between Hutu and Tutsi."[21] However, fearing that the Tutsi might use the state security services to repress the Hutu, the Belgians declared a state of emergency in 1959 and the country was placed under military rule with Colonel B.E.M. Guy Logiest in command. It soon emerged that the emergency measures under Colonel Logiest were meant not only to restore order, but to reshape Rwandan society. This became apparent when Colonel Logiest declared that "[b]ecause of the force of circumstances, we have to take sides. We cannot remain neutral and passive."[22] Invoking the emergency powers, Logiest began replacing Tutsi chiefs with Hutu, contending that the presence of Tutsi chiefs and subchiefs "disturbed the public order."[23] Over 300 Tutsi chiefs and subchiefs, who had either been killed or forced into exile, were replaced by Hutu chiefs. In order to strengthen the Hutu power base, the Belgian authorities created an African armed force, consisting of 85 percent Hutu and only 15 percent Tutsi. Communal elections were held in 1960, which saw the MDR-PARMEHUTU party wining 70.4 percent of the votes, compared to the mere 1.7 percent garnered by the pro-monarchist UNAR.[24]

In 1961 the predominantly Hutu MDR-PARMEHUTU, led by Gregoire Kayibanda, organized a rally of its supporters in the town of Gitarama and overwhelmingly voted to abolish the Tutsi monarchy. On July 1, 1962, Rwanda was declared a republic.[25] The councilors and burgomasters who had voted to abolish the monarchy elected Kayibanda the first president. UN-initiated elections and a referendum followed in 1962 during which MDR-PARMEHUTU won 77.7 percent of the vote in an outright rejection of the monarchy against 16.8 percent for UNAR.[26] The "revolution" that the Belgians had started in the mid-1950s was now complete. When Rwanda became formally independent on July 1, 1962, the country was in the firm grip of the new Hutu elite. In contrast, the majority of the former Tutsi elite were living in embittered exile in neighboring Congo, Burundi, Tanzania, and Uganda.

The Kayibanda Years, 1962–1973

Kayibanda ruled Rwanda from 1962 until 1973, when he was overthrown by his army. Although some Tutsi refugees had tried to make peace with Kayibanda, a group of refugees based in Burundi favored a military solution. They received the support of their Burundian Tutsi kinsfolk, who feared a fate similar to their Rwandan counterparts. Between 1961 and 1973 they and the growing numbers of Tutsi refugees elsewhere in neighboring states (the size of the exiled Tutsi community grew to about 600,000) launched attacks on Rwanda from bases in Burundi, Uganda, and north Kivu Province in Zaire (now the Democratic Republic of the Congo). These guerrillas called themselves *inyenzi,* or cockroaches, a term that has since been associated with the Tutsi and was invoked by pro-genocide propagandists in 1994. Their raids led to anti-Tutsi reprisals organized by the government in which thousands of innocent civilians were massacred. It was reported that well over 10,000 Tutsi were massacred by the government militia after the 1963 UNAR attack on Rwanda from Burundi. The Kayibanda government used this opportunity to eliminate Tutsi intellectuals, traders, and community leaders who had survived the massacres in 1959. Ten years later, in 1973, the massacre of Tutsi was repeated after another failed attack by Tutsi exiles on Kayibanda's government. Tutsi were hunted down and killed all over Rwanda in a campaign organized by the government. Tens of thousands of Tutsi civilians were massacred, and some in the international community felt compelled to label the killings genocide. It was in the midst of these massacres that a group of army officers led by General Juvenal Habyarimana overthrew president Kayibanda and set up the second republic.[27]

The Habyarimana Years, 1973–1994

General Habyarimana's coup was welcomed by large sections of Rwandan society who had had enough of the Kayibanda regime, characterized as it was by inter-clan rivalry, the marginalization of Hutu from the north of the country by the southern coterie around Kayibanda, and a worsening economic crisis. Moreover, some Hutu moderates were concerned with the regime's obsession with Tutsi conspiracies and the appalling manner in which it treated innocent Tutsi civilians. To these sections of the Hutu community, as well as to the remaining Tutsi population, the coup was a welcome development. In contrast to his predecessor's vicious rule, Habyarimana's appeared mild during his early years in power, even though the role of Tutsi in public life was highly regulated. During his years in power there were no Tutsi *bourgmestres* or *prefets,* and there was only one Tutsi officer in the army. Moreover, only two members of parliament out of over 75 were Tutsi; while only one out of approximately 25 to 30 cabinet ministers was a Tutsi. No national institution was more regulated than the military because of its crucial role in Rwandan politics. In addition to controlling the entry of Tutsi into the armed forces, serving members were prohibited from marrying Tutsi women—a policy aimed at denying the Tutsi any opportunity to penetrate the Hutu power base.[28] However, the new regime was prepared to leave the Tutsi largely alone so long as they steered very clear of politics. Heeding this policy of "don't mess around with politics," the Tutsi focused on the private sector, where a good number became very successful.

Habyarimana's military coup dealt a severe blow to all forms of political opposition within Rwanda. Immediately after seizing power, Habyarimana formed the Mouvement Revolutionnaire National pour le Development (MRND). Having outlawed all other political parties when he seized power, in 1974 he declared the country a one-party state with his MRND as the sole party. The MRND maintained a strong grip on power as Rwandans of all ages were compelled to be members of the party. As he consolidated his hold on power, Habyarimana courted international donors who responded favorably to his overtures. With substantial donor resources at his disposal, the president was able to appease both his supporters and opponents with this largesse. However, by the late 1980s the regime was faced with an unprecedented challenge due to a combination of factors.

First, the late 1980s witnessed a drastic fall in the price of agricultural commodities in the international market. Rwanda's predominantly agrarian-based economy was seriously affected by the sharp drop in the price of tea, the country's major export. This led to a sudden downturn in the economy, triggering political agitation. Second, with signs that the Cold War was coming to an end, the international donor community—which previously had patronized the Rwandan strongman—started to put pressure on him to liberalize his regime and, most importantly, to deal with the refugee problem in the region. It was clear by now to all that the Tutsi refugees were contributing to political instability in their host countries. Finally, the regime was growing increasingly uneasy about the large and influential role of Tutsi refugees in the National Resistance Army (NRA) in neighboring Uganda.[29] In 1980 the Ugandan dictator, Idi Amin, had been overthrown and Milton Obote (whom Amin had previously ousted in 1971) returned to power through a fraudulent vote count. His administration continued the violence of the Amin years and his security forces massacred an estimated 300,000 civilians, mainly in the south of the country in what had been the Bugandan kingdom, where opposition to Obote was concentrated. Hundreds of thousands more fled the country. As the killings escalated, so did the resistance of Yoweri Museveni's NRA, which had taken to the bush after the 1980 elections. The bulk of the refugee Tutsi cadres fought on the side of the NRA, because Obote's antagonism toward them was no secret. With their support the NRA won the bitter guerrilla war and overthrew Obote in 1986, heralding a new era in the region.

Fearing that the Tutsi refugees might use their influential role within the Ugandan armed forces to mount an invasion, and seeing the need to appease his international partners, Habyarimana rushed to "democratize" his regime by opening up the political space and dealing with the refugee problem by introducing wide-ranging reforms. However, observers of Rwanda largely dismissed these reforms as a cosmetic attempt by the regime to boost its rapidly sinking power base. And, if the reforms were meant to forestall an armed return of the refugees, they failed.

The RPF Invasion, 1990–1994

Following the NRA victory in Uganda in 1986, a number of Tutsi were compensated with senior positions in the new government of President Museveni. Using their strategic positions within the administration, these Tutsi officials recruited many young refugees into the Ugandan army. However, by the late 1980s Museveni was coming under intense domestic pressure over the presence of so many Tutsi officials in his administration. Consequently, at the very moment Habyarimana was making his "cosmetic" reforms in Rwanda, Museveni was being forced to cut down on the number of Tutsi within his administration. Tutsi soldiers within the NRA, now feeling rejected by their host community, began to prepare to defect from the Ugandan army in order to mount an armed return to Rwanda—a country that the bulk of them remembered only as small children before their exile. On October 1, 1990, a group of these disaffected Tutsi soldiers, calling themselves the Rwandan Patriotic Front (RPF), with its military wing known as the Rwandan Patriotic Army (RPA), invaded Rwanda from Uganda.

The invading RPF took the Kigali regime by surprise, unleashing initial panic among the government and the Rwandan Armed Forces (FAR). However, Habyarimana's government regained the upper hand when France, Belgium, and Zaire (then still under the dictatorial rule of Mobutu *Seso Seko,* "The All-Powerful," who enjoyed close relations with the West) intervened on its side to preserve the *status quo* and their established economic interests in Rwanda. The planning and logistical support provided to the Rwandan military by the 540 Belgian and 300 French troops, along with 500 of the Zairian elite Presidential Guard, dealt a serious blow to the invading RPF.[30] The Rwandan army, having recovered from its initial panic, and backed up by experienced troops, launched a counterattack, killing many RPF fighters and scattering thousands more. By November 1990, with the initial gains of their surprise attack rolled back and their forces in disarray, the RPF leadership fell out seriously among themselves over what strategy and tactics should best be adopted. To add to this disarray, the RPF suffered a serious setback when its legendary leader, General Paul Rwiygema, died in mysterious circumstances during the first weeks of the invasion. Rwiygema's death has been the subject of much speculation. While some believe that government forces shot him in an ambush, others think he was killed by his own men, the victim of the violent dispute over how best to continue the campaign. Whatever the truth of the case, it was essential for the RPF to act promptly to avoid a leadership vacuum and the final collapse of the invasion.

Major Paul Kagame (currently the president of Rwanda) hurriedly terminated his military training course in the United States and returned to Uganda to save the RPF from total disintegration. On his return, Kagame, who was both a trained military strategist and a tactful commander, reassembled the remnants of the RPF and retreated to the Virunga Mountains in northwest Rwanda in order to buy time to remold the RPF and increase its numbers. It is estimated that by mid-1991 he had put together a force of about 15,000 fighters. By the end of the year the RPF had successfully captured a strip of land along the Uganda–Rwanda border. From this point on, the RPF started making significant gains against the government forces. However, while its military operations were progressing well, the RPF was confronted with a serious political challenge stemming from lack of support by the predominantly Hutu civilian population. So when the RPF started "liberating" great swaths of territory, most of it was "empty" since the inhabitants had fled. Mamdani aptly captured the resulting dilemma when he wrote: "from the middle of 1991, the RPF entered a period in which every military victory brought home the same bitter lesson about the political realities of Rwanda. The RPF consistently failed to translate military victory on the field into political gains within the population."[31]

The Extremist Hutu Response

It is possible that the fleeing Hutu civilians were taking their cue from the reemerging Hutu nationalist extremists, whose activities had been temporarily moderated by Habyarimana's reconciliatory policies. For them, the invasion was a perfect opportunity to regain lost ground in their anti-Tutsi crusade. Taking advantage of the liberalization of the political scene, the Hutu nationalists established the Radio et Television Libres des Mille Collines (RTLM) and the newspaper *Kangura,* meaning "Wake Others Up." With these media at their disposal, they spread anti-Tutsi propaganda, invoking the past to justify the need for a united stand against the alien Tutsi who (they claimed) were bent on returning Rwanda to the days of the *ubuhake,* that much hated Tutsi-dominated patron-client relationship of the past. Immediately after the RPF invasion, *Kangura* published and widely circulated what have become known as the "Hutu Ten Commandments." The first of these warned all Hutu of the treacherous nature of the Tutsi woman, who always "works for the interest of her ethnic group,"[32] and declared any Hutu who married or employed a Tutsi woman to be a traitor. The "commandments" further called on Hutu not to enter into any form of business with Tutsi and insisted that all political, administrative, and educational institutions should be dominated and controlled by Hutu. In a chilling foretaste of the genocide that unfolded in 1994, the eighth "commandment" read: "The bahutu should stop having mercy on the batutsi."[33] This propaganda, which was tirelessly churned out by RTLM and *Kangura,* was directed at all Hutu who did not heed the "commandments." RTLM implored them to "defend your rights and rise up against those who want to oppress you."[34] Repeated messages of this kind led to a supercharged atmosphere that (as we shall see) boiled over in 1994.

In addition to spreading hate messages, the Hutu extremists also embarked on a project of training and arming civilians to "defend" themselves and to rid the country of the enemy "when the time comes." The creation of these civil defense militias was further meant to augment the limited number of soldiers in the armed forces. At the same time the military also established a commission to explore ways of defeating the Tutsi enemy "in the military, media and political domains."[35] The military consequently became involved nationwide in organizing and training the emerging civil defense militias in handling weapons and explosives. Most ominously of all, they trained them to kill expeditiously. The notorious *Interahamwe,* meaning "those who work closely together and who are united," became the militia of the president's ruling MRND party. They are believed to have been launched into action as early as 1991, and their activities increased as more civilians were drafted into the militia. By 1993 the *Interahamwe* had mastered their killing skills through their participation in the large-scale massacre of Tutsi across the country. The most appalling of these massacres took place in March 1992 when hundreds of Tutsi were slaughtered in the Bugesera area, in southeastern Rwanda. The implementation of massacre plans was closely coordinated between the *Interahamwe,* the military, and the local authorities in the area. Their activities were aided by the hate speech from RTLM, which told people that there were going to be collective work sessions to "clear the bush" (that is, kill the Tutsi) and to "pull out the bad weeds"—a chilling reference to Tutsi women and children to be exterminated.[36]

The Arusha Accords and the Establishment of UNAMIR

Meanwhile, in the midst of all these massacres, negotiations were in progress. At the beginning of 1993 pressure from the Organization of African Unity (OAU) and the Tanzanian government, with United Nations (UN) support and the support of Belgium, France, Germany, and the United States, brought Habyarimana to the negotiating table in Arusha in northern Tanzania. An agreement was reached in August 1993 for the creation in Rwanda of a Broad-Based Transitional Government (BBTG) made up of the Kigali regime, moderate Hutu in opposition, and the RPF. The Arusha Accords also provided for the repatriation of refugees, the integration of all military forces into a national army, and the holding of democratic elections in late 1995. The parties requested an international force to assist in the maintenance of public security in Rwanda during this delicate process, and to deliver humanitarian aid. On October 5, 1993 the Security Council of the United Nations adopted Resolution 872 establishing the United Nations Assistance Mission for Rwanda (UNAMIR). General Roméo Dallaire, a French-speaking Canadian officer, was appointed commander of the force and took up his command in Kigali on October 22, 1993.

THE GENOCIDE

The "100 Days"

Crucially, Hutu extremists were excluded from key positions in the BBTG, and those within the existing Rwandan government and army set about derailing the process, to preserve their power and privileges. By January 1994 the UN Secretariat had unequivocal warnings that a coup and genocide were being planned. However, it queried the sources of this intelligence and made no contingency plans.

On April 6, 1994, when Habyarimana and his presidential counterpart from Burundi, Cyprien Ntaryamira, were returning from the ongoing peace talks in Arusha, their jet was shot down as it approached Kigali. Both were killed. News of Habyarimana's death spread like wildfire and roadblocks were mounted in Kigali and the rest of the country. The spark had been struck that would ignite the most gruesome massacre of the last decade of the already blood-stained twentieth century.

RTLM automatically blamed the RPF for Habyarimana's death, and its announcers stridently urged the Hutu to rise and avenge his killing. Before anyone could even attempt to establish who was actually responsible for shooting down the president's plane (the finger of suspicion has been pointed most convincingly at Hutu extremists hoping to undo the Arusha settlement), the massacre of Tutsi was already in full swing. The speed and efficiency with which the killings were executed, and their scale, suggested the implementation of a plan that had been carefully prepared beforehand. In the space of a hundred days an estimated 800,000 Tutsi and moderate Hutu were killed by the Rwandan military, helped by scores of armed and drunk militia. These massacres, which took place before the very eyes of UNAMIR, were only finally brought to an end once the insurgent RPF had succeeded in establishing their control over the capital Kigali, and most of the rest of the country.

The International Response

In spite of having authorized the deployment of UNAMIR, the international community remained apparently indifferent and paralyzed throughout the genocide. The Security Council was divided on a suitable response, and its debates reflected this. Typical of its irresolution was the reluctance to refer to the events in Rwanda as "genocide," although that indubitably is what it was. On December 9, 1948 the United Nations had adopted the Genocide Convention, which required its signatories to prevent and punish such acts. However, to have acknowledged in 1994 that what was happening in Rwanda was genocide would have committed the members of the Security Council to robust intervention—precisely what they were wary of.[37]

Most observers at the time believed that at the crucial, early stage of the crisis it was not a question of whether or not the United Nations should intervene. Rather, it should have been a matter of deciding upon the right kind of mandate for immediate intervention, and agreeing upon the size, composition and command structure of the force to be deployed. General Dallaire, the commander of UNAMIR and a strong advocate for the people of Rwanda, certainly felt that merely to reinforce his hopelessly small and under-equipped force would be pointless. When interviewed on radio a month into the killings, he made it clear that he thought the United Nations should consider "modifying" his mandate "to carry out other activities."[38] It other words, what Dalliare was calling for was a strong interventionary force authorized by the United Nations with a mandate in terms of Chapter VII of the UN Charter to undertake enforcement actions to protect civilians facing massacre. He was destined to be sorely disappointed.

As a result of the confusion and inaction at the United Nations, it was only on April 20, 1994—three weeks into the genocide—that Boutros Boutros-Ghali, the secretary-general of the United Nations, presented the Security Council with three options: immediate and massive reinforcement of UNAMIR with a mandate that would allow it to coerce the parties into a cease-fire and restore law and order; a draw-down of the mission to a small group headed by the Force Commander, who would remain in Kigali with the UN Special Representative; or the complete withdrawal of UNAMIR. The Security Council adopted the least satisfactory option. In terms of its Resolution 912, UNAMIR's troop strength was reduced to 270, even though Dallaire had requested a residual force of 1,200. With this decision, it was clear that UNAMIR was to be no more than a "toothless bull dog,"[39] and that its capacity to be effective would be appreciably reduced. Justifiably feeling betrayed by the Security Council's decision, General Dallaire and his deputy, Brigadier Henry Kwami Anyidoho (the commander of the Ghanaian contingent in UNAMIR) took the unprecedented step of defying the council by allowing 456 soldiers to volunteer to stay in Rwanda instead of reducing their force to 270 as directed by the council.[40]

The secretary-general of the OAU, Ahmed Salim, deplored the timing of the UN decision to reduce the UNAMIR in Rwanda at the very moment when the massacre of Tutsi was in full swing. He pithily characterized it as typical of the world body's "lack of concern for African tragic situations."[41] Certainly, Salim's criticism touched on the lack of consistency in the international community's approach to conflicts and human tragedies in the post–Cold War era, and its greater readiness to commit resources to theaters of more immediate concern to the major powers than places in the Third World. Only six days after the council's decision to reduce UNAMIR, it authorized the strengthening of the United Nations Protection Force (UNPROFOR) in the former Yugoslavia with an additional 6,500 troops—5,000 more than Dallaire had been requesting to help stem the Rwandan genocide.

Yet the United Nations' failure to label the Rwandan killings genocide, or to heed Dallaire's pleas for reinforcements to stem the killings, must be understood to be at least partly a consequence of the reluctance of the United States and its western allies to become embroiled in another complex African conflict so soon after their Somali debacle in late 1993. That had ended with the humiliating collapse of the United Nations Operation in Somalia (UNOSOM). There is no doubt that the Somalia experience had a particularly negative impact on decision-making by the Security Council. It dampened the appetite for military entanglements and unacceptable casualties in what were considered to be areas of little or no strategic interests. The effects of the Somali withdrawal were clearly captured by Secretary-General Boutros-Ghali when he said: "Disillusion set in. Where peacekeepers were asked to deal with warfare, serious setbacks occurred. The first came in Somalia, and weakened the will of the world community to act against genocide in Rwanda."[42]

In Rwanda, Dallaire became the high priest of humanitarian intervention and urged western countries to leave their personnel in place since there was there was something left to fight for. He convinced Canada but could not hide his sense of betrayal by the Belgians. On April 12 their foreign minister ordered the Belgian contingent with UNAMIR to be withdrawn after 10 troops (who had vainly been attempting to protect the moderate acting prime minister, Agathe Uwilingiyimana, from death) had been abducted and killed. Dallaire declared: "I stood there as the Hercules left ... and I thought that almost exactly fifty years to the day my father and my father-in-law had been fighting in Belgium to free the country from Fascism, and there I was, abandoned by Belgian soldiers. So profoundly did I despise them for it ... I found it inexcusable."[43] With the departure of the Belgians and their equipment, UNAMIR's only lifeline was a Canadian C-130 plane that kept flying in essential supplies from Nairobi, Kenya.

The most serious indictment of the international community's response to the Rwandan emergency came with the Security Council authorization on May 17 of a unilateral French intervention (effectively UNAMIR II) with a mandate in terms of Chapter VII of the UN Charter—the very mandate Dallaire had been denied all along. To most observers, this decision was deplorable and confirmed the United Nations' clear disregard for the sensitivities on the ground. France's close relations with the Habyarimana regime and the role of the French military in defeating the initial RPF invasion in October 1990 had hardly endeared them to the RPF. As if to prove RPF suspicions right, news of the proposed French intervention was greeted with enthusiasm by FAR and its militia allies. RTLM immediately went into action, broadcasting that the French were intervening to assist the Hutu in defeating the "cockroaches." Certainly, some of the French officers who were deployed as part of *Opération Turquoise* (as their mission was called) had previously served as advisers to the genocidal Rwandan military, and their presence raised serious questions about the neutrality of the French force. France maintained close ties with its former colonies in Africa and was in the habit of intervening to bolster regimes that suited its interests. More generally, when playing their African regional politics, the French supported francophone countries. In the case of Rwanda, this meant rallying behind the francophone Hutu regime against the Tutsi of the RPF who were operating out of anglophone Uganda.

General Dallaire did not mince his words about France's biased and potentially "spoiling" tactics. Responding to news of the French intervention, Dallaire remarked: "I could not believe the effrontery of the

French. As far I was concerned they were using a humanitarian cloak to intervene in Rwanda, thus enabling the RGF [Rwandan Government forces] to hold on to a sliver of the country and regain a slice of legitimacy in the face of certain defeat." He added that "if France and its allies wanted to stop the genocide ... they could have reinforced UNAMIR instead."[44]

For its part, France strenuously emphasized the humanitarian rationale for its intervention. However, critics viewed the explanation as hypocritical because, in spite of clear evidence of the unfolding genocide, France had voted for the slashing of UNAMIR's strength. Moreover (so critics argued), if France had been genuine about a humanitarian intervention to save Rwandese lives, it could have offered to pay for the Armored Personnel Carriers (APCs) essential for helping people on the ground, or have airlifted Ethiopian and Ghanaian contingents prepared to bolster UNAMIR. Such initiatives would surely have saved thousands of lives. As it turned out, the victims of the genocide were sacrificed to suit France's interests, and when French intervention came it was to protect the *genocidaires,* the very people responsible for the genocide.[45]

The Congo Is Drawn into the Fray

As critics had predicted, France's unilateral intervention indeed bolstered FAR and the militia. When in late June the French landed in the city of Goma in eastern Zaire, it became immediately obvious they were taking the side of the remnants of the Habyarimana regime and military, which had fled to the town of Gisenyi, just across the border in western Rwanda. The presence of the French instantly attracted hundreds of thousands of the perpetrators of the genocide, whether military, militia, or civilian. The humanitarian protection zones set up by the French in terms of their UN mandate provided sanctuary to these *genocidaires,* who continued without hindrance to broadcast hate messages through RTLM. Most of the militia and soldiers who entered the camps were fully armed, but the French commanders did not disarm them, arguing that such action was outside their mandate.[46] The camps quickly became the launching pads for raids by the *genocidaires* against Rwanda in their attempt to demonstrate through a full-scale insurgency that the RPF could not run the country. Inevitably, this action took the form of atrocities committed against civilians such as Tutsi survivors of the genocide, moderate Hutu politicians, and aid workers. President Mobutu of Zaire supported them because he wanted to drive the indigenous Tutsi of eastern Zaire out for having supported the RPF. The Tutsi in Zaire thereupon rebelled, and this encouraged the RPF to lead a coalition against Mobutu, attack the Hutu refugee camps, and destroy FAR and the *Interahamwe.* Mobutu fell in 1997, but the RPF supported a second uprising against his successor, Laurent Kabila, whom they believed was not doing enough to suppress Hutu raids into Rwanda, which reached a peak in 1997–1998. In turn, Kabila incited his supporters to massacre the Tutsi in what was now renamed the Democratic Republic of the Congo. However, neither Kabila nor his successor have succeeded in regaining full control of the eastern DRC, where Rwandan forces and the Congolese rebels, the Congolese Rally for Democracy (Goma-RCD), continue to operate. There, besides harrying their enemies with routine torture and massacre, they control and exploit minerals and rare metals, which help keep their insurgency active.

The Lusaka Accords of 1999 between the DRC, Zimbabwe, Angola, Namibia, Rwanda, and Uganda did not succeed in settling this convoluted regional conflict. More practical has been the AU-sponsored agreement reached between the DRC and Rwanda on July 30, 2002 to create a security zone along their common border in order to prevent Hutu incursions. In return the RPF withdrew most of its troops from the DRC. However, the region remains volatile, and violence is endemic, with exiled Hutu such as the Armed People for the Liberation of Rwanda fighting it out with Congolese rebel groups loyal to the RPF. As always, civilians continue to be the victims. They are displaced, their camps are overrun and looted, and they are periodically massacred.[47]

THE AFTERMATH

The New Regime in Rwanda

By July 1994 the RPF had defeated the Hutu government and army in Rwanda itself, and a Government of National Unity was set up under a moderate Hutu, Pasteur Bizimungu, with Paul Kagame, the RPF leader, as vice president. Bizimungu resigned in 2000 and was replaced as president by Kagame, who has been reelected with huge majorities. His popularity is a measure of his success in promoting stability and reconciliation. It is also a consequence of heavy RPF pressure on voters.

The RPF victory persuaded some 800,000 Tutsi refugees to return to Rwanda between 1994 and 1996. Hundreds of thousands of Hutu exiles also returned between 1997 and 1999, bringing back the skill necessary to recreate the state. However, the victorious Tutsi monopolized the Government of National Unity, the administration, and the judiciary, and have taken over the property of Hutu who have fled. Hutu subsistence farmers find themselves subject once again to Tutsi landlords. The Hutu are marginalized politically as well as economically and are deeply divided over what they did—or did not—do during the genocide. For their part, the returning Tutsi who now run the country have been exiles for 35 years or were born out of the country. They are consequently different in outlook from the Tutsi who remained in Rwanda. The Tutsi fear the return of Hutu majority rule, but the Hutu want full democracy so that they can regain power. The Tutsi demand justice for the genocide, but the Hutu fear justice or deny that what took place was actually a genocide. It seems the country is as divided as ever.

National Unity and Reconciliation

The United Nations established the International Criminal Tribunal for Rwanda (ICTR) in November 1994 to bring closure to the genocide. Based in Arusha in Tanzania, it was intended to prosecute those responsible. With a budget of US$90 million and a huge staff of 800, its record has nevertheless been lamentable in sentencing perpetrators or getting to the roots of who masterminded the genocide.

The Rwandan government has taken its own initiative in dealing with the *genocidaires* and in 1996 set up Gacaca Community Courts, where the community participates in coming to terms with the genocide. There the retributive and punitive elements of justice are less important than the reparatory function and healing process. Of course, such courts have real shortcomings in terms of fairness, expertise, and so on, but they are widely accepted as the best means available of dealing with the wounds of the past and are seen by the people themselves as more culturally acceptable (and effective) than the ICTR.

The work of reconciliation is also being attempted through local churches (tarnished as they are because of their equivocal role during the genocide), women's organizations, and some international aid agencies. The government has done its best to repatriate refugees and has created a Commission for National Unity and Reconciliation as well as a National Human Rights Commission. Whether these initiatives will succeed in healing the deep wounds of the past remains to be seen.[48]

THE AFRICAN RESPONSE AND THE WAY FORWARD

Although the OAU—which was reorganized in 2002 as the African Union (AU)—and various African countries played a more positive role in Rwanda than did other members of the international community, the genocide also highlighted the dramatic failure of leadership in Africa. At the OAU meeting in Tunis in June 1994, President Nelson Mandela of South Africa used his inaugural speech to make precisely this point. Emphasizing the interlinked nature of human rights, stability, peace, democracy, and development, President Mandela said:

> Rwanda stands out as a stern and severe rebuke to all of us for having failed to address these inter-related matters.... +As a result of that, a terrible slaughter of the innocent has taken place and is taking place in front of our very eyes. We know it is a matter of fact that we must have it in ourselves as Africans to change all this. We must, in action, assert our will to do so.[49]

Ironically, the genocide coincided with the holding of the first nonracial elections in South Africa, marking the end of apartheid and the last colonial outpost on the continent. As I have argued elsewhere,[50] one of the enduring consequences of the genocide is the questioning by Africans of the principles of sovereignty and noninterference. The continued suffering of civilians in conflict zones, often at the hands of their governments—as was the case in Rwanda—raised fundamental questions regarding the virtue of blindly embracing these principles. In this, the newly constituted AU departs from its predecessor, the OAU, which enshrined the principle of noninterference in its Charter, formally adopted in 2002. While Article 3(b) of the Constitutive Act of the AU pledges to "defend the sovereignty, territorial integrity and independence of its member states," the act also gives member states the prerogative to intervene in cases of genocide, war crimes, or other gross violations of human rights. Thus Article 4(h) affirms the "the right of the Union to intervene in a Member State pursuant to a decision of the Assembly in respect of grave circumstances, namely war crimes, genocide and crimes against humanity."[51] Subsequent to the adoption of its Constitutive Act, the AU has intervened in Burundi through the African Mission in Burundi (AMIB), and also in Sudan through the African Mission in Sudan (AMIS I and II), which is still grappling with the conflict in the Darfur region. In spite of criticisms aimed at AMIS for its slow deployment, such interventions in what could qualify as domestic conflicts would have been extremely difficult—if not unthinkable—in the past under the OAU.[52] The political, legal, and diplomatic controversy that followed the initial military intervention by the Economic Community of West African States (ECOWAS) in Liberia in 1990 clearly demonstrates the complexity and divisive nature of such interventions. What is remarkable about the more recent interventions by the AU is the lack of controversy due to the growing general acceptance of the principle of African-led humanitarian interventions.

In addition to dealing with the normative aspects of humanitarian interventions, the AU has also proposed several mechanisms to help prevent African conflicts and to respond adequately when they nevertheless do break out. The shift in policy by the AU has led to the development of what is perhaps the most "interventionist" security regime in the post–Cold War era, namely the *Protocol Relating to the Establishment on the Peace and Security Council of the African Union*.[53] The Continental Early Warning System and the African Standby Force (ASF) would be the two principal organs of the AU's new security architecture. The Continental Early Warning System would be based in Addis Ababa in Ethiopia and would liaise with the regional early warning mechanisms in the various subregions in order to collect and analyze information about incipient conflicts. This information would be channeled to the AU headquarters for appropriate actions that could range from preventive diplomacy to intervention, particularly when civilians are under threat. The proposed ASF, which would consist of five regional standby brigades from East, West, Central, Northern, and Southern Africa, would be deployed to deal with a wide range of conflict situations, including enforcement actions.

The AU understands that to undertake effective Peace Support Operations (PSOs), thereby mitigating the effect of war on the civilian population and preventing another Rwanda-type scenario, these mechanisms must be made properly operational. That would lend credence to the notion of "African solutions to African problems" and would go a long way in dealing with the peacekeeping deficit due to the reluctance of major western powers to contribute troops to UN-led PSOs in Africa.

Efforts to develop accountability mechanisms by the AU and subregional organizations, such as ECOWAS, should be part of this process. Continental instruments such as the African Court of Human Rights and other subregional mechanisms such as the ECOWAS Court of Justice should be strengthened to deal with cases of war crimes and gross violations of human rights. The application of such mechanisms would go a long way in dealing with issues of impunity and provide the victims of conflicts a means of redress. Although the establishment of the ICTR to deal with those responsible for the 1994 genocide is an important (if flawed) step forward in the fight against impunity—as is that of the similar Special Court for Sierra Leone—both are nevertheless limited in duration and scope, and could have the unintended consequence of undermining long-term peace-building.

In fact, these ad hoc arrangements are seen by some Africans as mere compensatory mechanisms by the international community for having failed to take appropriate action to protect innocent civilians when they were under threat. While advocates for human rights have applauded the establishment of the International Criminal Court in The Hague, the poor record of compliance and the nonenforcement of international norms of justice leave much room for skepticism. In light of these challenges, Africa needs to embark on developing its own political, legal, and security mechanisms to ensure that it can prevent humanitarian disasters before they emerge, or can respond adequately when they do.

Finally, efforts should be made to deal with the democratic deficit in Africa that has resulted from years of one-party rule and military dictatorships. The implementation of continental governance mechanisms such as the African Peer Review Mechanism and the consolidation of individual human rights would go a long way in enhancing the protection of civilians. Protection of minority rights should be central to the democratic process, and in Rwanda, where 80 percent of the population is Hutu, efforts should be made to protect the rights of the minority Tutsi to avoid a "dictatorship of the majority." Maintaining a strong quota system in key national institutions such as the armed forces could be one way of ensuring that minority rights are protected.

As the most recent events unfolding in Darfur suggest, all these measures cannot guarantee that there will be no repetition in Africa of the horrific events in Rwanda. Nevertheless, there does seem to be a growing consensus that civilians must be protected from future abuse and massacre, and in Africa international mechanisms are being brought into being to ensure that they are.

ABBREVIATIONS

AMIB	African Mission in Burundi
AMIS	African Mission in Sudan
APC	Armored personnel carrier
APRM	African Peer Review Mechanism
ASF	African Standby Force
AU	African Union
ECOWAS	Economic Community of West African States
ICC	International Criminal Court
ICTR	International Criminal Tribunal for Rwanda
MDR	Rwandese Democratic Party
MRND	Mouvement Revolutionnaire National pour le Development
NRA	National Resistance Army
OAU	Organisation of African Unity
PARMEHUTU	Party of the Movement and of Hutu Emancipation
RPA	Rwandan Patriotic Army
RPF	Rwandan Patriotic Front
RTLM	Radio et Television Libres des Mille Collines
SCSL	Special Court for Sierra Leone
UNAMIR	United Nations Assistance Mission in Rwanda
UNAR	Union National Rwandaise
UNOSOM	United Nations Mission in Somalia
UNPROFOR	United Nations Protection Force

TIMELINE

1884–1885	Berlin Conference to partition Africa
1916	Belgium conquers Rwanda
1919	League of Nations mandates Belgium to administer Rwanda
1933	Belgium holds a referendum officially dividing the inhabitants of Rwanda into three distinct groups

1943	The *Mwami* converts to Christianity
1946	The *Mwami* consecrates Rwanda to Christ the King
1957	Hutu Manifesto is published
1959	The "social revolution" takes place and thousands of Tutsi flee to neighboring countries
1959	King Mutara III Rudahigwa dies
1961	MDR-PARMEHUTU abolishes the monarchy, declaring Rwanda a republic
1962	Rwanda attains independence with Gregorie Kiyabanda as president
1973	General Juvenal Habyarimana overthrows President Kiyabanda, heralding the second Republic
1974	MRND is formed and declared the sole party in Rwanda
1990	RPF Invades Rwanda from Uganda
1993	Security Council adopts Resolution 872 establishing UNAMIR
1994	April: Presidential plane is shot down, killing President Habyarimana Fighting breaks out, marking the start of the genocide United Nations orders a drawdown of UNAMIR to a skeletal force May: France launches *Opération Turquoise* July: RPF/A establishes control over most of Rwanda, ending the genocide November: United Nations establishes International Criminal Tribunal for Rwanda.

GLOSSARY

Names

Amin, General Idi. Uganda's notorious military dictator (1971–1979).

Boutros-Ghali, Boutros. Secretary-general of the United Nations (1992–1996).

Dallaire, Lt. General Roméo. Commander (1993–1994) of UNAMIR.

Habyarimana, General Juvénal. Second president of Rwanda (1973–1994) whose death sparked the genocide.

Kabila, Laurent. Leader of the Alliance of Democratic Forces for the Liberation of Congo, which overthrew Mobutu Seso Seko in 1997.

Kagame, General Paul. Military commander of the RPF in 1990, vice president of Rwanda in 1994 and president since 2000.

Kayibanda, Gregoire. First president of independent Rwanda (1961–1973).

Kigeri IV Rwabugiri. King of Rwanda (1853–1895).

Logiest, Colonel B.E.M. Guy. Belgian resident in Rwanda (1959–1962).

Mandela, Nelson. First black president of South Africa (1994–1999).

Mbonyumutwa, Dominique. PARMEHUTU leader in the 1950s.

Mobutu Sese Seko, General Joseph Désiré. Military dictator of Zaire (1965–1997).

Museveni, Yoweri. President of Uganda since 1986 and leader of the National Resistance Army/Movement.

Mutara III Rudahigwa. King of Rwanda (1931–1959). Known as *Mwami w'abazungu,* or the King of the Whites.

Ntaryamira, Cyprien. President of Burundi (February-April 1994) killed with his Rwandan counterpart in a plane crash in April 1994.

Obote, Milton. First prime minister (1962–1971) and later president (1980–1985) of Uganda.

Rwigyema, General Paul. Leader of the RPF; killed in the early days of the RPF invasion in 1990.

Salim, Salim Ahmed. Secretary-general of the Organisation of African Unity (OAU) (1989–2001).

Speke, John (1827–1864). English explorer and first European to set foot at the source of the Nile.

von Götzen, Count Adolf. Governor of German East Africa, 1901–1906.

Terms

Interahamwe. "Those who work closely together and who are united" (militia of the MRND party).

inyenzi. Cockroaches.

Kangura. Wake others up.

Mwami. King.

Mwami w'abazungu. King of the whites.

ubuhake. Contractual service in which a more powerful person provides protection in exchange for work.

ubuletwa. Forced labor system.

NOTES

1. At the time of the Rwandan genocide Salim Ahmed Salim was the secretary general of the Organization of African Unity (reorganized in 2002 as the African Union). For more information see Salim A. Salim "The Price of Peace," *The West African Bulletin* 3 (June 1995).

2. The Great Lakes of Africa consists of Lake Victoria, Lake Kivu, and Lake Tanganyika. The bordering countries are Rwanda, Burundi, the Democratic Republic of Congo, Uganda, and Tanzania.

3. Cited in Linda Melvern, *A People Betrayed: The Role of the West in Rwanda's Genocide* (London: Zed Books, 2000), 8.

4. For more information see J. B. Piolet, *Les Missions catholiques francaises au X1Xe siecle* (Paris: A. Colin, 1902).

5. Theorizing about the origins and relationship between the Hutu and Tutsi is discussed by Mahmood Mamdani, *When Victims Become Killers: Colonialisms,*

Nativism, and the Genocide in Rwanda (Princeton, NJ: Princeton University Press, 2001), 41.

6. Ibid., 57.

7. Melvern, *A People Betrayed,* 9.

8. See Gérard Prunier, *The Rwanda Crisis—History of a Genocide* (London: Hurst, 1995), 25.

9. Ibid., 26–27.

10. Ibid., 26.

11. Melvern, *A People Betrayed,* 10.

12. Prunier, *The Rwanda Crisis,* 31.

13. Ibid., 27–29.

14. Mamdani, *When Victims Become Killers,* 99.

15. Ibid.

16. Christian P. Scherrr, *Genocide and Crisis in Central Africa: Conflict Roots, Mass Violence, and Regional War* (Westport, CT: Praeger Publishers, 2002), 27.

17. Prunier, *The Rwanda Crisis,* 44–45.

18. Ibid., 47–48.

19. Ibid., 45–46.

20. The breakdown of refugees by country was as follows: Burundi 200,000; Uganda 78,000; Tanzania 36,000, and the Democratic Republic of Congo 22,000. For an in-depth analysis of the refugee issue, see ibid, 61–74.

21. Melvern, *A People Betrayed,* 14.

22. Cited in Prunier, *The Rwanda Crisis,* 51.

23. Cited in Mamdani, *When Victims Become Killers,* 124.

24. Ibid.

25. Prunier, *The Rwanda Crisis,* 48.

26. Mamdani, *When Victims Become Killers,* 125.

27. Scherrer, *Genocide and Crisis,* 38–39.

28. Prunier, *The Rwanda Crisis,* 74–75.

29. Alan J. Kuperman, *The Limits of Humanitarian Intervention: Genocide in Rwanda* (Washington, DC: The Brookings Institution, 2001), 8–9.

30. Ibid.

31. Mamdani, *When Victims Become Killers,* 186.

32. For a full text of the "Hutu Ten Commandments" see "Institutionalization of Ethnic Ideology and Segregation in Rwanda," Pan African Movement, http://www.panafricanmovement.org/R.Genocide2.htm. Last accessed 10/08/05.

33. Ibid.

34. Cited in Mamdani, *When Victims become Killers,* 191.

35. Des Forges and Alison Liebhafsky, *Leave None to Tell the Story* (New York: Human Rights Watch, 1999), 62.

36. For more information on the role of the Interahamwe in the genocide, see Linda Melvern, *Conspiracy to Murder—The Rwandan Genocide* (London: Verso, 2004), 19–47.

37. Norrie Macqueen, *United Nations Peacekeeping in Africa since 1960* (London: Longman, 2002), 75.

38. Interviewed by Radio France Internationale. Quoted on the BBC, *Summary of World Broadcasts,* AL/1991, 7 May 1994.

39. Ingrid A. Lehmann, *Peacekeeping and Public Information—Caught in the Crossfire* (London: Frank Cass: 1999), 91.

40. Following the Security Council's decision, the contingents who stayed behind with Dallaire were as follows: Ghana 334, Tunisia 40, Canada 11, Togo 18, Senegal 12, Bangladesh 11, Mali 9, Zimbabwe 8, Austria 7, Congo 7, Nigeria 7, Poland 3, Egypt 2, Malawi 2, and Fiji 1. For more on this momentous decision, see Merven, *A People Betrayed,* 174.

41. Tom Woodhouse, Robert Bruce, and Malcolm Dando, *Peacekeeping and Peacemaking—Towards Effective Intervention in Post Cold War Conflicts* (New York: St. Martin's Press, 1998), 60.

42. Lehmann, *Peacekeeping and Public Information,* 90. For an in-depth analysis of U.S. policy during this period see Samantha Powers, "Bystanders to Genocide," *The Atlantic Monthly* (September 2001), which can be accessed at: http://www.mtholyoke.edu/acad/intrel/power.htm; and Samantha Powers, *A Problem from Hell: America in the Age of Genocide* (New York: Basic Books, 2002).

43. See Melvern, *A People Betrayed,* 168.

44. For a personal and detailed account of the intricate and complex dynamics of the Rwanda genocide and the role of the international community, see Lt. General Romeo Dallaire, *Shake Hands with the Devil—The Failure of Humanity in Rwanda* (Toronto: Random House Canada, 2003), 425.

45. African Rights, *Rwanda: Death, Despair and Defiance,* revised edition (London: African Rights, August 1995), 1138.

46. See Melvern, *A People Betrayed,* 214–15.

47. See Macqueen, *United Nations Peacekeeping,* 86–92.

48. S'fiso Ngesi and Charles Villa-Vicencio, "Rwanda: Balancing the Weight of History," in *Through Fire with Water: The Roots of Division and the Potential for Reconciliation in Africa* , ed. Erik Doxtader and Charles Villa-Vicencio (Claremont, CA: David Philip, 2003), 19–26.

49. Cited in African Rights, *Rwanda,* 1137.

50. Alhaji M. S. Bah, "The Intervention Dilemma: The Dynamics of Civilian Protection in the Post-Cold War ERA," in *A Tortuous Road to Peace—The Dynamics of Regional, UN and International Humanitarian Interventions in Liberia,* ed. Festus Aboagye and Alhaji M. S. Bah (Pretoria: Institute of Strategic Studies, 2005), 21–43. This chapter can also be found at http://www.iss.co.za/pubs/Books/Tortuous-Road/Contents.htm.

51. See *Constitutive Act of the African Union* (Lome, Togo, July 2000), 5. The Constitutive Act was formally adopted by the AU at its first Summit Meeting in Durban, South Africa, 2002.

52. For more information on the African Union Mission in Sudan (AMIS), see Cdr. Seth Appiah-Mensah, "AU's Critical Assignment in Darfur—Challenges and Constraints," *African Security Review* 14, no. 2 (2005): 6–21. This article can be found at http://www.iss.org.za/pubs/ASR/14No2/F1.pdf.

53. For more on the protocol go to: http://www.africaunion.org/Official_documents/Treaties_ Conventions_ Protocols/Protocol_peace and security.pdf. Accessed 13/08/05.

SELECT BIBLIOGRAPHY

African Rights. *Rwanda: Death, Despair and Defiance.* Revised edition. London: African Rights, 1995.

Investigates the political dynamics of the Rwandan genocide and analyzes why and how the perpetrators embarked on their "final solution." Also illuminates the international response and the role of the media and concludes with a demand for justice.

Anyidoho, Brig. Gen. Henry. *Guns over Kigali.* Accra: Woeli Publishing Services, 1997.

A personal account from the perspective of a commander with one of the most difficult jobs in Rwanda during the genocide. Explores the contours of the crisis and the challenges faced by the skeletal UN peacekeeping force.

Appiah-Mensah, Cdr. Seth. "AU's Critical Assignment in Darfur: Challenges and Constraints." *African Security Review* 14, no. 2 (2005): 6–21. This article can be found at: http://www.iss.org.za/pubs/ASR/14No2/F1.pdf.

Analyses the opportunities and operational challenges facing the African Union's peacekeeping mission in Darfur, Sudan.

Bah, Alhaji M. S. "The Intervention Dilemma: The Dynamics of Civilian Protection in the Post-Cold War Era." In *A Tortuous Road to Peace: The Dynamics of Regional, UN and International Humanitarian Interventions in Liberia.* Edited by Festus Aboagye and Alhaji M. S. Bah. Pretoria: Institute for Security Studies, 2005. This chapter can also be found at: www.iss.co.za/pubs/Books/TortuousRoad/Contents.htm.

Interrogates the plight of civilians in the post–Cold War era and explores the evolution of the responses taken by African regional organizations and the United Nations to the deliberate targeting of civilians.

Clark, John, F. *The African Stakes of the Congo War.* New York: Palgrave/Macmillan, 2002.

Exposes the complex civil war that broke out in the Congo in the mid-1990s. Through incisive analysis it illustrates the motives that drove a large number of African states into the conflict, which has been dubbed Africa's First World War.

Dallaire, Lt. Gen. Roméo. *Shake Hands with the Devil: The Failure of Humanity in Rwanda.* Canada: Random House, 2003.

A personal and critical account from the perspective of the commander of the UN force in Rwanda of how the genocide was planned and executed. It presents in a painful manner the opportunities missed to end the genocide and criticizes the international community for its indifference.

Feil, Col. Scott. *Preventing Genocide: How the Early Use of Force Might Have Succeeded in Rwanda.* New York: Carnegie Commission, 1998.

An account of how timely military intervention could have ended the genocide and saved thousands of lives. It critically examines the military plan (which was not adopted) put forward by Lt. Gen. Dallaire to the United Nations to stem the tide of killings.

Kuperman, Alan J. *The Limits of Humanitarian Intervention: Genocide in Rwanda.* Washington, DC: The Brookings Institution, 2001.

Examines some of the political, legal, and operational challenges confronting humanitarian interventions in the post–Cold War era and explores possible options for interventions and the crucial role of early warning in preventing and dealing with conflicts when they erupt.

Lemarchand, René. *Burundi: Ethnic Conflict and Genocide.* Cambridge: Woodrow Wilson Center Press and Cambridge University Press, 1994.

An in-depth discussion of the ethnic cleavages in Burundi and their consequences for society. The analysis focuses on the massacres of 1972 and

1988 and how they shaped and continue to drive inter-ethnic relations in Burundi.

Melvern, Linda. *Conspiracy to Murder: The Rwandan Genocide.* London/New York: Verso, 2004.

Delves into the planning of the Rwandan genocide and the involvement of various state institutions such as the military, police, and civilian administrators who, with international connivance, planned and executed the massacre of the Tutsi population.

———. *A People Betrayed: The Role of the West in Rwanda's Genocide.* London: Zed Books: 2000.

Explores the background to the Rwandan genocide by skillfully analyzing the roles of various national and international actors and exposes the inaction by the international community.

Mamdani, Mahmood. *When Victims Become Killers: Colonialisms, Nativism, and the Genocide in Rwanda.* Princeton, NJ: Princeton University Press, 2001.

A sophisticated analysis of the colonial and postcolonial policies in Rwanda, which divided the people of Rwanda into separate and distinct "racial" groups, so laying the foundations for the genocide.

O'Halloran, Patrick, J. *Humanitarian Intervention and the Genocide in Rwanda.* London: Research Institute for the Study of Conflict and Terrorism, 1995.

Analyses the Rwandan genocide in the context of the wider security concerns of the post–Cold War era and investigates issues such as the use of force, refugees, and the responses of regional and international organizations to the genocide.

Powers, Samantha. *A Problem from Hell: America and the Age of Genocide.* New York: Basic Books, 2002.

Presents the often fractious decision-making process by the U.S. government in responding to issues not necessarily of national interest and exposes shortcomings of the Clinton administration's response to the genocide.

Prunier, Gerard. *The Rwanda Crisis: History of a Genocide.* London: Hurst and Co., 1995.

Traces the causes of the genocide in a chronological and sophisticated manner and shows how ethnic differences were manipulated by different administrations. Also investigates the consequences of the genocide on the central Africa region and further afield.

Scherrr, Christian P. *Genocide and Crisis in Central Africa: Conflict Roots, Mass Violence, and Regional War.* Westport, CT: Praeger Publishers, 2002.

An analytical picture of the interrelated conflicts in central Africa, focusing primarily on Burundi and Rwanda and the complex and contradictory roles played by the international community, the United Nations, and humanitarian agencies.

Woodhouse Tom, Robert Bruce, and Malcolm Dando. *Peacekeeping and Peacemaking: Towards Effective Intervention in Post Cold War Conflicts.* New York: St. Martin's Press, 1998.

Deals with the often divisive issue of military intervention, especially in the post–Cold War era, and investigates how peacemaking and peacekeeping can be made more effective.

Index

About the Editor and Contributors

Alhaji M. S. Bah is a Research Coordinator at the Center on International Cooperation at New York University. He holds a PhD in International Relations from Queen's University, Canada. He was previously a Senior Researcher with the Peace Missions Program at the Institute for Security Studies where he was responsible for a project on the protection of civilians. He specializes in regional security cooperation in Africa and has written widely in this field. His recent publications include a book co-edited with Festus Aboagye, *A Tortuous Road to Peace: The Dynamics of Regional, UN and International Humanitarian Interventions in Liberia* (2005).

Inge Brinkman is currently a researcher at the African Studies Centre in Leiden in The Netherlands. On the basis of her fieldwork she has undertaken research projects on the effects of violence and exile and other aspects of modern Angolan society and culture at Cologne University in Germany and subsequently at Ghent University in Belgium. Her publications include *Grandmother's Footsteps: Oral Tradition and South-East Angolan Narratives on the Colonial Encounter,* edited with Axel Fleisch (1999), *Singing in the Bush: MPLA Songs during the War for Independence in South-East Angola 1966–1975* (2001), and *"A War for People": Civilians, Mobility, and Legitimacy in South-East Angola during MPLA's War for Independence* (2005).

Jane Kani Edward is currently an external Research Associate with the Center for Refugee Studies at York University, Canada. Her research interests encompass refugee and immigrant women's experiences;

development, gender, equity and social justice issues; gender, race, and class in conflict; and postconflict societies in Northeast Africa and Central Africa with special focus on Sudan. Among her publications is "South Sudanese Refugee Women: Questioning the Past and Imagining the Future," in *Women's Rights and Human Rights: International Historical Perspectives,* eds. Patricia Grimshaw et al. (2001).

Lansana Gberie was until recently a Senior Research Fellow at the Kofi Annan International Peacekeeping Training Centre in Accra, Ghana. He covered the Sierra Leonean civil war as a journalist in 1991–1996 and has written extensively on contemporary Liberia and Sierra Leone. He is the author of *A Dirty War in West Africa: The RUF and the Destruction of Sierra Leone* (2005).

Amir Idris is Assistant Professor of African Studies at the Department of African and African American Studies, Fordham University in New York City, United States. His research interests focus on the history and politics of colonialism, on slavery and race, and on precolonial citizenship in Northeast Africa. He is the author of *Sudan's Civil War: Slavery, Race and Formational Identities* (2001) and *Conflict and Politics of Identity in Sudan* (2005).

David Killingray is Emeritus Professor of History at Goldsmiths College London, England. His recent books and articles have been on the history of Africa, the Caribbean, Empire, influenza, the black diaspora, and English local history. He has just completed a study of African soldiers in the Second World War.

John Laband is Professor of History at Wilfrid Laurier University, Canada. He has written extensively on the Zulu kingdom and on colonial warfare and society in Southern Africa. His publications include *Kingdom in Crisis: The Zulu Response to the British Invasion of 1879* (1992), *The Rise and Fall of the Zulu Nation* (1997), *The Atlas of the Later Zulu Wars 1883–1888* (2001), and *The Transvaal Rebellion: The First Boer War 1880–1881* (2005).

Paul E. Lovejoy is Distinguished Research Professor, Department of History, York University, Canada. He is holder of the Canada Research Chair in African Diaspora History and Director of the Harriet Tubman Resource Centre on the African Diaspora. He has published more than 20 books and is a Fellow of the Royal Society of Canada.

Bill Nasson is Professor of History at the University of Cape Town, South Africa. His publications include *Abraham Esau's War* (1991), *The South African War 1899–1902* (1999) and *Britannia's Empire* (2004). He is currently working on a history of South African participation in the First World War entitled *Springboks on the Somme.* He is a former editor of *The Journal of African History.*

Tim Stapleton is Associate Professor and Chair of the Department of History at Trent University, Canada. Previously, he taught history at Rhodes University and the University of Fort Hare in South Africa and was a research associate at the University of Zimbabwe. His publications include *Maqoma: Xhosa Resistance to Colonial Advance* (1994), *Faku: Rulership and Colonialism in the Mpondo Kingdom* (2001), and *No Insignificant Part: The Rhodesian Native Regiment in the East African Campaign of the First World War* (2006).